# The Social Context of Nonverbal Behavior

D0756786

This volume presents, in an integrated framework, the newest, most contemporary perspectives on the role of nonverbal behavior in social interaction. The book includes empirically grounded work and theories that are central to our understanding of the reciprocal influences between nonverbal behavior and social variables. In doing so, it contributes to the ongoing controversy now shaping the field regarding the degree to which nonverbal behavior represents social, as opposed to biological, forces.

The volume also highlights a number of recent subareas in the domain of nonverbal behavior that hold much promise, including the role of nonverbal behavior in group membership and media influences on nonverbal behavior. It also presents data and theories that have applied value, useful to people working in such fields as communication, psychotherapy, and counseling. Finally, the volume gathers contributors in different subfields that are rarely presented jointly, such as family and media socialization factors.

Pierre Philippot is Professor of Psychology at the University of Louvain at Louvain-la-Neuve, Belgium. He is also Senior Research Associate at the Belgium National Science Foundation.

Robert S. Feldman is Professor of Psychology at the University of Massachusetts, where he is Director of Undergraduate Studies and former head of the Personality and Social Psychology Division. He is editor of *Applications of Nonverbal Behavioral Theory and Research* and *Fundamentals of Nonverbal Behavior* (with Bernard Rimé).

Erik J. Coats is Assistant Professor of Psychology at Vassar College. His books include *Classic and Contemporary Readings in Social Psychology* and *Critical Thinking: General Principles and Case Studies*.

# STUDIES IN EMOTION AND SOCIAL INTERACTION
## Second Series

Series Editors

Keith Oatley
*University of Toronto*

Antony Manstead
*University of Amsterdam*


This series is jointly published by the Cambridge University Press and the Editions de la Maison des Sciences de l'Homme, as part of the joint publishing agreement established in 1977 between the Fondation de la Maison des Sciences de l'Homme and the Syndics of the Cambridge University Press.

Cete collection est publiée co-édition par Cambridge University Press et les Editions de la Maison des Sciences de l'Homme. Elle s'intègre dans le programme de co-édition établi en 1977 par la Fondation de la Maison des Sciences de l'Homme et les Syndics de Cambridge University Press.


Titles published in the Second Series:

*The Psychology of Facial Expression*
Edited by James A. Russell and José Miguel Fernández-Dols

*Emotions, the Social Bond, and Human Reality: Part/Whole Analysis*
Thomas J. Scheff

*Intersubjective Communication and Emotion in Early Ontogeny*
Stein Bråten

For a list of titles in the First Series of Studies in Emotion and Social Interaction, see the page following the index.

# The Social Context of Nonverbal Behavior

*Edited by*

Pierre Philippot

Robert S. Feldman

Erik J. Coats

CAMBRIDGE
UNIVERSITY PRESS

& Editions de la Maison des Sciences de l'Homme
*Paris*

PUBLISHED BY THE PRESS SYNDICATE OF THE UNIVERSITY OF CAMBRIDGE
The Pitt Building, Trumpington Street, Cambridge, United Kingdom
and EDITIONS DE LA MAISON DES SCIENCES DE L'HOMME
54 Boulevard Raspail, 75270 Paris Cedex 06, France

CAMBRIDGE UNIVERSITY PRESS
The Edinburgh Building, Cambridge CB2 2RU, UK   http://www.cup.cam.ac.uk
40 West 20th Street, New York, NY 10011-4211, USA   http://www.cup.org
10 Stamford Road, Oakleigh, Melbourne 3166, Australia

First published 1999

Printed in the United States of America

*Typeface* Palatino 10/13 pt.      *System* DeskTopPro$_{/UX}$® [BV]

*A catalog record for this book is available from
the British Library.*

*Library of Congress Cataloging-in-Publication Data*
The social context of nonverbal behavior / edited by Pierre Philippot,
Robert S. Feldman, Erik J. Coats.
p.   cm. – (Studies in emotion and social interaction)
Includes bibliographical references and indexes.
ISBN 0-521-58371-3 (hardcover). – ISBN 0-521-58666-6 (pbk.)
1. Body language.   I. Philippot, Pierre, 1960–   . II. Feldman,
Robert S. (Robert Stephen), 1947–   . III. Coats, Erik J., 1968–   .
IV. Series.
BF637.N66S63    1999
153.6'9 – dc21                                                        98-11637
                                                                            CIP
ISBN 0 521 58371 3 hardback
ISBN 0 521 58666 6 paperback
ISBN 2 7351 828 7 hardback (France only)
ISBN 0 7351 828 5 paperback (France only)

# Contents

# Acknowledgments

The impetus for this book came from a series of meetings that were held in Belgium and the United States over a period of several years. In our informal discussions, it became apparent that no unified source covering the social aspects of nonverbal behavior existed. Consequently, we embarked on a project that would bring together the best and most current work in the area.

We are grateful to all the contributors for their extraordinary chapters as well as their diligence in meeting our ambitious timelines and requests to circulate their drafts with one another. We are also very grateful to the editors of the series, Antony Manstead and Keith Oatley. Finally, Julia Hough, our editor, and William Grundy, our production supervisor, provided exceptional encouragement and support.

Our collaboration as editors would not have been possible without substantial financial support from our home universities. Specifically, the exchange program between the University of Louvain and the University of Massachusetts facilitated meetings among the three of us. Vassar College also provided travel support at a critical juncture during the editing of the book. We are particularly grateful to deans Glen Gordon and Guillaume Wunsch and former deans Seymour Berger and Jean Costermans for their unconditional support.

# Contributors

**D. Eric Anderson**  Department of Psychology, University of Virginia, Charlottesville, VA 22903-2477, USA

**Matthew E. Ansfield**  Department of Psychology, University of Virginia, Charlottesville, VA 22903-2477, USA

**Sylvie Blairy**  Département de Psychologie, Université du Québec à Montréal, CP 8888, Succ A, Montréal Qc H3C 3P8, Canada

**Erik J. Coats**  Department of Psychology, Vassar College, Raymond Avenue, Poughkeepsie, NY 12601, USA

**Valerie W. Crisp**  Department of Psychology, North Carolina State University, Raleigh, NC 27695-7103, USA

**Bella M. DePaulo**  Department of Psychology, University of Virginia, Charlottesville, VA 22903-2477, USA

**Kimberly L. Eaton**  Department of Psychology, North Carolina State University, Raleigh, NC 27695-7103, USA

**Judith A. Feeney**  Department of Psychology, University of Queensland, St. Lucia, Queensland 4067, Australia

**Robert S. Feldman**  Department of Psychology, University of Massachusetts, Amherst, MA 01003, USA

**José-Miguel Fernández-Dols**  Facultad de Psichologia, Universidad Autónoma de Madrid, Ctra. De Colmenar, KM 15, E-28049 Madrid, Spain

**Agneta Fischer**  Department of Psychology, University of Amsterdam, Roeterstraat 15, NL – 1018 WB Amsterdam, The Netherlands

**Amy G. Halberstadt**  Department of Psychology, Box 7801, North Carolina State University, Raleigh, NC 27695-7801, USA

**Marvin A. Hecht**  Department of Psychology, Harvard University, Cambridge, MA 02138, USA

**Ursula Hess**   Département de Psychologie, Université du Québec à Montréal, CP 8888, Succ A, Montréal Qc H3C 3P8, Canada

**Esther B. Jakobs**   Department of Psychology, University of Amsterdam, Roeterstraat 15, NL – 1018 WB Amsterdam, The Netherlands

**Gilles Kirouac**   Ecole de Psychologie, Université Laval, Pavillon Savard, Bur 1512, Québec G1K 7P4, Canada

**Kristie Kooken**   Department of Psychology, San Francisco State University, 1600 Holloway Ave., San Francisco, CA 94132, USA

**Cenita Kupperbusch**   Department of Psychology, University of California, Berkeley, 3210 Tolman Hall, Berkeley, CA 94720-1650, USA

**Marianne LaFrance**   Department of Psychology, McGuinn Hall 301, Boston College, Chestnut Hill, MA 02167-3807, USA

**Victoria Lee**   Department of Psychology, University of Manchester, Oxford Road, M13 9PL Manchester, England

**Sherry Loewinger**   California School of Professional Psychology – Alameda, 1918 Chestnut Street, Berkeley, CA 94720, USA

**Antony S. R. Manstead**   Department of Psychology, University of Amsterdam, Roeterstraat 15, NL – 1018 WB Amsterdam, The Netherlands

**David Matsumoto**   Department of Psychology, San Francisco State University, 1600 Holloway Avenue, San Francisco, CA 94132, USA

**Patricia Noller**   Department of Psychology, University of Queensland, St. Lucia, Queensland 4067, Australia

**Miles L. Patterson**   Department of Psychology, University of Missouri – St. Louis, St. Louis, MO 63121, USA

**Candida Peterson**   Department of Psychology, University of Queensland, St. Lucia, Queensland 4067, Australia

**Pierre Philippot**   Faculté de Psychologie, Université de Louvain, Place du Cardinal Mercier, 10, B-1348 Louvain-la-Neuve, Belgium

**Carolyn Saarni**   Department of Counseling, Sonoma State University, Rohnert Park, CA 94928, USA

**Grania Sheehan**   Department of Psychology, University of Queensland, St. Lucia, Queensland 4067, Australia

**Hideko Uchida**   Department of Psychology, San Francisco State University, 1600 Holloway Ave., San Francisco CA 94132, USA

**Hugh Wagner**   Department of Psychology, University of Manchester, Manchester, England

**Hannelore Weber**   University of Greifswald, Department of
Psychology, Greifswald, Germany
**Carinda Wilson-Cohn**   250 West 19th Street, Apt. 12C, New York,
NY 10011, USA
**Nathan Yrizarry**   Department of Psychology, San Francisco State
University, 1600 Holloway Avenue, San Francisco, CA 94132, USA

# Introduction

# 1. Introducing Nonverbal Behavior Within a Social Context

PIERRE PHILIPPOT, ROBERT S. FELDMAN, AND
ERIK J. COATS

"A face can tell many tales." This popular saying expresses well that
the information carried by nonverbal behaviors may be ambiguous
and may not always convey the intent or internal state of the individual who displays the behaviors. For instance, one of the most common
nonverbal behaviors, smiling, may express – or covary with – many
different emitter states. It may convey contentment, ecstasy, approval,
or seduction, but it may also express contempt, submissiveness, or
anxiety. Thus it is commonly agreed that nonverbal behavior cannot
be fully understood if contextual information is not taken into account.
As most nonverbal communication takes place within a social interaction – even if the interactants are not always physically present –
this contextual information is predominantly of a social nature.

In the last decade, the scientific community has generated an impressive wealth of data and theories pertaining to the interrelationships between nonverbal behaviors and their social contexts. The aim
of the present volume is to provide an extensive review of the most
contemporary theories and bodies of empirical research in this growing area. It provides an integrated account of the latest developments
in the field produced by researchers throughout the world. As such,
the book offers an overview of an exciting scientific domain that is
growing in influence and maturing rapidly.

## The Many Faces of Nonverbal Behavior in a Social Context

We have chosen to consider many aspects of social context as well as
several facets of nonverbal behavior. Indeed, if the facial expression
of emotion remains the predominant object of study in nonverbal behavioral research, other aspects, such as gestures and postures, are

3

addressed in several chapters to take full account of nonverbal behavior.

Similarly, a wealth of social contexts are investigated in the following chapters. In introducing a special issue of the *Journal of Nonverbal Behavior* devoted to the communicative function of facial expression, Arvid Kappas (1997) provided a modified Brunswikian lens model to identify the different factors involved in the communicative process. In this useful model, three kinds of social or situational determinants are considered: the situational context, social relationships, and cultural conventions. These factors can be considered as different aspects of the social context, and they are all reviewed in the present volume.

There are two types of interrelationships between nonverbal behavior and social contexts that need to be explored. On the one hand, the ways in which social contexts modulate nonverbal behavior are examined. For instance, the impact of cultures, display rules, and the presence of others, together with the status of these others, are considered in many chapters. On the other hand, we also consider how nonverbal behavior is an effective means to influence the unfolding of a social interaction, or to change a social context, or to regulate one's self-image or internal state within a social context.

### Different Perspectives in Nonverbal Behavioral Research

Our intention is also to reflect the different perspectives that have recently been taken in the study of these interrelationships. Indeed, identical behaviors within identical social contexts have sometimes been approached by researchers using very distinct perspectives, researchers who – quite remarkably – reported very different conclusions from their observations of the very same behaviors.

Consider, for instance, two recently published studies in which the same performing athletes were observed. Unknown to them, athletes at the 1992 Olympic games in Barcelona were under the keen scrutiny of several experts in nonverbal behavior. Several researchers observed the facial expressions of winning athletes as they were performing or receiving their prizes. It is instructive to compare the observations reported by Victoria Medvec and her colleagues with those of José Miguel Fernández-Dols and Maria Angeles Ruiz-Belda.

Victoria Medvec, Scott Madey, and Thomas Gilovich (1995) observed athletes' faces after their performance. They found that bronze medalists' faces expressed more "ecstasy" – on a 10-point "ecstasy to agony" scale – than silver medalists' faces. This effect was found both immediately after the performance and later while the athletes were standing on the podium. Further, the author controlled for expectations that had been placed on the athletes prior to the games. This coding of facial expressions converged with other data (athletes' reported satisfaction with their performance in postcompetition interviews) in showing that finishing third is, in some ways, easier to accept psychologically than finishing second. In sum, Medvec and her colleagues used the athletes' facial expressions as an index of their internal (emotional) state.

Fernández-Dols and Ruiz-Belda tell a different story about the same behavior (Fernández-Dols & Ruiz-Belda, 1995). They observed that at moments that are supposed to be the peak of athletes' emotional experience (e.g., when they are just learning that they have won), they do not display the prototypical facial expression of happiness but rather a disarticulated grimace. Based on such observations, the authors argue that the emotional display of smiling by the athletes, as they are standing on the podium, is a social signal that is not a direct index of their internal emotional state, but rather what they want to communicate to their social environment (see also Fernández-Dols, this volume).

The opposing viewpoints of Medvec and her colleagues and Fernández-Dols and Ruiz-Belda are illustrative of the current state of the field of nonverbal behavior in general, and of nonverbal expression of emotion in particular. In recent years, heated debates have developed concerning whether emotional facial displays are biologically rooted behaviors whose primary function is to express the internal state of an individual (e.g., Ekman, 1994) or social signals resulting solely from learning and socialization (e.g., Fridlund, 1994). This debate has stressed the theoretical importance of adequately conceiving the role of social factors in nonverbal behavior: Are social variables a primary determinant or are they mere modulators, affecting post hoc primary nonverbal signals, as nonverbal display rules are too often conceptualized (Kappas, 1996)?

The purpose of the present volume is not to take sides in the debate about whether nonverbal behavior represents social, as opposed to biological, forces. Rather, as stated above, our aim is to present the latest empirical and theoretical developments that connect nonverbal behaviors to the social contexts in which they appear, without taking a position about the cultural versus "natural" roots of nonverbal behavior. Our contention is that a wealth of empirical findings demonstrates that nonverbal behaviors serve many social functions and are shaped by many social forces. It is these social functions and determinants of nonverbal behavior that the following chapters aim to review. They consider many facets of social context and nonverbal behavior.

## Overview

This book is divided into four parts. The first is dedicated to the ways in which social norms shape nonverbal behavior. In part two, the social factors transmitting these social norms to individuals are examined. In part three, the specific microprocesses – e.g., mimicry or mere social presence – by which social contexts affect nonverbal behavior are analyzed. Finally, part four addresses the functions that nonverbal behavior serves in social interactions.

### The Impact of Social Norms on Nonverbal Behavior

The first section of this book considers the social norms that impact nonverbal behavior. It examines different sources of these norms (e.g., culture, gender, and status) as well as the processes by which these norms operate (e.g., via display rules).

One of the most obvious and fundamental sources of social norms is the culture in which nonverbal behavior is embedded. In the second chapter, Cenita Kupperbusch, David Matsumoto, and their co-workers cover several topics that reflect current knowledge and debates regarding the role of culture in the nonverbal expression of emotion. They start with a complete and structured review of the last 30 years of research on the influence of culture on the expression and perception of emotion. They show that the questions addressed by this research have recently evolved, focusing not only on recognition accuracy, but also on the emotional intensity attributed to facial expression and to the perception of secondary emotions in the face. The notion of culture has also shifted, today focusing more on the dimensions that define cultures. The authors discuss as well the current resurgence of the controversy surrounding the universality of emotion, and they rightfully plead for the development of empirical research directly addressing this question. They contend that universality and cultural relativity are not mutually exclusive and that a full picture of nonverbal behavior can only be grasped by jointly considering these two perspectives.

An important contribution of Kupperbusch et al.'s chapter is the development of a theory of how and why culture affects nonverbal expression of emotion. Indeed, cross-cultural research in nonverbal behavior may become a mere compilation of cultural differences and similarities if it is not guided by a theoretical framework. The authors propose that two dimensions are essential to understand cultural determinants of nonverbal display of emotion. Hofstede's (1983) dimension of individualism – the extent to which culture encourages the sacrificing of individual needs and desires for group goals – is suggested to be the primary cultural dimension related to nonverbal behavior. The distinction between ingroup and outgroup membership is the other dimension. Kupperbusch and her colleagues propose that in individualistic cultures several ingroups exist, and it is consequently less threatening for people to express and identify negative emotions with respect to both ingroup and outgroup members. In a collectivistic culture, however, where in general only one ingroup exists, the expression of negative emotion in the ingroup is more threatening and, consequently, regulated by social norms. In contrast, the expression of negative display toward the outgroup would even be encouraged. In their chapter, Kupperbusch and her colleagues report recent empirical findings in support of this theory.

Within every culture, two important determinants of social norms are gender and power. In chapter 3, Marianne LaFrance and Marvin Hecht review the literature pertaining to social power, gender, and smiling, a topic that is also addressed by Kirouac and Hess in chapter 7. LaFrance and Hecht present a model in which it is argued that in a power-asymmetrical relationship, the higher-power person has license to be expressive if he or she so chooses. In other words, high-power people smile if they are indeed positively disposed. In contrast, lower-power people have the obligation to smile a moderate amount, irrespective of their feelings. This amount is related to the need to please and not to their actual feelings. The norms for low-power people can also be applied to women. LaFrance and Hecht's data indicate that among high-status women, smiling is still related to the desire to please, as it is for low-status women and men but not for high-status men. Thus, it seems that smiling serves more and varied social functions for women than for men. These data clearly demonstrate that, given the social context, nonverbal behavior might be indicative of the "true" feeling state of individuals or might be disconnected from it.

One of the key concepts developed in the field of nonverbal behavior to account for the shaping of nonverbal displays by social norms is that of display rules. Carolyn Saarni is closely tied to the development of this concept and to its systematic empirical investigation. In chapter 4, together with Hannelore Weber, she elaborates the concept of display rules and its implications for emotional and social regulation. Linking their chapter to the contribution of Kupperbusch et al., Saarni and Weber propose that the functions of nonverbal emotional displays vary according to cultural ethnotheories of emotion. In Western societies, such displays have the important function of indicating how the social interaction will unfold. In other words, they act as indices that regulate social interaction.

Another important aspect of display rules is that, by acting on emotional display, they help regulate emotion. Thus, not only do they regulate social interaction, but, within the social interaction, they also function as affect regulators. In specific social contexts, nonverbal behavior is not determined by an inner feeling state; rather, the social context shapes nonverbal displays, which in turn impact the inner feeling state. The social context thus becomes the explanatory variable of the relation between feeling state and nonverbal display. Saarni and Weber provide an excellent review of the literature pertaining to how the ability to enact display rules is acquired and of individual differences in that domain. Finally, they integrate these different notions to demonstrate how nonverbal display rules, by taking into account both interaction and emotional regulation, play a key role in self-presentation during social interaction. This new area of nonverbal investigation certainly constitutes a promising field for future investigation.

### The Transmission of Social Norms Affecting Nonverbal Behavior

Whereas the first part of the book focuses on the social norms shaping nonverbal behavior, the second part examines the social factors that ensure the transmission of these social norms. Three transmission factors are considered in different chapters: family, media, and group belongingness.

In chapter 5, Amy Halberstadt and her colleagues offer an extensive review of the empirical findings on family nonverbal expressiveness.

They find striking similarities across the life span between family expressiveness style and children's own expressive style. Children's ability to express interpretable nonverbal displays is also related to family expressiveness style. Halberstadt and her colleagues also consider the impact of family expressiveness on many facets of individuals' development, including social, emotional, and cognitive development. Their in-depth and systematic analysis of the literature demonstrates that children clearly benefit from developing in a family high in positive nonverbal expressiveness. However, the association between developmental outcomes and negative expressiveness are more complex. Their analysis suggests many useful paths, at both theoretical and methodological levels, for the development of future research.

A new area of research is presented in chapter 6, which deals with the transmission of nonverbal social norms via the media, and more specifically by the most invasive medium: television. Erik Coats and his co-workers discuss the relationship between children's nonverbal behavior and the nature of their media exposure, focusing particularly on television viewing. They argue that media depictions of emotion are unrealistic (i.e., differ from real-world displays). In a series of follow-up studies, these authors find that television's portrayal of emotional displays appears to affect children's ability to effectively encode and decode nonverbal displays, as well as their ability to use nonverbal displays in the service of social goals. These findings provide a clearer picture of the ontogeny of children's understanding and use of nonverbal behavior.

A final factor involving transmission of the social norms affecting nonverbal behavior is considered by Gilles Kirouac and Ursula Hess in chapter 7. They examine how group membership affects both the display of emotion and the decoding of these displays. Their conception of group membership is broad and reflects the central psychosocial notion of in- and outgroup memberships. Although social cognitive research has amply demonstrated that group membership deeply impacts on the interpretation of many behaviors and individual-relevant information, and although a wealth of nonverbal research has established that during a social interaction considerable information is transmitted nonverbally, almost no empirical research has been devoted to the impact of this central social factor on nonverbal encoding and decoding. In their chapter, Kirouac and Hess develop the theoretical and empirical basis for this area of research. Specifically, they consider the influence of culture, gender, and social status, as group membership markers, on the encoding and decoding of emotional display. Their notion of nonverbal behavior as a self-presentation tool is consistent with that developed by Saarni and Weber and may open promising new fields of research.

## *Immediate Social Factors During Interaction*

The third section of the book is devoted to the analysis of the molecular processes by which the social context and nonverbal behavior interact. More specifically, the authors in this section examine the immediate effects of social context on nonverbal behavior.

In chapter 8, Ursula Hess, Pierre Philippot, and Sylvie Blairy examine how our interaction partners' nonverbal displays condition our own through a process of mimicry. Mimicry is a process by which individuals imitate, most often unconsciously, the nonverbal behaviors of other individuals with whom they interact or whom they observe. Hess et al. first review the empirical evidence establishing that, at least in some circumstances, people mimic the facial expressions of others. They then examine the social functions of this phenomenon. The authors show that there is no empirical evidence that mimicking other individuals enhances an understanding of their feeling states or fosters empathy – despite the fact that this claim is often encountered in the literature. However, mimicry has an effect on the individuals who are mimicked: They generally feel better understood by a mimicking partner than by a nonmimicking partner. The authors thus conclude that mimicry plays a function in social interaction by developing a feeling of rapport.

Another analysis of microphenomena is reported by José-Miguel Fernández-Dols in chapter 9. As mentioned earlier, Fernández-Dols observed the facial expressions of people during the seconds surrounding peak emotional experience. In his chapter, Fernández-Dols shows that these displays are transformed by the presence of social observers: The facial displays only take the form of interpretable facial expressions when the expressors know that they are being observed. The work of Fernández-Dols is grounded in a situationist approach of nonverbal behavior. This creative theoretical framework, developed and argued in the chapter, assumes that nonverbal behavior is largely determined by situational factors embedded in a dynamic tension system. According to Fernández-Dols, a nonverbal behavior can only make sense when considered with the social context in which it emerges. This original and thought-provoking theoretical approach is supported by intriguing data ranging from the observation of gold-medalists at the Olympic games to bullfighters "in the flow."

In chapter 10, Hugh Wagner and Victoria Lee examine how the presence of a social partner influences the intensity of nonverbal expression of emotion. They specifically focus on one dimension of this type of situation: whether the social partner is a friend or a stranger. A review of the literature and of the studies conducted in the authors' own laboratory reveals that the inhibition of or the facilitation of emotional display by a social audience depends on the type of relationship existing between the subject and the audience. More precisely, the authors argue that the most important dimension is uncertainty about the partner's role and attitude, coupled with a tendency to conformity in situations of uncertainty. This dimension has an impact not only on the intensity of the nonverbal display but also on its nature. The authors then consider that in most social interactions, nonverbal behavior often co-occurs with verbal utterance. Given the importance of both channels in alleviating the uncertainty inherent in most social situations, Wagner and Lee claim that nonverbal behavior cannot be understood without reference to verbal behavior. In support of this claim, they present preliminary data consisting of the micro-analysis of interviews in which both verbal and nonverbal channels are considered simultaneously.

Finally, in chapter 11, Antony Manstead, Agneta Fischer, and Esther Jakobs examine the effect on nonverbal behavior of the sociality of the context in which it appears. Within this perspective they address the debate evoked earlier in this chapter: Do facial displays express emotional states or do they communicate social motives? These authors carefully analyze both the theoretical arguments and the empirical evidence supporting each position. As often happens when resolving a polarized debate, their conclusion is that neither of the two positions is "right" or "wrong." Rather, our goal should be to identify the conditions that promote the "expressive" and "communicative" functions of facial displays. The authors develop a model that integrates these two functions. This model comprises four factors that determine the social or expressive function served by a nonverbal behavior: the intensity and the nature of the emotional situation, the type of nonverbal display at stake, and the social role of the expressor in the situation.

*The Role of Nonverbal Behavior in the Facilitation of Social Interaction*

In part four, the role of nonverbal behavior in social interaction is considered. In chapter 12, Miles Patterson provides a general model for this question. The role of nonverbal behavior during conflict in close relationships is examined by Judith Feeney and her collaborators in chapter 13. Finally, chapter 14, by Eric Anderson and his colleagues, also deals with close relationships, but from a different perspective: the role of nonverbal behavior in deception.

In chapter 12, Miles Patterson presents the latest version of his parallel process model of nonverbal behavior. He emphasizes the necessary interdependence of nonverbal behavior management and social cognition during social interactions. Patterson provides a personal account of the theoretical development of this domain in the last decades. Specifically, he shows how person perception theories and nonverbal exchange theory have shaped the present state of the field. The different components of the model, and their dynamic, make the link between social cognition and nonverbal behavior. Patterson's model offers a broad framework in which to root future research on nonverbal behavior in social interaction.

In chapter 13, Judith Feeney, Patricia Noller, and their collaborators analyze a more specific phenomenon: conflicts in close relationships. More precisely, they discuss the functions of nonverbal behavior in couples and families. They show that marital satisfaction is related to the type of nonverbal behaviors displayed during certain types of conflict. Further, they observe that nonverbal behavior indexing low involvement in the interaction (e.g., lack of gaze, head turn) is more typical of husbands than of wives. They then examine the effects of family conflict on children's perception of the different family members. The work they present in the chapter stresses the importance of nonverbal communication in family relations. A strength of this chapter is its demonstration of how nonverbal behavior has to be understood in the type of social context in which it occurs (the relationship satisfaction, the type of conflict discussed, and the way in which the conflict is typically handled in the family).

Finally, in the last chapter of the book, Eric Anderson, Matthew Ansfield, and Bella DePaulo argue that the social context in which deception occurs is an important consideration both for research and for everyday interaction. The conditions under which one lies to strangers and to close others differ, as do the kinds of lies one tells and the motivations behind them. The authors show that there is only a weak link between deception detection and closeness in the relationship. In other words, people are not really better at detecting intimate others' lies than strangers' lies. Anderson and his colleagues hypothesize that people in close relationships are more inclined to assume that their partners are telling the truth. They consider the differences between close and casual relationships in motivation for and consequences of lying.

## Conclusion

In sum, this volume considers many facets and levels of nonverbal behaviors and of social contexts. Nonverbal behaviors as diverse as emotional display, deception, mimicry, self-presentation, and conversation monitoring are studied. A similarly large variety of social contexts are reflected on: the presence of an audience, whether the audience is composed of strangers or friends, the level of intimacy between partners, group membership, culture, gender, power, and conflict. Whatever the facet considered, we are forced to conclude that nonverbal behavior can be fully understood only when considered within its social context.

Exciting theoretical advances are provided in many chapters. At the molar lever, in chapter 12 Miles Patterson provides an integrated theoretical framework that connects nonverbal communication with social cognition and the study of social interaction. In chapter 9, José-Miguel Fernández-Dols argues for a thought-provoking situationist approach to nonverbal behavior.

Regarding a more specific and contemporary debate, the dispute between "naturalists" and "nurturalists" is addressed in several other chapters and polarized oppositions are resolved. For instance, in chapter 1, Cenita Kupperbusch et al. convincingly argue that there is no necessary opposition between these two perspectives. In chapter 11, Antony Manstead et al. demonstrate that extreme positions on both sides are theoretically untenable and unsubstantiated by empirical data.

Other specific theoretical progress is reported in several contributions. Carolyn Saarni and Hannelore Weber provide a promising theoretical framework to integrate self-presentation, emotion regulation, and nonverbal behavior. Similarly, Gilles Kirouac and Ursula Hess offer a theoretical basis for studying the interactions between group membership and nonverbal decoding. Cenita Kupperbusch et al. propose a theoretical model to guide cross-cultural research in nonverbal behavior. Hugh Wagner and Victoria Lee develop a model that integrates verbal and nonverbal behaviors.

Theoretical advances are also provided for more specific phenomena such as smiling (LaFrance and Hecht), mimicry (Hess et al.), television influences on children's nonverbal behavior (Coats et al.), uncertainty and nonverbal expression (Wagner and Lee), and deception (Anderson et al.). Finally, extensive reviews of empirical findings are provided by Halberstadt et al. regarding family expressiveness and by Feeney et al. on the relationships between nonverbal behaviors and conflicts in families and couples.

It is clear that our understanding of nonverbal behavior within a social context has evolved dramatically in the last decade. Nevertheless, several exciting avenues of future research await further exploration. It is our hope that the present volume will help in this endeavor by providing an up-to-date and detailed account of the theoretical and empirical state of the art.

## References

Ekman, P. (1994). Strong evidence for universals in facial expressions: A reply to Russell's mistaken critique. *Psychological Bulletin, 115,* 268–287.

Fernández-Dols, J. M., & Ruiz-Belda, M. A. (1995). Are smiles a sign of happiness?: Gold medal winners at the Olympic Games. *Journal of Personality and Social Psychology, 69,* 1113–1119.

Fridlund, A. J. (1994). *Human facial expression: An evolutionary view.* San Diego, CA: Academic Press.

Hofstede, G. (1983). Dimensions of national cultures in fifty countries and three regions. In J. B. Deregowski, S. Dziurawiec, & R. C. Annis (Eds.), *Expiscations in cross-cultural psychology* (pp. 335–355). Lisse: Swets & Zeitlinger.

Kappas, A. (1996). The sociality of appraisals: Impact of social situations on the evaluation of emotion antecedent events and physiological and expressive reactions. In N. Frijda (Ed.), *IXth Conference of the International Society for Research on Emotions* (pp. 116–120). Toronto, ON: ISRE.

Kappas, A. (1997). The fascination with faces: Are they windows to our soul? *Journal of Nonverbal Behavior, 21,* 157–162.

Medvec, V. H., Madey, S. F., & Gilovich, T. (1995). When less is more: Counterfactual thinking and satisfaction among Olympic medalists. *Journal of Personality and Social Psychology, 69,* 603–611.

PART I

# Social Norms in Nonverbal Behavior

# 2. Cultural Influences on Nonverbal Expressions of Emotion

CENITA KUPPERBUSCH, DAVID MATSUMOTO,
KRISTIE KOOKEN, SHERRY LOEWINGER,
HIDEKO UCHIDA, CARINDA WILSON-COHN, AND
NATHAN YRIZARRY

## Introduction

We live in an increasingly diverse world. As a result, we often encounter people with whom we share various similarities, but about whom we may notice certain differences in communication styles. Similarities and differences in communication styles are readily apparent in verbal communication because different cultures have different languages and dialects within languages, and we often focus on language in communication. Many similarities and differences, however, also occur at the level of nonverbal behavior. Because the relative importance of nonverbal behaviors in communication is now well accepted in psychology, consideration of the influence of culture on those nonverbal behaviors has gained substantial importance in recent years. Our goal in studying how culture influences nonverbal behaviors is to investigate the origins of, and understand the implications of, those similarities and differences in communication. In this chapter, we discuss cultural similarities and differences in the expression, perception, and meanings of facial expressions of emotion. We focus largely on the role of the face in emotion communication, as that is the area most extensively studied and the area with which we are most familiar.

The development of research in the area of cultural influences on nonverbal expressions of emotion has been varied and interesting. Although most researchers now agree that the expression and perception of emotion is partially universal and partially culturally specific, there has been considerable debate regarding the extent of culture's influence. Debates about the influence of culture on emotion expression, emotion recognition, the language of emotion, and the antecedents of emotion across cultures suggest that the topic area is much more complex than it originally appeared. Although addressing all of the major issues that have appeared in the literature in the past three decades is beyond the scope of this chapter, we hope to clearly present the research that has been conducted to date and suggest future directions for continued understanding of the complex interaction of culture and emotion.

With that as our goal, we will cover five topics that reflect the current knowledge and debates regarding the role of culture in the nonverbal expression of emotion. First, we review early research on the universality and culture-specificity of facial expressions of emotion and the recognition of those faces. Second, we review new findings generated from studies in the past ten years. Third, we discuss current controversial issues regarding the universality of emotion expression. Fourth, we present a theory of how and why culture affects emotion, and we present two cross-cultural studies that support the theory. Finally, we suggest an agenda for future research in this area.

## Review of the Previous Literature

Although the bulk of the research on culture and emotion has been conducted within the past 30 years, the concept that facial expressions of emotion are universal is not new. Darwin is typically cited as the first to present a comprehensive theory on the universality of facial expressions of emotion in his book *The Expression of the Emotions in Man and Animals* (1872), in which he proposed that facial expressions of emotion were innate and evolutionarily adaptive. He presented examples of humans and animals that supported his theory. His data, however, were largely observational. Fortunately, since that time, a great deal of scientific research has been conducted with humans and nonhuman primates that supports Darwin's original theory (Ekman et al., 1987; Ekman & Friesen, 1971, 1986; Ekman, Sorenson, & Friesen, 1969; Izard, 1971; Sackett, 1966).

### *Universal Recognition of Facial Expressions of Emotion*

Some of the first evidence for the universal basis of facial expressions of emotion came from judgment studies in which observers in many different cultures were shown facial expressions of emotion considered to be universal and were asked to describe the emotion portrayed in the face. The theory underlying these early studies was that if the facial expressions of emotion were universal, observers in all cultures would agree on what emotion was being expressed in the faces. If disagreements within a culture, or across cultures, were found, it would be evidence against the notion of universality.

There are two research groups in particular who are responsible for collecting the first evidence supporting universality of facial expressions of emotion. Paul Ekman and Carroll Izard, influenced by the teachings of Silvan Tomkins (1962, 1963), began separate research programs with a similar goal – to test the universality hypothesis. Their studies, referred to as the "universality studies," produced the first scientific evidence in support of the universality hypothesis. Original data supporting universality of emotion recognition were collected in literate and preliterate cultures (see Ekman, 1972; Ekman & Friesen, 1971; Ekman, Sorenson, & Friesen, 1969; Izard, 1971). In these studies, subjects from twelve literate cultures and two preliterate cultures were shown pictures of facial expressions and asked to select the emotion being portrayed from a list of emotion terms that had been translated into their native language. In the studies conducted by Ekman and his colleagues, the photographs were selected based on their representing a single affect according to Ekman, Friesen, and Tomkins's (1971) Facial Affect Scoring Technique. The stimulus set included posed and spontaneous still photos. Izard's stimuli were similar in that they were selected still photos, but all photos were of posed expressions. For the literate cultures, agreement about the association of six emotion words – anger, disgust, fear, happiness, sadness, and surprise – with specific facial expressions was high, and agreement rates were well over chance. For the most isolated preliterate culture studied, the Fore in the South East Highlands of New Guinea, the methods were somewhat modified due to language differences. Subjects were told short stories (in their native language) that described an emotion, and were asked to point to the face (out of three possible choices) that portrayed the emotion being elicited. With the exception of fear, which was often mistaken for surprise, the New Guineans were able to correctly identify the emotion intended at levels well over chance. These findings have been replicated across many other cultures, using different methods and facial stimuli (e.g., see Ekman et al., 1987).

## Universal Expressions of Emotion

One of the limitations of the judgment studies with regard to their implications of universality was the assumption that cross-cultural agreements in *recognition* implicated pancultural *expression* of the same faces. The only way to address this limitation was to study the actual expressions themselves, examining cross-cultural similarities or differences in the components of the expressions for the different emotions.

One study attempting to do so was conducted by Ekman and Friesen (1971) and involved data collected in two preliterate cultures in New Guinea in order to control for the possibility that media exposure accounted for data favoring universality of emotion expression. Subjects were asked to show on their faces what they would look like if they felt the emotion elicited in simple stories designed to elicit the universally recognized emotions. Ekman and Friesen photographed the tribespeople's faces and showed the pictures to American subjects, who were able to recognize the intended facial expressions at accuracy well over chance rates (however, as in the judgment study findings, fear and surprise were often confused with each other). These results indicated that the New Guineans associated certain specific facial expressions with discrete emotions in the same way that subjects in Western cultures did in the judgment studies. Because the tribespeople were not exposed to the same visual input as literate cultures, those findings could only be explained in terms of the universality of emotion expression.

In spite of the evidence in favor of universality, Ekman and his colleagues' findings were not easily accepted by critics. One anthropologist even went so far as to call Ekman a fascist (Ekman, 1987). One of the major criticisms was of their use of posed, rather than spontaneous, facial expressions of emotion. In order to address that criticism, Ekman (1972) and Friesen (1972) conducted a cross-cultural study in the United States and Japan in which they collected spontaneous facial expression data. American and Japanese males were videotaped with a hidden camera while they watched video clips designed to elicit extreme disgust. Ekman and Friesen found that when the Japanese and American men believed they were alone, they showed no differences in the types and frequencies of their negative facial responses. That is, they exhibited the same facial behaviors in reaction to the stimulus clips. This study was very important in that it was the first of its kind to produce data that supported the universality hypothesis with spontaneous expressions of emotion in a controlled experimental setting.

*Cultural Differences in Expression: The Neurocultural Theory*

Although data primarily supported the universality of facial emotion expression, there was no explanation for why it seemed as though cultures differed. Nearly everyone has had some experience communicating with a person of another culture when it has seemed that facial expressions of emotion can't possibly be universal. To answer this apparent contradiction, Ekman and Friesen (1969) developed the Neurocultural Theory which accounts for both similarities and differences in the expression of emotion. According to this theory, universality of facial expressions of emotion occurs at the level of the facial muscles. That is, there are certain facial muscles associated with certain emotions that are constant across cultures. When a specific universal emotion is elicited, a specific set of facial muscles is activated by the Facial Affect Program, a biologically innate center that stores the facial configurations corresponding to the universal emotions. Thus the Facial Affect Program accounts for universality in emotional expression. Differences in facial displays occur, however, because of (1) learned cultural differences about the antecedents of emotion (i.e., the events that bring on particular emotions may differ across cultures), and (2) culturally learned rules regarding the appropriateness of showing certain expressions in certain situations. Ekman and Friesen (1969) coined the term *display rules* to refer to these learned rules of expression management. Display rules are socially learned habits regarding the control of facial appearance that act to intensify, deintensify, mask, or qualify a universal expression of emotion depending on the social circumstance (Ekman, 1972). Therefore, the facial expression shown in response to some stimulus is affected by a combination of biological and learned factors.

The most convincing evidence for the existence of display rules was gathered in another part of the Japanese–American cross-cultural study described above. After their initial viewing of the negative films, the Japanese and American men watched the films a second time. This time the experimenter stayed in the room with them while they watched the most emotionally intense portions of the film clips. Again, the subjects were videotaped with a hidden camera. In analyzing the videotaped records of the second viewing of the negative clips, Friesen (1972) found that the Japanese men showed considerably fewer negative facial expressions and even smiled when they were interviewed about their emotional reactions immediately following the viewing of the disgusting film. When compared to the results of the first part of the study, these findings strongly support Ekman's Neurocultural Theory. In the first condition, there were virtually no differences between the Japanese and the American men – they showed the same types of negative facial expressions when they believed they were alone. When an experimenter was in the room with them, however, the culturally learned display rules that differed for the two cultures (e.g., polite smiling for the Japanese) affected the natural or universal reactions of the Japanese subjects.

## Recent Research in Facial Expressions of Emotion

Recent studies have examined other components of expression and judgment and continue to indicate that there are universal as well as culture-specific aspects of facial expressions of emotion. Cultural differences do not necessarily refute the universality hypothesis, but suggest that biology and culture interact to affect emotion expression. Nearly all aspects of the communication of emotion examined in recent research are subject to the influence of culture. Some of the studies we will review address culture's influence on (1) the accuracy of recognition of universal emotions, (2) differences in attributions of intensity of emotional expression, (3) differences in what is judged the second most intense emotion in the case emotion blends, and (4) differences in the attributions of the meanings associated with certain emotions.

### Cultural Differences in Emotion Recognition

Although the data from the original universality research showed that subjects were able to recognize emotions at well over chance rates, no study ever reported perfect cross-cultural agreement. That is, cultures differed in the exact level of agreement in their judgments. Several recent studies have attempted to offer possible explanations for these differences. Matsumoto (1992a), for example, compared the ability of Japanese and American subjects to recognize what had been established as the six universal facial expressions of emotion. Although the study was not intended as a test of the universality hypothesis, he found that recognition rates ranged from 64% to 99%, which was consistent with the rates observed in earlier universality studies. He also found, however, that American subjects were better at recognizing anger, disgust, fear, and sadness than the Japanese subjects were but that the accuracy rates did not differ for happiness or surprise. Matsumoto interpreted these findings as demonstrating cultural rules about the perception of certain emotions that influence the recognition rates of basic universal expressions. He suggested that the differences in recognition rates were not due to the fact that the expressions were not universal. After all, both groups had recognized each of the emotions with accuracy rates well over chance. Rather, the differences in recognition rates were due to cultural differences in the socially learned rules about how universal emotions can be displayed, recognized, or felt. Specifically, he focused on the major cultural differences between Japan and the United States that have to do with the allowance for individuality or conformity. In Japan, because of the emphasis on group harmony and conformity, the presence of emotions that threaten group harmony (negative emotions) is discouraged. Therefore, a Japanese person would probably be careful not to show negative emotions and would tend not to recognize, or would attenuate their recognition of, negative emotion expressions in others. In contrast, an American, living in a country that encourages individuality, would be allowed, and possibly even encouraged in, the expression and therefore the perception of negative emotions.

*Cultural Differences in Attributions of Intensity of Facial Expressions of Emotion*

In an attempt to broaden the possible base of cultural dimensions (to go beyond individuality vs. group conformity) that could explain differences in agreement levels across cultures, Matsumoto (1989) reviewed data from four cross-cultural studies that reported differences in emotion recognition agreement rates. Fifteen cultures in which emotion recognition data had been collected were ranked on four of Hofstede's dimensions of culture (1980, 1983), including Power Distance (PD), the degree to which differences in power are maintained by the culture; Uncertainty Avoidance (UA), the degree to which a culture develops institutions and rituals to deal with the anxiety created by uncertainty; Individualism (IN), the degree to which a culture encourages the sacrificing of individual goals for the goals of the group; and Masculinity (MA), the degree to which a culture emphasizes sex differences (Hofstede, 1980, 1983). He then examined the correlations between these cultural dimensions and emotion accuracy and judged intensity levels. Two important findings suggested that cultural differences in intensity ratings may be accounted for by differences in the sociocultural dimensions. First, there was a negative correlation between PD and intensity ratings of certain negative emotions. Specifically, cultures that maintained status and power differentials among their members tended to rate the intensity of anger, fear, and sadness lower. Secondly, IN was positively correlated with the intensity ratings of anger and fear, with more individualistic cultures associated with higher ratings. Thus, cultures high on IN and low on PD (e.g., the American culture) have a tendency to perceive negative emotions at high intensities; cultures low on IN and high on PD (e.g., the Japanese culture) have a tendency to perceive negative emotions at lower intensities. These results suggest that understanding dimensions of culture could be the key to understanding cultural differences in the perception of negative emotions.

Matsumoto's (1989) study is not the first to report cultural differences in the attributed intensity of facial expressions. In Ekman et al.'s (1987) study of ten cultures, although overall recognition accuracy data supported the universality hypothesis, the authors found that certain cultural groups rated some universal emotions significantly more intensely than other groups. Specifically, subjects who were not Caucasian, judging the facial expressions of Caucasians (i.e., they were judging the facial expression of a person from a different culture), gave significantly lower intensity ratings on happiness, surprise, and fear. These data seemed to suggest that the subjects were acting according to culturally learned rules about how expressions are to be perceived. One possible explanation suggested by the researchers was that the non-Caucasian subjects may have rated the Caucasian subjects less intensely in order to be polite. To further examine this notion, Matsumoto and Ekman developed a stimulus set of facial expressions comprised of Asian and Caucasian posers and presented these stimuli to judges in the United States and Japan (Matsumoto & Ekman, 1989). They found that for all but one emotion (disgust), Americans rated the facial expressions more intensely than the Japanese, regardless of the culture of the person being judged. Because the differences in ratings were not specific to the race of the poser, Matsumoto and Ekman (1989) interpreted the differences as a function of learned rules of emotion decoding that are specific to each culture. Alternatively, decoders from different cultures may be using different base rates with which to compare the judged expressions. That is, there may be differences in the relative intensity with which a certain emotion is typically expressed in a particular culture. Future research should explore which of the two explanations is more accurate.

As recent research has demonstrated both cultural similarities and differences in judgments, a major consideration for the field is the question of what it is about the differences in the cultures that produce those differences in perception. We suggest that a mechanism similar to the Neurocultural Theory governing expressions also moderates emotion perception. This mechanism would imply that the judgment of an emotional stimulus will be affected by (1) a Facial Affect Recognition Program which is innate and universal, and (2) culturally specific decoding rules (a term defined by Buck, 1984) which will act to change, intensify, deintensify, or mask the perception of that emotion expression.

This theory suggests that, for some cultures, the expression of an emotion may not reflect exactly what the person is feeling. Or the emotion may be expressed at an intensity which does not reflect the true strength of the experience of that emotion. In other words, what you see may not be what you get. If a culture has rules about how a person is supposed to mask an expression based on, for example, the need to maintain group harmony, it is probable that judges will make different assumptions about the posers' actual emotional state and their facial expression. For example, a judge may perceive a person as showing a medium level of happiness; they may infer, however, that the poser is actually feeling higher levels of happiness because of rules about how much happiness it is appropriate to show in their culture.

In an unpublished study conducted in our laboratory, this notion was tested by comparing American and Japanese ratings of facial expressions in which separate ratings were obtained for expression intensity and inferred subjective experience. The findings indicated that American subjects rated intensity and subjective experience significantly differently, suggesting that they believed there was a difference between what was shown and what was felt. Interestingly, there were no significant differences between judgments of external display and subjective experience for the Japanese subjects. This finding may indicate that, for the Japanese subjects, there is no real difference between the subjective experience of an emotion and its facial expression. However, an alternative explanation is that, for the sake of maintaining social harmony, the Japanese subjects felt it would be impolite or disrespectful to assume that a person was not being honest in displaying his or her "true" emotional experience. A second important finding was a difference between the intensity judgments of American and Japanese judges. American judges rated greater intensities in display, while Japanese rated greater intensities in inferred subjective experience. The findings were interpreted in terms of culturally learned display rules which vary for Americans and Japanese. Having found significant differences between the experience and expression of an emotion, naive subjects are acknowledging social rules about the control of emotion expression. While some authors (see below) have opted to use cultural differences in judgments of emotion as evidence that refutes their universality, we consider differences as evidence of the importance of culture's role in influencing the interpretation and attributions of subjective experience of universal emotions.

## Cultural Similarities in Relative Intensity of Facial Expressions of Emotion

Despite the cultural differences found in the intensity ratings of judged facial expressions of emotion, both Ekman et al. (1987) and Matsumoto and Ekman (1989) found similarities in the relative intensity judgments of facial expressions of emotion. Ekman and his colleagues (1987) compared differences in relative intensity by pairing the intensity ratings of two expressions of the same emotion. Ninety-two percent of the time (out of 130 total comparisons), cultures agreed on which of two emotion expressions was the most intense. In a study by Matsumoto and Ekman (1989), the finding was extended to include comparisons of relative intensity across different poser types, as the stimulus set included both Caucasian and Japanese posers. Looking at emotion intensity comparisons separately for each emotion, within culture and across gender and then within gender across culture, findings indicated that the Americans and the Japanese agreed on which photo was more intense in 24 out of 30 comparisons. Differences were also tested more recently in the unpublished study described earlier examining relative intensity ratings in American and Japanese differences in judgments of expression intensity and subjective experience. Using more sophisticated tests, variance in expression ratings was systematically related to the variance in the experience ratings, separately for the American and Japanese subjects, and using both the observers and then the expressions as the units of analyses. They found no cultural differences in the relative relationships between experience and expression. These findings support the notion that emotional behavior is jointly influenced by universality of emotion expression and culturally learned rules defining the ways in which universal emotions are to be experienced, expressed, and judged.

## Cultural Similarities in the Second Modal Response in Emotion Recognition

Recent studies have also reported cultural similarities in the second modal response in emotion recognition. The second modal response is the emotion category that receives the second highest number of selections for any expression. This typically occurs when emotional expressions are judged as being blends of more than one emotion. The criticism that although there may be universality in the first modal response in facial expressions of emotion, culture may play a role in determining which emotion is judged as being the second possible emotion displayed was addressed in Ekman et al.'s (1987) cross-cultural study. Analyses strongly supported cultural agreement. For every culture in Ekman et al's (1987) study, the secondary emotion for the disgust expressions was contempt, and for fear expressions the secondary emotion was surprise. For anger, the second modal response varied depending on the anger photo, with disgust, surprise, and contempt as the second response choices. These findings suggest that universality of emotion recognition, at least for some emotions, goes beyond a simple first response.

## Ethnic Differences in Recognition and Intensity Attributions of Facial Expressions of Emotion

Having found certain similarities and differences across cultures, Matsumoto (1993) conducted a study that examined differences in affect intensity, emotion judgments, display rule attitudes, and self-reported emotional expression as a function of ethnic groups within the United States. The results indicated ethnic differences in the perceived intensity of certain emotions, as well as differences in display rule attitudes. Specifically, African Americans perceived anger more intensely than Asian Americans did and disgust more intensely than Caucasian Americans and Asian Americans; Hispanic Americans perceived Caucasian faces more intensely than Caucasian Americans and Asian

Americans did; and African Americans perceived female expressions more intensely than Asian Americans. Although these subjects all lived in the San Francisco Bay area, they showed the kinds of differences that one would expect to find across cultures. Findings such as these compel us, as cross-cultural researchers, to reevaluate the way we conceptualize culture and stress the importance of the need for psychologically meaningful dimensions of culture that are independent of ethnicity or country. Most cross-cultural research has been conducted with the assumption that a person living in a certain country is a member of the primary culture of that country. Finding differences within an American sample (a group which is nearly always considered culturally homogenous in cross-cultural studies) encouraged us to develop a theoretical explanation of cultural differences, using meaningful psychological dimensions (like Hofstede's cultural dimensions) measured on the individual level, to explain cultural and individual differences in emotion expression and perception not restricted by ethnicity or country. We will explain this theory in detail later in the chapter.

### Cultural Similarities in Perceived Expressivity

One recent study has also reported cultural similarities in perceived expressivity of people of different cultures (Pittam et al., 1995). In this study, Australian and Japanese subjects completed a questionnaire regarding the overall level of expressivity of Australian and Japanese people. The Japanese were rated as less expressive than the Australians by both Australian and Japanese subjects. These findings indicate that (1) people of different cultures believe that there are differences in intensity of emotion expression, and (2) they tend to agree about who is more or less expressive.

### Attributions of Personality Based on Smiles

Recent research has also shown that cultures can differ in the meanings they attribute to facial expressions of emotion. For example, in many cultures, the smile is a common signal for greeting, for acknowledgment, or for showing acceptance. Because the smile is one of the easiest facial movements to make, it can also often be employed to mask an inappropriate facial expression. Cultures may differ in the use of smiles for this purpose. This appeared to be the case in the study described earlier in which Japanese and American men watched disgust-eliciting video clips with an experimenter in the room with them. The Japanese men used smiling to cover up their negative expressions much more often than the American men did (Ekman, 1972; Friesen, 1972). To further investigate the meaning of those differences, Matsumoto and Kudoh (1993) tested the hypothesis that Japanese and American judges would make different assumptions about smiling versus nonsmiling (i.e., neutral) faces with regard to intelligence, attractiveness, and sociability. They found cultural differences on intelligence, with American judges rating smiling faces as more intelligent than neutral faces. The Japanese subjects, however, did not rate smiling and nonsmiling faces differently on intelligence. There was also a difference in degree of sociability. Although Americans and Japanese both found smiling faces more sociable than neutral faces, the difference for the Americans was to a greater degree. These differences suggest that cultural display rules cause Japanese and American subjects to attribute different meanings to the smile. Differences in the attributions of meanings to the smile of happiness and to other universal facial expressions of emotion serve as a good explanation for perceived major differences in communication styles across cultures.

## Evidence for a Universal Contempt Expression

Most recently, research has indicated the existence of a seventh universal facial expression of emotion, contempt. The initial evidence in support of contempt as a universally expressed emotion was collected from ten cultures including the non-Western culture of West Sumatra (Ekman & Friesen, 1986; Ekman & Heider, 1988). This evidence was later replicated by Matsumoto (1992b) in four cultures, three of which were different from Ekman and Friesen's original ten cultures. Like the previous findings concerning the universality of anger, disgust, fear, happiness, sadness, and surprise, the universality of a contempt expression received considerable attention and criticism (Izard & Haynes, 1988; Russell, 1991). For example, Russell (1991) suggested that the context in which the expression was shown greatly influenced the results in favor of data that supported the universality hypothesis. In his own study, he found that the contempt expression was more often labeled as either disgust or sadness when shown either alone or after showing a disgust or sadness picture (Russell, 1991). Ekman, O'Sullivan, and Matsumoto (1991) reanalyzed their data to address Russell's criticism and found no effect of context.

### Current Debate Regarding Universality of Facial Expression of Emotion

The debate over the contempt expression is a fitting example of the larger debate regarding the universality of *any* facial expression of emotion. For over thirty years, and as a result of a large body of evidence collected by many cross-cultural researchers, the notion of universality has gone from a possible explanatory hypothesis to a widely accepted psychological concept. Recently, however, some articles have appeared in the literature questioning the research underlying the basis of universality. Criticisms have generally been levied against the judgment studies described earlier, and have centered on their methods (Russell, 1991, 1994, 1995), interpretations (Russell, 1994), and the use of language specific terms for facial expressions of emotion (Wierzbicka, 1995).

Probably the greatest concern raised about universality has been about the methods employed in the judgment studies. Over the years, across many studies conducted independently by many laboratories around the world, many methods have been employed. In his review, Russell (1994) raised several criticisms of the methods, including (1) the nature of the stimuli: the fact that photos are often preselected and the expressions are often posed; (2) the presentation of stimuli: the fact that stimuli are previewed in some studies, are generally presented to subjects in a within-subjects design, and are generally in a particular order that creates a context in which subjects can make better "guesses"; and (3) the response format: the fact that the forced-choice methods are the predominant type of response alternative. In a recent paper, Russell (1994) reanalyzed judgment data across a number of studies, separating studies by method, and also employing a Western/non-Western distinction among the countries to demonstrate that the methods employed may have biased responses in favor of Western cultures.

Wierzbicka (1995) has raised a different type of concern, suggesting that emotions should not be referred to in terms of the six (or seven) basic emotions, because they are language specific terms. Alternatively, she suggests that one should only speak of universals in terms of "conceptual primitives." For example, she suggests that when a person recognizes a smile of happiness, he or she is reading the face as: "I think: something good is happening, I feel something good because of this." Her position, therefore, is that although facial expressions of emotion may indeed be universal, the methods we have used to study them, including the use of emotion terms as response alternatives in judgment tasks, are limited and bound by the culture in which those terms arise and cannot possibly be universal.

These concerns have been addressed in the literature by a number of writers. Ekman (1994) and Izard (1994), for example, both point out that although Russell's (1994) article appeared to be systematic in its presentation of evidence, it paid selective attention to those studies that helped to support Russell's thesis. In particular, Russell's (1994) article failed to cite those studies that controlled for the various flaws he suggested were responsible for skewing the previous universality findings. Russell's thesis was also flawed in that he used criticisms about one of several types of evidence for universality in facial expressions of emotion to argue against the entire basis of universality. Indeed, he failed to mention studies on nonhuman primates and with infants and the congenitally blind, all of which strongly indicate that certain facial expressions of emotion are innate and universal. Examples in the primate literature include a recent study by Geen (1992), in which he found that rhesus monkeys reared in isolation showed "more or less normal-appearing facial expressions" (Geen, 1992, p. 277) when they were later placed with other monkeys. Hauser (1993) found evidence that in rhesus monkeys, as in humans, emotion expression is lateralized in the right hemisphere of the brain. In a review of studies conducted with blind children, Charlesworth and Kreutzer (1973) concluded that the spontaneous expressions of blind children did not differ from the expressions of sighted children who had been exposed to visual examples of expressions their entire lives.

Wierzbicka's thesis is also not without criticism in the literature. Winegar (1995), for example, is somewhat critical of Wierzbicka's conceptual primitives, as they are also constrained by culture. He goes so far as to suggest that one cannot ever avoid cultural specificity in studying psychological phenomena, and that even if we could agree upon, for example, the universality of evaluation, we would not be able to avoid the effect of culture in our theory building. Another writer, VanGeert (1995), agrees that there is a need for a coding procedure for universal emotions similar to Wierzbicka's conceptual primitives. He believes that we need a more precise measure, one in which each universal has a "specific physical definition" (p. 265). He then presents three dimensions on which he suggests that universals can be named and organized. In his description of one dimension he eloquently suggests a distinction between what he calls "experiential" and "technical" universals. He believes that "emotions are experiential universals, that is, all people are in principle able to entertain a set of similar subjective experiences called the universal emotions. But the only way to refer to such shared emotions is by means of a technical language" (p. 206).

We agree with the basic premise of both Russell and Wierzbicka that researchers need to be more aware of how conscious and unconscious cultural biases may affect their methods of data collection, analysis, and interpretation with regard to this topic and others, for that matter. We do not believe, however, that the arguments they have proffered in the past are very convincing, for the very same reasons outlined by the writers we have just discussed. We would like to make two additional points germane to this topic.

First, concerns about the effect of different methodologies in the judgment studies conducted to date are empirical questions that can be addressed by research, not solely by argument. A piecemeal approach to the problem that addresses each issue in a separate study, however, would not be a solution, for the very reason Russell himself suggests: The interaction of multiple methodological parameters may contribute to results. Thus, the only possible empirical solution to this debate would be to conduct what we will call the "perfectly controlled and comprehensive study" (PCCS). The PCCS would systematically vary the following factors as independent variables in a multifactorial design: (1) type of subjects: literate and preliterate, and within literate, college and noncollege students; (2) type of stimuli: posed and spontaneous, and within both, emotional and nonemotional faces; (3) previewing and nonpreviewing of stimuli; (4) within- and between-subjects designs, and in within-subjects designs, different orders versus fixed orders; (5) type of response alternatives: open-ended, fixed responses, and scalar ratings; and (6) presence or absence of context manipulations, and if present, the exact type of manipulation. Any single study or group of single studies that combines bits and pieces of these crucial aspects would not address the question of methodological influences on judgment, as one would never know how different levels of one factor influenced different levels of another. Only a single PCCS would address the issue. Of course, the

PCCS is more fantasy than reality, and we will probably never see it in the literature. But it is important to understand what the parameters of an empirical study that addressed the issues raised by Russell would look like, if his points were to be fairly and rigorously evaluated. We suggest that claims concerning methodological influences on data have little merit in the absence of such evidence from a PCCS, vis-à-vis the preponderance of evidence that already exists.

Second, universality and cultural relativity are not mutually exclusive. Like its analogous nature versus nurture argument, by attempting to view a phenomenon from only one perspective, we are not able to see the whole picture. Culture and emotion is a complex topic involving multiple layers of influence. We feel that, as researchers in the area of culture and emotion, our energy should be focused not on whether culture affects emotion, but rather on understanding how and why biologically innate factors interact with learned, cultural factors to produce similarities and differences in emotion expression.

## How and Why Does Culture Affect Emotion?

Despite the wealth of cross-cultural research on emotion and the importance of cross-cultural studies to the field of emotion research, until recently there has been no theory about what it is about cultures that affects emotional expressions and perceptions, and why. To be sure, Ekman's Neurocultural Theory of Emotional Expression is a theory of the mechanics of facial expressions of emotion. While pivotal to describing the existence of universal and culture-specific aspects of emotion and explaining how they interact to produce emotional expressions, it does not tell us about the nature of the cultural influences on the expressions. We contend that the time is right for this area of inquiry to be guided by some kind of theoretical framework, if cross-cultural research is to go beyond mere "fact" compilation.

Recently, Matsumoto has suggested such a theory (1991). Some of the research presented thus far has alluded to this theory. Its development was based on understanding what the word *culture* means. By understanding what the term means, we can better understand the effect of culture on the expression and perception of emotion.

### Overview of the Theory

In most cross-cultural studies, culture is operationalized as either race (cross-ethnicity studies) or place of birth (cross-country studies). Culture is typically defined conceptually, however, as a set of shared beliefs, values, attitudes, and behaviors that are communicated from one generation to the next (Barnouw, 1985). In his often-cited study of IBM employees, Hofstede (1980) defined dimensions of culture that could discriminate cultural groups with respect to these beliefs, values, attitudes, and behaviors. The dimensions he defined (also discussed earlier in this chapter) are Power Distance (PD), Uncertainty Avoidance (UA), Individualism (IN), and Masculinity (MA) (Hofstede, 1980, 1983).

Of those four dimensions, we believed that Individualism (IN) would be primarily related to differences in emotion expression and perception. IN is defined as the degree to which a culture encourages the sacrificing of individual needs and desires for group goals. A person low on individualism (typically called a collectivist) is one who sacrifices his or her needs and desires for the needs of the group. An individualist is one who puts his or her personal needs over the needs of others (Matsumoto, 1996). American and Japanese cultures are often discriminated on this dimension. Japanese culture is considered to be on the lower end of individualism and more collectivist, while American culture is characterized as being high on individualism. In Hofstede's study of 40 countries, Japanese and American scores on individualism were 46 and 86, respectively (Hofstede, 1983).

A second important social distinction that is directly related to differences in the expression and perception of emotion is the distinction between ingroups and outgroups. Differences in ingroup and outgroup relationships will differ as a function of culture. Ingroup relationships are "relationships characterized by some degree of familiarity, intimacy, and trust" (Matsumoto, 1996, p. 159). Outgroup relationships are the opposite of ingroup relations. They are characterized by a lack of feeling of togetherness and may also be associated with negative feelings like hostility or aggression. Although the difference between outgroups and ingroups is suggested to be simply dichotomous, the distinction is not that simple and may vary as a function of context. For example, it is possible for someone to be a member of an ingroup in one circumstance but a member of an outgroup in another circumstance (Matsumoto, 1996).

The key to the theory is the interaction of IN and the ingroup–outgroup distinction. Triandis et al.'s (1988) paper describes the differences between individualistic and collectivistic cultures with regard to self-ingroup and self-outgroup relationships. In an individualistic culture, people have many ingroups and they are not as personally invested in any one ingroup, because the primary concern of an individualist is his or her own unique self-concept. In contrast, people in collectivistic cultures have fewer ingroups and feel strongly affiliated with those few ingroups. Maintaining harmony within their ingroup is very important – so important that collectivists often sacrifice their own personal needs for the needs of the group. There are also major differences between individualistic and collectivistic cultures with regard to self-outgroup relationships. Because the relationship of the self with the ingroup is so important to members of collectivistic cultures, the self-outgroup relationship is relatively less important. A collectivist will distance him- or herself from outgroups in order to maintain a cohesive ingroup. In contrast, people in individualistic cultures will make fewer distinctions between ingroup and outgroup members. Because ingroup membership is much more flexible, individualists are more likely to treat a member of their outgroup as an ingroup member.

*The Effect of IN and Self-Ingroup and Self-Outgroup Relationships on Emotion Expression*

Differences in self-ingroup and self-outgroup relationships will result in differences in display rules that will, in turn, affect emotional behavior. In an individualistic culture, due to the increased emphasis on individual needs, wishes, and desires, it will be more acceptable to express negative emotions, even within ingroups. Because people in individualistic cultures tend to have many ingroups, they may express their emotions freely, as there is less fear of exclusion from any particular ingroup. On the other hand, in a collectivistic culture, where group goals and needs are more important than individual wishes or desires, negative emotions will be less likely to be shown in order to maintain harmony within the ingroup. Also, because collectivists have fewer ingroups, the stability of their membership in an ingroup is very important and they will therefore avoid risking their place within that group. For outgroups, the expression of negative emotions will be the opposite. Because of the weaker distinction between ingroups and outgroups, individualists will be less likely to express negative emotions to their outgroups. For the same reason, they are more likely to treat outgroup and ingroup members more equally. Because there is a greater discrimination between ingroups and outgroups, and it is important to maintain ingroup cohesion, collectivists will be more inclined to express negative emotions toward outgroups and reserve positive emotions for ingroups.

Based on the above theory, one could learn the different cultural rules for communicating emotions. By knowing the display rules for cultures and social groups, we can predict variations as a function of culture in the ways in which emotions will be felt, expressed, perceived, and interpreted.

### Data Supporting the Theory

Two studies in particular support this theoretical explanation for cultural differences in the expression and perception of emotion. In a study assessing people's ideas of display rules (Matsumoto, 1990), Japanese and American subjects were shown universal facial expressions of emotion and rated the appropriateness of displaying each of the emotions in different social situations. The social situations described referred to interactions with ingroup or outgroup members. Americans rated the negative emotions of disgust and sadness as more appropriate in ingroups than did the Japanese, which supports the notion that in America (an individualistic culture) it is considered

Table 2.1. *Consequences for personal emotions in self-ingroup and self-outgroup relationships in individualist and collectivist cultures*

|  | Type of Culture | |
|---|---|---|
|  | Individualist | Collectivist |
| Self-ingroup relationships | OK to express negative feelings; less need to display positive feelings | suppress expressions of negative feelings; more pressure to display positive feelings |
| Self-outgroup relationships | suppress negative feelings; okay to express positive feelings as would toward ingroups | encouraged to express negative feelings; suppress display of positive feelings reserved for ingroups |

*Source:* Reprinted from *Culture and Psychology,* Matsumoto (1996).

more acceptable to express negative emotions within ingroups. In contrast, the Japanese subjects rated anger as more appropriate in outgroups than did the Americans. This finding supports the theory that in the Japanese culture (a collectivistic culture) it is more socially acceptable to show the negative emotion of anger toward members of outgroups. Americans also indicated that happiness in public (representative of an outgroup) was more appropriate than did the Japanese, further supporting the theory.

In a second study conducted by Matsumoto and Hearn (1991), subjects from three countries (the United States, Hungary, and Poland) were presented with the same facial stimuli as in the above study. Again, they rated the appropriateness of displaying each of the emotions in certain social circumstances. There were differences found between Hungarians (collectivists), Poles (collectivists), and Americans (individualists). For example, Poles and Hungarians felt that it was more appropriate than the Americans did to display negative emotions to casual acquaintances and in public (i.e., outgroups) and less appropriate to display negative emotions to close friends and family (i.e., ingroups). This type of support for the hypothesized differences between individualistic and collectivistic cultures with regard to display of positive and negative emotion toward ingroup and outgroup members illustrates the predictive strength of the theory.

**Future Research Agenda**

In developing and testing theories such as the one detailed here, we are slowly unraveling the complex effect that a construct as rich and multidimensional as culture has on nonverbal communication of emotion. Although the data support our theory, its predictive strength is limited inasmuch as the construct of individualism only explains one part of the possible differences between cultures. However, we are optimistic that we have the tools for addressing the still unanswered questions. We suggest some future research directions here.

*Measure Culture on the Individual Level in Order to Classify*
*Individuals on Meaningful Dimensions of Culture*

Future research on the influence of culture on emotion should operationalize culture on the individual level, using meaningful psychological dimensions. Up until now, most cross-cultural research has made assumptions about the culture of individuals based on the assumed culture of their country of birth or residence. However, a person from a specific culture may or may not share the values that are congruent with the cultural majority. Therefore, culture should be measured on the individual level as a sociopsychological construct that may be shared by many people but may also vary from person to person.

During the past ten years, researchers have developed questionnaires that measure the IN dimension of culture on the individual level. For example, individual measures of IN have been developed by Hui and Triandis (1986) and by Matsumoto and his colleagues (Matsumoto, Weissman, Preston, Brown, & Kupperbusch, 1997). Studies conducted using these individual measures of culture have been successful in helping to understand personality correlates of culture (Hui, 1988; Kupperbusch, Seban, & Matsumoto, 1995; Kupperbusch, Imai, & Matsumoto, 1996; Matsumoto et al., 1997) and also to predict individual differences in emotional expression as a function of culture as measured on the individual level.

### Refine Other Possible Social and Cultural Distinctions (in Addition to IN)

Culture is a multidimensional construct. Because IN is only one dimension of culture, it may account for only a small part of the variance in cultural differences in the experience, expression, and perception of emotion. Other dimensions of culture, such as Power Distance (PD) or Uncertainty Avoidance (UA) (Hofstede, 1980, 1983), may account for additional variance in differences in nonverbal expression and perception of emotion. Very recently, Schimmack (1996) found that UA was a significant predictor of recognition of fear and sadness, which suggests that UA is an important variable to be investigated in the future.

Our laboratory has begun to investigate the effect of Status Differentiation (SD), a construct very much like PD, on cultural differences in emotion communication. Matsumoto (1996) defines SD as the degree to which status differences are maintained by a culture. We believe that cultures high in SD may have rules about what emotions it is appropriate to communicate to higher- or lower-status others, which will manifest in behavioral differences in the expression and perception of certain emotions. We have developed a measure of SD to employ in future research to further predict and explain differences in nonverbal emotional behavior.

*Investigate the Effect of the Interaction of Cultural Dimensions on Differences in Expressions of Emotion*

Future hypotheses should also address the interactions of cultural dimensions to account for differences in nonverbal expressions of emotion. For example, the interaction of IN and SD would create four different subgroups: cultures high on IN and low on SD, high on IN and high on SD, low on IN and low on SD, low on IN and high on SD. Future studies could test a two (and more) factor model of the influence of culture on the expression and perception of emotion.

*Investigate the Effect of the Interaction of Cultural Dimensions with Interpersonal Dimensions on Differences in Expressions of Emotion*

Interpersonal styles of communication also vary and are related to cultural differences. Future hypotheses should address the interactions of intercultural and interpersonal factors. For example, considering the combined effect of IN and self-monitoring could further account for perceived individual differences in nonverbal expressions of emotion. The expression and perception of emotion would vary across the four different subgroups created: cultures high on IN and low on self-monitoring, high on IN and high on self-monitoring, low on IN and low on self-monitoring, low on IN and high on self-monitoring. Future studies could test models involving both intercultural and interpersonal factors.

*Define the Social Roles and Meanings of Emotion*

Understanding cultural influences on emotion requires more than just understanding differences in emotional expression and perception. It also requires understanding differences in the social meanings of emotion for that culture and the function that emotion serves in that culture. Emotions can function to communicate an internal state or to indicate social motives (see chapter by Manstead, Fischer, & Jakobs in this volume). The social function of emotion in general (or of specific emotions) may vary from culture to culture. For example, in some cultures, expressing a certain emotion may serve to indicate a person's relative social status. The expression of the same emotion may serve yet another function in a different culture. The research described earlier reporting Japanese and American differences in judgments of the meaning of smiles (Matsumoto & Kudoh, 1993) illustrates the importance of considering those differences when conducting future research.

## Consider the Emotion Target

The expression and perception of emotion may vary as a function of emotion target in the same way that it varies as a function of context. For example, display rules regarding the appropriateness of expressing emotion to certain target others will affect the expression behavior. Also, there may be positive or negative consequences as a result of expressing an emotion to a certain target person. Another interesting effect would be that of the interaction of context and emotion target.

## Refine the Distinction between Display Rules and Emotional Expression

It is important to define and maintain the distinction between display rules and emotional expression. Display rules are the values and attitudes that a person in a culture holds about the appropriateness of certain emotional displays. Emotional expression is the actual emotional behavior. Findings from our study comparing American and Japanese ratings of expression intensity and emotional experience indicated that people were aware of the fact that the emotional behavior may have been affected by display rules. Also, the consequence of display rules on emotional behavior may differ from culture to culture. For example, two different cultures may have a similar rule regarding the inappropriateness of a specific emotion. However, whether it is more appropriate to mask that emotion with another emotion or to show no emotion at all may differ in those two cultures. Cultures may also vary with regard to their adherence to display rules. For example, certain cultures may hold to display rules more rigidly while other cultures may allow for greater flexibility in actual display behaviors. Future research should continue to study both display rule attitudes and behaviors, being careful to distinguish between the two.

## Conclusion

The past 30 years of research on culture and nonverbal expressions of emotion have uncovered findings about many cultural similarities and differences in the experience, expression, and perception of emotion. We have attempted to cover the highlights in this chapter beginning with the "universality studies," covering more recent research (including findings which show that culture is a complex factor influencing every aspect of emotionality), discussing current debates concerning universality, and presenting a theoretical framework that attempts to explain the effect of culture on emotion. We also suggested directions for future research in this area.

Each individual's communication style is the result of a complex interaction of social, interpersonal, cultural, and biological influences. Universal facial expressions of emotion are one of the basic components of communication. Differences and similarities in the ways we display, perceive, interpret, and understand these universal modes of communication add color and variety to our everyday interactions. The next 30 years of research promises as many interesting and meaningful findings as the past 30.

## References

Barnouw, V. (1985). *Culture and personality*. Homewood, IL: Dorsey Press.

Buck, R. (1984). *The communication of emotion*. New York: Guilford Press.

Charlesworth, W., & Kreutzer, M. (1973). Facial expressions in infants and children. In P. Ekman (Ed.), *Darwin and facial expression* (pp. 91–168). New York: Academic Press.

Darwin, C. (1872). *The expression of the emotions in man and animals*. London: John Murray.

Ekman, P. (1972). Universals and cultural differences in facial expressions of emotion. In J. Cole (Ed.), *Nebraska Symposium of Motivation* (pp. 207–283). Lincoln, NE: University of Nebraska Press.

Ekman, P. (1987). A life's pursuit. In T. A. Sebeok & J. Umiker-Sebeok (Eds.), *The Semiotic Web '86: An International Yearbook* (pp. 3–45). Berlin: Mouton de Gruyter.

Ekman, P. (1994). Strong evidence for universals in facial expressions: A reply to Russell's mistaken critique. *Psychological Bulletin, 115*, 268–287.

Ekman, P., & Friesen, W. V. (1969). The repertoire of nonverbal behavior: Categories, origins, usage, and coding. *Semiotica, 1*, 49–98.

Ekman, P., & Friesen, W. V. (1971). Constants across cultures in the face and emotion. *Journal of Personality and Social Psychology, 17*(2), 124–129.

Ekman, P., & Friesen, W. V. (1986). A new pan-cultural expression of emotion. *Motivation and Emotion, 10*, 159–168.

Ekman, P., Friesen, W. V., O'Sullivan, M., Chan, A., Diacoyanni-Tarlatzis, I., Heider, K., Krause, R., LeCompte, W. A., Pitcairn, T., Ricci-Bitti, P. E., Scherer, K., Tomita, M., & Tzavaras, A. (1987). Universals and cultural differences in the judgments of facial expressions of emotion. *Journal of Personality and Social Psychology, 53*(4), 712–717.

Ekman, P., Friesen, W. V., & Tomkins, S. (1971). Facial Affect Scoring Technique: A first validation study. *Semiotica, 3*, 37–58.

Ekman, P., & Heider, K. G. (1988). The universality of a contempt expression: A replication. *Motivation and Emotion, 12*, 303–308.

Ekman, P., O'Sullivan, M., & Matsumoto, D. (1991). Confusion about context in the judgment of facial expression: A reply to "The contempt expression and the relativity thesis." *Motivation and Emotion, 15*, 169–176.

Ekman, P., Sorenson, E. R., & Friesen, W. V. (1969). Pan-cultural elements in facial displays of emotion. *Science, 164*, 86–94.

Friesen, W. V. (1972). *Cultural differences in facial expressions in a social situation: An experimental test of the concept of display rules.* Unpublished doctoral dissertation, University of California, San Francisco.

Geen, T. (1992). Facial expressions in socially isolated nonhuman primates: Open and closed programs for expressive behavior. *Journal of Research in Personality, 26*, 273–280.

Hauser, M. (1993). Right hemisphere dominance for the production of facial expression in monkeys. *Science, 261*, 475–477.

Hofstede, G. (1980). *Culture's consequences: International differences in work-related values.* Beverly Hills, CA: Sage.

Hofstede, G. (1983). Dimensions of national cultures in fifty countries and three regions. In J. B. Deregowski, S. Dziurawiec, & R. C. Annis (Eds.), *Expiscations in cross-cultural psychology* (pp. 335–355). Lisse: Swets & Zeitlinger.

Hui, C. H. (1988). Measurement of individualism-collectivism. *Journal of Research in Personality, 22*, 17–36.

Hui, C. H., & Triandis, H. C. (1986). Individualism-collectivism: A study of cross-cultural researchers. *Journal of Cross-Cultural Psychology 17*, 225–248.

Izard, C. (1971). *The face of emotion.* New York: Appleton-Century-Crofts.

Izard, C. (1994). Innate and universal facial expressions: Evidence from developmental and cross-cultural research. *Psychological Bulletin, 115*, 288–299.

Izard, C., & Haynes, O. M. (1988). On the form and universality of the contempt expression: A challenge to Ekman and Friesen's claim of discovery. *Motivation and Emotion, 12*, 1–16.

Kupperbusch, C., Imai, C., & Matsumoto, D. (1996, April). *Personality correlates of individualism/collectivism II.* Paper presented in poster at the annual meeting of the Western Psychological Association, San Jose, CA.

Kupperbusch, C., Seban, E., & Matsumoto, D. (1995, March). *Personality correlates of individualism/collectivism.* Paper presented in poster at the annual meeting of the Western Psychological Association, Los Angeles, CA.

Matsumoto, D. (1989). Cultural influences on the perception of emotion. *Journal of Cross-Cultural Psychology, 20*, 92–105.

Matsumoto, D. (1990). Cultural similarities and differences in display rules. *Motivation and Emotion, 14*(3), 195–214.

Matsumoto, D. (1991). Cultural influences in facial expressions of emotion. *Southern Journal of Communication, 56*, 128–137.

Matsumoto, D. (1992a). American–Japanese cultural differences in the recognition of universal facial expressions. *Journal of Cross-Cultural Psychology, 23,* 72–84.

Matsumoto, D. (1992b). More evidence for the universality of a contempt expression. *Motivation and Emotion, 16,* 363–368.

Matsumoto, D. (1993). Ethnic differences in affect intensity, emotion judgments, display rule attitudes, and self-reported emotional expression in an American sample. *Motivation and Emotion, 17*(3), 107–123.

Matsumoto, D. (1996). *Culture and psychology.* Pacific Grove, CA: Brooks/Cole Publishing Company.

Matsumoto, D., & Ekman, P. (1989). American–Japanese cultural differences in intensity ratings of facial expressions of emotion. *Motivation and Emotion, 13,* 143–157.

Matsumoto, D., & Hearn, V. (1991). Culture and emotion: Display rule differences between the United States, Poland, and Hungary. Unpublished manuscript.

Matsumoto, D., & Kudoh, T. (1993). American–Japanese cultural differences in attributions of personality based on smiles. *Journal of Nonverbal Behavior, 17,* 231–243.

Matsumoto, D., Weissman, M., Preston, K., Brown, B., & Kupperbusch, C. (1997). Context-specific measurement of individualism-collectivism on the individual level: The Individualism-Collectivism Interpersonal Assessment Inventory. *Journal of Cross-Cultural Psychology 28,* 743–767.

Pittam, J., Gallois, C., Iwasaki, S., & Kroonenberg, P. (1995). Australian and Japanese concepts of expressive behavior. *Journal of Cross-Cultural Psychology, 26,* 451–473.

Russell, J. A. (1991). Culture and the categorization of emotions. *Psychological Bulletin, 110,* 426–450.

Russell, J. A. (1994). Is there universal recognition of emotion from facial expression? A review of cross-cultural studies. *Psychological Bulletin, 115,* 102–141.

Russell, J. A. (1995). Facial expressions of emotion: What lies beyond minimal universality? *Psychological Bulletin, 118,* 379–391.

Sackett, G. (1966). Monkeys reared in isolation with pictures as visual input: Evidence for an innate releasing mechanism. *Science, 154,* 1468–1473.

Schimmack, U. (1996). Cultural influences on the recognition of emotion by facial expressions: Individualist or Caucasian cultures? *Journal of Cross-Cultural Psychology, 27,* 37–50.

Tomkins, S. (1962). *Affect, imagery, and consciousness* (Vol. 1). New York: Springer.

Tomkins, S. (1963). *Affect, imagery, and consciousness* (Vol. 2). New York: Springer.

Triandis, H. C., Bontempo, R., Villareal, M. J., Asai, M., & Lucca, N. (1988). Individualism and collectivism: Cross-cultural perspectives on self-ingroup relationships. *Journal of Personality and Social Psychology, 54,* 323–338.

VanGeert, P. (1995). Green, red, and happiness: Towards a framework for understanding emotion universals. *Culture and Psychology, 1,* 259–268.

Wierzbicka, A. (1995). Emotion and facial expression: A semantic perspective. *Culture and Psychology, 1*, 227–258.

Winegar, L. (1995). Moving toward culture-inclusive theories of emotion. *Culture and Psychology, 1*, 269–277.

# 3. Option or Obligation to Smile

## The Effects of Power and Gender on Facial Expression

MARIANNE LaFRANCE AND MARVIN A. HECHT

> *Sometimes I not only stand there and take it, I even smile at them and say I'm sorry. When I feel that smile coming onto my face, I wish I could take my face off and stamp on it.*
>
> Ursula K. Le Guin, *Very Far Away from Anywhere Else* (1983)

There may be no gesture with more diverse meanings and more varied forms than the human smile. Smiles convey delight and happiness, but people also smile when they feel anything but enjoyment. Researchers have documented, for example, that people smile when they are embarrassed and ashamed (Edelmann, Asendorpf, Contarello, & Zammuner, 1989; Keltner, 1995) and also when they are uncomfortable (Ochanomizu, 1991), miserable (Ekman & Friesen, 1982), and apprehensive (Ickes, Patterson, Rajecki, & Tanford, 1982).

And while it is true that smiles are often genuine and spontaneous (Ekman, Friesen, & Ancoli, 1980), it is also true that a smile can be among the most deliberate of facial actions. Anthropologists and sociologists have documented numerous instances of circumstances in which people smile because their role or situation requires them to do so. For example, Wierzbicka (1994) observed that cheerfulness is mandatory in many cultures. Within the United States, Hochschild (1983) noted that many job holders are required to smile as part of the work they do. For instance, airline flight attendants must smile and smile well. Thus a flight attendant is trained to "really work on her smiles"

Preparation of this chapter was supported by grants from the National Science Foundation, the Society for the Psychological Study of Social Issues, and the Social Science and Humanities Research Council of Canada, and portions of the research were presented at meetings of the American Psychological Association in 1995 and the Society for Research on Emotion in 1996.

and is expected to "manage her heart" in such a way as to create a smile that will both seem and be "spontaneous and sincere" (Hochschild, 1983, p. 105).

The present chapter is aimed at understanding when smiles are genuine signs of good feelings and when they are instead contrived displays required by one's role or situation. In this chapter, we explore whether the degree of power one has in a social situation and the sex that one is affects whether one smiles and whether such smiling is experienced as an option or an obligation.

## Candid and Contrived Smiles

At first blush, the human smile might seem to be the least ambiguous and most easily recognized facial expression. Upon closer scrutiny, however, it appears that there are many ways that people can smile and that many of these subtly different expressions are associated with different feelings and functions. For example, Ekman and Friesen (1982) distinguished the felt smile from the false smile and noted that the miserable smile is something else altogether. In fact, Ekman went on to describe a total of nineteen distinct smile varieties (Ekman, 1985).

Smiles can be distinguished by which facial muscles are used to produce them; whether the smile is displayed equally on both sides of the face or is more visible on one side of the face; and by various aspects of their timing, including how quickly they appear and disappear from the face (Frank, Ekman, & Friesen, 1993). Other investigators have also argued that there are many types of smiles and that each serves different communicative functions (Bänninger-Huber & Rauber-Kaiser, 1989; Blurton-Jones, 1967, 1972; Brannigan & Humphries, 1972; Bugental, 1986; Grant, 1969; Goldenthal, Johnston, & Kraut, 1981).

As far back as 1862, Duchenne noted that smiles of enjoyment involved not only the mouth muscle (*zygomatic major*) but also the muscle that circles the eyes (*orbicularis ocularis*) (Duchenne, 1862/1990). Subsequent research has confirmed that smiles with Duchenne's marker (crowfeet wrinkles at the edge of the eyes) show the strongest link to actually experienced positive affect (Ekman, 1992; Ekman, Davidson, & Friesen, 1990; Ekman, et al., 1980; Ekman, Friesen, & O'Sullivan, 1988; Matsumoto, 1986). The originally designated "false smile," now renamed the non-Duchenne smile, is actually any smile that does not involve contraction of the *orbicularis ocularis* muscle.

In fact, it is less a particular smile type than a class of smiles that appear to be more social in character and not necessarily reflective of positive feelings.

In sum, there are many types of smiles of which only one kind appears to be reliably associated with feeling good. Consequently, to know that a person is smiling, or smiles more than another, tells us only so much. To understand what a smile means we need to know more: We need to determine what type of smile is being displayed, and we need to assess whether the smile was elicited by feeling good or by feeling pressure to look the part.

## Smiles and Appeasement

One context in which human smiling may be required is a situation in which an individual has lower social standing relative to someone else. A recurrent idea in the nonverbal communication literature is that lower-power people smile more than those with higher power (Henley, 1973; 1977). The idea borrowed from the ethological literature argues that smiling, like the silent bared-teeth grin of primates, is an appeasement gesture (Andrew, 1965; Goldenthal, et al., 1981; Rowell, 1966). Research has examined this premise by asking (1) whether observers infer greater appeasement or submissiveness when they judge smiling versus nonsmiling faces, and (2) by examining whether low-power people actually smile more than their higher-power partners. In the former case, judgment studies have tended to show that nonsmiling faces are rated as more dominant than smiling faces (Keating, 1985; Keating & Bai, 1986; Keating, Mazur, & Segall, 1977). However, not every study has found this effect (Burgoon, Buller, Hale, & deTurck, 1984; Deutsch, LeBaron, & Fryer, 1987; Halberstadt & Saitta, 1987).

With regard to whether subordinates actually smile more than superiors, results also present a mixed picture. Both a laboratory experiment (Deutsch, 1990) and an observational study of status-discrepant interactions found that lower power was associated with more smiling (Denmark, McKenna, Juran, & Greenburg, 1976, cited in Denmark, 1977). Other studies, however, present more complex results. Data reported by Dovidio and his colleagues found the effect for males, but noted that females smiled the same high amount regardless of the power they possessed (Dovidio, Brown, Heltman, Ellyson, & Keating, 1988). Another study found that greater smiling was associated with low power when low power was defined as scoring low on trait measures of dominance, but it was not associated with power when power was experimentally manipulated (Hall & Payne, 1995). Still other studies find either no effect of power on smiling (Johnson, 1994; Kolaric & Galambos, 1995) or the opposite, namely, that high-power people smile more than low-power people (Halberstadt, Dovidio, & Davidson, 1988).

*Pressure to Smile*

Although the available evidence does not provide unequivocal evidence that those in low-power positions smile more than those in high-power positions, there are indications nonetheless that in power-unequal situations, low-power people likely experience more concern about impression management than high-power people (Tedeschi & Norman, 1985). This might translate into low-power people feeling more concerned about adopting an appropriate demeanor, which may entail feeling more pressure to smile. We tested this in a recent study in which participants responded to another person's "good news" with or without a smile. Specifically, 127 subjects were presented with a vignette in which they were asked to imagine interacting with a person who had higher power than themselves (a professor), equal power to themselves (a fellow classmate), or lower power than themselves (a student that the subject was supervising). In each case, the other person was presented as describing to the subject a recent success. After being asked to imagine that they either did or did not smile in response to this person's declared good news, participants indicated on several scales how they felt about their behavior and how they thought the other would react to it (LaFrance, 1997).

The assumption was that someone's good news deserves a smile in return and especially if the recipient of the news had lower power than the teller. Findings showed that everybody anticipated fewer rewards and more costs if they failed to smile when someone reported to them that they had recently been successful at something. But low-power people showed even more signs of obligation to smile. When low-power people did not smile, they expected that the other person would see them as less friendly and less caring than if they did smile, a reaction that was less manifest by those who had higher or equal power.

## Social Power and Nonverbal License

Communication researchers have long been interested in how nonverbal cues, in general, change when an interaction occurs between people possessing different levels of social power vis-à-vis each other. According to Brown (1965), all societies have some conception of differential social value, a vertical dimension termed *status*. This dimension is in addition to some conception of differential solidarity, a horizontal dimension in which relationships can be described as being close or remote. Brown noted, for example, that nonsymmetrical use of communicative behaviors by interactants indicated the likely presence of status differentials in the interaction. For example, with respect to the terms of address individuals use with each other, Brown noted that status equals adopted symmetrical terms, i.e., both used first names or both used formal surnames. Among status unequals, however, the higher-status individual would more likely refer to the lower-status person by his or her first name, a stance that would not be reciprocated by the lower-status person.

Goffman (1967) also drew a similar distinction and described a whole range of communicative behaviors that act as status reminders. In the nonverbal realm, Henley (1977) argued that the same nonverbal behavior can be used to express relationships between equals and unequals depending on whether it is asymmetrically or symmetrically used by the partners. For example, status equals touch each other about the same amount, but among status unequals, the superior has the option of touching the subordinate, an option the subordinate does not have.

In addition to more nonreciprocity where differences in social power are present, there are indications that those with greater power are given more license to adopt whatever communicative behaviors they choose. Clark (1990) noted that superiors have a right to have their feelings "count." In contrast, those with lower power operate with fewer options and more constraints. In short, power appears to give one more room to move, both literally and figuratively. High-power people are afforded more physical space and are allowed to determine how close others will approach (Henley, 1995). At the same time, they retain the prerogative to approach to whatever distance they choose (Lott & Sommer, 1967).

Those in power are also more likely to violate social norms with regard to gaze (Fehr & Exline, 1987), such as looking away while the other person is speaking (Ellyson & Dovidio, 1985), and to evidence more bodily relaxation (Mehrabian, 1969). In contrast, those with lower power evidence more hesitancy and greater obligation to accept the initiatives of those with more power (Baxter & Rosselle, 1975).

In sum, high-power people seem to have more license to behave as they choose, whereas low-power people appear to be under some obligation to express an appropriate set of verbal and nonverbal behaviors. With respect to facial expression, and particularly smiling, our thesis is that low-power people are under more obligation to smile than are those with more power. It may also be the case that women feel more pressure to smile than men.

### Gender and Smiling

While research has consistently shown that women smile more than men, controversy surrounds how best to interpret this difference. On the one hand, some have argued that women smile more than men because they are more socially affiliative or more socially anxious than men (Hall, 1984; 1987). On the other hand, social structural variations rather than individual differences have been claimed as the cause for sex differences in nonverbal communication. For example, others have argued that women smile more than men because of their lower power relative to men in U.S. society (LaFrance & Henley, 1994). Thus, women are said to smile more than men because it behooves those with lower status to be deferential, and smiling is a particularly effective sign of deference (Henley, 1977).

Another source of social causation for sex differences in smiling may be the fact that women and men tend to occupy different roles and occupations. If it is the case that some occupations and roles require those who hold them to show positive expressivity, and if it is the case that women tend to be more prevalent in these positions than men, then the greater smiling of women may not be gender based but role based (Nieva & Gutek, 1981). In fact, smiling appears to be a prerequisite for anyone whose job involves caring for others – nursing and teaching, for example – tasks typically carried out by women. As noted previously, Hochschild (1983) argued that workers such as flight attendants, receptionists, and personal assistants, who are also disproportionately women, are expected to show high degrees of positive expressivity as they perform their jobs.

*Women's Greater Obligation to Express Positive Emotion*

The notion of emotion display rules with their attendant obligatory aspects (Ekman, Friesen, & Ellsworth, 1972) presents a possible way to reconcile the various explanations for why women smile more than men and why low-power people may smile more than high-power people. Display rules guide what expressions people are to show on their faces in various cultural, situational, and personal situations. Depending on the situation, display rules indicate whether a particular emotion should be expressed and to what degree. This can be done by neutralizing, qualifying, or modulating the display of a felt emotion or by simulating an emotion that is not felt.

As noted elsewhere in this volume, with advancing years, children learn the display rules of their own culture and group (see Saarni & Weber, chapter 4 in this volume). Specifically, they learn that there is an important difference between their internal emotional experience and their external expressive behavior and that at the very least the latter needs to be socially regulated. In addition, cultures differ in the degree to which individuals are expected to mask some emotions with other emotions. See Kupperbusch et al., chapter 2 in this volume, for a description of how cultures vary in emotional expression. Specifically, there are indications that the Japanese inhibit overt negative displays more than Americans do. For example, Friesen (1972) reported that Japanese men showed fewer expressions of distress and smiled more than American men when they talked about their reactions to a distressing video, even though their expressions did not differ from those of the Americans when they were initially observed viewing the film in private.

With respect to gender display rules, research has shown that girls focus on inhibiting the display of negative feelings as they get older, while boys become better at neutralizing the display of all affect (Bugental & Shennum, 1982). With adults, Johnson and Shulman (1988) have shown people expect females and males to be similar in their *experience* of emotion, although they are expected to be dissimilar in what they express. In other words, people believe that women are more expressive than men even while they grant that women and men may be quite similar with respect to what they feel and how much they feel it.

There are also situation-based display rules. There are norms for what feelings should be expressed at events like weddings, funerals, graduations, and the like. Evidence shows that these norms clearly have a prescriptive character – people know that there are costs in not following expressivity display rules. In one study, subjects were asked to predict what kind of feedback they (or a person named "Terry") would get from others after having reacted appropriately (displaying happiness at a friend's successful campaign or sadness at a friend's funeral), or after having reacted inappropriately (displaying happiness at a funeral and sadness after a friend's successful campaign). Results showed that people expected fewer rewards and more punishment when they imagined themselves or another failing to display the appropriate emotion (Graham, Gentry, & Green, 1981). And women showed this even more than men.

In sum, women may smile more than men because there are gender-based display rules that obligate women to be more expressive than men (LaFrance & Banaji, 1992). Although people *believe* that there are some emotions which reverse the usual pattern – e.g., that men may display more anger than women (Fabes & Martin, 1991) – the available data are mixed as to whether there are actual sex differences in the expression of anger (Biaggio, 1989; Haynes, Levine, Scotch, Feinleib, & Kannel, 1978; Lerner, 1985). With respect to positive display, however, there is consensus with respect to what people believe and what the facts show. Women are thought to express more positive emotion than men (Fabes & Martin, 1991) and they actually do so. In one study, subjects were asked to predict what kind of feedback they would get after having expressed or failed to express positive emotion toward another or toward themselves. As predicted, females expected more rewards/fewer costs when they expressed positive emotion toward another person than when they did not express it. However, the feeling of having done the right thing by expressing positive emotion was limited for women to a situation in which they were reacting to someone else. Males, on the other hand, expected comparable benefits for expressing positive emotion to others and also if they directed it toward themselves (Stoppard & Gunn-Gruchy, 1993).

We extended this work by investigating whether this pattern would repeat if the expression specifically involved having smiled or not. Instead of describing a person as expressing positive emotion, we explicitly indicated that the target person *smiled*, or had a neutral expression, as they said "Congratulations" in response to another person's success. This was done in order to control for the possibility that participants in prior work had imagined different kinds of "positive emotion" being expressed by males and females. If so, then previous results may have confounded gender with different kinds of positive behavior. Specifically, the prediction was that women would feel more pressure to smile than men and anticipate more negative repercussions than men if they failed to do so (LaFrance, 1997).

Results strongly supported the idea that women feel more obligation to smile than men do. Specifically, nonsmiling females felt significantly less comfortable and less appropriate than nonsmiling men. They also reported that the other would regard them as significantly less friendly, less genuine, less caring, and less polite than the nonsmiling men reported, as well as colder and ruder. Finally, females also believed that the other's impression of them would change more if they didn't smile than if they did, while men reported that whether they smiled or not did not affect the other's impression of them.

These results along with the power-based results reported above strongly support the idea that smiling in response to another person's good news is expected of some people more than of others. Specifically, the data indicate that the absence of smiling is associated with higher costs for women than for men and for low-power people than for high-power. With respect to gender differences, these results corroborate previous work showing that women expect fewer rewards and higher costs when they are insufficiently positive in reaction to others' favorable outcomes (Graham et al., 1981; Stoppard et al., 1993). They are also consistent with much prior work in communication showing that it falls more to women to do the "conversational work" (Fishman, 1983) or provide the "emotion labor" (Hochschild, 1983) in social interaction.

With respect to the effect of power, the results are not as encompassing as those for gender but the pattern is clearly supportive of the idea that when low-power people do not display positive emotion in response to another's success, they experience more pressure to smile than high-power people do. They also expect that the impression that the other has of them will change more as a result.

To recapitulate, women and low-power people report more pressure to smile and expect that the other's impression of them will change more if they fail to smile. This similarity has been pointed out by others as evidence for the idea that women's expressive behavior is at least partly a function of their lower status (Henley, 1977). Moreover, in our study we found that low-power females report the least comfort and anticipate the most negative outcomes from not smiling.

This suggests the operation of two sets of display rules – those that are gender based and those that are power based. Women and low-power people appear to be under more obligation to smile than their respective counterparts. A position of high power appears to override the usual pressure to smile that women feel, but in a position of low power, gender and power-based display rules appear to be additive.

## Effect of Sex and Power on Amount and Type of Smiling

Despite these indications, those who study actual smiling do not reliably find that lower power necessarily leads to greater smiling. Nor has it been definitely settled that women smile more than men because they are less powerful and/or possess lower status. We contend that three factors may be primarily responsible for why research has failed to find a consistent relationship between the power one has and the amount of smiling one does. The first reason is that prior work has assumed that the relation between power and smiling is linear – lower power equals greater smiling. Instead, it may be the case that low-power people are obligated to smile some amount. Too much smiling by underlings might actually signal insubordination (Hall & Payne, 1995). Consequently, there may be occasions when lower-power people actually smile less than higher-power people, the latter having the option to do as they choose while the former are obligated to show some requisite amount.

A second and related reason for inconsistent findings is that insufficient consideration has been paid to the psychological underpinnings of the power–smile relation. Research has been rather mute on why smiling by subordinates is to be expected. Henley (1973, 1977) has argued that social conventions rather than individual motivations underlie differences in facial display. Thus smiles are direct signals of one's status. But the psychological state of individuals in power-marked relationships may be critical in determining when people with different levels of power smile. Those possessing greater power may smile when they are feeling positive and may not smile when they do not feel positive. In short, being in a position of high power would give one the option to smile or not. In contrast, when low-power people smile may be less directly linked to whether they are feeling particularly happy. Instead, their smiling may be associated more with feelings of needing to please than with feelings of pleasure (Hall & Halberstadt, 1996). In the study to be described, we assessed participants' positive affect and feelings of needing to please in order to see if these states differentially moderated the relation between power and smiling for high- and low-power people.

A third reason for the inconclusiveness of past research is that investigators have tended to treat smiling itself as unitary, despite growing evidence that there are many types of smiles. There has been no research examining whether high-power people experience more enjoyment than those with lower power but some evidence is suggestive. For example, people in a low-power position are more likely to be uneasy and insecure (Cohen, 1958; Kelley, 1951; Tjosvold, 1981). Thus, those with lower power might show significantly less Duchenne smiling and/or significantly more non-Duchenne smiling than those with higher power. The present study coded Duchenne and non-Duchenne smiles in order to address the relation between power and smile type.

We undertook another study to address these concerns as well as tackling the complicated relationship between sex and power (Hecht & LaFrance, 1998). It was our feeling that sex differences in smiling would be most manifest when people had equivalent status to each other in same-sex pairs. In contrast, we predicted that men and women would smile in comparable amounts when both had high power or both had low power, because power confers its own set of display rules that are presumed to operate in the same way on men and women. Support for this reasoning comes from work in other areas that has also found few or no sex differences given the presence of identical goals or expectations (Chase, 1988; Moskowitz, Suh, & Desaulniers, 1994; Ploutz-Snyder, Lassiter, & Snodgrass, 1995).

In brief then, the present study pursued several questions: (1) how does power affect the amount and type of smiling shown by participants in a dyadic interaction; (2) is the relationship between power and smiling mediated by positive affect for high-power people but by needing to please for low-power people; and (3) how does the sex of the participants impact their smiling behavior either alone or in conjunction with social power?

## Procedure

Seventy-two undergraduate psychology students were randomly assigned to 24 power-discrepant pairs (12 male dyads and 12 female dyads) and 12 power-equal pairs (6 male dyads and 6 female dyads).

Power in the power-discrepant condition was operationalized as reward power (French & Raven, 1959). The high-power person in each
dyad was designated as an interviewer, and the low-power person
was designated as an applicant. Both interviewers and applicants were
told that if at the completion of the five-minute interview, the interviewer indicated that the applicant was selected by the interviewer,
then the applicant's name would be entered into a lottery for a hundred-dollar reward. Precautions were taken to avoid prescribing particular nonverbal responses. Thus the instructions did not prescribe
that low-power participants "demonstrate their ability to interact with
others in a favorable way" (Deutsch, 1990, p. 533), which could be
interpreted as instructions to smile.

Instructions to high-power participants indicated they were responsible for finding the right person for the job. They were told to evaluate
the applicant carefully and discern whether the applicant was in fact
good for the position because a hundred-dollar reward was at stake.
Participants in the power-equal dyads were told to get acquainted and
in order to make the conversational content similar to that of the power-
discrepant dyads, participants were instructed to discuss past and future job plans as well as personal strengths and weaknesses.

Participants completed several self-report measures aimed at assessing perceived power, positive affect, needing to please, social anxiety, and liking. The presence or absence of smiling was coded every
5 seconds such that a subject's smiling score could range from 0 to 60,
although in practice no one smiled more than 38 times. Smiles were
further coded as being Duchenne or non-Duchenne using the Facial
Action Coding System (FACS; Ekman & Friesen, 1978) by a certified
FACS coder.

## Results

As intended, subjects assigned to the high-power position felt significantly more power than participants assigned to the low-power position. In addition, high-power participants reported significantly more
positive affect and significantly less feeling the need to please their
partners. Men and women in the same role reported comparable levels
of power, positive affect, and needing to please. Table 3.1 shows the
means on these self-report measures.

*Power and Smiling.*  We examined whether power directly affected how
much participants smiled and then followed that up by exploring

Table 3.1. *Means for the self-reported power, positive affect, and need to please by sex, condition, and role*

| | Males | | Females | | Row |
| --- | --- | --- | --- | --- | --- |
| | M | SD | M | SD | Mean |
| (a) Power | | | | | |
| Low power | 3.40 | 1.31 | 3.72 | 1.21 | 3.56 |
| High power | 7.42 | 1.17 | 7.37 | 1.13 | 7.40 |
| Equal power | 5.48 | 1.19 | 4.90 | 0.54 | 5.19 |
| Column Mean | 5.43 | | 5.33 | | 5.38 |
| (b) Positive affect | | | | | |
| Low power | 5.04 | 1.01 | 5.17 | 1.72 | 5.11 |
| High power | 5.63 | 0.48 | 5.67 | 1.34 | 5.65 |
| Equal power | 5.67 | 1.43 | 6.83 | 1.23 | 6.25 |
| Column Mean | 5.45 | | 5.89 | | 5.67 |
| (c) Trying to please | | | | | |
| Low power | 5.83 | 1.80 | 6.17 | 2.04 | 6.00 |
| High power | 5.42 | 1.78 | 4.58 | 2.35 | 5.00 |
| Equal power | 3.33 | 1.58 | 4.00 | 2.12 | 3.67 |
| Column Mean | 4.86 | | 4.92 | | 4.89 |

Note: $n = 12$ people per cell.

whether power affected smiling by way of positive affect and needing to please. We found that when people interact as equals, they smile more than when they interact as unequals. This pattern showed itself in both smile types. See Tables 3.2 and 3.3 for how power affected smile amounts. Equal-power participants showed more non-Duchenne smiles and more Duchenne smiles than unequals.

Within the power-discrepant condition, however, there were no significant differences between high-power and low-power participants in amount of smiling. In contrast to the prevailing wisdom that those who have lower power will, by necessity, smile more than their superiors, we did not find that to be the case. Both high- and low-power people smile less overall than those on equal footing, but high- and low-power participants smiled roughly the same amounts. This held true for both Duchenne and non-Duchenne smiles.

Although low-power and high-power people smiled similar amounts, their smiling was associated with different psychological states. We reasoned that if high-power people have more option to smile than low power people, then their smiling should be more

Table 3.2. *Mean amount of overall smiling by sex, condition, and role*

|  | Males | | Females | | Row |
|  | M | SD | M | SD | Mean |
|---|---|---|---|---|---|
| Low power | 8.83 | 7.67 | 13.50 | 5.30 | 11.17 |
| High power | 8.25 | 8.69 | 11.75 | 9.86 | 10.00 |
| Equal power | 12.92 | 8.69 | 23.50 | 8.05 | 18.21 |
| Column Mean | 10.00 | | 16.25 | | 13.13 |

*Note: n* = 12 people per cell.

Table 3.3. *Mean amount of Duchenne and non-Duchenne smiling by sex, condition, and role*

|  | Males | | Females | | Row |
|  | M | SD | M | SD | Mean |
|---|---|---|---|---|---|
| (a) Duchenne Smiling | | | | | |
| Low power | 1.33 | 1.56 | 1.33 | 1.30 | 1.33 |
| High power | 1.50 | 2.02 | 1.83 | 3.04 | 1.67 |
| Equal power | 1.58 | 2.75 | 5.92 | 3.78 | 3.75 |
| Column Mean | 1.47 | | 3.03 | | 3.38 |
| (b) Non-Duchenne smiling | | | | | |
| Low power | 7.50 | 6.72 | 12.17 | 4.86 | 9.84 |
| High power | 6.75 | 7.85 | 9.92 | 8.18 | 8.34 |
| Equal power | 11.33 | 8.36 | 17.58 | 7.20 | 14.46 |
| Column Mean | 8.53 | | 13.22 | | 10.88 |

*Note: n* = 12 people per cell.

strongly associated with positive affect than the smiling of low-power people. If, however, the smiling of low-power people springs from the obligation to smile, then their smiling should show a weak relationship with positive affect and a stronger relationship with needing to please than the smiling of high-power people.

These speculations were supported by the pattern of the correlations found between levels of power and each individual's reported positive affect. See Table 3.4 for these correlations. For high-power participants, smiling is significantly correlated with positive affect (*r*

= .55). For low-power participants, in contrast, smiling is unrelated to self-reported positive affect ($r = -.16$). The difference between these two correlations was statistically significant. Thus the smiling of high-power people corresponds to their feeling significantly more positive than the smiling of low-power people.

The pattern is repeated for the two types of smiles. For non-Duchenne smiling, there is a positive relationship between smiling and positive affect for the high-power participants ($r = .57$) but a non-significant negative association for low-power participants ($r = -.19$). The difference between the two correlations was also statistically significant. For Duchenne smiling, there is a positive relationship between smiling and positive affect for the high-power participants ($r = .22$) and a weak correlation for low-power participants ($r = .06$). Although these correlations were in the predicted direction, the difference between them was not statistically significant.

Several aspects of the correlations shown in Table 3.4 are worth noting. First, the correlations between positive affect and smiling for high-power people are not significantly different from those found for individuals in the power-equal condition. Both groups show positive relationships between positive affect and smiling that are consistent with prior work linking smiling to enjoyment (Ekman, 1992). The

Table 3.4. *Correlations of amount and type of smile with positive affect and trying to please*

|  | Duchenne | Non-Duchenne | Overall |
|---|---|---|---|
| (a) Positive affect |  |  |  |
|    Low power | .06 | −.19 | −.16 |
|    High power | .22 | .57 | .55 |
|    Equal power | .27 | .33 | .38 |
| (b) Trying to please |  |  |  |
|    Low power | .26 | .31 | .34 |
|    High power | .32 | .05 | .13 |
|    Equal power | −.06 | .07 | .04 |

*Note:* Correlations are based on $n = 24$ people. Using a two-tail test, correlations of $\pm.40$ are significantly different from zero at $p = .05$, and correlations of $\pm.34$ are significantly different from zero at $p = .10$.

exceptional group is that made up of those who possess relatively low power. On all three measures of smiling, there is no relationship between how positive these people feel and how much they smile. In two of three relationships, the direction of the correlation is such that greater positive affect is associated with less, not more smiling. A disjunction between positive affect and amount of smiling is unique for low-power people. For high-power people and equal-power people, there is no such disjunction between how positively they feel and how much positivity they show.

A second way to view the relationship between smiling and positive affect for groups varying in social power is shown in Figure 3.1. This figure shows the interaction between positive affect and power. The former variable was created by doing a median-split for positive affect in the power-discrepant condition. Positive feelings affected only those with high power. When positive affect is low, high-power people smiled less than the low-power people, but when positive-affect is high, high-power participants smiled more than low-power participants. In contrast, the smiling of low-power participants did not vary as a function of reported levels of positive feeling in the dyad. In sum, the smiling of high-power people is more variable than that of low-power people, and what underlies that variability is variability in positive affect.

Table 3.4 provides evidence relevant to the other half of the argument relating power to smiling, namely, that the smiling of low-power

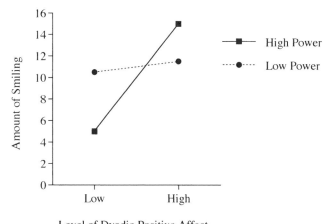

Figure 3.1. Amount of smiling as a function of social power and positive affect.

people would be related to their needing to please. Note that for low-power people, overall smiling is marginally positively correlated with their self-reports of needing to please their partner ($r = .34$, $p < .10$). For both high-power and equal-power participants, needing to please is uncorrelated with how much smiling they evidence ($r = .13$ and $r = .04$ respectively).

*Gender and Smiling.* Consistent with prior research, this study found a main effect for sex on all three smile measures. When power-equal and power-discrepant conditions were combined, women showed significantly more smiling than men. They also showed significantly more Duchenne smiling and significantly more non-Duchenne smiling than men.

In line with theorizing about the effect of context, results also show that sex differences are stronger in the equal-power condition than in the power-discrepant condition. The sex difference favoring women in the equal-power condition was statistically significant for overall smiling and for Duchenne smiling. Although equal-power women and men did not significantly differ from each other on non-Duchenne smiling, the effect size was still quite high for this variable ($r = .41$).

In contrast, sex differences for the power-discrepant dyads were negligible. In the high-power role, men and women smiled the same. High-power women and men also showed comparable amounts of Duchenne smiling and non-Duchenne smiling. For men and women in the low-power position, there were no significant differences in overall smiling or for Duchenne smiling. For non-Duchenne smiling, there was a marginally significant gender difference favoring women. Thus, when we look at a situation in which men and women have high or low power, their level of smiling is almost comparable. It only diverges when power differences are not expressly imposed on same-sex pairs.

### Discussion

This study clearly demonstrated that social power affects the propensity to smile. But the effect of having greater or lesser power did not directly translate into the display of less or more smiling. It was not the case across the board that low-power people smiled more than those with greater power. Rather, greater social power seems to provide its holders with the option to display what they feel, at least with respect to positive feelings. When high-power people felt positive, they smiled, but when they did not feel positive, they did not smile. In contrast, whether lower-power people smiled or not was unconnected to how positive they felt and much more connected to how much they felt they needed to please their partner.

These findings resolve some of the contradictions in prior work. The prevailing assumption has been that low-power people evidence more smiling than high-power people. As it turns out, low-power people smile more than high-power people only when the interaction is characterized by low positive affect. To the extent power-discrepant interactions in the "real world" are often marked by low positive affect, then greater smiling by low-power people might be the norm (Henley, 1973, 1977). However, these results show that it is possible to find high-power people smiling more than low-power people. This occurs when high-power people are enjoying themselves. No such variability characterizes the smiling of low-power people, who display the same level of smiling regardless of the affective quality of the interaction. The consistency in smiling for low-power people, irrespective of positive emotional tone, may contribute to the intuitive sense that low-power people usually smile.

Secondly, the fact that positive feelings and needing to please mediated the relationship between power and smiling is supportive of the idea that power provides options or enforces obligation. It should be noted, however, that we did not experimentally manipulate positive affect and needing to please, and thus the correlations between psychological states and smiling do not imply causation. Although our interpretation is that high-power participants' greater positive affect led to greater smiling, and low-power participants feeling of needing to please led to what smiling they did, it is also possible that smiling (for whatever reason) led to greater positive affect for high-power people and needing to please for low-power people as predicted by the facial feedback hypothesis (Laird, 1974; Strack, Martin, & Stepper, 1988). Regardless of the actual causal direction, the important point is that associations between feelings and smiling varied as a function of experimentally manipulated social power.

This study also explored the distinction between two smile types and their relationship to power. It seemed possible that high-power people would show more Duchenne smiling and low-power people would show more non-Duchenne smiling. Neither was the case. In addition, the correlations of the two smile types with positive affect were very similar, thus calling into question the idea that only Duchenne smiling is related to positive emotion. But it seems reasonable that people enjoying an interpersonal interaction would show both types of smiles. The Duchenne smiles may be an authentic expression of positive affect, while the non-Duchenne smiles may act as a signal of goodwill toward the partner. This interpretation coincides with recent work suggesting that the functional differences between Duchenne and non-Duchenne smiles in actual social situations may not be as strict as once thought (Fernández-Dols & Ruiz-Belda, 1995).

Finally, this study went some way toward understanding sex differences in smiling. In short, whether women smile more than men is significantly modified by context. Specifically, women smile more than men only in the power-equal condition. Within the power-discrepant condition, there were no differences on any measure of smiling between high-power men and high-power women or between low-power men and low-power women. These results are compatible with contextual models of gender-related behavior (Deaux & LaFrance, 1998; Deaux & Major, 1987). Specifically, the argument is that gender-related behavior depends on the nature of the social-psychological situation. Some situations (e.g., a job interview), and some positions (e.g., having less power than one's partner), impose requirements for appropriate behavior (Schutte, Kenrick, & Sadalla, 1985; Snyder & Ickes, 1985). In less defined, getting-acquainted situations, gender norms (even in same-sex dyads, as was the case in this study) may specify who is obliged to do what. In that situation, women smile much more, and their smiling was found to be slightly but positively correlated with needing to please; men smiled much less, and their smiling was negatively correlated with needing to please.

## Conclusions

In summary, differences in social power are manifested in facial display, although in ways quite different from what was previously thought. In a relationship characterized by asymmetric power, the more powerful person, whether male or female, appears to have the option to smile when he or she feels positively inclined and not to smile when he or she does not feel so inclined. Low-power people, whether they are female or male, appear to be under some obligation to display some level of smiling regardless of whether they are feeling good or not.

Low power appears to impose some expressive obligations; high power appears, on the other hand, to confer expressive options. These results corroborate ideas that power conveys the option to act at will (Fiske, 1993; Huston, 1983). Goffman observed, for example, that "the superordinate has the right to exercise certain familiarities which the subordinate is not allowed to reciprocate" (Goffman, 1967, p. 64). In the language of display rules, it thus appears that expressivity norms at least with respect to smiling apply more to some people than to others.

The license to act at will appears to operate at the micro level of nonverbal behavior as well as at macro level social behavior. Having greater power, defined here as having the imagined capacity to reward someone with a desirable job, gives one the option not to smile if feelings don't warrant it. Having lower power means that one is obligated to smile even if, or especially if, one is not feeling positively inclined. It is worth a reminder that people in a power-equal relationship also showed a significant positive correlation between positive affect and smiling. It thus appears that having the same power or possessing more power than one's partner means that one is more likely to show what one feels or feel what one shows. However, having lower power than one's partner means that smiling is unrelated to feeling good. In fact, the negative direction of the positive affect and smiling relationship for low-power people suggests that low-power people might be suppressing the expression of the positive affect that they do feel or accentuating positive display that they do not feel.

Sociologists who study emotion have for some time speculated that higher social status brings the privilege of freer, more spontaneous emotional expression but that lower status brings with it inhibition of expression (Gordon, 1990). The self-report data on pressure to smile and the amount of smiling shown by high- and low-power people clearly corroborate such thinking. Micropolitics has to do with the creation and negotiation of hierarchy (Clark, 1990); smiling and the feeling that one should smile show one way these things are accomplished.

Similarly, body politics is substantially concerned with the creation and negotiation of gender distinctions (Henley, 1977). See chapter 7 by Kirouac and Hess in this volume for a discussion of how gender group membership affects how such emotional expressions are perceived. Smiling, in particular, appears to be a gendered expression. In same-sex pairs, women smile significantly more than men. Even in high-power pairs, where women and men smile pretty much the same amount, and where smiling is related for both groups to positive affect, the smiling of women is also positively correlated with needing to please ($r = .38$) while it is uncorrelated with this feeling for men ($r = -.12$). In sum, it appears that smiling serves more and varied functions for women, and hence it would be incorrect to say that for them it means one thing: low status, high attraction, or social anxiety.

Nonverbal cues can contribute to gender and power distinctions even while remaining conveniently implicit and apparently incontrovertible. Power and gender do not merely modify the display of nonverbal behavior, they are the ubiquitous context for it, even when gender appears not to be particularly salient and even when people appear to be operating on an equal basis with each other. The implication of such findings, as attested to by the title of this volume, is that context always matters.

## References

Andrew, R. J. (1965). The origins of facial expression. *Scientific American, 213*, 88–94.

Bänninger-Huber, E., & Rauber-Kaiser, S. (1989). Die Differnzierung verschiedener Lächeltypen: FACS-Codierung und Einschätzungen eine Untersuchung zur Eindrucksbildung. *Schweizerische Zeitschrift für Psychologie, 48*, 21–34.

Baxter, J. C., & Rosselle, R. M. (1975). Nonverbal expression as a function of crowding during a simulated police-citizen encounter. *Journal of Personality and Social Psychology, 32*, 40–54.

Biaggio, M. K. (1989). Sex differences in behavioral reactions to provocation of anger. *Psychological Reports, 64*, 23–26.

Blurton-Jones, N. (1967). An ethological study of some aspects of social behavior of children in nursery school. In D. Morris (Ed.), *Primate ethology* (pp. 347–368). London: Weidenfeld & Nicholson.

Blurton-Jones, N. (1972). Nonverbal communication in children. In R. Hinde (Ed.), *Non-verbal communication* (pp. 271–296). Cambridge: Cambridge University Press.

Brannigan, C. R., & Humphries, D. A. (1972). Human nonverbal behavior, a means of communication. In N. B. Jones (Ed.), *Ethnological studies of child behavior* (pp. 37–64). Cambridge: Cambridge University Press.

Brown, R. (1965). *Social psychology*. New York: The Free Press.

Bugental, D. B. (1986). Unmasking the "polite smile": Situational and personal determinants of managed affect in adult–child interaction. *Personality and Social Psychology Bulletin, 12*, 7–16.

Bugental, D. B., & Shennum, W. A. (1984). Difficult children as elicitors and targets of adult communication patterns: An attributional-behavioral-transactional analysis. *Monographs of the Society for Research in Child Development, 49*, 79–99.

Burgoon, J. K., Buller, D. B., Hale, J. L., & deTurck, M. A. (1984). Relational messages associated with nonverbal behaviors. *Human Communication Research, 10*, 351–378.

Chase, S. E. (1988). Making sense of "The woman who becomes man." In A. D. Todd & S. Fisher (Eds.)., *Gender and discourse: The power of talk* (pp. 275–295). Norwood, NJ: Ablex.

Clark, C. (1990). Emotions and micropolitics in everyday life: Some patterns and paradoxes of "place." In T. D. Kemper (Ed.), *Research agendas in the sociology of emotions* (pp. 305–333). Albany, NY: State University of New York Press.

Cohen, A. R. (1958). Upward communication in experimentally created hierarchies. *Human Relations, 11*, 41–53.

Darwin, C. (1872). *The expression of the emotions in man and animals*. London: Murray.

Deaux, K., & LaFrance, M. (1998). Gender. In D. Gilbert, S. Fiske & G. Lindzey (Eds.), *Handbook of social psychology*, 4th edition (Vol. 1 (pp. 788–828). New York: McGraw Hill.

Deaux, K., & Major, B. (1987). Putting gender into context. *Psychological Review, 94*, 369–389.

Denmark, F. L. (1977). Styles of leadership. *Psychology of Women Quarterly, 2*, 99–113.

Denmark, F. L., McKenna, W., Juran, S., & Greenburg, H. M. (1976). *Status and sex differences in nonverbal behavior*. Unpublished manuscript, City University of New York.

Deutsch, F. M. (1990). Status, sex, and smiling: The effect of role on smiling in men and women. *Personality and Social Psychology Bulletin, 16*, 531–540.

Deutsch, F. M., LeBaron, D., & Fryer, M. M. (1987). What is in a smile? *Psychology of Women Quarterly, 11*, 341–352.

Dovidio, J. F., Brown, C. E., Heltman, K., Ellyson, S. L., & Keating, C. F. (1988). Power displays between women and men in discussions of gender-linked tasks: A multichannel study. *Journal of Personality and Social Psychology, 55*, 580–587.

Duchenne de Bologne, G. B. (1862). *The mechanism of human facial expression*. (R. A. Cuthberton, Trans.). New York: Cambridge University Press, 1990.

Edelmann, R. J., Asendorpf, J., Contarello, A., & Zammuner, V. (1989). Self-reported expression of embarrassment in five European cultures. *Journal of Cross-Cultural Psychology, 20*, 357–371.

Ekman, P. (1985). *Telling lies*. New York: Norton.

Ekman, P. (1992). Facial expressions of emotion: New findings, new questions. *Psychological Science, 3*, 34–38.

Ekman, P., Davidson, R. J., & Friesen, W. (1990). The Duchenne smile: Emotional expression and brain physiology II. *Journal of Personality and Social Psychology, 58*, 342–353.

Ekman, P., & Friesen, W. V. (1978). *The Facial Action Coding System. A technique for the measurement of facial movement.* Palo Alto: Consulting Psychologists Press.

Ekman, P., & Friesen, W. V. (1982). Felt, false, and miserable smiles. *Journal of Nonverbal Behavior, 6*, 238–252.

Ekman, P., Friesen, W. V., & Ancoli, S. (1980). Facial signs of emotional experience. *Journal of Personality and Social Psychology, 39*, 1125–1134.

Ekman, P., Friesen, W. V., & Ellsworth, P. (1972). *Emotion in the human face.* New York: Pergamon.

Ekman, P., Friesen, W. V., & O'Sullivan, M. (1988). Smiles when lying. *Journal of Personality and Social Psychology, 54*, 414–420.

Ellyson, S. L., & Dovidio, J. F. (1985). Power, dominance, and nonverbal behavior: Basic concepts and issues. In S. L. Ellyson & J. F. Dovidio (Eds.), *Power, dominance, and nonverbal behavior* (pp. 1–28). New York: Springer.

Fabes, R. A., & Martin, C. L. (1991). Gender and age stereotypes of emotionality. *Personality and Social Psychology Bulletin, 17*, 532–540.

Fehr, B. J., & Exline, R. V. (1987). Social visual interaction: A conceptual and literature review. In A. W. Siegman & S. Feldstein (Eds.), *Nonverbal behavior and communication* (pp. 225–326). Hillsdale, NJ: Lawrence Erlbaum.

Fernández-Dols, J. M., & Ruiz-Belda, M. A. (1995). Are smiles a sign of happiness?: Gold medal winners at the Olympic Games. *Journal of Personality and Social Psychology, 69*, 1113–1119.

Fishman, P. M. (1983). Interaction: The work that women do. In B. Thorne, C. Kramarae, & N. M. Itenley (EDs.). *Language, gender, and society* (pp. 89–101). Rowley, MA: Newbury House.

Fiske, S. (1993). Controlling other people: The impact of power on stereotyping. *American Psychologist, 48,* 621–628.

Frank, M., Ekman, P., & Friesen, W. V. (1993). Behavioral markers and recognizability of the smile of enjoyment. *Journal of Personality and Social Psychology 64*, 83–93.

French, J. R. P., Jr., & Raven, B. H. (1959). The bases of social power. In D. Cartwright (Ed.), *Studies in social power.* Ann Arbor: University of Michigan Press.

Friesen, W. V. (1972). *Cultural differences in facial expressions in a social situation: An experimental test of the concept of display rules.* Unpublished doctoral dissertation, University of California, San Francisco.

Goffman, E. (1967). *Interaction ritual.* Garden City, NY: Doubleday.

Goldenthal, P., Johnston, R. E., & Kraut, R. E. (1981). Smiling, appeasement, and the silent bared-teeth display. *Ethology and Sociobiology, 2*, 127–133.

Gordon, S. L. (1990). Social structural effects on emotions. In T. D. Kemper (Ed.), *Research agendas in the sociology of emotions* (pp. 145–179). Albany, NY: State University of New York Press.

Graham, J. W., Gentry, K. W., & Green, J. (1981). The self-presentational nature of emotional expression: Some evidence. *Personality and Social Psychology Bulletin 7*, 407–474.

Grant, E. C. (1969). Human facial expression. *Man, 4*, 525–536.

Halberstadt, A. G., Dovidio, J. F., & Davidson, L. A. (1988, October). *Power, gender, and smiling*. Paper presented at the annual meeting of the Society for Experimental Social Psychology.

Halberstadt, A. G., & Saitta, M. B. (1987). Gender, nonverbal behavior, and perceived dominance: A test of theory. *Journal of Personality and Social Psychology, 53*, 257–272.

Hall, J. A. (1984). *Nonverbal sex differences: Communication accuracy and expressive style*. Baltimore: Johns Hopkins University Press.

Hall, J. A. (1987). On explaining gender differences: The case of nonverbal communication. In P. Shaver & C. Hendrick (Eds.), *Sex and gender* (pp. 177–200). Beverly Hills: Sage.

Hall, J. A., & Halberstadt, A. G. (1996). Subordination and nonverbal sensitivity: A hypothesis in search of support. In M. R. Walsh (Ed.), *Women, men, and gender: Ongoing debates* (pp. 120–133). New Haven, CT: Yale University Press.

Hall, J. A., & Payne, R. M. (1995). *Smiling in relation to trait and manipulated dominance/status*. Unpublished manuscript, Northeastern University.

Haynes, S., Levine, S., Scotch, N., Feinleib, M., & Kannel, W. B. (1978). The relationship of psychosocial factors to coronary heart disease in the Framingham Study. I. Methods and risk factors. *American Journal of Epidemiology, 107*, 362–383.

Hecht, M. A., & LaFrance, M. (1998). License or obligation to smile: The effect of power and gender on amount and type of smiling. *Personality and Social Psychology Bulletin, 24*, 1332–1342.

Henley, N. M. (1973). Power, sex, and nonverbal communication. *Berkeley Review of Sociology, 18*, 1–26.

Henley, N. M. (1977). *Body politics: Power, sex, and nonverbal communication*. Englewood Cliffs, NJ: Prentice-Hall.

Henley, N. M. (1995). Body politics revisited: What do we know today? In P. J. Kalbfleisch and M. J. Cody (Eds.), *Gender, power, and communication in human relationships*. Hillsdale, NJ: Lawrence Erlbaum.

Hochschild, A. R. (1983). *The managed heart: Commercialization of human feeling*. Berkeley, CA: University of California Press.

Huston, T. L. (1983). Power. In H. H. Kelley, E. Berscheid, A. Christensen, J. H. Harvey, T. L. Huston, G. Levinger, E. McClintock, L. A. Peplau, & D. P. Peterson (Eds.), *Close relationships* (pp. 169–219). New York: Freeman.

Ickes, W., Patterson, M. L., Rajecki, D. W., & Tanford, S. (1982). Behavioral and cognitive consequences of reciprocal versus compensatory responses to preinteraction expectancies. *Social Cognition, 1*, 160–190.

Johnson, C. (1994). Gender, legitimate authority, and leader–subordinate conversations. *American Sociological Review, 59*, 122–135.

Johnson, J. T., & Shulman, G. A. (1988). More alike than meets the eye: Perceived gender differences in subjective experience and its display. *Sex Roles, 19*, 67–79.

Keating, C. F. (1985). Human dominance signals: The primate in us. In S. L. Ellyson & J. F. Dovidio (Eds.), *Power, dominance, and nonverbal behavior* (pp. 89–108). New York: Springer.

Keating, C. F., & Bai, D. L. (1986). Children's attribution of social dominance from facial cues. *Child Development, 57*, 1269–1276.

Keating, C. F., Mazur, A., & Segall, M. H. (1977). Facial gestures which influence the perception of status. *Sociometry, 40*, 374–378.

Kelley, H. H. (1951). Communication in experimentally created hierarchies. *Human Relations, 4*, 39–56.

Kolaric, G. C., & Galambos, N. L. (1995). Face-to-face interactions in unacquainted female-male adolescent dyads: How do girls and boys behave? *Journal of Early Adolescence, 15*, 363–382.

LaFrance, M. (1997). Pressure to be pleasant: Effects of sex and power on reactions to not smiling. *International Review of Social Psychology, 2*, 95–108.

LaFrance, M., & Banaji, M. (1992). Towards a reconsideration of the gender emotion relationship. In M. S. Clark (Ed.), *Review of Personality and Social Psychology, 14*. Beverly Hills, CA: Sage.

LaFrance, M., & Henley, N. M. (1994). On oppressing hypotheses or sex differences in nonverbal sensitivity revisited. In L. Radtke & H. Stam (Eds.), *Power and gender*. London, England: Sage.

Laird, J. D. (1974). Self-attribution of emotion: The effects of expressive behavior on quality of emotional experience. *Journal of Personality and Social Psychology, 29*, 475–486.

Lerner, G. (1985). *The dance of anger*. New York: Harper & Row.

Lott, D. F., & Sommer, R. (1967). Seating arrangements and status. *Journal of Personality and Social Psychology, 7*, 90–95.

Matsumoto, D. (1986). *Cross-cultural communication of emotion*. Unpublished doctoral dissertation, University of California, Berkeley.

Moskowitz, D. S., Suh, E. J., & Desaulniers, J. (1994). Situational influences on gender differences in agency and communion. *Journal of Personality and Social Psychology, 8*, 249–270.

Nieva, V. F., & Gutek, B. A. (1981). *Women and work: A psychological perspective*. New York: Praeger.

Ochanomizu, U. (1991). Representation forming in Kusyo behavior. *Japanese Journal of Developmental Psychology, 2*, 25–31.

Ploutz-Snyder, R., Lassiter, G. D., & Snodgrass, S. E. (1995). *Expectancies overcome gender effects in leader emergence*. Unpublished manuscript.

Rowell, T. E. (1966). Hierarchy in the organization of a captive baboon group. *Animal Behaviour, 14*, 430–433.

Schutte, N. A., Kenrick, D. T., & Sadalla, E. K. (1985). The search for predictable settings: Situational prototypes, constraint, & behavioral variation. *Journal of Personality and Social Psychology, 49*, 121–128.

Snyder, M., & Ickes, W. (1985). Personality and social behavior. In G. Lindzey & E. Aronson (Eds.), *Handbook of social psychology*, Vol. 2, 3rd ed. (pp. 883–947).

Stoppard, J., & Gunn-Gruchy, C. D. (1993). Gender, context, and expression of positive emotion. *Personality and Social Psychology Bulletin, 19*, 143–150.

Strack, F., Martin, L., & Stepper, S. (1988). Inhibiting and facilitating conditions of the human smile: A nonobtrusive test of the facial feedback hypothesis. *Journal of Personality and Social Psychology, 54,* 768–777.

Tedeschi, J. T., & Norman, N. (1985). Social power, self-presentation and the self. In R. R. Schlenker (Ed.), *The self and social life* (pp. 293–322). New York: McGraw-Hill.

Tjosvold, D. (1981). Unequal power relationships within a cooperative or competitive context. *Journal of Applied Social Psychology, 11,* 137–150.

Wierzbicka, A. (1994). Emotion, language, and cultural scripts. In S. Kitayama and H. R. Markus (Eds.), *Emotion and culture: Empirical studies of mutual influence* (pp. 133–196). Washington, DC: American Psychological Association.

# 4. Emotional Displays and Dissemblance in Childhood

## Implications for Self-Presentation

CAROLYN SAARNI AND HANNELORE WEBER

We begin with an extended (and, hopefully, entertaining) vignette about an incident involving two children well-known to Carolyn Saarni, which should provide an intuitive foundation for the reader for understanding how emotional displays function for children in social interaction. Not only does the expressive behavior described below give us some idea of what feelings might be felt, it gives us perhaps an even better idea of how children shape their social exchanges with others by the emotional cues they produce, not that this "shaping" is necessarily conscious, nor are the emotional cues necessarily genuine.

> Ned and Jack, identical 12-year-old twins, were enrolled in a class to learn how to kayak on the San Francisco Bay during their summer vacation. An older know-it-all kid, Steve, frequently harassed them and tried to ridicule them in front of the other kids, but the twins' faces registered nothing of his insults. Even the camp counselor seemed a bit intimidated by the arrogant and hostile youth. Finally, Ned and Jack got their chance for revenge against the older boy. They had spent part of a lunch break exploring the tide pools along the rocky edge of the Bay and had caught a small rock crab. Ned engaged Steve in some berating and put-downs, while behind Steve's back Jack dropped the crab into the bully's wetsuit.
>
> The twins fairly leapt into their wetsuits and paddled out onto the water to watch what Steve would do. He donned his wetsuit, seemingly nothing amiss. He too paddled out, and then he let out a scream that revealed his adolescent changing voice, as it oscillated back and forth between a young boy's soprano shriek and a youth's guttural bellow. He clutched his crotch, rocking the kayak violently and dumping it

Portions of this chapter have been adapted from C. Saarni, *The Development of Emotional Competence* (New York: Guilford).

over. As he bobbed up and down in the water, furiously trying to loosen his wetsuit under the chilly water (which is nearly impossible to do), the twins paddled over, with great effort suppressing their laughter and substituting expressions of concern and worry, and asked what was wrong and if they should get help. Steve said he was pretty sure a scorpion was in his wetsuit or maybe a snake or perhaps it was a yellow jacket that got in there. Yeah, he needed to be towed back to shore because his kayak had also drifted away.

Ned and Jack artfully played out their rescue role, and Steve's performance in the water became the source of much comic repetition by the other boys on shore. Steve looked balefully around for the perpetrator of the trick and, not finding a ready target, vented his anger and chagrin by making a great show of offering the now squashed crab that had been retrieved from his wetsuit to the ever-hovering seagulls.

He never suspected the twins; after all, they had been right in front of him because he had been arguing with them before getting into his wetsuit. For once, it paid off for Jack and Ned to be perceived as one, and they nodded with astute commiseration over Steve's ostensible suffering and added sympathetically, with perhaps just a trace of ruefulness, "What a terrible thing to do to that crab, too."

At age 11, Ned and Jack possess a well-developed competence in concealing their genuine feelings when it would be disadvantageous to them to reveal them; indeed, not only did they conceal their feelings by adopting neutral expressions when Steve insulted them, but they were also able to adopt misleading expressive behavior that was intended to influence another to believe something about them that was not true (i.e., the seeming commiseration with the bully Steve so as to avoid his suspecting them of any trick). Steve appeared to use a strategy of expressive amplification of his hostility to intimidate others, and the other children who witnessed the incident similarly exaggerated their expressive behavior in mockery of Steve's plight. With this introduction to children's emotional displays and some of their possible functions in social interaction, we will consider in this essay (a) how different types of emotional displays have different functions relative to the social transaction at hand; (b) how emotional display management may also represent a strategy for regulating emotional experience itself; (c) how children develop strategies for emotional dissemblance; (d) how individual differences, most notably gender differences, may manifest themselves in emotional displays; and (e) how self-presentation represents a culminating integration of emotion management, dissemblance, and coping.

## Functions of Emotional Displays

*Emotions and Social Context*

The theoretical perspective that we take is that emotional-expressive behavior is inseparable from social context, whether it is an immediate or a historical social context. This embeddedness of emotional-expressive behavior in social contexts further suggests that emotional displays can have dual functions: They are both visible cues as to what we are feeling as well as social signals to others about our probable actions (see also the chapters by Manstead and Fernández-Dols in this volume; Lewis & Michalson, 1985). In the course of our socialization, we learn what likely motives and action tendencies are associated with assorted emotions (e.g., Frijda, 1987) as well as what likely circumstances gave rise to the emotional reaction (e.g., Barden, Zelko, Duncan, & Masters, 1980; Harris, 1985). From our observations of others' emotional displays we also learn to infer what they might be feeling as well as how they might subsequently act (e.g., Beeghly, Bretherton, & Mervis, 1986; Dunn, Brown, & Beardsall, 1991; Harris, 1989; Harris & Olthof, 1982). However, understanding others' emotions is not always this simple: Much expressive behavior is ambiguous and does not seem tied in a one-to-one fashion to the presumed emotional state being experienced. As observers, we are often left in a quandary, not being certain how to infer our interactant's feelings nor his or her likely behavior, and we must use other information to guide us in the unfolding transaction (e.g., we might possess unique personal information about our interactant; Gnepp, 1989).

*Folk Theories and Emotions*

The fact that we anticipate some actions as being more likely to follow some expressive displays than others is also an illustration of cultural beliefs. Most societies have tacit belief systems that have been referred to as folk theories about the mind (D'Andrade, 1987), naive theories of emotion (Weiner, 1987), or ethnotheories of emotion (Lutz, 1987; Wellenkamp, 1995), which are integrated with larger networks of knowledge about psychosocial functioning within a given culture. Most relevant to our discussion of emotional-expressive displays is Lutz's view, which emphasizes that ethnotheories of emotion function as pragmatic guidelines for daily social-emotional exchanges among people. Lutz also argues that ethnotheories of emotion have implicit goals, the first being *action tendency goals* and the second being *disclosure goals*. Her first-mentioned goal is very similar to what we discussed above about emotions being probabilistically linked to subsequent actions. But what those actions specifically are is contextualized by the cultural beliefs surrounding the emotional experience. Thus, Western children when feeling angry might be prone to strike out at someone, but an angered Japanese child would be much less likely to act out such feelings (e.g., Kitayama & Marcus, 1994). The second type of goal refers to the acceptability of the emotion to oneself and within one's society (i.e., is the felt emotion one that may be disclosed or expressed, or is it "taboo," indicative of "weakness," or otherwise undesirable?). However, norms of acceptability for emotions are themselves contextualized. For example, Western girls appear to be socialized to avoid anger-provoking conflicts, perhaps because of the reduced acceptability of anger in girls, and as a consequence, the frequency of their physical aggression is relatively low compared to that of boys (e.g., Brody & Hall, 1993; Crick & Grotpeter, 1995; Golombok & Fivush, 1994).

The action tendency goal has particular importance for how one's emotional-expressive behavior will function interpersonally. Most significant displays of emotional-expressive behavior carry messages of impending interpersonal interaction. Indeed, smiling may be relatively unassociated with emotional experience and may function more as a nonverbal indicator of social involvement. As an illustration, in their observational research with Olympic athletes, Fernández-Dols and Ruiz-Belda (1995) argued for the heterogeneity of happiness displays which begin to resemble prototypical displays only when social interaction commences (see also Camras, 1992; Fernández-Dols, this volume; Kraut & Johnston, 1979). For our purposes, what we want to argue here is that our emotional-expressive behavior demonstrates multidimensionality and that our study of such behavior must examine at least two of those dimensions, namely, the meaning of the emotional experience conveyed by the expressive behavior (regardless of its genuine or dissembled status) and the socially meaningful cue for subsequent social interaction (cf. Fridlund, 1991).

In summary, functions of emotional-expressive behavior vary according to cultural ethnotheories of emotion. In Western societies emotional-expressive behavior can function as a cue or signal for what is felt, but perhaps more importantly, the behavior functions interpersonally to suggest how the social transaction will unfold. However, this relationship may be attenuated or simply different in some non-Western societies; for example, Potter (1988) contended that the significance of emotional behavior in China differed from that in Western societies in that emotional experience was irrelevant to formal or institutionalized "socially significant action" (p. 185). On an informal, more directly personal level (in China as well, according to Potter), emotional-expressive behavior often has very instrumental goals, whether self-serving, other oriented, or both. Among adults, tacit messages of dominance and responsiveness are also often carried by nonverbal expressive behavior as metacommunications (LaFrance, this volume; Mehrabian, 1972; Saarni, 1982; Watzlawick, Beavin, & Jackson, 1967), but this topic is virtually unresearched among children (for an exception, see von Salisch, 1991). We turn next to a discussion of what could be thought of as yet another function of emotional-expressive behavior, that is, to regulate the experience of emotion itself; however, our perspective will be less on functionality and more on the process of how children come to cope with their feelings.

## Display Management and Emotion Regulation

### *Definition of Emotion Regulation*

We make the distinction between emotional display *management* and emotion *regulation* in that the former refers to controlling one's expressive behavior, that is, what others will observe about one's emotional experience, which can be strategically or habitually dissembled. The latter term we use to refer to how we deal with the subjective experience of our emotions. For display management, we saw in the opening vignette examples of both suppression and substitution of emotional-expressive behavior by the twins Ned and Jack, whereas the term emotion regulation is more often applied to internally experienced affect. We offer a brief definition of *effective* emotion regulation: *It is the recruitment of those processes (including deployment of attention, response inhibition, and modulation of emotional arousal) that facilitate one's monitoring, evaluating, and changing one's emotional reactions so as to maximize one's efficacy.* Efficacy is used here to refer to mastery and competence vis-à-vis one's environment, and thus this definition integrates the regulation of internal subjective emotional experience with the context in which it occurs. People vary in how effective they are in regulating their negative emotions, with the result that they can get "stuck" in their misery as in depression, or they may escalate anger into destructive rage. High intensity of feeling and a high frequency of negative feelings (or a low threshold for experiencing aversive emotions) appear to be aspects of emotional experience that interfere with effective emotion regulation (see, for example, Fox's edited *Monograph*, 1994; Garber & Dodge, 1991; Meerum Terwogt & Olthof, 1989; Thompson, 1991, 1994, among others). A considerable research literature has emerged in recent years that examines individual differences in emotion regulation, and this research overlaps with research on coping (e.g., Aldwin, 1994; Compas, Phares, & Ledoux, 1989; Cramer, 1991; Miller & Green, 1985; Skinner & Wellborn, 1994; Sorensen, 1993). Indeed, Brenner and Salovey (1997) view coping and emotion regulation as the same construct since both terms are concerned with how people manage stressful encounters.

## Does Adoption of Managed Displays Help Regulate Emotion?

Let us look at the particular instance of how we might regulate our emotional experience by managing our emotional-expressive behavior. Probably the most commonly encountered way that Westerners strive to manage their negative emotions is by adopting the "emotional front" of smiling (e.g., Ekman & Friesen, 1975). Not that such smiles are especially gracious or authentic, but they are intended to influence a social situation in such a way that one's emotional experience does not get worse. Indeed, LaFrance (this volume) presents data that show that those with less power smile genuinely less often than those with high power, suggesting that they mask some degree of discomfort about their discrepant power by smiling "falsely."

There has been virtually no systematic developmental research on recruitment of emotional-expressive behavior that is used specifically or solely for the purpose of internal emotion regulation; yet our Western ethnotheory of emotion suggests that many people adopt stoic (or poker-faced) emotional fronts so as to feel "in control" or at least to reduce the likelihood of their becoming "upset." A few investigations have been undertaken with children which suggest that by managing their expressive behavior, children may have more effectively prevented overarousal in the sense that interpersonal conflicts were defused or at least not escalated. In one study of German preadolescents, von Salisch (1991) studied the verbal and facial expressions of pairs of best friends as they played a rigged computer game. The computer game had been constructed so that when it "crashed," one of the pair of friends appeared to have caused the failure by being unskilled or inattentive. These game failures reliably triggered conflicts or disputes among the children. Von Salisch found that girls were inclined to use a strategy whereby they blamed their friend verbally, yet gave them a particularly cordial smile at the same time. Expressions of contempt also appeared but were followed almost immediately by smiles. It appeared as though the reproaching girl wanted to reassure her friend that the friendship was not threatened. Similarly, Vespo and Caplan (1993) also found that female school-age friends used more conciliatory gestures with one another when involved in a conflict together. However, the boys in von Salisch's sample tended to deal with the conflict (and the potential for escalating arousal) differently: They simply avoided it by adopting "flat" expressive behavior that revealed little about their feelings, yet they did show some signs of tension in that they touched their faces and bodies and fidgeted in their chairs more.

It remains to be determined whether emotional-expressive behavior management actually affects physiological indices of emotional experience. On one hand, some research with adults suggests that suppression of facial expression by adopting a "poker face" may amplify physiological responding (e.g., Gross & Levenson, 1997); on the other hand, if one monitors one's expressive behavior in order to achieve a desired interpersonal outcome and indeed succeeds, then emotion regulation has probably also been achieved in that aversive arousal is less likely if one has just succeeded in reaching a social goal. School-age children wisely appreciate that some degree of management of emotional-expressive behavior will more reliably provide emotional equilibrium as well as help one to have more satisfying social relations (Saarni, 1988): Too much expressive suppression or substitution (by adopting not-felt emotional-expressive behavior) was viewed as problematic, socially alienating, and even as an indicator of possible emotional disturbance (e.g., from a 13-year-old girl: "If she kept everything inside herself all the time, she'd consume all her anger, jealousy, whatever, and then one day she'd explode, commit suicide, and get emotionally disturbed"). But the other extreme, always showing one's feelings, was viewed as "babyish" and likely to get one rejected or in trouble, and with such outcomes one's emotional state would presumably not be effectively regulated.

In summary, although we have little empirical research that directly examines management of emotional-expressive behavior in order to regulate emotional experience, what we do have is a growing body of research that shows that children manage their emotional-expressive behavior so as to regulate their social interaction. Indeed, Gottman and Mettetal (1986) have theorized that preschool children react to aversive levels of emotional arousal by leaving or avoiding social interaction, whereas by middle childhood the construction of implicit and explicit rules for social interaction helps to contain emotional arousal. We argue that these rules for social interaction include strategies for managing emotional-expressive behavior, and thereby their adaptive use should also facilitate emotional regulation. We turn next to a discussion of their development.

## Development of Strategies for Emotional Dissemblance

By the preschool years, if not earlier, young children learn how to introduce disparities between their internal emotional experience and their external expressive behavior (e.g., Cole, 1986). Such discrepancies indicate that the young child has begun to differentiate her inner emotional experience from what she expresses in her behavior – especially to others. Impressively enough, by middle childhood children have learned and constructed for themselves a sometimes implicit, sometimes explicit, set of expectancies and contingencies for figuring out under what conditions which emotions get expressed and to whom (e.g., Saarni, 1989). This growth in complexity of emotional expression is inseparable from the sorts of relationships children have. Thus, for example, children growing up in homes with alcoholic parents or who are abused may well operate with a somewhat different set of expectations about how and with whom to express their feelings than do children who grow up in more functional families (e.g., Adams-Tucker, 1985; Copans, 1989; Putnam & Trickett, 1991). When we show our feelings indirectly or deceptively in our faces, in our tone of voice, and in our body movement, we are dissembling our emotional communication to others, which is very much related to whom we are with, what the social risks are, and what we are really feeling.

*Forms of Expressive "Manipulation"*

Perhaps the earliest form of this differentiation between internal state and external expression is the *maximization* of emotional-expressive behavior in order to gain someone's attention (a trivial injury becomes the occasion to howl loudly and solicit comfort and attention); readers who are parents are likely to think that this occurs in the second year, if not earlier. More systematic observational research supports this anecdotal view: Blurton-Jones (1967) reported that children, ages 3 to 4, in a free-play situation were more likely to cry after injuring themselves if they noticed a caregiver looking at them; they were less likely to cry if they thought they were unattended. Maximization can also be used functionally to amplify an emotional response to impress or intimidate others, to emphasize a point, or to mock others by exaggerating their emotional response.

*Minimization* may be the next to appear; it consists of dampening the intensity of emotional-expressive behavior, despite feeling otherwise. Socialization is likely to be highly influential here, such as when we admonish children to calm down their rambunctiousness or control their upsetness (e.g., "boys don't cry," or "don't act like a baby"). Minimization appears to be used functionally to avoid some onerous social reaction or to appear relatively unmoved (e.g., the boys in von Salisch's research, 1991, described above).

*Neutralization* describes the adoption of a "poker face," but it is probably relatively difficult to carry off, and what we may see more often are minimized displays. If neutral expressions are adopted, they appear to function similarly to minimization: to stay in control, to keep options open, to appear unaffected. Ekman and Friesen (1975) have suggested that substitution of another expression that differs from what one genuinely feels is probably a more successful strategy (e.g., smiling despite feeling anxious) from a social reaction standpoint. Functionally speaking, not only might one retain control or avoid something onerous, one can more actively mislead others to believe something positive about oneself (e.g., that one is self-confident, capable, etc.).

*Prerequisites of Emotional Dissemblance*

As summarized by Shennum and Bugental (1982), in North America children gradually acquire *knowledge* about when, where, with whom, and how to express behaviorally their feelings. They also need to have the *ability to control* the skeletal muscles involved in emotional-expressive behavior. Very significantly, they need to have the *motivation* to enact display rules in the appropriate situations. Lastly, they also need to have reached a certain complexity of *cognitive representation*. An elaboration of these issues follows.

*Knowledge.* In an early study (Saarni, 1979a), the author interviewed elementary school children about when and why they would conceal their own feelings of hurt/pain and fear. The majority of their reasons referred to wanting to avoid embarrassment or derision from others for revealing vulnerable feelings. Getting attention, making someone feel sorry for oneself, and getting help were also among the reasons mentioned for dissembling one's emotional-expressive behavior. Significant age difference appeared only when children were questioned about when it would be appropriate to express one's genuine feelings. Older children were more likely to cite many more such occasions than younger children – suggesting that the older children (10 to 11 years) perceived the expression of emotion, whether genuine or dissembled, as a regulated act. The older children were more likely to make reference to the degree of affiliation with an interactant, status differences, and controllability of both emotion or circumstances as contextual qualities that affected the genuine or dissembled display of emotion. However, across all ages, the most common reason cited for when genuine feelings would be expressed was if they were experienced as very intense (and thus less controllable).

More recent research by Zeman and her associates (Zeman & Garber, 1996; Zeman & Shipman, 1996) confirms and extends the above findings. Using structured interviews and hypothetical vignettes, Zeman and Garber examined children's appraisal of how important the audience or interactant was for controlling the display of emotional-expressive behavior. Across all age groups (first, third, and fifth grades) children expected that they would control their expressive behavior more with peers than with parents (cf. Saarni, 1988). The reason that was most commonly cited for doing so was to avoid a negative social interaction. Older children also anticipated that they would be less likely to display negative feelings with their fathers and would be more likely to reveal sadness and pain to their mothers than to peers. Echoing Zeman and Garber, we clearly need more research that addresses how children experience disapproval for their genuine displays of negative emotion within these different relationships (mother, father, peer).

*Ability to Implement Emotional Dissemblance.* Control of skeletal muscles, especially in the face, is critical to being able to modify one's emotional-expressive behavior and thus dissemble the outward expression of one's feelings. Children begin to be able to do this modification voluntarily at a young age (2 to 3 years), and it is readily apparent in their pretend play; e.g., they mimic postures, expressions, vocal qualities, and the like of assorted fantasy characters. However, when it comes to deliberately adopting emotional expressions, the posing of facial expressions proves to be difficult, especially negatively toned expressions (e.g., Lewis, Sullivan, & Vasen, 1987; Odom & Lemond, 1972). The difficulty in posing fear, disgust, sadness, and the like may be due to the fairly consistent socialization pressure in our culture to inhibit negative displays of emotion (see Zeman's research above; also Malatesta & Haviland, 1982). A smiling expression is considerably easier for children to produce "on demand," but even then only partially "happy" facial expressions may be produced, perhaps partly due to self-consciousness. As Lewis et al. point out, when asked to produce a scared face, the young children in their sample produced scary faces instead.

*Motivation.* In another early study with elementary school children (Saarni, 1979b), expectations about what motivated story characters to manage their emotional-expressive behavior were examined. Four broad categories of motivation for emotional dissemblance were apparent in their interview responses. Given that most human behavior has multiple determinants, similarly any given instance of emotional dissemblance may have more than one of these motivational categories underlying it.

(a) The first category of motivation was to avoid negative outcomes, as succinctly illustrated by a 6-year-old boy's response: "He wouldn't show that he thought it [a trick played on another child] was funny, because he'd be scared that the kid would beat him up." This sort of rationale – to avoid some anticipated bad outcome – is generally found to be the most frequently offered as a justification for expressive dissemblance, and it would appear to be the one to develop first (see also Zeman & Garber, 1996).

(b) The second motivation category for dissemblance is to protect one's self-esteem or to cope more effectively with how one feels. An 8-year-old boy said the following: "He could show that he could stand up to stuff like that" in reference to being the target of criticism. Particularly when children or youth adopt stoic or smiling emotional fronts, they may have as their motive the desire to protect their vulnerability, self-image, or self-esteem. In this boy's comment what may be alluded to is being able to control stoically one's feelings, despite the threat to self-esteem implied by being criticized.

(c) The third motivation category for expressive dissemblance concerns relationships. It has a more elementary version as well as a more sophisticated version. The simpler level is to dissemble one's feelings so as not to hurt someone else's feelings (e.g., Saarni, 1987, 1989), and even children of ages 5 to 6 years old are able to understand this sort of motive for dissembling their feelings (not that they reliably perform it, however). The more complex level of this motive category is to regulate relationship dynamics, and it was more likely to appear in preadolescent children's justifications for expressive dissemblance. Examples from another study (Saarni, 1991) include, "He didn't want to let the other kids down, so he didn't show his disappointment [at losing the game that he had coached]." Concern for others' well-being is a prominent theme among such rationales, both simpler and more complex levels, and is generally associated with relatively close relationships or the desire to increase the closeness of a relationship.

(d) The fourth motivation category concerns norms and conventions; these are the cultural display rules that provide us with consensually agreed-upon scripts for how to manage our emotions. A couple of 9- to 10-year-old children's responses illustrate their notions of what the norms are for emotional dissemblance: "You shouldn't yell at a grown-up" and "You should apologize, even though you don't feel like it." It is probably noteworthy that cultural display rules often have "shoulds" associated with them. Parenthetically, children may readily articulate culturally accepted scripts for emotional dissemblance, but that does not mean that they will actually perform such scripts, for example, apologizing when they would rather not. At least a couple of factors might account for why children do not consistently perform cultural display rule scripts, despite knowing them: First, the social stakes may not be sufficiently high for them to feel motivated to do so; and, second, their distressed, hurt, or angry feelings may be experienced as too intense to allow for emotional dissemblance. As mentioned earlier (Saarni, 1979a), intensity of feeling was cited by school-age children as the chief reason for genuinely expressing feelings.

These four categories of motivation for emotional dissemblance are not necessarily exhaustive, but they all have one significant feature in common: They are concerned with interpersonal consequences, and it is the varying nature of these social consequences that yields the differences among motives. Even the self-esteem motive for dissemblance does not occur in a social vacuum, for the self is embedded in a history of social relationships. As we shall see in the latter part of this essay, these motives affect self-presentation strategies.

*Cognitive Representation.* A pragmatic or implicit knowledge of emotional dissemblance is likely to precede an articulated and verbalized understanding of expressive dissimulation, as suggested by Josephs's (1993) research with 4- and 5-year-olds. Within the "theory of mind" literature, a large body of research has emerged concerned with children's understanding of real versus apparent phenomena, and this distinction has been applied to inner emotional state as "real" and external expressive behavior as "apparent." (One could quibble over the distinction, since the social message of the dissembled expressive behavior may be what is "real.")

By the time they enter school, children generally understand that how one looks on one's face is not necessarily how one feels on the inside (e.g., Harris & Gross, 1988). Thus, relatively young children understand that the appearance of one's facial expression can be misleading about the actual emotional state experienced. By age 6 many children can provide justifications for how appearances can conceal reality, in this case, the genuine emotion felt by an individual. Harris and Gross (1988) examined young children's rationales for why story characters would conceal their emotions by adopting misleading facial expressions. A significant number of the 6-year-olds interviewed gave very complex justifications that included describing the intent to conceal their feelings and to mislead another to believe something other than what was really being emotionally experienced (e.g., "She didn't want her sister to know that she was sad about not going to the party"). Children younger than 6 can readily adopt pretend facial expressions, but they are not likely to be able to articulate the embedded relationships involved in deliberate emotional dissemblance. These embedded relationships refer to how the self wants another to perceive an apparent self, not the real self. In other words, by age 6 children readily grasp that emotional dissemblance has as its basic function the creation of a false impression on others, and this is where self-presentation strategies are relevant. Before considering this topic in greater detail, we will next examine some of the rich research on individual differences in management of emotional-expressive behavior.

## Individual Differences in Emotional Displays

Children acquire many idiosyncratic mannerisms of nonverbal behavior that may become evident in their gestures, body kinesics and posture, vocal intonation, patterns of eye contact, and facial expression. What we are interested in here are those broader categories of influence that generate differences in the patterning of emotional-expressive behavior. Gender and the accompanying processes of sex-role socialization is one such category; other broad categories are social-emotional adjustment status and (sub-)cultural influences. Relatively few studies have examined these categories as they influence children's emotional-expressive displays, but we will discuss several of these here.

### Influence of Gender

Meerum Terwogt and Olthof (1989) have argued that knowledge of when to control emotional-expressive displays may be gender-related when the specific emotion is culturally sanctioned for one sex but not for the other. Specifically, the school-age girls in their Dutch sample said they would not express anger as readily as the boys would, and conversely, the boys were reluctant to express fear. The justifications for the girls included disapproval from adults for showing anger, and the boys worried they would be viewed as cowards by their peers if they expressed fear. Fuchs and Thelen (1988) also report that school-age boys were loathe to reveal their sadness to their fathers but might consider doing so with their mothers.

A study by Davis (1995) attempted to tease apart whether boys and girls differed in their emotion management strategies because of differences in motivation or differences in ability. The young elementary school children (grades 1 and 3) in her study participated in the "disappointing gift" scenario (see Saarni, 1984; Cole, 1986), in which children receive an undesirable gift and are faced with the predicament of feeling disappointed with what they have received yet under some pressure to be polite toward the gift-giver (usually the experimenter) and thus to suppress or minimize the expression of their disappointment. The boys showed more negative expressive behaviors than the girls upon receiving the disappointing gift, an outcome that parallels earlier research (Saarni, 1984; Cole, 1986). However, in the next task Davis had the children play a game in which a desirable prize and an undesirable one were placed in two boxes, visible only to the child. The children were told to deceive the experimenter by pretending to like both prizes, and if they succeeded in "tricking" the experimenter to believe they really liked both, they would be able to keep both prizes. If they did not succeed, then the experimenter took both prizes. Thus, for the children to get the attractive prize, they had to persuasively manage their expressive behavior so as to look positive for both attractive and unattractive prizes.

The results showed that the girls were more successful at suppressing negative expressive behaviors toward the unattractive prize than the boys. Interestingly, the girls also revealed a greater number of social monitoring behaviors (e.g., rapid glancing at the experimenter) as well as tension behaviors (e.g., touching one's face; the coding scheme may be found in Saarni [1992] and in Davis [1995]). In comparing the children's expressive behavior in the two situations (gift and game), the children were given a clear incentive and were explicitly instructed to produce positive behaviors in the game situation. Indeed, compared to the disappointing gift situation, both boys and girls did reduce the number of their negative expressive behaviors in the game situation. However, the girls' level of negative responses to both attractive and unattractive prizes was virtually indistinguishable. Instead, they appeared to monitor the social exchange more closely than the boys, which may have facilitated their expression management. Davis concludes that girls do have more ability in managing the expression of their negative feelings, and she suggests that individual differences (e.g., temperament) may interact with sex-role socialization to yield the gender pattern she observed.

An observational study by Casey (1993) also yielded intriguing gender effects. She investigated the relations among children's ability to report their emotions and their ability to describe their own facial expression under two different social feedback conditions. The children, ages 7 to 12 years, were given a variety of tasks and then told that there was another child of their age and gender who might be brought in later to interact with them. The experimenter then left the room, and a video monitor in the subject child's room then began to show this other child (a confederate) with the experimenter talking with her/him. The confederate child then gave either disparaging social feedback or positive social feedback about the subject child in the first room. The monitor then went dark, and the experimenter shortly returned to the subject child in the first room. The subject children were interviewed as to how they felt hearing the feedback, how they knew what they felt, and how they believed they looked in their faces when they heard the feedback. Their expressive behavior had also been videotaped throughout the whole episode, and thus their verbal reports could be compared with what they had indeed displayed. Although Casey was not investigating emotional dissemblance, she found that girls were facially more responsive to conditions of negative and positive social feedback than were boys. The latter tended to maintain a low level of constant negative expressive behavior under both conditions of positive and negative feedback. Casey argued that in comparison to boys, girls may embellish their facial displays so as to better regulate their social communications, and thus this skill may have contributed to their greater awareness and accuracy in also knowing how their faces looked upon hearing the feedback. Interestingly, there were few significant age differences in children's expressive behavior or their understanding of how they felt upon receiving the positive or negative feedback, but older children were more likely than younger children to report more sophisticated explanations for what they felt, which was an expected outcome.

Brody and Hall's (1993) excellent review of sex differences in emotion is oriented toward adult functioning, and they too emphasize that the type of emotion felt and expressed is itself influenced by sex role socialization, via the family and peer group. Thus, they suggest that girls end up "cultivating" the expression of feelings like happiness, shame, fear, and warmth, whereas boys attend more to the expression of feelings of anger, aggression, contempt, and pride. Brody and Hall also contend that through a multitude of influences (which they describe in their review at length), by adolescence boys may end up expressing their emotions more through their physiology and their overt action (e.g., aggression, withdrawal, avoidance). In contrast, adolescent girls may end up subjectively experiencing both negative and positive emotions more intensely, expressing them more intensely in facial and other nonverbal behaviors, and using emotion-laden language more often.

## Social-Emotional Adjustment Status

*Emotional Disturbance.* Few studies have directly addressed what sorts of deficits or differences in emotional-expressive behavior management strategies may exist among children who are functioning well in their social relationships as opposed to those who are not. Insofar as emotion management, emotional dissemblance, and self-presentation may also be considered part of a larger "package" of coping skills, it would be expected that children with identified problems in coping with stress and conflict would not use adaptive emotion management strategies in an appropriate way or would do so only some of the time. One study that did empirically examine understanding of display rule usage among school-age children identified as emotionally disturbed was done by Adlam-Hill and Harris (1988). They found that emotionally disturbed children of average intelligence showed a distinct deficit compared to their nondisturbed peers in understanding that internal emotional state and external expressive behavior can be incongruent. As a consequence, such children were also less likely to think that story characters would modify their facial expressions if showing how they really felt would hurt the feelings of another. Adlam-Hill and Harris speculate about why this deficit occurred and suggest that emotionally disturbed children may not understand how to protect others' feelings, or they may not be motivated to do so, or they do not even predict that the display of genuine emotion can impact another in the first place.

*Depression.* If children nominate intense feelings as those least likely to be controlled and thus least amenable to management strategies, how would a depressed child make use of smiling displays to create smooth and engaging social transactions if he were feeling very sad and hopeless? Not surprisingly, Harris and Lipian (1989) found that school-age children who were hospitalized for acute medical conditions showed a regression or slippage in their understanding of emotion management in hypothetical situations (elicited in an interview held in the hospital). In contrast to comparable healthy children, these sick children were less likely to say they could conceal their feelings or to consider that they might have mixed feelings. Harris and Lipian argued that these children's strongly negative and depressive emotional feelings "exert a pervasive filtering effect on consciousness. Other more positive concerns are either subverted to fit this one central preoccupation or are ignored" (p. 255).

*At-risk Children.* Cole, Zahn-Waxler, and Smith (1994) investigated how 4- to 5-year-old children, who had been categorized as at low, moderate, and high risk for developing behavior problems (e.g., oppositional behavior, excessive aggression), would respond to the "disappointing gift" scenario. At-risk boys showed more angry, disruptive, and generally negative behavior while the examiner was present than low-risk boys. An interesting gender difference occurred in that the at-risk girls showed a flattening of affect compared to the low-risk girls during the examiner's absence. More specifically, when the examiner was absent, the low-risk girls readily expressed their disappointment or aggravation with the lousy gift, but the at-risk girls expressed only minimal distress or negative behavior. These girls were primarily diagnosed as having attention deficit disorder, and Cole et al. speculate that possibly their overinhibition of negative affect may be related to deficits in instrumental coping and appropriate emotion management.

## Cultural Influence

Mesquita and Frijda's (1992) review of cultural variation in emotions suggests that one of the most significant sources of variation in emotional experience lies in regulatory processes, whether these be the sort that prohibit certain emotions from being experienced and/or expressed or the sort that prescribe what one should feel and express emotionally under certain circumstances (e.g., where, what, when, and with whom). In short, ethnotheories regarding emotional displays may be as variable as cultures are. To illustrate how these ethnotheories reveal themselves in children's responses to researchers investigating understanding of misleading expressions and display rules, we will describe several studies done with African American, Italian, and Indian children. All of these studies are social cognitive investigations; comparative observational studies have not been undertaken to our knowledge.

*African American Children.* Underwood, Coie, and Herbsman (1992) examined children's expectations of when to mask expressions of anger in response to videotaped hypothetical vignettes that featured a child interacting with either a teacher or another child. The children were all urban African American children in a low-income neighborhood; they ranged in age from 8 to 13. Children were asked to put themselves in the protagonist's shoes and respond with what they would do. They generally suggested genuine expressions of anger toward peers but were more likely to inhibit the expression of their anger toward teachers; this audience difference makes sense strategically, because teachers have authority over children, and the display of anger toward a peer is not the sort of expression of emotion that renders one vulnerable or "weak." If anything, in American culture, displaying anger may well facilitate making the impression on one's peers that one is strong and invincible.

*Italian and British Children.* Manstead (1995) investigated whether British and Italian children would differ from one another in understanding display rules; his supposition was that given greater socialization pressure in England to inhibit emotional expression, British children would both adopt and understand the usage of display rules at a younger age than would Italian children. The participating children were ages 6 to 7 and 10 to 11 years old. The procedure followed was to present the children with audiotaped vignettes about a disappointing gift and about disgusting food and then to follow up with questions that asked the children what they would do if they were in the protagonists' position relative to expression management. The children were also asked about whether one's genuine feelings could be concealed from another (i.e., the appearance-reality distinction). The results indicated a significant main effect of age group in that older children were more likely to suggest concealment of disappointment upon receiving an undesirable gift as compared to the younger children. In addition, the culture comparison was also significant: British children were considerably more likely to ascribe concealment of disappointment to themselves than the Italian children, with this effect being most pronounced among the younger children. By age 7 the proportion of British children suggesting inhibition of disappointment was nearly as high as at age 11, whereas a majority of the younger Italian children advocated genuine expression of disappointment upon receiving the undesirable gift. Relative to the appearance-reality distinction, Italian children were also less likely to contend that appearance of expression might not coincide with internally felt emotion than British children. Thus, cultures that differ in their expectations about controlling certain emotions under certain circumstances also differ in the socialization pressure brought to bear upon children to acquire such emotion management strategies.

*Indian and British Children.* Joshi and MacLean (1994) compared 4- and 6-year-old children in Bombay and England on their understanding that expressive behavior need not be congruent with subjectively felt emotion. They systematically varied child–child stories and child–adult stories, since children are more likely to endorse genuine displays of emotion with peers (e.g., see the study by Underwood et al., 1992, mentioned above). More than three times as many 4-year-old Indian girls than English girls endorsed the idea that children would inhibit or use misleading facial expressions to conceal a negative emotion when interacting with an adult. Indian and English boys did not differ. The authors emphasize a socialization interpretation of their findings, describing the sort of intense pressures applied to young Indian girls to adopt deferential and highly regulated decorum in the presence of adults. They also highlight the fact that this early acquisition of understanding that negative emotions are to be concealed from adults, especially by girls, is brought about not by greater concern for the feelings of others but by fear of punishment for acting improperly.

In summary, the investigation of individual differences in emotional displays and in understanding the relations between what we express and what we feel in social contexts continues to be a rich area for further research. Most conspicuously absent are systematic observational studies that focus on children and compare different cultural contexts for how emotion-eliciting situations are managed from an expressive standpoint. However, there are a number of relevant anthropological studies that are informative as to how children in different societies manage their emotions (e.g., Lutz & White, 1986; Ochs, 1986; Russell, 1991; Weisz, Sigman, Weiss, & Mosk, 1993), and these studies simultaneously provide us with an understanding of how emotion management is embedded in the particular cultural ethnotheory of emotion.

We turn next to the final section of this essay in which we attempt to integrate what we know about emotion management and expressive behavior from a developmental perspective with how self-presentation functions as a coping resource in interpersonal contexts. We present this material with an emphasis on self-presentation as functioning *in service of* emotion regulation and coping.

## Self-Presentation: An Integration of Emotion Management and Coping

*Emotion Management and Coping*

Coping with stressful situations is a context in which regulation of emotional arousal and management of emotional-expressive displays are strongly linked. When internal or external demands are appraised as taxing or exceeding one's resources (Lazarus & Folkman, 1984), we experience stress; if this stressful experience occurs in an interpersonal setting (as it often does), then we also experience especially great demands on our ability to manage subjectively experienced emotion and to control our emotional expression when appropriate. Coping with one's emotional experience *and* with the stress-producing circumstances is a complex process indeed and requires further discussion of the functions of coping and its role in emotional dissemblance.

*The Functions of Coping.* The crucial role that emotions play in stressful experience becomes apparent by the functions that generally are ascribed to coping. We will first describe four basic coping functions and then delineate how emotional displays fulfill these coping functions. Consensus can be found for the first two functions of coping: (1) problem solving (e.g., change the situation or avoid it), and (2) regulating emotional distress (e.g., Lazarus & Folkman, 1984; Weber & Laux, 1993). However, there are at least two additional functions that have to be met when coping with stress, both of which emphasize the *interpersonal* nature of coping, namely, regulating social interaction (and relationships) and regulating self-esteem and self-concept (Weber & Laux, 1993). Regulating interactions and relationships is crucial because most, if not all, stressful episodes somehow involve other persons. For example, other individuals can be the source of stress (e.g., a good friend's betrayal), or they can be affected by the stress that the person close to them experiences (e.g., the mother commiserating with her daughter who fell unhappily in love), or they can get involved as mere observers (e.g., being among the first to come upon a serious car accident). The regulation of interactions includes the short-term interaction (e.g., communicating genuine or pretended feelings, giving feedback, communicating desired self-images, influencing the behavior of interactants), and the long-term relationship that one wants to establish in the long run (e.g., maintaining, fostering, or challenging a relationship).

Regulation of self-esteem and self-concept have been proposed as the final function of coping with stress in that self-esteem and highly regarded aspects of one's self-concept are threatened, or even damaged, in many stressful episodes. Protecting one's self-esteem and restoring vulnerable aspects of one's self-concept demand coping responses that convey favorable self-images in order to compensate for an otherwise negative impression. For example, failing a task in front of others might be coped with by bragging about one's successful performances in other areas. We will come back to this point in a later section when we apply the concept of self-presentation to interpreting coping behavior.

These four functions of coping with stress can also be viewed as having embedded in them goal-directed behavior. However, the goals need not be consciously planned; it is likely that much of the striving has become virtually automatic by repeated experience. As an illustration, in coping with a personal failure, maintaining one's face in front of an audience becomes an overriding concern that need not be deliberately developed at that moment. In considering the overriding importance that goals have for explaining behavior, it becomes obvious that theory and research on coping are astonishingly deficient in studying the goals persons pursue in coping with stress (Laux & Weber, 1991; Weber & Laux, 1993). In other contexts, however, personal goals have become an expanding research issue, especially questions regarding how the structure of a personal goal system and the status of its achievement relate to psychological well-being (e.g., Brunstein, 1993; Klinger, 1987; Little, 1983).

*Emotional Display and Dissemblance as Part of Coping Processes*

Coping behavior typically includes overt behavioral acts, cognitive processes, and expressive behavior that are oriented toward the stress-related goals. Together, these three components build an inseparable *coping behavior pattern*. Depending on the personal goals set, a coping behavior pattern can serve any or all of the four basic coping functions described above. For example, an outburst of anger can be guided by the intention to prevent the occurrence of future insults (solving the problem by regulating the situation), to discharge the feelings of anger (regulating the emotion), to demonstrate strength and reestablish the balance of power that had existed before (regulating the interaction and relationship), and finally to protect the part of one's self-concept that has been injured by the offending remark (regulating self-esteem and self-concept). As an integral part of coping patterns, expressive reactions, whether genuine or dissembled, contribute their share to serving the coping functions and thus contribute to achieving personal coping goals. Expressive reactions are also particularly well suited to the appearance of a coping pattern and thus shape the message that is sent, and we elaborate this function below.

*Shaping the Appearance of a Coping Behavior Pattern.* Since cognitive processes are not visible, the impression that a coping behavior pattern conveys will be dependent on overt behavioral acts and on expressive reactions. In contrast to overt behavioral acts that can either be performed or not (e.g., a criticism that can either be uttered or not), the seemingly unlimited subtleness and variability of expressive reactions allow the individual to convey more finely attuned, nuanced, or, as the case may be, even more forceful messages. The rich repertoire of expressive reactions encompasses variants of the genuine expression of what one is feeling, as well as mechanisms of dissemblance of which four basic forms have already been mentioned (i.e., maximization, minimization, substitution, and neutralization). It is the expressive reaction (genuine or not) that carries the urgent plea for help (by displaying utter despair) or its opposite, the impression of mastery (by displaying coolness and perfect emotional control), and it is the expressive reaction that plays a significant role in collusive relationships in which the two partners play out a reciprocally protective script (see also Saarni & Lewis, 1993). Besides sending its own messages, the display of emotions can be used either to stress the significance of an overt behavioral act (as is usually the case when throwing a tantrum), or to modify an overt behavioral act (as was the case with the girls in the study by von Salisch [1991] who smiled at their friends while scolding them). Thus, the impression that any coping behavior pattern conveys, and thus the way it is interpreted by others, relies heavily on the display and the dissemblance of emotion. This is not to deny that overt behavior is not important, too, for creating a certain impression. For example, enacting a facial expression that conveys competence, while at the same time trying to escape the situation is not very convincing. Nevertheless, in achieving desired impressions, it is the emotional display that makes the difference. Perhaps one could say that the "medium is the message" when it comes to the way emotion-laden expressions are the most potent contributors to nonverbal communication (e.g., Mehrabian, 1972).

## Coping, Self-Presentation, and Emotional-Expressive Behavior

In analyzing the goals that can be pursued in coping with stressful situations, it has become apparent that to a great extent they are achieved by communicating desired self-images, for example, strength or mastery, and thereby influencing the way one is treated by other people. For example, by projecting the image of helplessness, one wants others to commiserate and to feel obliged to help with solving the problem. This suggests that the concept of self-presentation can be adopted as an approach to understanding coping behavior. Coping behavior, with emotional-expressive reactions as a vital part, can be interpreted as a way of presenting oneself in order to achieve stress-related goals. Self-presentation is maneuvering one's behavior so as to influence another's response to oneself, that is, to render it more favorable or conducive to one's own goals (e.g., E. Jones, 1990; DePaulo, 1991). The strong ties that exist between coping and self-presentation become apparent if one looks at the motivations that are ascribed to presenting oneself and apply these motives to the functions and goals of coping. According to Baumeister (1993), self-presentation is motivated by three basic needs, which have in common the interpersonal orientation of human behavior.

The first need is to belong to social groups, to form and maintain attachments to other people. Self-presentations that fulfill expectancies and values are more likely to maintain or strengthen social bonds. Depending on the role others play in a stressful encounter, for example, as opponent, as supporter, or as observer, maintaining relationships demands different ways of presenting oneself. If others are the source of stress, a form of self-presentation must be chosen that fulfills the twofold task of challenging the interaction by influencing others to change their behavior and, at the same time, preserving existing relationships. The situation is different if others are sought for emotional, cognitive, or material support. In this case, strengthening attachments to significant others or to a social group and making them feel obliged to help becomes a critical part of the coping motivation. In both cases, however, in managing conflicted interactions as well as in seeking social support, the ability to maneuver between genuine expression of feelings and appropriate expressive dissembling is needed. For example, minimizing the expression of distress and misery seems quite paradoxically to be a prerequisite for getting social support. Others are more inclined to help if they perceive the person in need as a good coper who makes great efforts for control and mastery (Silver, Wortman, & Crofton, 1990).

The second need, according to Baumeister (1993), that underlies self-presentation is the construction of self-identity. In this case, self-presentation goes beyond trying to convey self-images to others in order to influence the way they treat us. Instead, self-presentation serves as a tool to build a desired identity, to construct oneself as the person one wants to be. To assure an identity it is necessary to convince others to validate one's claims. But a desired identity is not only created by convincing others to accept a claim, one must also convince oneself of possessing desired qualities. A quality that is especially desirable for coping with stress is self-efficacy (e.g., Bandura, 1995). Since stress arises if internal or external demands are appraised as taxing or exceeding one's resources or capacities, the construction of oneself as a person who is able to cope with adversities and master difficult situations is a key determinant for not giving up, for maintaining effort and hope. The belief in self-efficacy is one of the basic personal resources for successful coping. It seems that the self-construction of self-efficacy relies heavily on successful emotion management and on the perception that one is in control of one's feelings, especially anxiety (Bandura, 1995).

The third need ascribed to one's self-presentation is protecting and enhancing one's self-esteem by presenting oneself in a favorable light to others. Tedeschi and Norman (1985) differentiate between two strategies in presenting oneself: asserting positive self-images, such as appearing competent, or friendly, or trustworthy, or projecting defensive self-images that are self-protective. In coping with stress both strategies might be pursued, assertive as well as defensive ones. Obviously, in many stressful situations the need to protect threatened self-images, for example, not appearing anxious, nervous, out of control, or helpless, will be a matter of priority. In regard to assertive self-presentation, presenting oneself in a positive light can be used as a kind of buffer that prevents (additional) damage. For example, one can prepare oneself for an impending conflicted interaction by appearing particularly competent, relaxed, and inoffensive.

The strategies and tactics of self-presentation that are discussed in self-presentational approaches mainly involve cognitive processes (e.g., self-serving reappraisals, making excuses, giving accounts, or denying that a self-threatening incident has happened). Like theories and research on coping, research on self-presentation is seriously deficient in studying emotional-expressive reactions as the most obvious means of conveying impressions. Considering the crucial importance that display of emotions and dissemblance have for shaping coping behavior patterns and thus the way one wants to be seen and treated by others, one can hardly understand why both research areas are preoccupied to such an extent with cognitive processes and overt behavioral acts. Clearly, there is a need for research that bridges the gap that exists between emotion theory and applied fields such as coping and self-presentation.

### Social Rules and Self-Presentation

The display or presentation of emotions is not only a matter of personal decision, it is also subject to collective definitions and social construction about the "proper" way to experience and express emotion (e.g., Averill, 1979; 1982). We have already addressed the learning of display rules in childhood, but there are also *feeling rules* (Hochschild, 1979). According to Hochschild, feeling rules prescribe which emotion should be felt or not be felt, depending on the person, the interactant, the relationship, and the situation. Compared to display rules that require expressive control or "surface acting" in order to comply with the rule, conformity with feeling rules demands "deep acting" so as to change the feelings themselves.

The third set of rules that apply to the display of emotion are *coping rules* which circumscribe the proper way to interpret and to handle aversive situations and emotions (Weber, 1996). Such consensually defined coping rules apply to all three of the constituents of a coping behavior pattern. They prescribe proper overt behavioral acts (e.g., restraining oneself from becoming aggressive when treated unfairly by an authority), proper cognitions (e.g., looking at the bright side), and proper expressive reactions (e.g., hiding anger).

The results of an interview study by Hannelore Weber, the second author, on the social construction of stress and coping support the significance of consensually defined rules for "proper" emotional displays as part of coping. As part of a semistructured interview, adult subjects were asked to report a stressful episode in which they did *not* do what they wanted to do. After describing the incident, they were asked why they suppressed their action impulses. One of the most frequently cited actions that had been suppressed was the open expression of emotion. Other action impulses that had been suppressed were acting selfishly, acting immorally, acting assertively, and giving up. The fact that the open expression of genuine feeling was mentioned along with selfish and immoral behavior suggests the extent to which our Western societies loathe the loss of emotional control. The reasons subjects gave for not executing their action impulses were concern for others, preventing social conflicts, maintaining harmony, preventing loss of face, and conformity with existing rules. It is remarkable that children as young as 7 years old already give very similar reasons for concealing their feelings (Saarni, 1979a), that is, they already know about the tacit social rules. However, although research with North American school-age children confirmed that "losing one's cool" would result in teasing and humiliation (Saarni, 1988), this same research also suggested that an absolute suppression of genuine emotions would result in "emotional disturbance" (recall the quote from the 13-year-old girl cited earlier). Coping rules, like display and feeling rules, can be understood as tacit knowledge. They become explicit, however, in lay theories and in common sayings and proverbs, for example, "if angry, count to ten." In a similar vein, rules can be understood as part of the ethnotheories of emotions (Lutz, 1987), which includes the idea that the expression of genuine feelings is also socially regulated (see also Doubleday, Kovaric, & Dorr, 1990, for research confirming school-age children's knowledge of norms for expression of genuine feelings).

These culture-based coping rules serve a couple of purposes in social life. The more obvious one is that if there is consensus about "appropriate" ways of dealing with stress, then personal and social predictability will be maintained. In stressful situations, the behavioral and expressive conduct that is usually controlled and constrained may be jeopardized, and the capacity for self-control may be reduced. In societies that value control, losing control means losing one's face, thus ending up with perhaps a worse presentation of oneself. With societal rules, the scope for legitimate behavior and appropriate self-presentation is considerably limited, thereby lessening the risk of maladaptive behavior.

A second purpose met by culturally determined coping rules is the provision of ready-made plans. Rules provide plans and strategies on which one can rely. Rules tell us which coping behavior pattern and which form of self-presentation will be expected and reinforced by others. Rules save us from designing a favorable self-presentation anew each time we face a stressful situation and a conflicted interaction. Instead, we can draw on a repertoire of prototypical, tested forms of favorable self-presentations. Prototypes tell us which presentation will work best for which goal and for which interaction. For example, children learn that appearing "cool" is the best impression to convey if they do not want to be subjected to mockery (Gottman, Katz, & Hooven, 1997).

We learn the different sets of rules for displaying and dissembling emotions in the course of our socialization. One of the major problems that arises in managing behavior according to rules is that the rules carry benefits as well as costs. The benefits are that rules provide assistance and ready-made plans for dealing with taxing circumstances. The costs are that the scope for legitimate behavior is seriously narrowed and what might in fact prove to be highly adaptive and productive is instead labeled by society as a personal failure (Weber, 1996). Thus, for coping with stressful situations, rules can be a support as well as a burden and are sometimes even a source for emotional disorder. This might be the case if rules prescribing emotional control lead to chronic and rigid concealing of feelings and to becoming alienated from one's experiences. Each of us can expect considerable conflict when the costs for obeying the "rules" exceed the benefits.

## Conclusion

We thought to close this chapter in a fashion parallel to the way we began, namely, with a narrative that captures the rather abstract and theoretical material we have just presented. The vignette has been adapted from a family counseling case supervised by Carolyn Saarni.

Fifteen-year-old Jason had enjoyed a warm and affectionate relationship with his father until his Dad was diagnosed with an inoperable brain tumor and died a short while later. In the first few weeks after his father's death, Jason was able to cry and emotionally express his grief around his mother and sister, but he revealed nothing of his sadness among his male peers at school. Some might not even have known that his father had recently died. "Big boys don't cry" was definitely the controlling display rule of his peer group, and Jason managed his expressive behavior with diligence.

Jason maintained his stiff upper lip and his dry eyes throughout that school year. He did experience periodic bouts of nonspecific dermatitis. When the following summer his boyhood pal, his dog, also abruptly died, Jason stoically excavated the hole in which to bury him. The next day Jason awakened to find himself covered with scaly, itchy hives from head to toe, and it wasn't poison oak. Managing his self-presentation so well appeared to have penalized his autoimmune system, and, cruelly, it came out in a most visible manner, upsetting his careful attempts at self-presentation. His mother and his physician both agreed that family counseling would help both Jason and the family as a whole to cope more adaptively with the father's death.

Jason's reaction illustrates how compelling an individual may perceive emotion management to be in coping with a very serious and stressful experience, even when it may not be in the individual's best interest to deny how he feels in his attempt to put on a persuasive external display. Somewhere in coping with one's feelings, with one's self-image, with interpersonal demands, and with situational exigencies lies an emotion-laden balance between having respect for one's genuine emotional-expressive behavior and an awareness of and ability to adopt "strategic finesse" in managing one's emotional behavior when the social situation calls for it. Perhaps this is in part what the elusive construct of subjective well-being consists of, and we suspect that a healthy sense of self-efficacy is inherent in such emotional balance as well (see also Lazarus, 1992).

In closing, we have also noted the dearth of research using observational studies to evaluate individual differences in children's self-presentations that are simultaneously directed at coping with interpersonally stressful circumstances. The multiple roles played by emotion-laden expressive behavior in adults' self-presentation strategies are similarly underinvestigated. As authors, one of us is a developmental psychologist and the other a social psychologist, and in this collaborative essay we have sought to sketch the likely links between emotion regulation and strategies for self-presentation, enriched by a developmental perspective.

## References

Adams-Tucker, C. (1985). Defense mechanisms used by sexually abused children. *Children Today, 14*, 8–12.

Adlam-Hill, S., & Harris, P. L. (1988). Understanding of display rules for emotion by normal and maladjusted children. Unpublished paper, Department of Experimental Psychology, University of Oxford.

Aldwin, C. (1994). *Stress, coping, and development*. New York: Guilford.

Averill, J. R. (1980). A constructivist view of emotion. In R. Plutchik & H. Kellerman (Eds.), *Emotion. Theory, research, and experience* (Vol. 1, pp. 305–339). New York: Academic Press.

Averill, J. R. (1982). Anger and aggression. *An essay on emotion*. New York: Springer Verlag.

Bandura, A. (1995). Exercise of personal and collective efficacy in changing societies. In A. Bandura (Ed.), *Self-efficacy in changing societies* (pp. 1–45). Cambridge: Cambridge University Press.

Barden, R. C., Zelko, F., Duncan, S. W., & Masters, J. C. (1980). Children's consensual knowledge about the experiential determinants of emotion. *Journal of Personality and Social Psychology, 39*, 968–976.

Baumeister, R. (1993). Self-presentation: Motivational, cognitive, and interpersonal patterns. In G. van Heck, P. Bonaiuto, I. J. Deary, & W. Nowack (Eds.), *Personality psychology in Europe* (Vol. 4, pp. 257–280). Tilburg: Tilburg University Press.

Beeghly, M., Bretherton, I., & Mervis, C. (1986). Mothers' internal state language to toddlers: The socialization of psychological understanding. *British Journal of Developmental Psychology, 4*, 247–260.

Blurton-Jones, N. (1967). A ethological study of some aspects of social behaviour of children in nursery school. In D. Morris (Ed.), *Primate ethology*. London: Weidenfeld and Nicolson.

Brenner, E., & Salovey, P. (1997). Emotion regulation during childhood: Developmental, interpersonal, and individual considerations. In P. Salovey & D. Sluyter (Eds.), *Emotional literacy and emotional development* (pp. 168–192). New York: Basic Books.

Brody, L., & Hall, J. A. (1993). Gender and emotion. In M. Lewis & J. Haviland (Eds.), *Handbook of emotions* (pp. 447–460). New York: Guilford.

Brunstein, J. C. (1993). Personal goals and subjective well-being: A longitudinal study. *Journal of Personality and Social Psychology, 65*, 1061–1070.

Camras, L. (1992). Expressive development and basic emotions. *Cognition and Emotion, 6*, 267–283.

Casey, R. (1993). Children's emotional experience: Relations among expression, self-report, and understanding. *Developmental Psychology, 29*, 119–129.

Cole, P. M. (1986). Children's spontaneous control of facial expression. *Child Development, 57*, 1309–1321.

Cole, P. M., Zahn-Waxler, C., & Smith, K. D. (1994). Expressive control during a disappointment: Variations related to preschoolers' behavior problems. *Developmental Psychology, 30*, 835–846.

Compas, B., Phares, V., & Ledoux, N. (1989). Stress and coping preventive interventions for children and adolescents. In L. Bond & B. Compas (Eds.), *Primary prevention and promotion in the schools* (pp. 319–340). London: Sage.

Copans, S. (1989). The invisible family member: Children in families with alcohol abuse. In L. Combrinck-Graham (Ed.), *Children in family contexts: Perspectives on treatment* (pp. 277–298). New York: Guilford.

Cramer, P. (1991). *The development of defense mechanisms.* New York: Springer Verlag.

Crick, N., & Grotpeter, J. (1995). Relational aggression, gender, and social-psychological adjustment. *Child Development, 60,* 710–722.

D'Andrade, R. (1987). A folk model of the mind. In D. Holland & N. Quinn (Eds.), *Cultural models in language and thought* (pp. 112–148). New York: Cambridge University Press.

Davis, T. (1995). Gender differences in masking negative emotions: Ability or motivation? *Developmental Psychology, 31,* 660–667.

DePaulo, B. (1991). Nonverbal behavior and self-presentation: A developmental perspective. In R. S. Feldman & B. Rime (Eds.), *Fundamentals of nonverbal behavior* (pp. 351–397). Cambridge: Cambridge University Press.

Doubleday, K., Kovaric, P., & Dorr, A. (1990). *Children's knowledge of display rules for emotional expression and control.* Paper presented at the annual meeting of the American Psychological Association, August, Boston.

Dunn, J., Brown, J., & Beardsall, L. (1991). Family talk about feeling states and children's later understanding of others' emotions. *Developmental Psychology, 27,* 448–455.

Ekman, P., & Friesen, W. (1975). *Unmasking the face.* Englewood Cliffs, NJ: Prentice-Hall.

Fernández-Dols, J., & Ruiz-Belda, M. (1995). Expression of emotion versus expressions of emotion. In J. Russell, J. Fernández-Dols, A. Manstead, & J. Wellenkamp (Eds.), *Everyday conceptions of emotion: An introduction to the psychology, anthropology, and linguistics of emotion* (pp. 505–522). Hingham, MA: Kluwer.

Fox, N. (Ed.) (1994). The development of emotion regulation. *Monographs of the Society for Research in Child Development, 59,* Serial No. 240.

Fridlund, A. (1991). Evolution and facial action in reflex, social motive, and paralanguage. *Biological Psychology, 32,* 3–100.

Frijda, N. (1987). Emotion, cognitive structure, and action tendency. *Cognition and Emotion, 1,* 115–143.

Fuchs, D., & Thelen, M. (1988). Children's expected interpersonal consequences of communicating their affective states and reported likelihood of expression. *Child Development, 59,* 1314–1322.

Garber, J., & Dodge, K. (Eds.) (1991). *The development of emotion regulation and dysregulation.* New York: Cambridge University Press.

Gnepp, J. (1989). Children's use of personal information to understand other people's feelings. In C. Saarni & P. Harris (Eds.), *Children's understanding of emotion* (pp. 151–180). Cambridge: Cambridge University Press.

Golombok, S., & Fivush, R. (1994). *Gender development.* New York: Cambridge University Press.

Gottman, J., Katz, L., & Hooven, C. (1997). *Meta-emotion*. Mahwah, NJ: Lawrence Erlbaum.

Gottman, J., & Mettetal, G. (1986). Speculations about social and affective development: Friendship and acquaintanceship through adolescence. In J. M. Gottman & J. G. Parker (Eds.), *Conversations with friends: Speculations on affective development* (pp. 192–237). New York: Cambridge University Press.

Gross, J., & Levenson, R. (1997). Hiding feelings: The acute effects of inhibiting negative and positive emotion. *Journal of Abnormal Psychology, 106*, 95–103.

Harris, P. L. (1985). What children know about the situations that provoke emotion. In M. Lewis & C. Saarni (Eds.), *The socialization of affect* (pp. 161–185). New York: Plenum.

Harris, P. L. (1989). *Children and emotion: The development of psychological understanding*. Oxford: Basil Blackwell.

Harris, P. L., & Gross, D. (1988). Children's understanding of real and apparent emotion. In J. W. Astington, P. L. Harris, & D. R. Olson (Eds.), *Developing theories of mind* (pp. 295–314). Cambridge: Cambridge University Press.

Harris, P., & Lipian, M. S. (1989). Understanding emotion and experiencing emotion. In C. Saarni & P. Harris (Eds.), *Children's understanding of emotion* (pp. 241–258). Cambridge: Cambridge University Press.

Harris, P. L., & Olthof, T. (1982). The child's concept of emotion. In G. Butterworth & P. Light (Eds.), *Social cognition* (pp. 188–209). Brighton, Sussex: The Harvester Press.

Hochschild, A. (1979). Emotion work, feeling rules, and social structure. *American Journal of Sociology, 85*, 551–575.

Jones, E. E. (1990). *Interpersonal perception*. New York: W. H. Freeman.

Josephs, I. (1993). *The regulation of emotional expression in preschool children*. Munster, Germany/New York, NY: Waxmann.

Joshi, M. S., & MacLean, M. (1994). Indian and English children's understanding of the distinction between real and apparent emotion. *Child Development, 65*, 1372–1384.

Kitayama, S., & Marcus, H. (Eds.) (1994). *Emotion and culture*. Washington, DC: American Psychological Association.

Klinger, E. (1987). Current concerns and disengagemant from incentives. In F. Halisch & J. Kuhl (Eds.), *Motivation, intention, and volition* (pp. 337–347). Berlin: Springer.

Kraut, R., & Johnston, R. (1979). Social and emotional messages of smiling: An ethological approach. *Journal of Personality and Social Psychology, 37*, 1539–1553.

Laux, L., & Weber, H. (1991). Presentation of self in coping with anger and anxiety: An intentional approach. *Anxiety Research, 3*, 233–255.

Lazarus, R. (1992). *Emotion and adaptation*. New York: Oxford University Press.

Lazarus, R. S., & Folkman, S. (1984). *Stress, appraisal, and coping*. New York: Springer Verlag.

Lewis, M., & Michalson, L. (1985). Faces as signs and symbols. In G. Zivin (Ed.), *The development of expressive behavior* (pp. 153–180). New York: Academic Press.

Lewis, M., Sullivan, M., & Vasen, A. (1987). Making faces: Age and emotion differences in the posing of emotional expressions. *Developmental Psychology, 23*, 690–697.

Little, B. R. (1983). Personal projects: A rationale and method for investigation. *Environment and Behavior, 15*, 273–309.

Lutz, C. (1987). Goals, events, and understanding in Ifaluk emotion theory. In D. Holland & N. Quinn (Eds.), *Cultural models in language and thought* (pp. 290–312). New York, NY: Cambridge University Press.

Lutz, C., & White, G. M. (1986). The anthropology of emotions. *Annual Review of Anthropology, 15*, 405–436.

Malatesta, C., & Haviland, J. (1982). Learning display rules: The socialization of emotion expression in infancy. *Child Development, 53*, 991–1003.

Manstead, A. (1995). Children's understanding of emotion. In J. Russell, J. Fernández-Dols, A. Manstead, & J. Wellenkamp (Eds.), *Everyday conceptions of emotion: An introduction to the psychology, anthropology, and linguistics of emotion* (pp. 315–331). Hingham, MA: Kluwer.

Meerum Terwogt, M., & Olthof, T. (1989). Awareness and self-regulation of emotion in young children. In C. Saarni & P. Harris (Eds.), *Children's understanding of emotion* (pp. 209–240). New York: Cambridge University Press.

Mehrabian, A. (1972). *Nonverbal communication.* New York: Aldino Atherton.

Mesquita, B., & Frijda, N. (1992). Cultural variations in emotions: A review. *Psychological Bulletin, 112*, 179–204.

Miller, S. M., & Green, M. L. (1985). Coping with stress and frustration: Origins, nature, and development. In Michael Lewis & Carolyn Saarni (Eds.), *The socialization of emotions* (pp. 263–314). New York: Plenum Press.

Ochs, E. (1986). From feelings to grammar: A Samoan case study. In B. B. Schieffelin & E. Ochs (Eds.), *Language socialization across cultures* (pp. 251–272). Cambridge, UK: Cambridge University Press.

Odom, R., & Lemond, C. (1972). Developmental differences in the perception and production of facial expressions. *Child Development, 43*, 359–369.

Potter, S. H. (1988). The cultural construction of emotion in rural Chinese social life. *Ethos, 16*, 181–208.

Putnam, F., & Trickett, P. (1991, May). *Dissociation in sexually abused girls.* Paper presented at the annual meeting of the American Psychiatric Association, New Orleans, LA.

Russell, J. A. (1991). Culture and the categorization of emotion. *Psychological Bulletin, 110*, 426–450.

Saarni, C. (1979a). *When not to show what you feel: Children's understanding of the relations between emotional experience and expressive behavior.* Paper presented at the meeting of the Society for Research in Child Development, San Francisco.

Saarni, C. (1979b). Children's understanding of display rules for expressive behavior. *Developmental Psychology, 15*, 424–429.

Saarni, C. (1982). Social and affective functions of nonverbal behavior: Developmental concerns. In R. Feldman (Ed.), *Development of nonverbal behavior in children* (pp. 123–147). New York: Springer Verlag.

Saarni, C. (1984). An observational study of children's attempts to monitor their expressive behavior. *Child Development, 55*, 1504–1513.

Saarni, C. (1987). *Children's beliefs about parental expectations for emotional-expressive behavior management.* Paper presented at the biennial meeting of the Society for Research in Child Development, Baltimore.

Saarni, C. (1988). Children's understanding of the interpersonal consequences of dissemblance of nonverbal emotional-expressive behavior. *Journal of Nonverbal Behavior, 12*, 275–294.

Saarni, C. (1989). Children's understanding of strategic control of emotional expression in social transactions. In C. Saarni & P. Harris (Eds.), *Children's understanding of emotion* (pp. 181–208). New York, NY: Cambridge University Press.

Saarni, C. (1991). *Social context and management of emotional-expressive behavior: Children's expectancies for when to dissemble what they feel.* Paper presented at the biennial meeting of the Society for Research in Child Development, Seattle, WA.

Saarni, C. (1992). Children's emotional-expressive behaviors as regulators of others' happy and sad states. *New Directions for Child Development, 55*, 91–106.

Saarni, C., & Lewis, M. (1993). Deceit and illusion in human affairs. In M. Lewis & C. Saarni (Eds.), *Lying and deception in everyday life* (pp. 1–29). New York: Guilford.

Shennum, W. A., & Bugental, D. B. (1982). The development of control over affective expression in nonverbal behavior. In Robert S. Feldman (Ed.), *Development of nonverbal behavior in children* (pp. 101–118). New York: Springer Verlag.

Silver, R. C., Wortman, C. B. & Crofton, C. (1990). The role of coping in support provision: The self-presentational dilemma of victims of life crises. In B. R. Sarason, I. G. Sarason, & G. R. Pierce (Eds.), *Social support: An interactional view* (pp. 307–426). New York: Wiley.

Skinner, E., & Wellborn, J. (1994). Coping during childhood and adolescence: a motivational perspective. In R. Lerner (Ed.), *Life-span development and behavior* (pp. 91–133). Hillsdale, NJ: Erlbaum.

Sorensen, E. S. (1993). *Children's stress and coping.* New York: Guilford.

Tedeschi, J. T., & Norman, N. (1985). Social power, self-presentation and the self. In B. R. Schlenker (Ed.), *The self and social life* (pp. 293–322). New York: McGraw-Hill.

Thompson, R. A. (1991). Emotional regulation and emotional development. *Educational Psychology Review, 3*, 269–307.

Thompson, R. A. (1994). Emotion regulation: A theme in search of definition. In N. Fox (Ed.), *Emotion regulation: Behavioral and biological considerations. Society for Research in Child Development Monographs, 59*, Serial No. 240, 25–52.

Underwood, M., Coie, J., & Herbsman, C. (1992). Display rules for anger and aggression in school-age children. *Child Development, 63*, 366–380.

Vespo, J., & Caplan, M. (1993). Preschoolers' differential conflict behavior with friends and acquaintances. *Early Education and Development, 4*, 45–53.

von Salisch, M. (1991). *Kinderfreundschaften*. Gottingen, Germany: Hogrefe.

Watzlawick, P., Beavin, J., & Jackson, D. (1967). *Pragmatics of human communication: A study of interactional patterns, pathologies, and paradoxes*. New York: Norton.

Weber, H. (1996). Social constructivist approaches to understanding how we cope with stress. In N. Frijda (Ed.), *Proceedings of the IX Conference of the International Society for Research on Emotion*. Toronto, Canada.

Weber, H., & Laux, L. (1993). Presentation of emotion. In G. van Heck, P. Bonaiuto, I. J. Deary, & W. Nowack (Eds.), *Personality psychology in Europe* (Vol. 4, pp. 235–256). Tilburg: Tilburg University Press.

Weiner, B. (1987). The social psychology of emotion: Applications of a naive psychology. *Journal of Social and Clinical Psychology, 5*, 405–419.

Wellenkamp, J. (1995). Ethnotheories of emotion. In J. Russell, J. Fernández-Dols, A. Manstead, & J. Wellenkamp (Eds.), *Everyday conceptions of emotion: An introduction to the psychology, anthropology, and linguistics of emotion* (pp. 169–179). Hingham, MA: Kluwer.

Weisz, J., Sigman, M., Weiss, B., & Mosk, J. (1993). Parent reports of behavioral and emotional problems among children in Kenya, Thailand, and the United States. *Child Development, 64*, 98–109.

Zeman, J., & Garber, J. (1996). Display rules for anger, sadness, and pain: It depends on who is watching. *Child Development, 67*, 957–973.

Zeman, J., & Shipman, K. (1996). Children's expression of negative affect: Reasons and methods. *Developmental Psychology, 32*, 842–849.

# PART II

# Transmission of Social Norms Regulating Nonverbal Behavior

# 5. Family Expressiveness

## A Retrospective and New Directions for Research

AMY G. HALBERSTADT, VALERIE W. CRISP, AND
KIMBERLY L. EATON

In the 20 years since Balswick and Avertt (1977) published their study on family expressiveness, over 75 studies have investigated relationships between family expressiveness and a host of social and interpersonal variables relevant to individual family members. Early theory focused on socialization processes; for example, Balswick and Avertt (1977) predicted that gender differences emerge from parents' differential expressive behaviors with daughters versus sons, and Jones (1950, 1960) and Lanzetta and Kleck (1970) hypothesized that individuals who were disciplined for overtly expressing emotion would learn to inhibit emotional expression. In these early years, family socialization of emotion expression was thought to predict developing individuals' own levels of expressiveness (Balswick & Avertt, 1977; Malatesta & Haviland, 1982), their levels of emotionality (Jones, 1950, 1960), and their nonverbal sending and receiving skills (Lanzetta & Kleck, 1970). Those questions have continued to be of interest to researchers (witness the 34 studies on expressiveness, the 14 studies on emotionality, and the 26 studies on sending and receiving that we review below). However, the research areas that family expressiveness touches upon have expanded considerably. In fact, the borders now reach far beyond what one of the chapter authors ever imagined almost two decades ago when she began to study whether the particular patterns and skills she was noticing in her own major relationships would be replicated in others' relationships. (They were.) Apparently the con-

We thank Susanne Denham and Julie Dunsmore for their comments on this chapter. Correspondence regarding this chapter should be sent to the first author at the Department of Psychology, North Carolina State University, Raleigh, NC, 27695–7801 or via e-mail at Halbers@unity.ncsu.edu.

cept of family expressiveness has also been compelling to others, and research on family styles of expressiveness now includes, but is not restricted to, the study of developing individuals' own expressiveness styles, sending skills, emotion experience and regulation, knowledge about and ability to understand others' displays of emotion, social competence, interpersonal relationships, social adjustment, and academic competence. In this chapter we review the research on family expressiveness and suggest directions for future research.

We begin with some definitions. Then, we describe our methods for finding and reviewing the studies, and we provide some general, descriptive information about the corpus of research as a whole. Third, we review the studies, organized by topics, from emotion expressiveness to academic achievement. Finally, we comment on what we have learned, based on our review of these studies, and we suggest new and continued directions for future theory and research.

## Definitions of Family Expressiveness

*Expressiveness* is a persistent pattern or style of exhibiting facial, body, vocal, and verbal expressions that are often but not exclusively emotional in nature (Halberstadt, 1991; Halberstadt, Cassidy, Stifter, Parke, & Fox, 1995). Our judgments about a person's style of expressiveness are based on aggregates of that individual's facial, body, vocal, and verbal expressions over time and across situations (Halberstadt, 1991).

*Family Expressiveness (FE)* is best described as the predominant pattern or style of nonverbal and verbal expression found in the family (Halberstadt et al., 1995). In some families, all or most members share the same style; however, in other families, different members may represent distinct styles within the family, and thus, may need to be studied separately (Halberstadt et al., 1995). This chapter reviews both types of studies – those that consider the family as a whole, and those that consider various family members (in these cases, usually one or two parent members). In all cases, the expressiveness of family members, either individually or as a family group, is understood within the social context of the family.

Finally, it is important to distinguish expressiveness from emotionality and expressiveness from personality, at least at the theoretical level. As pointed out by Halberstadt (1991), expressiveness and emotionality are different in that individuals do not always (or even often) show what they feel, nor do they always (or even often) feel what they show (see also Saarni and Weber, this volume). And, although the links between expressiveness styles and personality characteristics are sometimes put forth intuitively (e.g., assuming expressive individuals tend to be more extroverted and nonexpressive individuals more reserved), these linkages have not been well tested. Thus, in this chapter we maintain a stance that considers expressiveness and family expressiveness as variables quite distinct from emotionality and personality. We recognize, however, that although they are distinct variables, there are good theoretical reasons for expecting that they are also somewhat related, thus; we examine the links between these variables in the research currently available.

## Method

### Data Collection and Reduction

The studies in this chapter were obtained by searching the APA's PsychInfo database using terms related to family expressiveness. In addition, reprints and preprints were requested from researchers active in this area. Conference presentations from 1990 to 1997 were included, as were unpublished manuscripts written in 1996 or 1997. In total, we found 77 manuscripts on family expressiveness, with 72 independent samples. Nonindependent samples were included when additional measures and/or substantially different kinds of analyses of the data were reported in separate publications.

Findings from each article were identified by one author and verified by at least one other author. Failures to support hypotheses as well as significant effects were included in the data set whenever possible. Many studies had multiple methods and multiple findings per study. Group rubrics summarizing these findings emerged rather naturally, and findings, for the most part, were easily organized within groups. Altogether, nine groups emerged and these, along with the subgroups nested within them, are listed in the Appendix and in Table 5.1.

### Participants

Participants in these studies spanned a broad spectrum of age, race, class, and family structure. The age of participants, however, was

Table 5.1. *Ns of Studies investigating family expressiveness and Ns of participants within age groups*

| Domain | N of studies | N of Ps | Infant/ toddler | Preschool | K & elementary | High school | College | Adult |
|---|---|---|---|---|---|---|---|---|
| | | | | | | | *Ns of participants within age groups* | |
| Expression of emotion | | | | | | | | |
| Spontaneous expressiveness | 35 | 2832 | 475 | 435 | 405 | 40 | 1441 | 36 |
| Posed sending | 5 | 322 | — | 120 | 59 | — | 143 | — |
| Experiencing emotion | | | | | | | | |
| Feeling emotion | 14 | 1384 | 55 | 92 | 471 | — | 730 | 36 |
| Emotion regulation | 4 | 516 | 115 | — | 322 | — | 43 | 36 |
| Understanding emotion | 26 | 1405 | — | 544 | 350 | — | 511 | — |
| Children's social competence | | | | | | | | |
| Aggregate social | 7 | 460 | — | 104 | 356 | — | — | — |
| Prosocial behavior | 6 | 547 | 24 | 48 | 475 | — | — | — |
| Popularity | 4 | 210 | — | 56 | 154 | — | — | — |
| Aggression | 3 | 220 | 50 | — | 50 | 120 | — | — |

| | | | | | | | | | |
|---|---|---|---|---|---|---|---|---|---|
| Parent–child and sibling relationships | | | | | | | | | |
| Parenting styles | 1 | 437 | — | — | — | — | — | 437 | — |
| Attachment | 4 | 288 | 172 | 44 | — | — | — | 72 | — |
| Sibling relationships | 1 | 64 | — | — | 64 | — | — | — | — |
| Parent–adolescent relationships | 4 | 235 | — | — | — | 196 | — | — | 39 |
| Adult friendships and romance | 3 | 242 | — | — | — | — | — | 142 | 100 |
| Temperament and personality | 6 | 459 | — | 102 | 293 | — | — | 64 | — |
| Personal adjustment | | | | | | | | | |
| Self-Esteem | 4 | 1118 | — | — | 43 | 111 | — | 964 | — |
| Adjustment | 10 | 954 | 124 | 56 | 446 | 40 | — | 188 | 100 |
| Cognitive correlates | 4 | 467 | 46 | 56 | 365 | — | — | — | — |

*Note:* The total number of manuscripts included in this review is 72, however because of multiple questions and multiple outcome measures, many studies are included in more than one section.

dependent upon the particular outcome being examined. For example, studies of family expressiveness and social competence included mostly preschoolers and kindergartners, whereas studies of family expressiveness and romance included only college-age and adult samples. The vast majority of participants were white, middle-class Americans. Only a few studies actually reported family structure or included enough information to infer structure; in these studies, the families are generally headed by two parents. The family size was rarely reported, although the number of present family members may well affect expressiveness levels in the family (R. Kuersten & P. H. McHale, personal comm. April 8, 1997). Overall, the number of female and male children included in the studies was roughly equal. However, there are usually more female adult participants because mothers were often the only family member asked to complete questionnaires and participate in observations (see Table 5.1).

*Family Expressiveness Measures*

Family expressiveness was measured using a variety of methods, including self-reported and other-reported questionnaires, home and laboratory observations, interviews, and diaries (see Table 5.2). Family expressiveness was conceptualized along affect dimensions (total, positive and negative), subcomponents of these dimensions (positive-dominant, positive-submissive, negative-dominant, and negative-submissive), or in terms of discrete emotions such as happiness, anger, fear, sadness, tension, love, and warmth. Both dimensional and discrete measures of expressiveness were primarily assessed by their frequency of occurrence and occasionally by the clarity and/or intensity of expression, or by contingent responding.

Although we know little about family structure and family size, Table 5.2 reports who was measured as "family." Researchers defined the family as all family members, the parents together, the parents separately, or parent–child dyads or triads. The expressiveness of these family units was reported by mothers, fathers, adolescent or adult children, close friends, relatives, significant others, and/or unrelated observers.

*Outcome Measures*

Outcome measures are briefly reported in terms of method and informant in Table 5.3. Because of space limitations we do not list these in detail but do try to hint at the multiple and rich choice of measures as we describe the outcomes section by section.

## Review of the Literature

*Overview of Our Review Strategies*

In each of the nine sections and subsequent subgroupings, we first describe the "consensual" predictions (i.e., the basic predictions that are agreed upon by most of the researchers who conducted the studies to be reviewed) about family expressiveness and that particular set of outcome variables. We next describe the results, first summarizing the studies that assess total family expressiveness, without differentiating between positive and negative expressiveness, and, second, summarizing the studies that allow us to study positive and negative expressiveness separately, because positive and negative expressiveness are often unrelated (e.g., Burrowes & Halberstadt, 1987; Fabes et al., 1994; Satsky & Bell, 1996). Within the sections on positive FE and negative FE, we also report outcome differences based on types of positive and negative expressiveness (e.g., sadness versus anger, or negative-submissiveness versus dominance) when they were available. When developmental shifts seem to be occurring, we also include results differentiated by age. Because of space limitations we reference studies only when discussing their specific findings. Lists of the studies used in each section are provided in the Appendix; additional information as to how we scored the directionality of effects is available from the first author.

*Spontaneous and Posed Expression of Emotion*

*Emotion Expressiveness (35 Studies).* It makes sense to predict that children growing up in expressive homes will themselves be expressive. Thus the consensual prediction in this area is that children's expressiveness will be positively associated with FE, and that observational learning is the implicit underlying mechanism. Although we still don't know much about the mechanisms, the relationship between FE and children's expressiveness has been well tested. For total FE, the prediction is well supported in 10 of 13 studies examining various kinds of self-expressiveness, and with children ranging in age from infancy through college.

For positive FE, 18 of 20 studies found positive associations with

Table 5.2. *Types of measurements of family expressiveness*

| Domain | N of studies | FE measure method | | | | | | Who is family | | | |
|---|---|---|---|---|---|---|---|---|---|---|---|
| | | Q-Self | Q-Parent | Q-Teacher/ other | Lab observation | School/ home observation | Interview/ diary | Family | Parents | Mother separately | Father separately |
| Expression of emotion | | | | | | | | | | | |
| Spontaneous expressiveness | 35 | 10 | 9 | 1 | 16 | 4 | 2 | 12 | 3 | 23 | 5 |
| Posed sending | 5 | 2 | 3 | — | — | — | — | 4 | — | 1 | — |
| Experiencing emotion | | | | | | | | | | | |
| Feeling emotion | 14 | 6 | 5 | 1 | 3 | — | 1 | 8 | — | 6 | 1 |
| Emotion regulation | 4 | 1 | 2 | 1 | 1 | — | — | 3 | — | 1 | — |
| Understanding emotion | 26 | 8 | 9 | — | 6 | 6 | 1 | 14 | — | 14 | 3 |
| Children's social competence | | | | | | | | | | | |
| Aggregate social | 7 | 1 | 4 | — | 2 | 2 | 1 | 2 | — | 5 | 2 |
| Prosocial behavior | 6 | — | 2 | — | 2 | 2 | 2 | 2 | — | 4 | 1 |
| Popularity | 4 | 1 | 4 | — | 1 | 2 | — | 1 | — | 3 | 2 |
| Aggression | 3 | 1 | 1 | — | — | 2 | — | 2 | — | 2 | 1 |
| Parent–child and sibling relationships | | | | | | | | | | | |
| Parenting styles | 1 | 1 | — | — | — | — | — | 1 | — | — | — |
| Attachment | 4 | 1 | 2 | — | 1 | — | — | 1 | — | 3 | — |
| Sibling relationships | 1 | 1 | 1 | — | — | — | — | 1 | — | — | — |

| | | | | | | | | | | |
|---|---|---|---|---|---|---|---|---|---|---|
| Parent–adolescent relationships | 4 | — | 1 | — | 3 | — | — | — | 3 | 4 |
| Adult friendships and romance | 3 | 3 | — | 1 | — | — | — | 2 | 2 | 2 |
| Temperament and personality | 6 | 1 | 3 | — | 1 | 1 | — | 4 | 4 | — |
| Personal adjustment | | | | | | | | | | |
| Self-Esteem | 4 | 2 | 2 | — | 1 | 1 | — | 2 | 2 | 2 |
| Adjustment | 10 | 4 | 4 | — | 3 | 3 | — | 5 | 6 | 1 |
| Cognitive correlates | 4 | 1 | 3 | — | 1 | 1 | — | 2 | 2 | — |

*Note:* The total number of manuscripts included in this review is 72, however because of multiple questions and multiple outcome measures, many studies are included in more than one section.

117

Table 5.3. *Types of measurements of "outcome" variables*

| Domain | N of studies | Q-Self | Q-Parent | Q-Teacher/other | Lab observation | School/home observation | Interview/diary |
|---|---|---|---|---|---|---|---|
| Expression of emotion | | | | | | | |
| Spontaneous expressiveness | 35 | 8 | — | 4 | 19 | 8 | 3 |
| Posed sending | 5 | — | — | — | 5 | — | — |
| Experiencing emotion | | | | | | | |
| Feeling emotion | 14 | 7 | 1 | 3 | 4 | 1 | 1 |
| Emotion regulation | 4 | 1 | 1 | 1 | 2 | — | — |
| Understanding emotion | 26 | 2 | 1 | — | 16 | 6 | 2 |
| Children's social competence | | | | | | | |
| Aggregate social | 7 | — | 1 | 6 | — | 1 | 1 |
| Prosocial behavior | 6 | — | 3 | 3 | 1 | 2 | 1 |
| Popularity | 4 | — | — | 4 | — | — | — |
| Aggression | 3 | 1 | — | 1 | 1 | — | — |
| Parent–child and sibling relationships | | | | | | | |
| Parenting styles | 1 | 1 | — | — | — | — | — |
| Attachment | 4 | — | 1 | — | 3 | — | 1 |
| Sibling relationships | 1 | — | — | — | — | — | 1 |
| Parent–adolescent relationships | 4 | 4 | — | — | 1 | — | 1 |

| | | | | | | | | |
|---|---|---|---|---|---|---|---|---|
| Adult friendships and romance | 3 | 3 | — | — | — | 3 | — | — |
| Temperament and personality | 6 | 1 | 4 | — | 4 | 2 | — | — |
| Personal adjustment | | | | | | | | |
|   Self-Esteem | 4 | 4 | 1 | 1 | 1 | — | — | — |
|   Adjustment | 10 | 3 | 3 | 4 | 3 | 2 | 2 | — |
| Cognitive correlates | 4 | — | 1 | 3 | 1 | 1 | 1 | — |

*Note:* The total number of manuscripts included in this review is 72, however because of multiple questions and multiple outcome measures, many studies are included in more than one section.

individuals' positive self-expressiveness throughout the life span. So we know that positive expressiveness in the family is associated with positive expressiveness in children; what then happens, when families are positively expressive, to children's negative expressiveness? Four studies found no effects through the life span. However, 4 other studies found *reduced* negative expressiveness in infants and young children when mothers were positively expressive; 1 study found increased sadness (Weissbrod & Kendziora, 1997); another found increased anger, but not sadness, in boys (Jones, Eisenberg, & Fabes, 1996); and yet another found associations between FE and adolescents' self-expressiveness 7 years later for negative emotional expressions traditionally associated with the other gender (Bronstein, Briones, Brooks, & Cowan, 1996). That is, boys from more positively expressive families were more expressive of sadness (crying) than boys from less expressive families, and girls from more positively expressive families were more expressive of anger than girls from less expressive families. Thus, there is some evidence to suggest that children may be less negatively expressive in positively expressive homes because they feel less negative affect. However, when they do feel negative emotions, they may be more willing to express the negative feelings they have because parental positivity may signal a safe and supportive environment for emotional expression. And positively expressive homes may provide the opportunity and freedom for adolescents to express negative emotions thought to be largely associated with the other gender.

For negative FE, the 18 studies show increasingly clear associations with age. The 4 infant/toddler studies each show a different relationship between negative FE and various kinds of expressiveness, but 6 of 10 studies of preschool through elementary-school children, and 3 of 4 studies of college students and adults indicate that negative FE is positively associated with children's self-expressiveness of negative affect. Of interest are the intriguing but highly contradictory associations between negative maternal expressiveness and children's positive expressiveness. Four studies show no effect for infants and children. However, 3 studies report that maternal negativity is associated with less happy-looking children, but 2 other studies suggest that negative FE is associated with children's greater positive expressiveness. Whether the negative FE is directed at the child or at another family member may influence how the children respond; for example, when children see someone else affected by negative expressiveness they may develop strategies that include positive expressiveness in their attempts to ameliorate family distress.

In summary, we find substantial associations between expressiveness styles in the family and children's own developing styles. The development and the persistence of these similarities across the life span is striking. The cross-positivity findings (that is, the associations of positive FE with negative self-expressiveness and of negative FE with positive self-expressiveness), however, are not supportive of the overall prediction, and much theoretical work remains to be done. For example, does positive FE increase children's negative expressiveness (e.g., because the children come to expect support and comfort when they do feel negatively) and/or reduce negative expressiveness (e.g., by impacting children's actual feelings of negativity or their beliefs about not showing negative expressions)? And (or) is positive FE more an outcome of children's behavior (e.g., because parents are themselves more positive when their children are less negatively expressive, and/or because they increase their positivity in response to children's distress by assuming a cheerful countenance as an emotional regulation strategy)? These hypotheses are consistent with at least some of the cross-positivity data reported above, and so this area is ripe for studies designed to specifically test competing hypotheses. Similarly, hypotheses need to be developed and then tested for how and why negative FE becomes associated with children's positive expressiveness.

*Posed Sending (5 Studies).* Posed sending concerns how well one sends emotional information when one intends to. An early prediction about posed sending suggested that children from more expressive homes would be better at sending emotional communications than children in less expressive homes, simply because they would have more practice at communicating emotional messages (Halberstadt, 1986).

Five different studies examined the relationship between FE and sending skill. Two studies of young children found no support for the hypothesis (Coats & Feldman, 1995; Ludemann, 1993), but in a study of masking negative feelings following a disappointment (not sending what you are feeling), children with more positively expressive mothers were better at masking negative feelings and tended to provide more sophisticated responses regarding how they hide emotions compared to children with less expressive mothers (Nixon, 1997). It may be that more positively expressive parents are better able to use negative affect situations as teachable moments (Dunn & Brown, 1994). Interestingly, children with more negatively expressive mothers were the ones who thought they hid their emotions. Perhaps high negative FE children think they are hiding their feelings because they are, but they have so much more negative affect than low FE children that some negative affect is still leaking out (as college students report in Fabes, Martin, Rose, & Karbon, 1990); alternatively, high negative FE children might just think they ought to hide their emotions because only adult members are free to express negative affect and children are not.

Among college students, one study reported a positive relationship between total FE and posed sending skill (Halberstadt, 1983), and another reported complex interactions between the two (Halberstadt, 1986). Low FE students were actually better at posed encoding compared to high FE students, however, when items were judged in terms of their difficulty, high FE students were relatively better at encoding the more difficult items, compared to the low FE students who performed best on the less difficult items.

In summary, that significant results are emerging in these studies suggests that FE *is* related to sending skill, but the "when," "what," and "why" remain unclear. We now know that sending emotional communications is highly complicated and involves several processes, including: noticing that a message needs to be sent, knowing what to communicate and what not to communicate, and being able to effectively send a message within the constraints of the ongoing flow (Halberstadt, Denham, & Dunsmore, 1999). An ideal study in this domain would examine the relations between both positive and negative FE and the distinct processes for both posing and masking. There may also be curvilinear relations, such that high expressive families may help young children develop early skill in posing, because the children are more familiar with and have good models of emotion expression. But by adolescence, children from low expressive families may obtain the advantage; having lived for many years with low expressive others, they may have had to learn how to communicate "economically" but clearly with their family members. Alternatively, the type of measurement may matter; high FE children may pose more intense and/or more enduring expressions, whereas low FE children may pose less intense or enduring expressions which are, however, more pure and concise, and therefore more understandable.

## Experiencing Emotion

*Feeling Emotion (14 Studies).* As mentioned earlier, expressiveness and emotionality are often intertwined, and expressiveness is often thought to be a window into individuals' emotionality. Some families may be highly expressive, precisely because they are comprised of highly emotional individuals. Children developing in those families may then be more emotional themselves, either because of some enduring biological substrate that is shared by most or all of the family members, because of "contagion" (whereby children developing around emotional others become emotionally aroused themselves), or because children develop belief systems about the acceptability and importance of emotionality and are, therefore, more willing to experience and value emotion. The studies summarized below test the degree of association between family expressiveness and children's positive and negative emotionality.

The 1 study on total FE indicates a positive relationship, with college students from more expressive homes feeling emotion more intensely and experiencing less ambivalence about expressing emotion in general than students from less expressive homes (King & Emmons, 1990). For positive FE, the 11 studies indicate increasingly clear associations with age. Among children, only 1 of 3 studies on children's positive emotions found an association. Of the 6 studies on children's negative emotions, none favor the hypothesis that children from more expressive families are more emotional, and one finds an inverse relationship between positive maternal expressiveness and emotionality (Fabes et al., 1994). Among college students, both studies on positive FE and students' positive emotions report a positive relationship, but 2 of the 3 studies on positive FE and negative emotions suggest highly interesting relations regarding women's experience of negative emotions: Women from high positively expressive families may be more able or willing to experience negative emotions (Eisenberg et al., 1991), but they are also less prone to depression (Cooley, 1992). Perhaps positive FE enables individuals to be less defensive against negative emotionality, so that they can experience the emotions effectively and then move on. In combination with the interaction of FE, gender, and emotion expression reported above (Bronstein et al., 1996), these results suggest that it may be worth testing whether high FE women, compared to low FE women, may more readily experience the emotions that are not traditionally associated with their gender.

For negative FE, 13 studies again show increasingly clear associations with age. Among young children, 4 of 8 studies on either positive or negative emotionality show an association between FE and children's emotions, but not always in the same direction. However, all 5 studies on college students and adults report increased emotionality (primarily negative emotionality) associated with greater FE. Whether the negative affect involves negative submissiveness or negative dominance also makes a difference, at least for some emotional experiences. Specifically, negative-submissive FE is associated with experiencing dependent depression (Satsky, Bell, & Garrison, 1998), sadness, sympathy, and distress for women, but not for men (Eisenberg et al., 1991). And negative-dominant FE is associated with self-critical depression (Satsky et al., 1998) and depression proneness (Cooley, 1992).

In summary, family expressiveness appears to be associated with developing individuals' emotionality only in adulthood, which suggests that if lessons are learned in childhood, time is needed for them to become internalized and manifested in the individual's own psychological world. Alternatively, it may be that highly emotional children impact their families' expressiveness and that these stylistic or emotional changes develop only slowly over time. The associations with FE are fairly specific; positive FE is associated with both positive and negative emotionality, and negative FE is associated with negative emotionality, with specific variations based on whether the negative FE is submissive or dominant.

*Emotion Regulation (4 Studies).* We tend to think of emotionally expressive families as more spontaneous and free, and less expressive families as more controlled and careful in their underlying feelings as well as demeanor. If less expressive parents tend to be more emotionally regulated themselves, it is likely that they work to inculcate those skills in their children. Less expressive parents may value emotional regulation, and they may have greater skills in that area to teach their children than parents who are more expressive.

Only one study examines the relationships between total FE and emotion regulation, and although this study requires some extrapolation – family expressiveness was evaluated in terms of mother's level of verbal, facial, and body activity during peekaboo, and emotional regulation was evaluated in terms of infant's gaze aversion – the analytic strategy and results are especially worth noting. A curvilinear relationship best described the relationship between maternal expressiveness and emotion regulation, such that moderately active mothers elicited greater gaze aversion among their infants than either low- or high-activity mothers (Stifter & Moyer, 1991).

For positive FE, the relationship with emotion regulation is positive in two studies: Toddlers left alone in a lab setting with an older sibling, or with an older sibling and a stranger, engaged in more self-soothing behavior (Garner, 1995) and kindergartners were rated as having greater emotion regulation by their teachers, when they were from more positively expressive families (Greenberg, Lengua, Coie, & Pinderhughes, in press). These studies suggest another mechanism by which positive FE might provide increased resiliency against negative emotionality; if children from positively expressive families develop greater emotion regulatory skills, they are able to cope more quickly with their feelings and regulate them when they do begin to feel negative emotions.

For negative FE, the relationship is unclear in three studies. Kindergartners from more negatively expressive families were rated as having greater emotion regulation (Greenberg et al., in press); however, toddlers with more negative-submissive families engaged in less self-soothing than those with less negative-submissive families, and levels of negative-dominance in the family had no impact (Garner, 1995). Finally, college students and adults from more negatively expressive families reported less actual control over feeling angry (Burrowes & Halberstadt, 1987). One might think that these individuals had less control over their anger because their anger was more intense; however, the relation between FE and control over the anger experience held even when level of intensity was partialled out of the correlation.

Several points can be made about further exploration of the relationship between negative FE and emotion regulation. First, although positive FE and emotion regulation may be linearly related, the confusing results for negative FE should be explored with curvilinear analyses. Children who observe moderate amounts of negative expressiveness followed by their family members' use of coping techniques may learn more about emotion regulation than young children in homes where negative feelings are not overtly expressed and thus resolution of them is not salient. However, more intense negative expressiveness in the family may become overly arousing for children, and a pathway of FE to arousal (rather than of FE to coping) may become established instead. Second, the type of negative FE may also be of importance: A lot of maternal sadness, embarrassment, apology, and other self-focused emotion expressions may preclude maternal attention to children's emotion displays, may inhibit guidance regarding possible coping strategies (Garner, 1995), and/or may provide children with the message that there are no successful resolutions when one is feeling bad. Third, these relationships are surely bidirectional: When children are able to self-regulate successfully, family members may tend to be more positively expressive, but when children are unable to regulate their own emotions, negative expressiveness in the family, especially sadness, may increase. Fourth, because, as shown above, feeling emotions more intensely may be a correlate of family expressiveness, research on the relationship of FE with emotion regulation needs to assess and control for the intensity of the emotional experience. Finally, more complex definitions of emotion regulation (see Saarni and Weber, this volume) may also help to clarify how different aspects of emotion regulation may be differently related to negative FE.

### Understanding (26 Studies)

It was originally hypothesized that socialization pressures for communication skills would function in different directions for children growing up in differentially expressive homes. As described above, children from more expressive families would have greater opportunities than children from less expressive families to practice their sending skills. However, children from less expressive homes would need to become more sensitive to subtle displays of emotion in their families and, thus, would develop greater judging skill, compared with children from more expressive homes, who would not need to look far to know how the other family members were feeling (Halberstadt, 1983, 1984, 1986). Thus, we would predict a negative association between FE and skill in understanding others' emotional communications.

For total FE, the 13 studies indicate clear age differences in the relationships between FE and understanding. Among young children, 5 of the 6 studies report *positive* associations between maternal expressiveness and children's skills in understanding emotion in others, including skill in labeling emotions, greater emotion situation knowledge, and greater perspective-taking/role-taking ability. However, among college students, all 7 studies tend toward *negative* associations between family expressiveness and students' skills in labeling emotions that were communicated aurally or by video, or in taking others' perspectives. Although not all of these studies were individually significant, a meta-analysis of the 6 labeling studies showed a clear and significant pattern of negative association: Students from less expressive families were more skilled in identifying facial and vocal emotion communications than students from more expressive families (Halberstadt, 1984). The difference is especially clear for difficult and negative expressions (Halberstadt, 1986). To summarize, it appears most likely that parents' obvious and clear expressions are associated with better understanding of emotion expressions early in life, but that as children get older, those who come from less expressive homes develop a greater advantage; whereas adolescents and adults in highly expressive families might not have had to work very hard to understand their family members' clear, frequent, intense, and/or enduring communications, adolescents and adults in less expressive families may have needed to develop skill in understanding the subtle, masked, or blended communications that occurred less frequently and for only abbreviated duration in their families.

For positive FE, the 12 studies suggest positive associations between positive FE and skill in understanding emotion expression and experience of others. Six of the 11 studies of young children found significant relationships between positive FE and knowledge of emotion expressions and situations, affective perspective-taking ability, but not use of display rules. In 1 study on deaf children, positive paternal expressiveness was actually a better predictor of children's understanding than any other predictor in that study, including family talk, family climate, parental sign-language skills, and children's own emotion vocabularies (Cantor, 1995). However, another of these studies suggests that the positive association between positive FE and children's understanding of emotion may be specific to European American families only, and the relationship may be weaker and may actually be reversed in Japanese American families (Mirch-Kretschmann, Alvarez, Gerbi, & Piker, 1996). The 1 study of college students reported a finding that was in accord with results for young children; FE was positively associated with less difficulty in identifying and communicating emotions (Berenbaum & James, 1994).

For negative FE, the 13 studies assessing understanding of emotional experience report less consistent results than for positive FE.

Five of the 10 studies of young children found significant positive relationships between negative FE and labeling of emotion expressions and/or knowledge of emotion situations, though not for all measures. However, 1 of these and 3 others also found negative relationships between negative maternal expressiveness and understanding of emotion, and another study found no effects in either direction. Paternal expressiveness was again the best predictor of children's understanding in the study on deaf children (Cantor, 1995). When negative FE was examined by subscales, negative-dominant FE was associated with children's use of more self-protective display rules, and negative-submissive FE was associated with fewer prosocial display rules (Jones, Bowling, & Cumberland, 1997).

A last, intriguing study on young children indicated that mothers and their children in more negatively expressive families were more similar in their predictions of the children's responses to angry situations than were mothers and children from less negatively expressive families. What is not clear, however, is whether high expressive mothers are better at predicting their children's responses, or whether the children have better self-knowledge of their own experiences and expressive styles (Casey & Fuller, 1994). The one study of college students was consistent with the studies on total FE; although negative-dominant FE had little impact specifically, high negative-submissive FE was associated with greater difficulty in identifying one's own emotions (Berenbaum & James, 1994).

Together these studies suggest that positive FE is clearly associated with positive outcomes in children's understanding of emotion, and that negative FE may also impact positively on children's understanding of emotional experience and expression. The results for negative FE and children's understanding may be less clear because the relationship may not be linear, such that mild to moderate negative expressiveness provides a learning experience but intense displays of negative affect, particularly directed at the child, are associated with such distress that the development of understanding is deterred (Dunn & Brown, 1994; Jones, Bowling, & Cumberland, 1997).

In adulthood, with one exception, the results suggest that FE is negatively associated with understanding. The contrast between the results for young children and young adults suggests a shift in skill as a consequence of long-term experiences with different levels of family expressiveness. A longitudinal, or even a cross-sectional, study investigating children's, adolescents', and young adults' skills on similar measures would provide a very useful test of this intriguing phenomenon.

## Children's Social Competence

How does the emotional expressive style of a child's family relate to the child's social acceptance, prosocial behaviors, and problem behaviors in school? In this section, we discuss the relations between family expressiveness and aggregate measures of social competence, followed by an examination of the separate measures of social competence that are available. The consensual predictions are similar across types of social competence, though the actual outcomes vary somewhat, as we shall see. The predictions are that positive FE will be positively associated with children's social competence, possibly because children develop social skills by watching their parents positively negotiate the inevitable conflicts in family life, and/or because positive FE helps young children develop greater emotion regulation and skill in understanding others' emotional communications, as suggested by the research already described above. Negative FE, however, is generally predicted to be negatively associated with children's social competence, perhaps because negative FE tends to intensify children's own negative experience, thus, precluding development of their ability to regulate their own negative emotions, and/or because reciprocal negative interactions teach children to respond negatively toward distressed or angry others, thereby escalating peer conflicts and lowering their social competence in peer relationships (Carson & Parke, 1996; Denham & Grout, 1992). All studies on social competence assessed preschoolers or kindergartners, except for one study on elementary school children and one on college students' aggressive behavior.

*Aggregate Social Competence (7 Studies).* This domain includes general social skills and composites of prosocial, nonaggressive, nondisruptive, sociable, and likeable behaviors in school. The only study on total FE found no relationship with general social competence (Coats & Feldman, 1995). For positive FE, however, four of five studies report clear positive associations with children's social competence. Results for negative FE in four of five studies indicate poor outcomes when parents are highly negatively expressive. Two of these studies on negative FE also suggest that some negative affect from parents may afford children an opportunity to develop socially competent behaviors in response to their parents. In one study, mothers' low-level expressions of anger, compared to high-level expressions of anger, were associated with children's greater social competence (Denham & Grout, 1992), and in another study there was a positive relationship between mothers' negative-submissive expressiveness and minority children's social competence (but not European American children's competence) (Jones et al., 1996). It may be that low levels of negative FE gets a child's attention so that s/he can learn about emotions, but the emotions are not so overwhelming that the child's physiological arousal impedes sophisticated cognitive processing (Davies & Cummings, 1994; Denham & Grout, 1992; Dunn & Brown, 1994; Dunsmore & Halberstadt, 1997a; Eisenberg et al., 1992). Through this process and children's empathic and guilt responses, they may learn about emotions and the appropriate reactions to them, thus increasing social competence (Denham & Grout, 1992). The finding of a minority/majority status difference also suggests that cultural expectations about what is "socially competent" may vary by race (and possibly gender), in that some people may still expect blacks (and females) to be relatively more submissive than whites (and males); thus, even though it is not morally right, negative-submissive FE may be a pathway for increased perceived social competence of blacks (and possibly girls) in some elementary school settings.

In summary, positive FE is associated with children's greater social competence. However, negative FE may be more complexly related to children's social competence, such that intense negative FE contributes negatively to children's social competence, whereas negative-submissive and low-level negative expressiveness may contribute positively to children's social competence. The relationship between negative FE and social competence may also be dependent upon parents' explanations of their own expressiveness (Denham & Grout, 1992) and the meanings and degree of personal responsibility children attach to specific parental emotional expressions.

*Prosocial Behavior (6 Studies).*  Positive parental expressiveness (or positive FE relative to negative FE) was associated with children's greater prosociality (e.g., helpfulness, concern, attention to others, and empathy) in all four studies on this topic, though not for all tests of the relationship. Results for negative FE varied: Maternal (but not paternal) anger, sadness, and general negative expression were associated with less prosocial behavior, but maternal clarity of negative expression with their daughters (Boyum & Parke, 1995) and negative FE with sons and daughters were associated with more prosocial behavior (Greenberg et al., in press). Two kinds of processes may be co-occurring: When children are overly aroused by negative expression in the family, they may look inward and be less effective at dealing with others' distress (Eisenberg et al., 1992; Jones, Bowling, & Cumberland, 1997). However, less intense but frequent or clearly communicated negative expressions in the family may allow children opportunities to practice interpreting and responding to emotion more prosocially.

*Popularity (4 Studies).* Parents' total expressiveness was positively related to children's popularity, and may be partially mediated by children's understanding of emotions (Cassidy, Parke, Butkovsky, & Braungart, 1992). For positive FE, all three studies report a positive association between parental expressiveness and children's popularity in the classroom; in one of these studies, mothers' positive expressiveness was the only family variable that predicted children's popularity (Nixon, 1997). The two studies on negative FE were less clear. Negative maternal expressiveness and/or father's negativity toward the mother (but not to the child) were negatively related to children's ratings of popularity (Boyum & Parke, 1995). However, mothers who expressed less anger, but more disgust, had boys who were more liked by their peers, and relatively greater neutral affect (perhaps reflecting inattention) toward girls was related to unpopularity (Boyum & Parke, 1995). Another study found no relation between negative maternal expressiveness and popularity (Nixon, 1997). Thus, although the relation between positive FE and popularity is clear, more research on various aspects of negative FE (including dimensions, directionality, and type of affect) and popularity needs to be conducted.

*Aggression (3 Studies).* Positive FE was negatively related to children's and adolescents' aggressive behavior and negative FE was positively related to children's and female adolescents' aggressive behavior in the classroom in two studies. Negative FE was also related to adolescents being victimized more often (Selkirk & Galligan, 1997). Parents' neutral expressions were positively correlated with children's negative social behaviors, especially for daughters (Boyum & Parke, 1995). Negative maternal expressiveness was related to a reduced amount of family talk about feelings when children were upset or angry, but was not related to young children's style of reasoning during conflict situations (Dunn & Brown, 1994). As suggested above, positive FE may increase children's self-regulation and understanding of others' feelings. These skills may allow children to reason more effectively during conflicts, rather than resort to aggression. However, the impact of negative FE on children's self-regulation, understanding of others, and use of aggressive tactics may be more complex, and future studies will most likely need to assess types of parental expression (e.g., sadness, anger, or contempt; negative submissiveness or negative dominance), who the negative affect is directed at (a child or another person), and the amount of and quality of family talk about feeling after conflicts (Davies & Cummings, 1994; Gottman, Katz, & Hooven, 1996).

To conclude this section on social competence: The relations between positive FE and children's social competence are clearly and persistently positive across the various domains of competence. The relations with negative FE are less clear and suggest the importance of distinguishing level of intensity or frequency (low versus high), type of negativity (e.g., negative submissiveness versus dominance, or anger, sadness, contempt, or no affect at all), who the expressor is and the direction of the anger (mother versus father, and directed at child or not), and clarity of communication. These relations between FE and children's social competence are especially interesting in that the nonverbal and verbal expressive behaviors of the family in the home context seem to influence children across other social contexts, such as those involving peers and school activities.

## Parent–Child and Sibling Relationships

*Parenting Styles (1 Study).* Because of the higher levels of warmth and supportiveness found in authoritative parenting, and the lower levels of warmth associated with high demandingness found in authoritarian parenting, it makes sense that positive FE would be associated positively with authoritative parenting and negatively with authoritarian parenting, and that negative FE would be associated with authoritarianism. In the one study assessing FE and parenting styles, much of this was confirmed. Positive FE was positively related to authoritative parenting and negatively associated with authoritarian parenting (Satsky & Bell, 1996). Distinct patterns emerged for negative FE, such that negative-dominant FE was negatively related to authoritative parenting, but positively associated with authoritarian parenting, and negative-submissive FE was positively related with both authoritative and authoritarian parenting. Family expressiveness was not related to permissive parenting (Satsky & Bell, 1996).

*Attachment (4 Studies).* Several predictions have been made regarding FE and attachment security, with parents' moderate contingency (being responsive but not smothering), positivity (being loving and supportive), and predictability (both in terms of consistency over time and in the type of response one would expect) as important aspects of attachment security. In the one study on maternal contingency, mothers' low to moderate contingent expressiveness was more often associated with secure attachment in the Strange Situation than mothers' highly contingent expressiveness (Malatesta, Culver, Tesman, & Shepard, 1989). Maternal variability in expressiveness across three measurements in a 5-month period was also associated with attachment security, such that mothers who maintained a more consistent style (were more predictable) had more secure infants (Malatesta et al., 1989).

For positive FE, two studies suggest that more positively expressive mothers were more likely to have securely attached children than less positively expressive mothers. Positive FE was also associated with fewer dismissing strategies toward attachment issues in college students' interviews, and this effect held even when perceived support from one's family was partialled out (Bell, 1998).

For negative FE, two studies indicated that mothers who were more openly negatively expressive tended to be *more* likely to have securely attached children than mothers who suppressed their negative feelings. Negative FE, particularly negative-dominance FE, was also associated with greater preoccupation with attachment issues in the college student interviews (Bell, 1998).

Finally, an interesting association between maternal experience and expression was identified. Although mothers with more securely attached children reported feeling less negative and more positive emotion overall, they were more openly expressive of their negative feelings when they did have them; mothers of less securely attached children reported feeling more negative emotion, but suppressed their negative feelings and overrode them with positivity that they were not feeling (Izard, Haynes, Chisholm, & Baak, 1991). Thus, attachment security may relate to this form of parental predictability, and the match/mismatches between maternal experience and expression of emotion may be as important as intensity and frequency of negative expressions and experience of emotion.

*Sibling Relationships (1 Study).* From a simple social learning perspective, it makes sense that children from more positively expressive homes will be more positively expressive toward their siblings, and children from more negatively expressive homes will be more negatively expressive toward their siblings. The one study on this topic supports the claim: Children reported that positive maternal expressiveness was associated with more sibling warmth and less sibling conflict; both mothers and children reported that negative maternal expressiveness was associated with less sibling warmth, more sibling conflict, and greater sibling rivalry (Stocker, Ahmed, & Stall, 1997). Also, the relationship between marital satisfaction and sibling relationships appears to be mediated by negative maternal expressiveness; either a mother's marital relationship affects her negative expressiveness which then affects the sibling relationship, or the sibling relationships affect her negative expressiveness which then affects her marital relationship (Stocker et al., 1997).

*Parent–Adolescent Relationships (4 Studies).* Again, the consensual prediction is for positive associations between positive FE and good family relationships, and negative associations between negative FE and good family relationships. The one study on total expressiveness found that fathers' expressiveness (no mothers were in the study) was related to greater parent–adolescent relationship quality (Julian, McKenry, & McKelvey, 1991). For positive (and neutral) parental expressiveness, three studies suggested positive trends with family problem solving when discussing "hot" topics, adolescents' perceptions of communication quality and reduced conflict, but also reduced psychological autonomy. Negative parental expressiveness, on the other hand, was clearly related to poorer parent – adolescent communication quality, increased conflict, and difficulty in problem solving, yet perceptions of greater autonomy, in these three studies. Gender differences for perceptions of control also emerged. When fathers expressed more negative affect, sons perceived that fathers exercised more control in the relationship; however, when mothers expressed more negative affect, daughters perceived that mothers exercised less control (Flannery, Montemayor, & Eberly, 1994). In sum, positive FE seems positively associated with relationship quality, and negative FE seems negatively related to quality. Nevertheless, some positive outcomes, such as psychological autonomy, do seem to be associated with negative FE.

## *Adult Friendships and Romance (3 Studies)*

Two kinds of questions are represented in this literature: (1) Does FE affect individuals' choices of friends and romantic partners, e.g., for similarity or complementarity? and (2) Is FE associated with marital satisfaction? FE was associated with college students' relational choices in two studies. Both positive FE and negative FE of college students were associated with their close friends' self-expressiveness, and total FE was a better predictor of their friends' expressiveness compared to the target student's own self-expressiveness or affect intensity (Halberstadt, Hoeft, & Tesh, 1990). Students may feel even more comfortable with people like their family members than they do with people like themselves; alternatively, FE may impact students' interaction styles with others, thereby influencing the type of person who will respond positively to them. Similarly, both positive and negative dyadic expressiveness in the mother–child and father–child relationships was related to college students' expressiveness in their dating relationships (Barth & Steingard, 1994). However, interparental expressiveness was not related to expressiveness in the dating relationship, therefore college students' styles and choices for romantic partners may be influenced more by personal interactions with parents than by observing parents in their spousal relationship. And, in the marital relationship, spouses' perceptions of their partners' expressiveness was positively related to their own marital satisfaction (King, 1993; see also Feeney, Noller, Sheehan, & Peterson, this volume, for the importance of perceptions of nonverbal behavior in family relationships).

## *Temperament and Personality (6 Studies)*

As described in Halberstadt (1991), expressiveness is sometimes considered to be a personality characteristic that emerges as a consequence of either genetic or socialization factors. Researchers who find this view congenial would predict positive associations between FE and various aspects of temperament and personality, particularly those related to emotion experience and expression. Additionally, temperament may affect the degree to which and manner in which parental socialization of emotion influences children's behavior (Dunsmore & Halberstadt, 1997a). That is, does children's temperament mediate the associations between parental behavior and values and children's internalization and adoption of those behaviors and values?

One study on total FE indicates no relation between FE and children's classification into inhibited, uninhibited, or moderately inhibited groups at 31 months, nor any relationships with maternal reports of temperament or various laboratory measures of exuberance, impulsivity, or activity level of these children in first grade (Pfeifer & Goldsmith, 1996). In college, however, conversation partners tended to describe students from more expressive homes as more warm, friendly, loud, assertive, outgoing, and excitable than students from less expressive homes (Halberstadt, 1984).

For positive FE, three studies report positive relations between FE and young children's positive temperament (smiling, laughing, approach), emotional intensity, and emotional reactivity to negative emotions (for kindergartners but not second graders), with all temperament measures based on maternal report. And for negative FE, these studies suggest positive relations with negative temperament (a trend) and emotional intensity, possibly because parents are moderating their own behavior with children they perceive to be emotionally reactive.

In summary, FE and children's temperament may be related (although the one study that assessed temperament behaviorally, as opposed to through maternal report, found no relationships). Whether there is a biological basis for FE that is then shared with children genetically is unclear; relationships did not appear for inhibition in toddlers and were weak for young children and college students. These results tend to suggest more socialization and socially constructed influences, but only further research can clarify parental mechanisms of influence, as well as the ways in which family expressiveness and temperament may be bidirectional, i.e., how child temperament and parent temperament impact the expressiveness of each family member, as well as how FE may influence and direct the temperament of the individuals over time.

We know of only one study that examines the role of temperament as a mediator between FE and a child outcome (but see Garner &

Power, 1996; Jones et al., 1996, for other interesting approaches regarding relations between temperament and emotion socialization). In that study, children who were highly impulsive and whose mothers were highly negatively expressive recalled more information about an event during which the mother expressed delight at her child than did less impulsive children with less negatively expressive mothers (Dunsmore & Halberstadt, 1997a). These results suggest that children's temperament may influence the associations between family styles of expressiveness and various kinds of outcomes for those children.

### *Self-Esteem (4 Studies)*

It is an implicit assumption that positive FE and children's self-esteem would be positively associated and negative FE and children's self-esteem would be negatively associated, probably because of children's internalizations of parental expressiveness as self-evaluations. These studies report clear associations between FE and self-esteem in older children and college students.

For positive FE, all four studies indicated that parents' self-reported affect (but not home observations) was associated with their children's self-esteem. These effects may be especially strong for daughters and appear to have a lasting impact on developing children's self-esteem (Bronstein, Fitzgerald, Briones, Pieniadz, & D'Ari, 1993). FE was a stronger predictor of college students' self-esteem than parenting style or support (Barber & Thomas, 1986; Satsky & Bell, 1996).

For negative FE, the two studies on the negative relationship with self-esteem show clear results. Fathers' hostility during discussions of "hot," conflictual topics in the family were negatively associated with eighth-grade boys' self-esteem (Capaldi, Forgatch, & Crosby, 1994), and parents' reported negative affect was negatively associated with college students' self-esteem (Satsky & Bell, 1996). Future research may need to distinguish whether self-esteem is most associated with the overall expressiveness of the family or evaluations directed at particular individuals.

### *Adjustment (10 Studies)*

The relationships between FE and various aspects of adjustment were somewhat surprising to the present authors, as we had not initially hypothesized that expressive styles of family members would impact adjustment. Thus, we report these findings first and theorize about them afterward.

One longitudinal study assessed total FE and adjustment; mothers' active style (including ratings of dominance, energy, expressiveness) during pregnancy was positively related to infants' and toddlers' adaptation and competence, energy level, goal-directedness, and sense of self at various points in the infants' first two years of life (Diskin & Heinicke, 1986). Maternal activity was the single most prominent prebirth variable to be associated with infant and toddler adjustment indices.

For positive FE, six of seven studies indicate clear positive relations between FE and adjustment, with diverse measures of both constructs. Family expressiveness was associated with toddlers' positive mutuality with mother (Diskin & Heinicke, 1986), toddlers' socioemotional competence in settings without mother present (Denham, 1989), constructive coping in preschool (Nixon, 1997), and acceptance of teacher authority and lower levels of ADHD in kindergarten (Greenberg et al., in press). In kindergarten, FE was a better predictor of these teacher-rated variables than the social support parents received and their marital adjustment (but not interviewer-rated quality of the home environment and neighborhood risk). Positive FE when children were in fifth grade was associated with parent-rated measures of school-aged children's psychological problems and distress and teacher-rated measures of boys' social, emotional, and academic functioning (Bronstein et al., 1993) in a 3-year study, though not again when these children were studied 5 years later upon graduating from high school (Bronstein et al., 1996). College students, however, particularly girls, report less loneliness, more satisfaction with professors, and more successful adjustment to college life (Ludemann, 1995). Thus, the overall picture for positive FE suggests clear positive relations with various measures for adjustment and that positive FE somehow increases resiliency against psychological stress. We suspect that the mechanisms mediating this relationship may be children's greater emotion regulation and/or greater self-esteem.

One last study on primarily positive FE involves married couples: Interestingly, the wives' ratings of husbands' expressiveness (but not the husbands' self-reported expressiveness) were negatively associated with wives' depression, hostility, and negative affect, and husbands' ratings of wives' expressiveness (but not the wives' self-reported expressiveness) were positively correlated with husbands' interpersonal sensitivity, obsessive compulsive tendencies, and phobic anxiety (King & Emmons, 1991). Thus, it may be that perceptions of family expressiveness may be more relevant than actual levels of expressiveness.

For negative FE, the six studies provide a confusing picture. There were no relationships between FE and preschoolers' constructive coping (Nixon, 1997) or pretend play (Dunn & Brown, 1994). However, negative FE was associated with toddlers' reduced socioemotional competence in settings without mother present (Denham, 1989) and increased loneliness in college males (Ludemann, 1995). In contrast, negative FE or maternal negative expressiveness in response to children's own anger, sadness, or joy blends was associated with preschoolers' lower levels of risk for externalizing disorders and conduct disorders, and oppositional behavior and ADHD in girls in one study (Teti & Cole, 1995), and lower levels of kindergartners' ADHD in a four-city study (Greenberg et al., in press). Negative FE was also associated with acceptance of teacher authority (Greenberg et al., in press). That so many findings emerged suggests that negative FE has a significant impact on adjustment or results from children's adjustment difficulties, and that these paths will vary depending on the kinds of FE and adjustment being evaluated. One promising distinction may be between typical and atypical negative FE (Dunsmore & Halberstadt, 1997). When parents are negatively expressive in general, children may not think about parental negativity as relevant about themselves; however, when parents are negatively expressive in response to children's specific behaviors, children may well internalize that information as self-relevant. Their subsequent self-beliefs as being uncooperative or as unable to sit still, and so forth, may then affect their own attempts at engaging in more positive behaviors.

Further, as suggested above, when parents are highly negatively expressive in response to their children's behavior, a cyclicity may develop such that children become more emotionally negative themselves and subsequently have difficulty changing inappropriate behaviors or feelings. However, when parents are positively expressive (e.g., warmly redirecting, or acknowledging causal factors while instituting corrective action) in response to children's specific behaviors, especially negative ones, children may be able to emerge from negative emotionality more quickly and move on to other feelings and behaviors.

*Cognitive Correlates and Academic Achievement (4 Studies)*

We did not anticipate any findings with cognitive correlates, so this set of four studies and the emerging pattern was a surprise to the present authors. Total maternal expressiveness, measured in terms of activity (energy, expressiveness, etc.), was associated with several aspects of cognitive development in infants tested 1 year later (Diskin & Heinicke, 1986).

For positive FE, three of four studies suggested positive associations with various aspects of cognitive performance, including preschool and kindergarten children's abilities in several theory-of-mind tasks and teacher-rated cognitive concentration (Greenberg et al., in press; Nixon, 1997), and better functioning in a teacher-rated composite that included academics as well as social and emotional aspects for elementary-school boys (but not girls) over a 3-year period (Bronstein et al., 1993). Positive FE had no association with kindergartners' reading achievement and was negatively related with math achievement in a four-sample study (Greenberg et al., in press). Like positive FE, negative FE was positively related with teacher-rated cognitive concentration, had no association with kindergartners' reading achievement, and was negatively related with math achievement (Greenberg et al., in press).

Together, these studies suggest generally positive aspects of family expressiveness for overall cognitive functioning. Dunsmore and Halberstadt (1997a) have proposed that family expressions of emotion may function as cues to children to "be alert, and pay attention!"; perhaps children in more expressive families have more signals at home that help them focus during teachable moments. At school, the more expressive style that teachers are encouraged to develop in elementary school may also be more familiar and comfortable for children from more expressive families. An interesting exception, however, is math calculations; these may require more careful, nondistracted thinking that may be more often available in low-expressive families. These surprising and intriguing results are well worth further examination.

## Discussion

As always, there is more to be done. We have tried to suggest fruitful avenues for research that are specific to each section; here, we attempt to address some of the larger issues. These include the methodological issues that are relevant across sections; caveats about the review in general; and the interrelations between sections, other aspects of family socialization, and cultural norms and values.

## Some Methodological Issues

First, how should we measure family expressiveness? FE has traditionally been measured in terms of frequency and occasionally in terms of intensity and duration. There are, however, numerous relevant dimensions, such as: purity (showing only one emotional expression at a time versus showing emotion blends), clarity or "interpretability" of expression (the degree to which expressions are idiosyncratic or conventional for a particular group), changeability (how quickly emotion expressions change from one moment to the next), sequential order (the degree to which one emotion, such as delight, is predictably followed by another emotion, such as disappointment), consistency (the degree to which the same context elicits the same expression at different times), situational relevance (whether all expressions pertain to the immediate interaction or whether some expressions are passing glimpses of internal states that are not related to the interaction), and genuineness (the degree to which an expression is a true account of the expressor's feelings rather than a social maneuver). Studying these dimensions can enhance our understanding of relations between FE and various outcomes. For example, Cantor (1995) found different relationships between FE and understanding of emotion when expressions were pure versus complex; Boyum and Parke (1995) found different relationships between FE and prosocial behavior for frequency and clarity; and Malatesta et al. (1989) found that consistency in maternal expressiveness across contexts was associated with secure attachment in infancy.

In this chapter, many channels were reviewed but space constraints did not allow for an examination of differences across facial, vocal, verbal, and body channels. It is important to note that channels may be differentially associated with outcomes. For example, activity in mother's face and body cues, but not vocal cues, was associated with several measures of infant adaptation and competence, whereas warmth in mother's voice, but not face and body, was associated with other measures of infant adjustment (Diskin & Heinicke, 1986). Further, the interrelations between channels of expressiveness have not been well examined in terms of consistency across channels and the consequences of matches and mismatches. We know that differences in consistency exist, and vary by gender and situation (Halberstadt, Hayes, & Pike, 1988), but we know little about their impact on developing individuals in family contexts.

Second, *where, when*, and *with whom* should FE be measured? We can only touch briefly on these issues, but: (a) the situational context of interactions between parents and children seems to influence the impact of family expressiveness (e.g., Camras et al., 1990; Cassidy et al., 1992; Denham & Grout, 1993); (b) associations with FE may well change over time, as is suggested by the reversing pattern of results for understanding emotion from early childhood to adulthood; and (c) whether expressiveness is directed at the child rather than at other family members seems to make a difference. For example, children whose fathers expressed happy affect toward mothers (but not necessarily directly to the children themselves) were rated as more popular (Boyum & Parke, 1995), however parents' expressiveness in direct relationship with their college-age children (rather than their expressiveness with each other) was most closely related to the expressive style between the child and his/her romantic partner (Barth & Steingard, 1994). Thus, several aspects of the context need to be considered in assessing the impact family expressiveness has upon various outcomes.

Third, what kinds of expressiveness should be measured, particularly regarding the qualities of negative expressiveness? Gottman, Katz, and Hooven (1996) provide a convincing argument for the importance of distinguishing contempt and anger, and many studies identified different outcomes for negative submissiveness versus negative dominance and for different emotions, such as sadness, disgust, and anger. Thus, we strongly recommend distinguishing different kinds of negative expressiveness in future research.

Fourth, the question to address now is: "How *does* family expressiveness impact these various outcomes?" As suggested above, early theorizing focused almost exclusively on social learning pathways involving simple modeling effects; more recently, a variety of mechanisms and pathways have been posited. For example, Isley, O'Neil, Clatfelter, and Parke (in press) found that FE was associated both directly and indirectly (via children's own expressiveness) with children's social acceptance and competence; Jones, Bowling, and Cumberland (1997) found that FE was associated with children's choice of display rule goals, and that these display rule goals were associated with other aspects of children's social competence. We suspect that there are numerous pathways between FE and the various outcomes identified in this review; an important next step is to develop greater theory and analysis of the processes by which FE actually does influence outcomes.

Fifth, we need to consider more complex models of relationship. For example, curvilinear relationships need to be examined, particularly for negative FE in association with emotion regulation, understanding of emotion, and social competence. The relationship between positive and negative FE is also of interest for many outcomes. Although an "affective balance" ratio has been used in several studies, our preference is to keep positive and negative scores separate, so as to assess both their independent and interactive effects.

*Caveats*

Although our orientation is to disentangle experience and expression, as described above, few studies actually attempt to do so. Consequently, the boundary between the experience and expression sections was fuzzy, and we had some difficulty sorting studies into one or the other of the sections. (However, we never flipped a coin.) Our claim that this distinction is a useful one is justified by significant results found in the studies that actually do attempt to disentangle these (e.g., Burrowes & Halberstadt, 1987; Fabes et al., 1990; Halberstadt et al., 1990). Further, theoretical developments in understanding family socialization of emotion suggest the importance of distinguishing low negative FE that occurs because negativity is not felt from low negative FE that occurs because of suppressed emotion (e.g., when negative emotion is thought to be dangerous), and also distinguishing high positive FE that occurs because of felt joyousness from high positive FE that is not felt (e.g., when positive expression is thought to be required social behavior). Thus, we recommend that future studies attempt to disentangle these important but conceptually separate constructs.

Space constraints have permitted only a glimpse of the gender effects in FE. There are reasons to expect differences in the levels of FE that boys and girls experience, because parents may be more openly expressive with their daughters. Likewise, there may be differential consequences that FE may have for boys and girls, because of our cultural beliefs that girls are more openly expressive, emotional, intuitive about emotion, and socially skilled. For example, open and frequent expressiveness in their families may provide support for boys to develop more traditionally "feminine" skills and styles, and for girls to develop more traditionally "masculine" skills and styles (e.g., Bronstein et al., 1996).

Perhaps most importantly, children need to be brought back into the theorizing and research about the socialization process, both as agents of socialization and as recipients of others' attempts to socialize them. Two considerations emerge. First, many studies ask how children's individual differences (e.g., children's gender, age, pubertal status, and temperament) affect both their abilities to socialize others in their families and to be socialized by them (e.g., Fabes et al., 1994; Montemayor, Eberly, & Flannery, 1993; Stocker et al., 1997). Second, the questions about family expressiveness have been traditionally "top-down," with the implied direction of influence being from parent to child. Although parent-to-child influence certainly does occur, we need to more effectively study the bidirectionality of family expressiveness. For each set of outcomes, we need to consider children as active participants in family relationships with reciprocal and transactional influences reverberating through family life. We know of no studies that actually assess the impact of children's expressiveness styles upon parental outcomes, although anecdotal reports about parents' expressiveness, emotionality, understanding of emotion, personality development, and personal adjustment strongly suggest this as a fruitful area of research.

*Interrelationships*

*Interrelationships between the Nine Domains of Findings.* So far we have examined how FE is related within domains, and we have only touched on a few of the implications that the findings from one section have for subsequent research in the other sections. There are multiple connections, however, between sections. For example, the greater expressiveness found in individuals from more expressive families may be a result and/or cause of greater emotionality in those individuals. Further, the relations between family expressiveness and understanding others' emotions may be affected by whether an individual also becomes more self-expressive and/or emotional as a consequence of his or her emotionally expressive heritage. And the relations between family expressiveness and social competence may be affected by linkages with those other variables influenced by FE, such as self-expressiveness, emotionality, and understanding of emotion. Thus it is important to consider the linkages between the different kinds of variables and in relation to FE. Again, space constraints preclude a complete discussion here, but the studies described above include multiple examples of research investigating interrelationships across more than one domain associated with FE.

*Interrelationships between the Other Aspects of Family Socialization.* When FE is compared to other aspects of family socialization or emotional life, it tends to stand out as relatively important (e.g., Burrowes & Halberstadt, 1987; Cantor, 1995; Cassidy et al., 1992; Greenberg et al., in press; Halberstadt et al., 1990; but see also Fabes et al., 1994). However, family expressiveness styles are only one aspect of family socialization of emotion. We suggest thinking about family socialization in terms of family beliefs as well as behaviors and in terms of the emotions themselves as well as their expression and their resolution. There are many ways to proceed; for example, researchers have investigated parental beliefs about emotion (Dunsmore & Halberstadt, 1997a; Hyson & Lee, 1996); regulation of children's emotion expression, apologies, and explanations for their own expressiveness, reaction to children's negative emotions, derogation of and intrusiveness about children's emotions and emotional expression (Casey & Fuller, 1994; Denham & Grout, 1992; Eisenberg & Fabes, 1994; Gottman, Katz, & Hooven, 1996; Saarni, 1985); and parental responsiveness and support for emotion, emotional security, validation and scaffolding of positive emotion responses, and reaction to positive emotion (Bronstein et al., 1996; Crockenberg, 1985; Davies & Cummings, 1994; Gottman et al., 1996; Ladouceur & Reid, 1996).

How can we use these numerous aspects of socialization? We advocate more theorizing about the rich sources of information and influence available to children. For example, Dunsmore and Halberstadt (1997a, 1997b) provide an account of the ways in which family expressiveness behavior and beliefs about emotion and emotion expression can influence children's understanding of the world; they found that maternal beliefs about emotions as controllable and positive maternal expressiveness interact with children's activity levels, leading to different levels of children's memory for an event. And in another study, parental expression of anger and styles of responding to children's emotions were both associated with less popular and socially skilled children; these parental variables together may provide a more complete picture regarding children's outcomes (Jones et al., 1996).

*Interrelationships with Culture.* Family expressiveness styles (and other related aspects of family socialization of emotion) may be influenced by more global aspects of the culture, but there is very little research on family expressiveness and ethnicity, occupation, parental education, socioeconomic status, and so forth, and little theorizing about how culture might affect our interpretations and acceptance of family expressiveness (but see Dunn & Brown, 1994; Dunsmore & Halberstadt, 1997b; Mirch-Kretschmann et al., 1996; Nixon, 1997; Potter, 1988; and Wierzbicka, 1994, for exceptions). Thus, comprehensive models including the interrelations between various aspects of family socialization of emotion and their interrelations and match with individuals and with culture are needed, followed by research assessing those hypothesized relationships.

To conclude: In the twenty years of research on family expressiveness, we have learned a great deal about the positive associations of positive family expressiveness with a host of other variables, and we have learned a lot about the complexity of associations between various kinds and levels of negative family expressiveness with various outcomes. It was somewhat surprising to us that negative family expressiveness fared as well as it did, given the current cultural ideology favoring parental restraint of negative emotion expression. It is also quite interesting how diverse the variables are that are associated with family expressiveness; nonverbal behavior in the social context of the family appears to influence, and perhaps is also influenced by, developing individuals' emotional and expressive behavior and skill, interpersonal relationships in other contexts, and even intrapsychic and cognitive development.

For the future we recommend a three-pronged attack. First, an initial assumption that expressiveness and emotionality are related but distinct constructs appears verified, and we need to further examine the relationships between "outcome" variables and what is felt and not felt, as well as what is expressed and not expressed. Second, we need to create bidirectional models of processes that can be assessed across time. And third, we need to begin to examine the other aspects of the elephant, that is, to examine the multiple aspects of family socialization, including matches and mismatches between family beliefs and behavior and cultural socialization, and between family socialization and individual beliefs and behavior. We look forward to this new wave of increasingly complex and informative research.

## Appendix: Studies Reviewed

*Spontaneous and Posed Expression of Emotion*

*Expressiveness*: Balswick & Avertt, 1977 (T); Barth & Steingard, 1994 (P, N); Berenbaum & James, 1994 (P, N); Bronstein et al., 1996 (P); Burrowes & Halberstadt, 1987 (P, N); Camras et al., 1990 (P, N); Cassidy et al., 1992 (P, N); Coats & Feldman, 1995 (T); Cummings, Zahn-Wahler, & Radke-Yarrow, 1981 (N); Denham, 1989 (P, N); Denham & Grout, 1993 (P, N); Denham, Renwick-DeBardi, & Hewes, 1994 (P, N); Denham, Zoller, & Couchoud, 1994 (T); Diskin & Heinicke, 1986 (P, N); Dunn, Bretherton, & Munn, 1987 (T); Fabes et al., 1990 (P, N); Garner & Power, 1996 (P, N); Garner, Jones, Gaddy, & Rennie, 1997 (T); Garner, Robertson, & Smith, 1997 (P, N); Halberstadt, 1984 (T); Halberstadt, 1986 (T); Halberstadt, Fox, & Jones, 1993 (T); Isley et al., in press (P, N); Jones et al., 1996 (P, N); King & Emmons, 1990 (T); Kring & Gordon, 1998 (T); Lacks & Uzgiris, 1995 (T); Malatesta & Haviland, 1982 (P, N); Malatesta et al., 1989 (T); Malatesta, Grigoryev, Lamb, Albin, & Culver, 1986 (P, N); Nixon, 1997 (P, N); Stifter & Grant, 1993 (P, N); Stifter & Moyer, 1991 (T); Weissbrod & Kendziora, 1997 (P, N).

*Posed Sending*: Coats & Feldman, 1995 (T); Halberstadt, 1983 (T); Halberstadt, 1986 (P, N); Ludemann, 1993 (P, N); Nixon, 1997 (P, N).

*Experiencing Emotion*

*Feeling Emotion*: Berlin, 1994 (P, N); Burrowes & Halberstadt, 1987 (P, N); Cassidy et al., 1992 (P, N); Cooley, 1992 (P, N); Denham & Grout, 1992 (P, N); Eisenberg et al., 1991 (P, N); Eisenberg et al., 1992 (P, N); Fabes et al., 1990 (P, N); Fabes et al., 1994 (P, N); Garner, 1995 (P, N); Jones et al., 1996 (P, N); King & Emmons, 1990 (T); Satsky et al., 1998 (N); Teti & Cole, 1995 (N).

*Emotion Regulation*: Burrowes & Halberstadt, 1987 (P, N); Garner, 1995 (P, N); Greenberg et al., in press (P, N); Stifter & Moyer, 1991 (T).

*Understanding Emotion*

Berenbaum & James, 1994 (P, N); Camras et al., 1990 (P, N); Cantor, 1995 (P, N); Casey & Fuller, 1994 (N); Cassidy et al., 1992 (T); Daly, Abramovitch, & Pliner, 1980 (T); Denham & Grout, 1992 (P, N); Denham, Cook, & Zoller, 1992 (T); Denham, Zoller, & Couchoud, 1994 (P, N); Dunn & Brown, 1994 (P, N); Dunn, Brown, & Beardsall, 1991 (T); Dunn, Brown, Slomkowski, Tesla, & Youngblade, 1991 (T); Dunsmore & Smallen, 1998 (P, N); Eisenberg et al., 1991 (T); Garner et al., 1997 (T); Garner & Power, 1996 (P, N); Halberstadt, 1983 (studies 1 and 2) (T); Halberstadt, 1984 (studies 3, 4 and 5) (T); Halberstadt, 1986 (T); Jones et al., 1997 (P, N); Ludemann, 1993 (P, N); Mirch-Kretschmann et al., 1996 (P, N); Nixon, 1997 (P, N).

*Children's Social Competence*

*Aggregate Social Competence*: Bronstein et al., 1993 (P); Carson & Parke, 1996 (N); Coats & Feldman, 1995 (T); Denham & Grout, 1992 (P, N); Isley et al., in press (P, N); Jones et al., 1996 (P, N); Nixon, 1997 (P, N).

*Prosocial Behavior*: Boyum & Parke, 1995 (P, N); Crockenberg, 1985 (N); Denham & Grout, 1992 (P, N); Denham et al., 1994 (N); Fabes et al., 1994 (P, N); Greenberg et al., in press (P, N).

*Popularity*: Boyum & Parke, 1995 (P, N); Bronstein et al., 1993 (P); Cassidy et al., 1992 (T); Nixon, 1997 (P, N).

*Aggression*: Boyum & Parke, 1995 (P, N); Dunn & Brown, 1994 (N); Selkirk & Galligan, 1997 (P, N).

*Parent–Child and Sibling Relationships*

*Parenting Styles*: Satsky & Bell, 1996 (P, N).
*Attachment*: Bell, 1998 (P, N); Berlin, 1994 (P, N); Izard et al., 1991 (P, N); Malatesta et al., 1989 (P, N).
*Sibling Relationships*: Stocker, Ahmed, & Stall, 1997 (P, N).
*Parent–Adolescent Relationships*: Capaldi et al., 1994 (P, N); Flannery et al., 1994 (P, N); Flannery, Montemayor, Eberly, & Torquati, 1993 (P, N); Julian et al., 1991 (T).

*Adult Friendships and Romance*

Barth & Steingard, 1994 (P, N); Halberstadt et al., 1990 (P, N); King, 1993 (T).

*Temperament and Personality*

Casey & Fuller, 1994 (P, N); Dunsmore & Halberstadt, 1997a (P, N); Fabes et al., 1994 (P, N); Garner & Power, 1996 (P, N); Halberstadt, 1984 (study 6) (T); Pfeifer & Goldsmith, 1996 (T).

*Personal Adjustment*

*Self-Esteem*: Barber & Thomas, 1986 (P); Bronstein et al., 1993 (P); Capaldi et al., 1994 (P, N); Satsky & Bell, 1996 (P, N).

*Adjustment*: Bronstein et al., 1996 (P); Bronstein et al., 1993 (P); Denham, 1989 (P, N); Diskin & Heinicke, 1986 (T, P); Dunn & Brown, 1994 (N); Greenberg et al., in press (P, N); King & Emmons, 1991 (P); Ludemann, 1995 (P, N); Nixon, 1997 (P, N); Teti & Cole, 1995 (N).

*Cognitive Correlates*

Bronstein et al., 1993 (P); Diskin & Heinicke, 1986 (T, P); Greenberg et al., in press (P, N); Nixon, 1997 (P, N).

## References

Balswick, J., & Avertt, C. P. (1977). Differences in expressiveness: Gender, interpersonal orientation, and perceived parental expressiveness as contributing factors. *Journal of Marriage and the Family, 39,* 121–127.

Barber, B. K., & Thomas, D. L. (1986). Dimensions of fathers' and mothers' supportive behavior: The case for physical affection. *Journal of Marriage and the Family, 48,* 783–794.

Barth, J. M., & Steingard, B. (1994, April). *Family expressivity and college students' intimate relationships.* Poster presented at the Conference for Human Development, Pittsburgh, PA.

Bell, K. L. (1998). Family expressiveness and attachment. *Social Development, 7,* 37–53.

Berenbaum, H., & James, T. (1994). Correlates and retrospectively reported antecedents of alexithymia. *Psychosomatic Medicine, 56,* 353–359.

Berlin, L. J. (1994). *Attachment and emotions in preschool children.* Unpublished doctoral dissertation, Pennsylvania State University, University Park.

Boyum, L. A., & Parke, R. D. (1995). The role of family emotional expressiveness in the development of children's social competence. *Journal of Marriage and the Family, 57,* 593–608.

Bronstein, P., Briones, M., Brooks, T., & Cowan, B. (1996). Gender and family factors as predictors of late adolescent emotional expressiveness and adjustment: A longitudinal study. *Sex Roles, 34,* 739–765.

Bronstein, P., Fitzgerald, M., Briones, M., Pieniadz, J., & D'Ari, A. (1993). Family emotional expressiveness as a predictor of early adolescent social and psychological adjustment. *Journal of Early Adolescence, 13,* 448–471.

Burrowes, B. D., & Halberstadt, A. G. (1987). Self- and family-expressiveness styles in the experience and expression of anger. *Journal of Nonverbal Behavior, 11,* 254–268.

Camras, L. A., Ribordy, S., Hill, J., Martino, S., Sachs, V., Spaccarelli, S., & Stefani, R. (1990). Maternal facial behavior and the recognition and production of emotional expression by maltreated and nonmaltreated children. *Developmental Psychology, 26,* 304–312.

Cantor, E. (1995). *The socialization of emotion understanding in deaf children: The role of the family.* Unpublished doctoral dissertation, University of Denver, Denver.

Capaldi, D. M., Forgatch, M. S., & Crosby, L. (1994). Affective expression in family problem-solving discussions with adolescent boys. *Journal of Adolescent Research, 9,* 28–49.

Carson, J. L., & Parke, R. D. (1996). Reciprocal negative affect in parent-child interactions and children's peer competency. *Child Development, 67,* 2217–2226.

Casey, R. J., & Fuller, L. L. (1994). Maternal regulation of children's emotions. *Journal of Nonverbal Behavior, 18,* 57–89.

Cassidy, J., Parke, R. D., Butkovsky, L., & Braungart, J. M. (1992). Family-peer connections: The roles of emotional expressiveness within the family and children's understanding of emotions. *Child Development, 63,* 603–618.

Coats, E. J., & Feldman, R. S. (1995). The role of television in the socialization of nonverbal behavioral skills. *Basic and Applied Social Psychology, 17,* 327–341.

Cooley, E. L. (1992). Family expressiveness and proneness to depression among college women. *Journal of Research in Personality, 26,* 281–287.

Crockenberg, S. (1985). Toddlers' reactions to maternal anger. *Merrill-Palmer Quarterly 31,* 361–373.

Cummings, E. M., Zahn-Waxler, C., & Radke-Yarrow, M. (1981). Young children's responses to expressions of anger and affection by others in the family. *Child Development, 52,* 1274–1282.

Daly, E. M., Abramovitch, R., & Pliner, P. (1980). The relationship between mothers' encoding and their children's decoding of facial expressions of emotion. *Merrill-Palmer Quarterly, 26,* 25–33.

Davies, P. T., & Cummings, E. M. (1994). Marital conflict and child adjustment: An emotional security hypothesis. *Psychological Bulletin, 116,* 387–411.

Denham, S. A. (1989). Maternal affect and toddlers' social-emotional competence. *American Journal of Orthopsychiatry, 59,* 368–376.

Denham, S. A., Cook C., & Zoller, D. (1992). Baby looks very sad: Implications of conversations about feelings between mothers and preschoolers. *British Journal of Developmental Psychology, 10,* 301–315.

Denham, S. A., & Grout, L. (1992). Mothers' emotional expressiveness and coping: Relations with preschoolers' social-emotional competence. *Genetic, Social, and General Psychology Monographs, 118,* 75–101.

Denham, S. A., & Grout, L. (1993). Socialization of emotion: Pathway to preschoolers' emotional and social competence. *Journal of Nonverbal Behavior, 17,* 205–227.

Denham, S. A., Renwick-DeBardi, S., & Hewes, S. (1994). Emotional communication between mothers and preschoolers: Relations with emotional competence. *Merrill-Palmer Quarterly, 40,* 488–508.

Denham, S. A., Zoller, D., & Couchoud, E. A. (1994). Socialization of preschoolers' emotion understanding. *Developmental Psychology, 30,* 928–936.

Diskin, S. D., & Heinicke, C. M. (1986). Maternal style of emotional expression. *Infant Behavior and Development, 9,* 167–187.

Dunn, J., Bretherton, I., & Munn, P. (1987). Conversations about feeling states between mothers and their young children. *Developmental Psychology, 23,* 132–139.

Dunn, J., & Brown, J. (1994). Affect expression in the family, children's understanding of emotions, and their interactions with others. *Merrill-Palmer Quarterly, 40,* 120–137.

Dunn, J., Brown, J., & Beardsall, L. (1991). Family talk about feeling states and children's later understanding of others' emotions. *Developmental Psychology, 27,* 448–455.

Dunn, J., Brown, J., Slomkowski, C., Tesla, C., & Youngblade, L. (1991). Young children's understanding of other people's feelings and beliefs: Individual differences and their antecedents. *Child Development, 62,* 1352–1366.

Dunsmore, J. C., & Halberstadt, A. G. (1997a, April). Emotional communication in children's schema development. In Karen Caplovitz Barrett (Chair), *New directions in the communication of emotion.* Symposium conducted at the meeting of the Society for Research in Child Development, Washington, DC.

Dunsmore, J. C., & Halberstadt, A. G. (1997b). How does family emotional expressiveness affect children's schemas? In K. C. Barrett (Ed.), *The communication of emotion: Current research from diverse perspectives, 77,* 45–68. San Francisco: Jossey Bass.

Dunsmore, J. C., & Smallen, L. S. (1998). *Are young children able to identify their parents' emotions better than those of strangers?* Manuscript submitted for publication, Hamilton College, Clinton, NY.

Eisenberg, N., & Fabes, R. A. (1994). Mothers' reactions to children's negative emotions: Relations to children's temperament and anger behavior. *Merrill-Palmer Quarterly, 40,* 138–156.

Eisenberg, N., Fabes, R. A., Carlo, G., Troyer, D., Speer, A. L., Karbon, M., & Switzer, G. (1992). The relations of maternal practices and characteristics to children's vicarious emotional responsiveness. *Child Development, 63,* 583–602.

Eisenberg, N., Fabes, R. A., Schaller, M., Miller, P., Carlo, G., Poulin, R., Shea, C., & Shell, R. (1991). Personality and socialization correlates of vicarious emotional responding. *Journal of Personality and Social Psychology, 61,* 459–470.

Fabes, R. A., Eisenberg, N., Karbon, M., Bernzweig, J., Speer, A. L., & Carlo, G. (1994). Socialization of children's vicarious emotional responding and prosocial behavior: Relations with mothers' perceptions of children's emotional reactivity. *Developmental Psychology, 30,* 44–55.

Fabes, R. A., Martin, C. L., Rose, H., & Karbon, M. (1990). *We don't cry in our family: Family expressiveness styles and offsprings' emotionality.* Poster presented at the meeting of the National Council on Family Relations, Seattle, WA.

Flannery, D. J., Montemayor, R., & Eberly, M. B. (1994). The influence of parent negative emotional expression on adolescents' perceptions of their relationships with their parents. *Personal Relationships, 1,* 259–274.

Flannery, D. J., Montemayor, R., Eberly, M. B., & Torquati, J. (1993). Unraveling the ties that bind: Affective expression and perceived conflict in parent-adolescent interactions. *Journal of Social and Personal Relationships, 10,* 495–509.

Garner, P. W. (1995). Toddlers' emotion regulation behaviors: The roles of social context and family expressiveness. *Journal of Genetic Psychology, 156,* 417–430.

Garner, P. W., Jones, D. C., Gaddy, G., & Rennie, K. M. (1997). Low-income mothers' conversations about emotions and their children's emotional competence. *Social Development, 6,* 37–52.

Garner, P. W., & Power, T. G. (1996). Preschoolers' emotional control in the disappointment paradigm and its relation to temperament, emotional knowledge, and family expressiveness. *Child Development, 67,* 1394–1407.

Garner, P. W., Robertson, S., & Smith, G. (1997). Preschool children's emotional expressions with peers: The roles of gender and emotion socialization. *Sex Roles, 36,* 675–691.

Gottman, J. M., Katz, L. F., & Hooven, C. (1996). Parental meta-emotion philosophy and the emotional life of families: Theoretical models and preliminary data. *Journal of Family Psychology, 10,* 243–268.

Greenberg, M. T., Lengua, L. J., Coie, J., & Pinderhughes, E. (in press). Predicting developmental outcomes at school entry using a multiple-risk model: Four American communities. *Developmental Psychology.*

Halberstadt, A. G. (1983). Family expressiveness styles and nonverbal communication skills. *Journal of Nonverbal Behavior, 8,* 14–26.

Halberstadt, A. G. (1984). Family expression of emotion. In C. Z. Malatesta & C. E. Izard (Eds.), *Emotion in adult development* (pp. 235–252). Beverly Hills, CA: Sage.

Halberstadt, A. G. (1986). Family socialization of emotional expression and nonverbal communication styles and skills. *Journal of Personality and Social Psychology, 51,* 827–836.

Halberstadt, A. G. (1991). Socialization of expressiveness: Family influences in particular and a model in general. In R. S. Feldman & B. Rimé (Eds.), *Fundamentals in nonverbal behavior* (pp. 106–160). New York: Cambridge University Press.

Halberstadt, A. G., Cassidy, J., Stifter, C. A., Parke, R. D., & Fox, N. A. (1995). Self-expressiveness within the family context: Psychometric support for a new measure. *Psychological Assessment, 7,* 93–103.

Halberstadt, A. G., Denham, S. A., & Dunsmore, J. C. (1999). *Affective social competence.* Unpublished manuscript, North Carolina State University.

Halberstadt, A. G., Fox, N. A., & Jones, N. A. (1993). Do expressive mothers have expressive children? The role of socialization in children's affect expression. *Social Development, 2,* 48–65.

Halberstadt, A. G., Hayes, C. W., & Pike, K. M. (1988). Gender and gender role differences in smiling and communication consistency. *Sex Roles, 19,* 589–604.

Halberstadt, A. G., Hoeft, S., & Tesh, M. (1990, March). *Self- and family expressiveness and emotionality correlates in friendship choices.* Poster presented at the Conference for Human Development, Richmond, VA.

Hyson, M., & Lee, K. M. (1996). Assessing early childhood teachers' beliefs about emotions: Content, contexts, and implications for practice. *Early Education and Development, 7,* 57–78.

Isley, S., O'Neil, R., Clatfelter, D., & Parke, R. D. (in press). Parent and child expressed affect and children's social acceptance and competence: Modeling direct and indirect pathways. *Developmental Psychology.*

Izard, C. E., Haynes, O. M., Chisholm, G., & Baak, K. (1991). Emotional determinants of infant-mother attachment. *Child Development, 62,* 906–917.

Jones, D. C., Bowling, B. J., & Cumberland, A. (1997). *The development of display rule knowledge: Linkage with family expressiveness and social competence.* Manuscript submitted for publication, University of Washington, Seattle.

Jones, H. E. (1950). The study of patterns of emotional expression. In M. L. Reymert (Ed.), *Feelings and emotions* (pp. 161–168). New York: McGraw-Hill.

Jones, H. E. (1960). The longitudinal method in the study of personality. In I. Iscoe and H. W. Stevenson (Eds.), *Personality development in children* (pp. 3–27). Austin: University of Texas Press.

Jones, S. M., Eisenberg, N., & Fabes, R. A. (1996). *Parents' emotion behaviors and children's social competence: The mediating role of children's affective displays.* Unpublished manuscript, Arizona State University, Tempe.

Julian, T. W., McKenry, P. C., & McKelvey, M. W. (1991). Mediators of relationship stress between middle-aged fathers and their adolescent children. *The Journal of Genetic Psychology, 152,* 381–386.

King, L. A. (1993). Emotional expression, ambivalence over expression, and marital satisfaction. *Journal of Social and Personal Relationships, 10,* 601–607.

King, L. A., & Emmons, R. A. (1990). Conflict over emotional expression: Psychological and physical correlates. *Journal of Personality and Social Psychology, 58,* 864–877.

King, L. A., & Emmons, R. A. (1991). Psychological, physical, and interpersonal correlates of emotional expressiveness, conflict, and control. *European Journal of Personality, 5,* 131–150.

Kring, A. M., & Gordon, A. H. (1998). Sex differences in emotion: Expression, experience, and physiology. *Journal of Personality and Social Psychology, 74,* 686–703.

Lacks, J. M., & Uzgiris, I. C. (1995, March). *Affective imitation in relation to the genesis of empathy.* Paper presented at the meeting of the Society for Research in Child Development, Indianapolis, IN.

Ladouceur, C., & Reid, L. (1996, August). *Reliability and construct validity of the parents' reactions to children's positive emotion scale*. Paper presented at the meeting of the International Society for the Study of Behavioral Development, Quebec City.

Lanzetta, J. T., & Kleck, R. E. (1970). Encoding and decoding of nonverbal affect in humans. *Journal of Personality and Social Psychology, 16,* 12–19.

Ludemann, P. M. (1993, March). *Family factors and preschoolers' facial expression production and recognition*. Paper presented at the meeting of the Society for Research in Child Development, New Orleans, LA.

Ludemann, P. M. (1995, Spring). Sex differences in patterns of college adjustment. Framingham State College: Family and Parent Press, 3–4.

Malatesta, C. Z., Culver, C., Tesman, J. R., & Shepard, B. (1989). The development of emotion expression during the first two years of life. *Monographs of the Society for Research in Child Development, 54,*(1–2, Serial No. 219).

Malatesta, C. Z., Grigoryev, P., Lamb, C., Albin, M., & Culver, C. (1986). Emotion socialization and expressive development in preterm and full-term infants. *Child Development, 57,* 316–330.

Malatesta, C. Z., & Haviland, J. M. (1982). Learning display rules: The socialization of emotion expression in infancy. *Child Development, 53,* 991–1003.

Mirch-Kretschmann, S. E., Alvarez, M. M., Gerbi, S. A., & Piker, R. A. (1996). *Japanese American and White mothers' self-expressiveness and beliefs regarding their children's understanding of emotions*. Poster presented at the meeting of the Southwestern Society for Research in Human Development, Park City, UT.

Montemayor, R., Eberly, M. B., & Flannery, D. J. (1993). Effects of pubertal status and conversation topic on parent and adolescent affective expression. *Journal of Early Adolescence, 13,* 431–447.

Nixon, C. L. (1997). *Family experiences and early social-cognition: Links to social behavior*. Unpublished doctoral dissertation, Pennsylvania State University, Erie.

Pfeifer, M. A., & Goldsmith, H. H. (1996, May). *Inhibited and uninhibited toddlers as first graders: Temperamental continuity and change*. Paper presented at the meeting of the Midwestern Psychological Association, Chicago, IL.

Potter, S. H. (1988). The cultural construction of emotion in rural Chinese social life. *Ethos, 16,* 181–208.

Saarni, C. (1985). Indirect processes in affect socialization. In M. Lewis & C. Saarni (Eds.), *The socialization of emotions* (pp. 187–209). NY: Plenum.

Satsky, M. A., & Bell, K. L. (1996, June). *Dimensions of family emotional expressiveness predict self-esteem*. Poster presented at the meeting of the American Psychological Society, San Francisco, CA.

Satsky, M. A., Bell, K. L., & Garrison, S. A. (1998, February). *Dimensions of negative family expressivity discriminate self-critical and dependent depression in late adolescence*. In K. L. Bell (Chair), Family socialization and expression of emotion. Symposium presented at the biennial meeting of the Society for Research on Adolescence, San Diego, CA.

Selkirk, J., & Galligan, R. F. (1997). *Family background characteristics of bullying and victimization in young adolescents.* Unpublished manuscript, Swinburne University of Technology, Melbourne, Australia.

Stifter, C. A., & Grant, W. (1993). Infant responses to frustration: Individual differences in the expression of negative affect. *Journal of Nonverbal Behavior, 17,* 187–204.

Stifter, C. A., & Moyer, D. (1991). The regulation of positive affect: Gaze aversion activity during mother-infant interaction. *Infant Behavior and Development, 14,* 111–123.

Stocker, C., Ahmed, K., & Stall, M. (1997). Marital satisfaction and maternal emotional expressiveness: Links with children's sibling relationships. *Social Development, 6,* 371–383.

Teti, L. O., & Cole, P. M. (1995, April). *Emotion regulation in the preschool years: Relations to socialization and psychopathology.* Paper presented at the meeting of the Society for Research in Child Development, Indianapolis, IN.

Weissbrod, C. S., & Kendziora, K. T. (1997, April). *Parental positive socialization and emotion in the prediction of children's emotional expression.* Poster presented at the meeting of the Society for Research in Child Development, Washington, DC.

Wierzbicka, A. (1994). Emotion, language, and cultural scripts. In S. Kitayama and H. R. Markus (Eds.), *Emotion and culture: Empirical studies of mutual influence* (pp. 133–196). Washington, DC: American Psychological Association.

# 6. The Influence of Television on Children's Nonverbal Behavior

ERIK J. COATS, ROBERT S. FELDMAN, AND
PIERRE PHILIPPOT

Researchers working in the area of nonverbal behavior often trace their intellectual roots to Charles Darwin. In his third book on the theory of evolution, *The Expression of the Emotions in Man and Animals*, Darwin (1872) brought renewed attention to the study of facial expressions. Like many people working in the field today, Darwin sought to understand human expressions of emotion by examining their development in childhood. Yet more than 120 years after the publication of *Expression*, we are only beginning to understand how children build a vocabulary of facial expressions.

The need to understand the development of expressive behavior has taken on a new importance because of the considerable impact nonverbal displays have in children's daily lives. It is now clear that there is a relationship between expressive behavior and social success (Feldman, Philippot, & Custrini, 1991). The ability to communicate emotional information to others using facial expressions – termed *encoding ability* – has been shown to correlate positively with ratings of interpersonal warmth (Sabatelli & Rubin, 1986), with ratings of sociometric status among peers (Coats & Feldman, 1996), and with parental ratings of general social competence (Custrini & Feldman, 1989). Similarly, the ability to read emotional information on others' faces – termed *decoding ability* – has been shown to correlate positively with friendliness ratings of peers (Edwards, Manstead, & MacDonald, 1987), with popularity ratings of classroom teachers (Spence, 1987), and with parental ratings of general social competence (Philippot & Feldman, 1990).

Despite the importance of nonverbal skills in social interactions, most children are never formally taught how to encode and decode nonverbal expressions. The techniques of nonverbal communication are not included in the school curriculum, nor are they explained by parents to their children. Yet in classrooms and homes everywhere, some children are more effective encoders and decoders, and they have a social advantage because of it.

Uncertainty about exactly why some children are better nonverbal communicators, coupled with certainty about the importance of this skill, makes this an important area of research. It is likely that differences in encoding and decoding are partially the result of biology. At very young ages, differences in children's temperament have been shown to influence emotion-related behavior (Field, 1982). And among adults, there is evidence that individuals differ in how they respond to emotional events (Cacioppo et al., 1992; Manstead, 1991). Some people respond to emotions more externally (e.g., changes in face and voice); some people respond more internally (e.g., changes in GSR and heart rate). Whether the tendency to respond to emotions internally is inversely correlated or orthogonal to the tendency to respond externally is still debated. In any event, it seems likely that there are biologically based individual differences in the extent to which people respond to emotional events with nonverbal expressions.

However, most, if not all, leading theories of the development of expressive behavior presume that differences in encoding and decoding are partially the result of socialization experiences. For example, most theorists believe that people actively control their facial expression in accordance with cultural norms or display rules (see, for instance, Saarni and Weber, this volume, and Kupperbusch et al., this volume). Although most theories of the development of expressive behavior presume that socialization plays an important role, empirical evidence for social learning has been surprisingly scarce. The goal of this chapter is to review recent evidence that extends our understanding of the socialization of expressive behavior. We begin by briefly discussing research on the influence of family members and of peers. We then focus on evidence from our own laboratory on the influence of television. This evidence suggests that television has a powerful and wide ranging impact on children's expressive behavior. Finally, we compare research in the three areas and call attention to some important commonalities.

## Review of Relevant Prior Research

When we began this research, we were not aware of any previous research that had attempted to demonstrate the impact of television viewing on children's nonverbal behavior. However, research on other agents of socialization was helpful in guiding our research. In particular, research on the influence of family members and of peers provided insights into the possible impact of television. We review this research briefly for two reasons. First, to explicate the basis of our predictions about television's impact. Second, and more importantly, to allow us to compare television's impact to that of the family and of friends.

## Influences of Family Members

The family is probably the most widely acknowledged agent in the socialization of nonverbal behavior (for an extensive review, see Halberstadt, Crisp, and Eaton in this volume). Halberstadt (1991) argues that families can have four types of influence on children's expressive behavior. First, children may naturally imitate other family members' facial expressions. Second, family members may communicate expectation about expressive behavior to children by labeling them. A mother may call her son a big boy, thus communicating to him certain expectations for his behavior. Third, family members may reinforce certain expressions in children. A father may tell his daughter that he is proud of her for not crying when a favorite toy broke. Fourth, family members may occasionally explicitly coach children to perform certain behaviors, although this does not appear to happen very often.

Because the level of emotionality shown within families varies widely, children who grow up in different families will not have the same socialization experiences. Halberstadt's empirical research has focused on family differences in global emotional expressivity as measured by the Family Expressiveness Questionnaire (FEQ, Halberstadt, 1986). Using this instrument, she has found that college students who report growing up in a highly expressive family are themselves very expressive. However, these students tend not to be especially sensitive to others' nonverbal expressions. A person accustomed to seeing a wide grin as an expression of happiness may not notice this emotion when it is represented by a subtle smile. In other words, people raised in expressive families tend to be good nonverbal encoders but poor nonverbal decoders.

Interestingly, the effect on decoding ability of growing up in an expressive home appears to change over time (Halberstadt, 1991). Although adults who grew up in highly expressive homes are poorer decoders than adults who grew up in less expressive homes, among young children the opposite pattern is found. Young children whose mothers are highly expressive appear to be more knowledgeable of display rules (Denham & Couchoud, 1988) and to be better nonverbal decoders (Daly, Abramovitch, & Pliner, 1980). We will reconsider this interesting interaction in subsequent sections of this chapter and propose two possible explanations for it.

Other research suggests that the influence of the family environment on expressive behavior may be emotion-specific (Camras, 1985). Families may not be equally expressive of all emotions. Children of families that express only a limited range of emotions may become proficient at recognizing only those emotions. For example, abusive parents have fewer positive interactions with their children than nonabusive parents (Burgess & Conger, 1978). Perhaps consequently, abused children are particularly bad at recognizing expressions of positive emotions (i.e., happiness) (Camras, Grow, & Ribordy, 1983). We should, however, be cautious in interpreting these correlational studies. Although their results are consistent with emotion-specific family influences, they do not constitute a direct test of the hypothesis.

Finding that children's nonverbal style is associated with the style of their family environment cannot be taken as conclusive evidence for social learning. Many of the observed associations between children's expressive behavior and their family environment could be reinterpreted as demonstrating biological influence. For example, perhaps children grow up to be as expressive as their family members because of their shared biology. The case for social learning would certainly benefit by finding that children's nonverbal style is associated in similar ways with socialization forces outside of the family.

*Influences of Peers*

Less research has examined the possibility that children's expressive behavior is influenced by their peers. Yet it would appear that all, or at least most, of the methods by which children are influenced by their families (modeling, labeling, reinforcement, coaching) should also operate among peers (Halberstadt, 1991). Additionally, peers may broaden the range of context in which children witness emotions. When interacting with peers, children are likely to see emotions expressed in situations different from those in which they have seen family members (Camras, 1985).

Several researchers have demonstrated that even very young children can and do attend and respond to one another's nonverbal displays (Ekman & Friesen, 1971; Michalson & Lewis, 1985, Morency & Krauss, 1982). For example, children in conflict situations can effectively encode and decode facial expressions of hostility (e.g., Camras, 1977). Children may also express emotions differently when they are with peers and when they are alone. For example, children smile and laugh more when watching an entertaining cartoon with a friend than when watching alone (Foot, Chapman, & Smith, 1977). In sum, children's behavior in a specific situation has been shown to change as a result of the presence and expressive behavior of peers.

However, evidence that stable qualities of children's understanding or use of expressive behavior are affected by peer interactions has yet to be shown. One study that could be taken as suggestive of such an effect was reported by Ansfield, DePaulo, and Bell (1995), who found that women's nonverbal sensitivity (i.e., decoding ability) was strongly correlated with the sensitivity of a close same-sex friend. They suggest as one possible explanation that the intimacy shared between close women friends leads to a growing similarity in how they interpret social events. However, similarity in perceiving social events could equally be a cause, and not a consequence, of close friendship.

### The Influence of Television

We now turn to evidence that children's expressive behavior is influenced by the social models of a different group of nonfamily members: actors on television. On one hand, we might expect television's impact to be considerably less than that of either families or peers. Unlike family members and peers, television cannot coach specific behavior. Neither can it reinforce behaviors with direct rewards and punishments, nor communicate expectations via labeling. However, like family members and peers, television can provide salient models to be imitated, and it certainly may expose children to a broader range of emotions and emotional contexts than they are likely to see anywhere else (Dorr, 1985).

Television may also share another form of social influence with families and peers – the influence of display rules. According to Saarni (1982; 1985), children's beliefs about emotionality function as expectations that affect both how children feel and how and whether they express emotions. Display rules can come from many sources, including television (Saarni & Borg, 1990). Dorr (1985) suggests that television can teach children a great deal about the "American emotional landscape." For example, television may give children names for labeling emotional displays as well as information about what types of situations give rise to them. By influencing children's understanding of emotions and emotional expressions, television may influence expressive behavior through its impact on the development of display rules.

The theories discussed thus far can be summarized as suggesting that television may have some impact on children's expressive behavior yet possesses only a subset of the weapons in the arsenal of social influence. Of the four types of social influence available to families and peers (imitation, labeling, reinforcement, and coaching), television can make use of only one. Of the four kinds of situations in which children learn about emotions discussed by Dorr (1985; participating, observing an interaction between real people, observing an interaction between actors playing a role, and remembering a prior event), television viewing provides only one.

On the other hand, there are some reasons to suspect that television's impact would not be trivial. Because of the tremendous amount of time that children spend watching television, it has the potential to be one of the most influential sources of information regarding emotions and emotional expressions. The average American child will, by the age of 18, have spent more time watching television than engaged in any other waking activity: more, even, than playing with friends or interacting with parents or siblings (Liebert & Sprafkin, 1988).

Two additional observations about television suggest the usefulness of examining its role in shaping children's nonverbal behavior. First, research in other areas has demonstrated that children are affected by what they see on television (e.g., Potter & Chang, 1990; Signorielli, 1991). Although not universally accepted, a preponderance of evidence suggests that children become more aggressive because of watching television violence (Berkowitz, 1993; Donnerstein, Slaby, & Eron, 1994; Wood, Wong, & Chachere, 1991). Strong evidence also exists to suggest that children normally assume that television's portrayals of life are accurate (Zillmann, 1991). They are not aware that it exaggerates, overgeneralizes, and misrepresents (Gerbner, Gross, Morgan, & Signorielli, 1986).

Second, nonverbal behavior may be the most salient aspect of television for young viewers. Children as old as third-graders are unable to follow the plots of television shows (Collins, 1983), or to recall significant details about the storylines (Rule & Ferguson, 1986). Consequently, television's socializing effects, at least for young viewers, may be largely socioemotional (Noble, 1983).

For these reasons, television appears to possess the potential to influence children's expressive behavior. We began our investigation by comparing emotional displays on television with those seen in the real world (more specifically, on a college campus).

We began our investigation of television's impact on nonverbal behavior by examining its depiction of emotional displays. If television's depictions of displays are accurate, we should not expect frequent viewing to have much impact on children. If, for example, the intensity of violence on television were the same as in everyday life, there would be no reason to worry about the impact of viewing televised violence: Turning off the television would not turn off the violence. However, to the extent that television's depictions of emotional displays are unrealistic, frequent viewers should be expected to develop a style of nonverbal behavior that differs from infrequent viewers.

## Nonverbal Displays on Television

To examine the nature of nonverbal displays on television, Houle and Feldman (1991) examined 5 shows that were among the 10 most favorite for children between the ages of 6 and 11. At this age, most of children's favorite shows are situation comedies; consequently, each show examined was of that genre. Five randomly selected episodes from each of the 5 shows were recorded for 10 minutes (commercial breaks were excluded). The 250 minutes of programming provided by this procedure was then broken into 1,000 15-second segments. Each segment was viewed and its emotional content recorded. Specifically, segments were coded for which, if any, displays of emotion appeared, and the context in which displays occurred.

To compare emotional displays on television with displays in the real world, Coats & Feldman (1994, 1997) conducted two studies employing the experience sampling method (Larson & Csikszentmihalyi, 1983). In the first study, trained observers were paged at randomly selected, predetermined times throughout the day. Each time they were paged, observers spent 15 seconds looking at people around them and recorded which, if any, emotional expressions they saw. In the second study, trained observers wore watches that were programmed with five alarms that went off daily. Each time their alarm went off, observers looked at the first five people they saw and recorded which, if any, emotional expressions they displayed. Three aspects of our comparison of emotional displays on television and on a college campus stand out.

*Frequency of Emotional Displays.* Our analysis suggests that television depicts emotional displays at an unrealistically high rate. The percentage of 15-second intervals in which at least one emotional display was observed was substantially higher on television than on a college campus. Fifty-five percent of intervals on campus contained an emotional display, compared with 70% on television. On television, the rate with which emotional displays occurred was some 200 per hour.

*Context of Emotional Displays.* We observed that characters on television generally show facial expressions that are consistent with the situational context (i.e., angry characters show angry faces; happy characters show happy faces). In other words, characters do very little dissembling or masking. And although our comparison studies did not provide data on how frequently people in the real world respond to emotional events by displaying their felt emotions versus a socially appropriate response, we know from previous research that people often engage in nonverbal dissemblance in the service of social goals (DePaulo, 1991; 1992). In contrast, television characters appear to do very little dissembling or masking of emotions.

*Range of Emotional Displays.* Our analysis also suggests that the relative frequency with which specific emotions are displayed on television is inconsistent with the real world. Compared with a college campus, television depicts expressions of sadness and anger more frequently and expressions of fear and disgust less frequently. Happy expressions were extremely frequent on both television and on campus.

Finding that depictions of emotions on television are unrealistic (i.e., differ from the real world), we suspected that children who watched a great deal of television would differ in predictable ways from children who watched less television. We therefore undertook a series of studies to compare the nonverbal behaviors of children who watch television frequently and those of children who watch infrequently. Currently, we have examined three types of nonverbal behaviors: encoding, decoding, and display rules of dissemblance.

## Television and Encoding

When considering television's potential impact on children's nonverbal encoding, we focused on the potential consequences of modeling highly expressive characters. If children do imitate the people they see on television, the effect of watching television should mirror the effect of living in a highly expressive family environment: Both should socialize children to develop a highly expressive encoding style.

Based on Halberstadt's (1983; 1986) research on encoding ability and family expressiveness, we predicted that frequent television viewers would encode emotions differently from infrequent viewers. Interestingly, highly expressive people exhibit relatively unambiguous nonverbal cues when genuinely experiencing an emotion but are not particularly effective when attempting to feign an emotion they are not feeling. Thus, children raised in a highly expressive family tend to be better encoders under spontaneous conditions, but worse encoders under posed conditions (Halberstadt, 1986). We therefore hypothesized that frequent television viewers would similarly be more effective spontaneous encoders but less effective posed encoders.

Moreover, because television's range of emotions is largely limited to happiness, sadness, and anger, frequent and infrequent viewers should not be equally able to encode all emotions. Because expressions of fear and disgust are shown on television less often than in the real world, children who watch television most often may be less experienced encoders of these emotions. We therefore hypothesized that frequent viewers would be more effective encoders of anger, happiness, and sadness, but less effective encoders of fear and disgust.

These hypotheses were tested in a study of 59 children enrolled in grades 2 through 6 at a public elementary school (Coats & Feldman, 1995). Children's effectiveness in posing and spontaneously encoding five emotions (anger, disgust, fear, happiness, and sadness) was investigated. In order to record posed expressions, children sat in front of a camera and simply tried to look as if they were feeling each emotion.

In order to record spontaneous expressions, children's faces were recorded with a hidden camera as they viewed emotional scenes from movies that had been selected to elicit one of the five emotions under investigation. As a manipulation check, participants were asked to indicate after watching each scene what emotion it made them feel. This check indicated that our movies were effective in eliciting four of the five intended emotions but were not effective in eliciting anger. After watching the movies selected to elicit anger, nearly a third of the participants reported feeling an unintended emotion. We therefore dropped anger from our analysis, leaving two TV-frequent emotions (happiness and sadness) and two TV-infrequent emotions (disgust and fear).

To create discrete posed expressions, 5-second segments were excerpted from the camera's recording of participants' attempts to feign each emotion. To create discrete spontaneous expressions, 5-second segments were excerpted from the camera's recording as participants viewed the most emotional scene of the stimulus film clips. (The decision about what scene was the most emotional was made a priori and was the same for all participants.) To evaluate both types of expressions, college-student judges viewed each and tried to identify which of the five emotions under investigation it represented. The percentage of judges who correctly identified which emotion a facial expression represented constituted our measure of that expression's effectiveness. This procedure resulted in eight encoding scores for each participant (4 emotions $\times$ 2 types of encoding).

To measure children's television viewing habits, we called participants every evening for seven days and asked them what shows they had watched the previous day. This information was collected for all participants during the same 7-day period. Participants were divided by a median split of the number of hours spent watching television into an infrequent-viewing group (10 hours or less per week, $M = 6$ hours) and a frequent-viewing group (10.5 hours or more per week, $M = 19$ hours).

The results of this study supported both hypotheses. First, as shown in Table 6.1, compared with infrequent viewers, frequent viewers' spontaneous expressions were more effective (37% vs. 34%), yet their posed expressions were less effective (64% vs. 70%), resulting in a significant TV-viewing by type-of-encoding interaction, $F(1,39) = 4.00$, $p = .052$. Second, as also shown in Table 6.1, frequent viewers were better able to encode those emotions seen commonly on television, but not emotions seen uncommonly, resulting in a significant TV-viewing by type-of-emotion interaction, $F(1,39) = 5.57$, $p < .025$.

These results suggest that television's effect on encoding is similar

Table 6.1. *Encoding effectiveness of infrequent and frequent TV viewers by type of encoding and type of emotion*

|  | Level of TV-Viewing | |
| --- | --- | --- |
| Type of Encoding | Frequent | Infrequent |
| Spontaneous | 37% | 34% |
| Posed | 64% | 70% |
| Type of Emotion | | |
| TV-Common (Happy/Sad) | 57% | 51% |
| TV-Uncommon (Disgust/Fear) | 44% | 53% |

to the effect of growing up in an expressive home environment. This raises the possibility that family expressiveness affects both television viewing and encoding. If family expressiveness and television viewing are strongly correlated, it could be argued that measuring television viewing is simply another way to measure family expressiveness. In this case, the import of our research would be greatly reduced.

To examine this possibility, we asked each participant's parents to complete the Family Expressiveness Questionnaire (Halberstadt, 1986). The bivariate correlation between scores on the FEQ and television viewing did not approach significance, $r(59) = .13, p > .25$. Further, our analyses included family expressiveness as an additional grouping variable. Thus, encoding's relationship with family expressiveness was accounted for and statistically independent of its relationship with television viewing. If television viewing were merely a rough estimate of family expressiveness, then including the better measure of FEQ would have eliminated the apparent association between television and expressive behavior. It does not appear that the relation between television viewing and encoding is an artifact caused by family expressiveness.

*Television and Decoding*

When considering the potential influence of television on children's ability to decode facial expressions, three qualities of televised emotional expressions seemed relevant. First, faces on television are exaggerated prototypes of how people in our culture express emotions nonverbally. If each facial expression represents a decoding problem to be solved, the problems that television presents are relatively easy. Second, characters on television almost always display emotional expressions that are consistent with their presumed emotional state. Thus, viewers are told when a character is "feeling" some emotion through the situational context and are then shown a prototypical expression of that emotion on the character's face. In other words, each of the decoding problems that television presents comes with the equivalent of an answer key. Finally, television gives viewers these easy decoding problems at a rate of some 200 per hour. It seems likely that these qualities of television would make it an excellent, if inadvertent, tool for teaching young children how to decode emotional facial expressions.

An example may help to show how television's portrayal of emotional scenes differs from more real-life situations. Imagine that a young girl named Andrea is watching as her friend, a young boy named David, works on a math problem at the front of a classroom. When the teacher announces that David has made a mistake, some children in the class laugh at his public embarrassment. Andrea looks at her friend to try to see how he is feeling.

Compare how this situation might unfold in a real classroom and on television. If this scenario occurred in a real classroom, Andrea would be faced with several difficulties in trying to understand David's feelings. Aware that others are watching him, David will likely try not to show an embarrassed expression. And after Andrea makes a decision about David's feelings, she will probably never know if it was correct. Even if she asks David what he was feeling, he may not answer honestly. Without corrective feedback, any erroneous beliefs she holds about the faces of embarrassed people will go uncorrected.

If Andrea had instead seen this scenario on her favorite television program, she would have had an easier time. David's reaction would likely have been an exaggerated prototype of embarrassment. Further, the story line of the program would likely have included definitive information that he had indeed been embarrassed by the event. Thus, even if Andrea had never seen an embarrassed expression before, she would understand its connotations in the current situation.

Some empirical support for the hypothesis that children who watch television frequently should be better nonverbal decoders can be found in the literature on family expressiveness. As mentioned earlier, young children whose mothers are highly expressive have been found

Table 6.2. *Decoding ability by grade and TV-viewing*

| Grade in School | Percent correct |
| --- | --- |
| Second | 61 |
| Third | 66 |
| Fourth | 70 |
| Fifth | 69 |
| Sixth | 73 |
| Frequency of TV-Viewing | |
| Low | 65 |
| Medium | 68 |
| High | 70 |

to be more knowledgeable of display rules (Denham & Couchoud, 1988) and to be better nonverbal decoders (Daly, Abramovitch, & Pliner, 1980). It therefore seems likely that frequent viewers would similarly be better nonverbal decoders.

To test this hypothesis, we examined the decoding ability and television-viewing habits of 66 children enrolled in grades 2 through 6 at a public elementary school (Feldman, Coats, & Spielman, 1996; Study 2). We employed a standardized decoding procedure in which 20 facial expressions were presented to participants on a videotape at the rate of 4 per minute. These expressions had been previously recorded as two male and two female college students experienced five different emotions. After viewing each expression, participants selected which of the five possible emotions they believed it portrayed. The percentage of facial expressions that participants correctly identified constituted our measure of their decoding ability.

To measure television viewing we used the same television log format described earlier. On the basis of this log, children were divided into three TV-viewing groups: low frequency (7 hours or less per week, $M = 4.5$ hours), medium frequency (7.5 to 14 hours per week, $M = 10$ hours), and high frequency (14.5 hours or more per week, $M = 22.8$ hours).

The results of this study showed that both grade in school and viewing habits predicted decoding ability. The means presented in the top of Table 6.2 show that older children were better decoders, $F(4,51) = 2.69$, $p < .05$. This finding is consistent with previous research showing that the ability to decode facial expressions improves with age and, presumably, experience (e.g., Morency & Krauss, 1982; Philippot & Feldman, 1990).

More importantly for the current discussion, the means presented in the bottom of Table 6.2 show that children who watched more television were better decoders, $F(2,51) = 4.55$, $p < .05$. Once again, family expressiveness was measured using the FEQ and used as an additional grouping variable. Thus the relation between television viewing and decoding is statistically independent of the relationship between family expressiveness and decoding. In this study, only the former was significant.

*Television and Display Rules*

Thus far we have talked about encoding and decoding as abilities, something that all people do but with different levels of skill. However, being nonverbally skilled requires more than knowing how to communicate emotional information via nonverbal channels, it also requires knowing *when* to communicate *what* information.

For example, imagine a young child opening presents at her birthday party. Upon opening the gift from her favorite uncle, she is disappointed to see that he has bought her an unwanted toy. The uncle looks at his niece to see her reaction, and she is aware of his gaze. What should she do? Should she show her genuinely felt disappointment, or should she mask her feelings with a socially appropriate smile? Social life is full of situations like this – times when showing our feelings might hinder a social goal (e.g., not to hurt a favorite uncle's feelings). In order to navigate the social waters successfully, children must learn that facial expressions reflect social norms as well as felt emotions (see Saarni and Weber in this volume).

Characters on television often seem unaware of the need for nonverbal dissemblance. Our analysis indicated television characters generally show their "felt" emotions. If frequent viewers adopt this spontaneous style of expressivity, their responses to nonverbal dilemmas should differ from those of infrequent viewers. Specifically, frequent viewers should be more likely to advocate showing true feelings even when doing so would violate a social norm. Frequent viewers may also hold relatively simplistic views about the relationship between the experience and expression of emotions, whereas infrequent viewers may hold more complex views.

Table 6.3. *Categorization of display rules among light, moderate, and heavy television viewers*

| Display Rule Categorization | Frequency of TV-Viewing | | |
|---|---|---|---|
| | Low | Medium | High |
| Simple | 7 | 9 | 13 |
| Complex | 7 | 4 | 0 |

In order to test these hypotheses, we examined the relationship between television viewing and display rules of dissemblance (Feldman, Coats, & Spielman, 1996; Study 1). Forty children enrolled in the sixth grade at a public middle school participated. After completing a display rule procedure, their viewing habits were recorded in the same television-log format described earlier. On the basis of this log, children were divided into three TV-viewing groups: low frequency (17 hours or less per week, $M = 11.2$), medium frequency (17.5 to 29 hours per week, $M = 23.5$), and high frequency (29.5 hours or more per week, $M = 38.8$).

To study children's beliefs about nonverbal dissemblance, we employed a task developed by Saarni (1979). In this task, participants are presented with four photo-accompanied stories depicting a protagonist in a nonverbal dilemma. In stories such as the disappointing birthday gift story described above, protagonists are seen in situations in which showing one's true emotions would conflict with some social goal. In the final photo of each story, depicting the denouement, the protagonist's face cannot be seen. Participants' first task was to select from among three photographs what the protagonist's face would likely display (e.g., a disappointed or a happy expression). Participants' second task was to answer a series of questions about their choice.

To assess the complexity of participants' knowledge of nonverbal dissemblance, their responses to the following questions were categorized as being either simple or complex: "Would people suspect that he/she was not showing his/her true emotions?" and "What would happen if someone did suspect?" Responses that were single answers – such as "No, people will not suspect" or "Yes, people will suspect"

– were coded as simple. Responses that considered multiple factors or reported more than one specific possible outcome – such as "They might suspect if she is not good at hiding her feelings, but if she is good at it then maybe no one would suspect" – were coded as complex.

The results of this study supported only one of the two experimental hypotheses. When asked to select the photograph showing protagonists' most likely facial display, all 40 children picked the "masking" photo that displayed the socially appropriate response. It appears that all children have by the sixth grade learned the necessity of masking emotions, at least in the specific situations depicted in our investigation.

However, support was found for the second hypothesis. As expected, frequent viewers were the most likely to give simple explanations for the protagonists' behavior, whereas infrequent viewers were the most likely to give complex explanations. As shown in Table 6.3, all children in the highest viewing group gave simple explanations for how the protagonist might respond. In contrast, children in the lowest viewing group were equally likely to give complex and simple answers. Children in the moderate group fell in between. A chi-square showed that children in the three TV-viewing groups were not equally likely to give simple versus complex explanations, $X^2(2) = 8.56$, $p < .025$.

*Summary*

We began by identifying three aspects of television's depiction of nonverbal emotionality that are somewhat unrealistic (i.e., unlike nonverbal emotionality in the real world): the high rate of displays, the limited range of emotions displayed, and the simplified relation between emotional experience and expression. In a series of subsequent studies, these qualities where shown to be associated with children's understanding and use of nonverbal behavior. Compared with children who watched television only infrequently, children who watched frequently – who watched as much as 40 hours per week or more – exhibited different nonverbal strengths and weaknesses.

With respect to encoding, frequent viewers were more expressive when genuinely experiencing emotions but less expressive when trying to pose an emotion. Further, unlike infrequent viewers, frequent viewers were better able to encode emotions common on television (happiness and sadness) than emotions uncommon on television (fear and disgust).

With respect to decoding, frequent viewers were better than infrequent viewers at decoding others' facial expressions. The ability to decode nonverbal expressions is a skill that requires practice (Rosenthal, Hall, DiMatteo, Rogers, & Archer, 1979). Whatever else television may do, by bombarding young viewers with 200 emotional expressions each hour, it certainly gives them ample opportunity to practice decoding.

With respect to display rules, frequent viewers appear to share television's oversimplified view of the relationship between the experience and expression of emotion. Nonverbal dissemblance does not appear as a theme in the modal television show. Consequently, children whose primary source of information about nonverbal behavior is learned from television do not appear to fully appreciate the complexities of emotional dissemblance.

## Comparison of Influences

In this section, we address themes that research on television, family, and peer influence share in common. Observing similar effects in different areas of investigation should provide important clues into the more general principles of socialization.

### Impact of Highly Expressive Models on Encoding

Research on the development of posed and spontaneous encoding abilities has shown an interesting interaction with age. Compared with younger children, older children's spontaneous expressions are less effective (i.e., are harder to read) but their posed expressions are more effective (Feldman, Jenkins, & Popoola, 1979; Shennum & Bugental, 1982). This pattern suggests that older children are more engaged in active regulation of their nonverbal displays. This increases the communication effectiveness of conscious attempts to pose emotions but decreases the effectiveness of spontaneous expressions. It thus appears that as children grow up in our culture, they become aware of the need to self-regulate nonverbal displays.

It now appears that this message of self-regulation is not uniformly socialized in all children. Some children are more encouraged to express their genuine emotions. These children become more effective spontaneous encoders but less effective posed encoders. One such group of expressive children are those raised in highly expressive families. Such children are better spontaneous encoders but worse posed encoders (Halberstadt, 1986). Similarly, children who watch a great deal of television – which is likely more expressive than even the most expressive families – are also better spontaneous encoders but worse posed encoders (Coats & Feldman, 1995).

### Impact of Highly Expressive Models on Decoding

Our finding that children exposed to highly expressive models on television are better decoders (Feldman, Coats, & Spielman, 1996) is consistent with research on the decoding ability of children raised in highly expressive families (e.g., Daly, Abramovitch, & Pliner, 1980). Yet these results appear inconsistent with the finding that college students from highly expressive families are worse decoders than college students from less expressive families (Halberstadt, 1983; 1984).

Two explanations for the interaction between age and exposure to expressive models are possible, one motivational and one cognitive. Both assume that children exposed to highly expressive models of emotional display initially get more practice decoding facial expressions and so are initially better skilled. It is possible that the initial difficulties faced by children raised in an unexpressive environment would motivate them to work on developing this skill. Their later advantage, in this view, is due to increased motivation.

Additionally, a more straightforward learning principle may be at work. We have suggested that decoding facial expressions is similar to other problem-solving skills. Further, we have argued that highly expressive models constitute relatively easy decoding problems, whereas inexpressive models constitute relatively difficult decoding problems. When first learning how to decode, children should benefit most by working on easier problems. During childhood, the easy decoding problems presented by expressive models should serve to accelerate learning. However, as older children begin to become more proficient, more difficult problems may be needed to sharpen and hone this skill. In adulthood, the easy decoding problems presented by expressive models may not be adequate to further learning. The later advantage of people raised in low expressive environments, in this view, is the result of different learning curves.

### Impact of Highly Expressive Models on Display Rules

The display rules task we used in our study included four stories about children who were feeling some emotion but who did not want to reveal their emotions to others. In a previous study using this task with children in first, third, and fifth grade, Saarni found that older children were more likely to believe that protagonists would choose to hide their emotions. Further, when asked to explain their choices, older children gave more complex responses and spontaneously gave more reasons for their decisions (Saarni, 1979). This age effect is consistent with the developmental trend to encode spontaneous expression less effectively and posed expressions more effectively. Both suggest that children are socialized to self-regulate nonverbal displays.

Once again, it appears that children who watch large amounts of television are less responsive to the message of self-regulation. The sixth graders who participated in our study were slightly older than the oldest children in Saarni's initial study, and all believed that the stories' protagonists would choose to hide their emotions. But when asked to explain their choice, frequent viewers spontaneously gave fewer reasons for their decisions, just as younger children did in Saarni's investigation.

### Do Expressive Environments Affect Nonverbal Behavior?

One of the most difficult aspects of uncovering the processes involved in the socialization of expressive behavior is sorting out causal pathways. Because of the impossibility of manipulating socialization experiences, most of the research we have reviewed here, including our own, is correlational. Although we believe that the convergence of research on television with research on family and peer influences most strongly supports the hypothesis that exposure to highly emotional environments affects children's nonverbal behavior, other explanations cannot be ruled out.

First, it may be that some family dynamic – for example, socioeconomic status – affects children's nonverbal behavior as well as their television-viewing habits. We have attempted to identify potential family-dynamic third variables by asking our participants' parents to provide a variety of demographic information, including parents' education and occupation, family income, ethnicity, number of older and younger siblings, and (as mentioned earlier) family expressiveness. If such factors were found to correlate with television viewing, they might be responsible for the observed correlation between viewing and nonverbal behavior. Of the variables examined, only the number of older siblings was correlated with viewing, such that children with more older siblings watched television more often. Thus it is possible that having more older siblings (or some other as yet unstudied variable) causes children both to watch more television programs and also to develop a highly expressive style of nonverbal behavior.

Second, it may be that some temperamental individual difference exists that creates in some children both an expressive nonverbal style and a preference for highly expressive television programs. This type of explanation is sometimes used to argue against the causal role of television in the observed relationship between television viewing and aggression. In response to this type of argument, aggression researchers have employed longitudinal designs and time-lagged correlations in order to demonstrate temporal precedence (e.g., Eron, Huesmann, Lefkowitz, & Walder, 1972). Finding that early television viewing predicts later aggression (i.e., a tendency to watch more television precedes a tendency to behave aggressively) suggests that television viewing affects aggressive behavior. Following this tradition, we have begun a longitudinal study of television-viewing and nonverbal behavior. This project should help us identify whether television viewing habits develop before or after nonverbal behavior style. Finding that television habits develop first would strengthen the case for its causal role in the observed correlations.

Finally, it may be that intelligence, either global I.Q. or some specific subtype, may be responsible for the observed correlations between television viewing and nonverbal behavior. If amount of viewing were found to correlate negatively with intelligence, it is possible that the apparent effects of viewing were actually caused by level of intelligence. Although we would agree that some sort of intelligence does likely correlate with encoding and decoding ability, the observed pattern of results is not easily explained by intelligence alone. Recall that frequent viewers were better able to encode happiness and sadness but not as able to encode fear and disgust. Recall also that frequent viewers were better decoders but gave less complex answers in response to a display rules task. Because the nonverbal behaviors associated with frequent viewing are neither consistently better nor worse than average, intelligence alone seems insufficient to explain them. Nevertheless, the relationship between nonverbal and other cognitive abilities certainly deserves further attention.

## Emotion-Specific Expressivity

In the preceding sections we have discussed expressivity as if it were a unitary dimension. But it is clear that families and friends are not equally expressive of every emotion, and these differences can have emotion-specific effects. For example, it appears that children are more willing to express sadness if their parents demonstrate support through positive expressions (Halberstadt, Crisp, and Eaton, this volume). Our initial investigation of television indicates that it, too, is not equally expressive of all emotions (Houle & Feldman, 1991).

It seems likely, then, that the influence of any social agent would also be emotion-specific. Camras (1985) makes this argument when considering the impact of growing up in an abusive home. She suggests that the difficulty abused children have in decoding happy faces may be the result of seeing very few of them in their home.

This argument is consistent with our analysis of the encoding abilities of children who watch large amounts of television. These children are more effective encoders of happiness and sadness, emotions shown frequently on television, than of disgust and fear, emotions shown infrequently. In contrast, children who watch television less, and presumably interact with friends and family more, are equally effective encoders of both types of emotions (Coats & Feldman, 1995).

Converging evidence appears to bear out the prediction that social influences can be emotion-specific. And although it has often been useful at this early stage of research to measure emotionality more globally, researchers must remain cognizant that social influences may not have the same impact on all types of expressive behavior. An example from research on peers' influences serves as a warning.

As discussed earlier, research published in the 1970s showed that people smiled and laughed more at humorous stimuli when in the presence of a friend than when alone (e.g., Foot, Chapman, & Smith, 1977; Smith, Foot, & Chapman, 1977). Fridlund et al. (1990) extended this approach by showing that the imagined presence of a friend was sufficient to increase smiling. He concluded from this that smiling was a social signal and not the concomitant of a pleasant feeling. In part on the basis of this, Fridlund went on to argue that all facial expressions must also represent social signaling (Fridlund, 1991, 1994).

However, subsequent research has shown that the presence of a friend does not have the same influence on all expressive behavior. In two studies published later, the presence of a friend was shown to increase expressive behaviors during positive experiences but to decrease expressive behavior during negative experiences (Buck, Losow, Murphy, & Costanzo, 1992; Wagner & Smith, 1991; see Wagner and Lee in this volume for a review of more recent data that demonstrate an even more complicated relationship between the presence of others and expressiveness). This is inconsistent with Fridlund's assertion that expressive behavior is entirely a social signal. If it were, the presence of a friend would increase all signals. It may have been erroneous to assume that the presence of a friend would affect all expressive behavior in the same way. (Concerning the critique of Fridlund's stand, see also Manstead, Fischer, and Jakobs in this volume.)

## Conclusion

This research provides the first empirical evidence that children's expressive behavior is influenced by viewing television. Although some theories of emotional development have recognized that the mass media may play a role in shaping children's expressive behavior, the role suggested has often been small or poorly elaborated. This is somewhat surprising considering that social influence theories in other domains of emotion have examined the influence of television more actively. Perhaps the most researched emotional domain is anger and aggression (e.g., Averill, 1982; Berkowitz, 1993; Eron, Gentry, & Schlegel, 1994). For more than 25 years, researchers in this area have devoted considerable attention to the study of television (Donnerstein, Slaby, & Eron, 1994). We believe that this research is also important for its contribution to our growing understanding of the more general processes of socialization. In at least one respect Darwin seems to have been right – the answers to important questions about human facial expressions will likely come from observing their development in children.

### References

Ansfield, M. E., DePaulo, B. M., & Bell, K. L. (1995). Familiarity effects in nonverbal understanding: Recognizing our own facial expressions and our friends'. *Journal of Nonverbal Behavior, 19*, 135–150.

Averill, J. R. (1982). *Anger and aggression: An essay on emotion.* New York: Springer-Verlag.

Berkowitz, L. (1993). *Aggression: Its causes, consequences, and control.* New York: McGraw-Hill.

Buck, R., Losow, J. I., Murphy, M. M., & Costanzo, P. (1992). Social facilitation and inhibition of emotional expression and communication. *Journal of Personality and Social Psychology, 63,* 962–968.

Burgess, R., & Conger, R. (1978). Family interaction in abusive, neglectful, and normal families. *Child Development, 49,* 1163–1173.

Cacioppo, J. T., Uchino, B. N., Crites, S. L., Snydersmith, M. A., Smith, G., Berntson, G. G., & Lang, P. J. (1992). Relationship between facial expressiveness and sympathetic activation in emotion: A critical review, with emphasis on modeling underlying mechanisms and individual differences. *Journal of Personality and Social Psychology, 62,* 110–128.

Camras, L. A. (1977). Facial expressions used by children in conflict situations. *Child Development, 48,* 1431–1435.

Camras, L. A. (1985). Socialization of affect communication. In M. Lewis and C. Saarni (Eds.), *The socialization of emotions* (pp. 141–160). New York: Plenum.

Camras, L. A., Grow, G., & Ribordy, S. C. (1983). Recognition of emotional expressions by abused children. *Journal of Clinical and Child Psychology, 12,* 325–328.

Coats, E. J., & Feldman, R. S. (1994, August). *Nonverbal expressions of emotion in naturalistic and media settings.* Paper presented at the meeting of the American Psychological Association, Los Angeles.

Coats, E. J., & Feldman, R. S. (1995). The role of television in the socialization of nonverbal behavioral skills. *Basic and Applied Social Psychology, 17,* 327–341.

Coats, E. J., & Feldman, R. S. (1996). Gender differences in nonverbal correlates of social status. *Personality and Social Psychology Bulletin, 22,* 1014–1022.

Coats, E. J., & Feldman, R. S. (1997). Nonverbal expressions of emotion in the "real world." Manuscript in preparation.

Collins, W. A. (1983). Interpretation and inference in children's television. In J. Bryant & D. R. Anderson (Eds.), *Children's understanding of television.* New York: Academic Press.

Custrini, R., & Feldman, R. S., (1989). Children's social competence and nonverbal encoding and decoding of emotion. *Journal of Child Clinical Psychology, 18,* 336–243.

Daly, E. M., Abramovitch, R., & Pliner, P. (1980). The relationship between mothers' encoding and their children's decoding of facial expressions. *Merrill-Palmer Quarterly, 26,* 25–33.

Denham, S. A., & Couchoud, E. A. (1988, March). Knowledge about emotions: Relations with socialization and social behavior. In J. Gnepp (Chair), *Emotion knowledge and emotional development.* Symposium conducted at the meeting of the Conference on Human Development, Charleston, SC.

Darwin, C. (1872). *The expression of the emotions in man and animals.* London: Murray.

DePaulo, B. M. (1991). Nonverbal behavior and self-presentation: A developmental perspective. In R. S. Feldman & B. Rimé (Eds.), *Fundamentals of nonverbal behavior* (pp. 351–400). Cambridge: Cambridge University Press.

DePaulo, B. M. (1992). Nonverbal behavior and self-presentation. *Psychological Bulletin, 111*, 203–243.

Donnerstein, E., Slaby, R. G., & Eron, L. D. (1994). The mass media and youth aggression. In L. D. Eron, J. H. Gentry, & P. Schlegel (Eds.), *Reason to hope: A psychosocial perspective on violence and youth* (pp. 219–250). Washington, DC: American Psychological Association.

Dorr, A. (1985). Contexts for experience with emotion, with special attention to television. In M. Lewis and C. Saarni (Eds.), *The socialization of emotions* (pp. 55–88). New York: Plenum.

Edwards, R., Manstead, A. S. R., & MacDonald, C. J. (1987). The relationship between children's sociometric status and ability to recognize facial expressions of emotion. *European Journal of Social Psychology, 14*, 235–238.

Ekman, P., & Friesen, W. V. (1971). Constants across cultures in the face and emotion. *Journal of Personality and Social Psychology, 17*, 124–129.

Eron, L. D., Gentry, J. H., & Schlegel, P. (1994). *Reason to hope: A psychosocial perspective on violence and youth.* Washington, DC: American Psychological Association.

Eron, L. D., Huesmann, L. R., Lefkowitz, M. M., & Walder, L. O. (1972). Does television cause aggression? *American Psychologist, 27*, 253–263.

Feldman, R. S., Coats, E. J., & Spielman, D. A. (1996). Television exposure and children's decoding of nonverbal behavior. *Journal of Applied Social Psychology, 26*, 1718–1733.

Feldman, R. S., Jenkins, L., & Popoola, O. (1979). Detection of deception in adults and children via facial expressions. *Child Development, 50*, 350–355.

Feldman, R. S., Philippot, P., & Custrini, R. (1991). Social competence and nonverbal behavior. In R. S. Feldman & B. Rimé (Eds.), *Fundamentals of nonverbal behavior* (pp. 329–350). Cambridge: Cambridge University Press.

Field, T. (1982). Individual differences in the expressivity of neonates and young infants. In R. S. Feldman (Ed.), *Development of nonverbal behavior in children* (pp. 279–298). New York: Springer-Verlag.

Foot, H. C., Chapman, A. J., & Smith, J. R. (1977). Friendship and social responsiveness in boys and girls. *Journal of Personality and Social Psychology, 35*, 401–411.

Fridlund, A. J. (1991). Sociality of solitary smiling: Potentiation by an implicit audience. *Journal of Personality and Social Psychology, 60*, 229–240.

Fridlund, A. J. (1994). *Human facial expression: An evolutionary view.* San Diego, CA: Academic Press.

Fridlund, A. J., Sabini, J. P., Hedlund, L. E., Schaut, J. A., Shenker, J. I., & Knauer, M. J. (1990). Audience effects on solitary faces during imagery: Displaying to the people in your head. *Journal of Nonverbal Behavior, 14*, 113–137.

Gerbner, G., Gross, L., Morgan, M., & Signorielli, N. (1986). Living with television: The dynamics of the cultivation process. In J. Bryant & D. Zillmann (Eds.), *Perspectives on media effects* (pp. 17–40). Hillsdale, NJ: Lawrence Erlbaum.

Halberstadt, A. G. (1983). Family expressiveness styles and nonverbal communication skills. *Journal of Nonverbal Behavior, 88*, 258–261.

Halberstadt, A. G. (1984). Family expression of emotion. In C. Z. Malatesta & C. E. Izard (Eds.), *Emotion in adult development* (pp. 235–252). Beverly Hills, CA: Sage.

Halberstadt, A. G. (1986). Family socialization of emotional expression and nonverbal communication styles and skills. *Journal of Personality and Social Psychology, 51*, 827–836.

Halberstadt, A. G. (1991). Toward an ecology of expressiveness. In R. S. Feldman and B. Rimé (Eds.), *Fundamentals of nonverbal behavior* (pp. 106–160). Cambridge: Cambridge University Press.

Houle, R., & Feldman, R. S. (1991). Emotional displays in children's television programming. *Journal of Nonverbal Behavior, 15*, 261–271.

Larson, R., & Csikszentmihalyi, M. (1983). The experience sampling method. In H. T. Reis (Ed.), *Naturalistic approaches to studying social interactions*. San Francisco: Jossey-Bass.

Liebert, R. M., & Sprafkin, J. (1988). *The early window: Effects of television on children and youth* (3rd ed.). New York: Pergamon.

Manstead, A. S. R. (1991). Expressiveness as an individual difference. In R. S. Feldman and B. Rimé (Eds.), *Fundamentals of nonverbal behavior* (pp. 329–350). Cambridge: Cambridge University Press.

Michalson, L., & Lewis, M. (1985). What do children know about emotions and when do they know it? In M. Lewis and C. Saarni (Eds.), *The socialization of emotions* (pp. 117–140). New York: Plenum.

Morency, N. L., & Krauss, R. M. (1982). Children's nonverbal encoding and decoding of affect. In R. S. Feldman (Ed.), *Development of nonverbal behavior in children*. New York: Springer-Verlag.

Noble, G. (1983). Social learning from everyday television. In M. Howe (Ed.), *Learning from television*. New York: Academic Press.

Philippot, P. & Feldman, R. S. (1990). Age and social competence in preschoolers' decoding of facial expressions. *British Journal of Social Psychology, 29*, 43–54.

Potter, W. J., & Chang, I. J. (1990). Television exposure measures and the cultivation hypothesis. *Journal of Broadcasting and Electronic Media, 34*, 313–333.

Rosenthal, R., Hall, J. A., DiMatteo, M. R., Rogers, P. L., & Archer, D. (1979). *Sensitivity to nonverbal communication: The PONS test*. Baltimore, MD: Johns Hopkins University Press.

Rule, B. G., & Ferguson, T. J. (1986). The effects of media violence on attitudes, emotions, and cognitions. *Journal of Social Issues, 42*, 29–50.

Saarni, C. (1979). Children's understanding of display rules for expressive behavior. *Developmental Psychology, 15*, 424–429.

Saarni, C. (1982). Social and affective functions of nonverbal behavior: Developmental concerns. In R. Feldman (Ed.), *Development of nonverbal behavior in children* (pp. 123–147). New York: Springer-Verlag.

Saarni, C. (1985). Indirect processes in affect socialization. In M. Lewis and C. Saarni (Eds.), *The socialization of emotions* (pp. 187–212). New York: Plenum.

Saarni, C., & Borg, V. (1990). *Television's influence on children's understanding of emotions and social control.* Unpublished manuscript. Sonoma State University, California.

Sabatelli, R. M., & Rubin, M. (1986). Nonverbal expressiveness and physical attractiveness as mediators of interpersonal perceptions. *Journal of Nonverbal Behavior, 10,* 120–133.

Shennum, W., & Bugental, D. (1982). The development of control over affective expression in nonverbal behavior. In R. Feldman (Ed.), *Development of nonverbal behavior in children* (pp. 101–122). New York: Springer-Verlag.

Signorielli, N. (1991). *A sourcebook on children and television.* New York: Greenwood Press.

Smith, J. R., Foot, H. C., & Chapman, A. J. (1977). Nonverbal communication among friends and strangers sharing humor. In A. J. Chapman & H. C. Foot (Eds.), *It's a funny thing humor.* Oxford: Pergamon.

Spence, S. H. (1987). The relationship between social-cognitive skills and peer sociometric status. *British Journal of Developmental Psychology, 5,* 347–356.

Wagner, H. L., & Smith, J. (1991). Facial expression in the presence of friends and strangers. *Journal of Nonverbal Behavior, 15,* 201–214.

Wood, W., Wong, F. Y., & Chachere, J. G. (1991). Effects of media violence on viewers' aggression in unconstrained social interaction. *Psychological Bulletin, 109,* 371–383.

Zillmann, D. (1991). Empathy: Affect from bearing witness to the emotions of others. In J. Bryant and D. Zillmann (Eds.), *Responding to the screen: Reception and reaction processes.* Hillsdale, N.J.: Lawrence Erlbaum.

# 7. Group Membership and the Decoding of Nonverbal Behavior

GILLES KIROUAC AND URSULA HESS

## Objectives

Imagine you see someone spill red wine over someone's expensive pair of white pants. What does the "victim" feel? Anger, chagrin, sadness? The research on display rules presented by Saarni and Weber (chapter 4 in this volume) suggests that the type and intensity of the emotion display depends on whether the person is male or female, which culture they belong to, whether they are interacting with friends or strangers, and what type of hierarchical relationship the two interaction partners have. In short, the social group membership of the two protagonists will influence the emotion displays. The goal of the present chapter is to show that the interaction partners' social group membership influences not only the *display* of emotion but also the *decoding* of these displays. In other words, whether you will interpret the victim's reaction to the ruined pants as anger or sadness may depend on whether the victim is male or female, on the culture to which both you and the victim belong, and on the type of relationship between the two people you observe. That is, emotion display rules are complemented by emotion decoding rules. Specifically, we argue that knowledge regarding a sender's social group membership and the associated stereotypical knowledge regarding the norms regulating the emotion displays of members of this group influence the attribution of emotions.

Preparation of this chapter was supported in part by a grant to the authors from the Conseil de Recherche en Science Humaine. We would like to thank the volume editors for helpful suggestions on previous drafts of this chapter.

## Introduction

The exchange of emotional information in human interactions serves not only to inform interaction partners of each other's emotional state but also to regulate aspects of the social relationship such as intimacy or status (e.g., Steimer-Krause, Krause, & Wagner, 1990). On one hand, appraisal theories of emotion emphasize the importance of the social construal of the emotion eliciting event (e.g., Frijda, 1986; Frijda, Kuipers, & ter Shure, 1989). On the other hand, the expression of emotions in a given social context provides information regarding certain aspects of the social relationship of the interaction partners such as relative power (Frijda & Mesquita, 1994). Thus, elements of the social situation are both constituent elements of emotion experiences and important sources of information regarding the interpretation of emotion expressions in a particular context. That is, the interpretation of emotion expressions can be modulated depending on the social relationship between the sender and the receiver. One important element of the social relationship between interaction partners is the social group they belong to, in particular, the social role expectations associated with being a member of a particular group defined by such salient characteristics as social power, sex, or cultural background.

In the context of this chapter, we want to focus on this particular aspect and its influence on the decoding of emotional messages. In particular we argue that norms regarding the appropriateness of displaying certain emotions in certain contexts influence not only the encoding of emotions but also the decoding. Specifically, we argue that knowledge regarding a sender's social group membership and the associated stereotypical knowledge regarding the norms regulating the emotion displays of members of this group influence the attribution of emotions.

The first part of the chapter presents the theoretical framework that underlies our reflections and discusses the role of emotion displays in human interactions. The second part briefly summarizes some findings on emotion norms as well as their influences on the *encoding* of emotions. Finally, the last section summarizes the relatively scarce literature on the issue of the influences of group membership on the *decoding* of emotions and outlines the importance of future research.

## Theoretical Framework

Before going on to discuss the influence of group membership on the decoding of emotional messages, it is useful to present in more detail some of the theoretical underpinnings from which we attempt to understand the decoding process and the influence of social context variables on this process.

### Emotion Displays: Signals, Symptoms, or Both?

Generally, emotion displays have been interpreted as symptoms of an underlying emotional state (e.g., Buck, 1984; Ekman, 1984; Frijda, 1986). The notion that emotional expressions reflect an underlying emotional state and have evolved through adaptive value has been supported by findings regarding the similarities between human and nonhuman emotional facial expressions already described by Darwin (1872) and, more recently, by Chevalier-Skolnikoff (1973) and by Redican (1982) who compared the expressions of human and nonhuman primates. Findings that chimpanzees react differentially to different human expressions (Itakura, 1994) and that human children's ability to interpret monkey vocalizations of aggression, fear, dominance, positive emotions, and submission develops simultaneously with their ability to interpret human emotional behavior (Linnankoski, Laasko, & Leinonen, 1994) also suggest similarities between the expressions of human and nonhuman primates. Further, specific facial displays can be linked to self-reports of specific affective states (e.g., Cacioppo, Petty, Losch, & Kim, 1986; Pope & Smith, 1994; Rosenberg & Ekman, 1994). Similarly, vocal expressions have been linked to emotional states. For example, Banse and Scherer (1996) could show that vocal parameters index the valence and intensity for different emotions.

Yet, the relationship between emotion displays and the emotional state experienced by the sender has been questioned (e.g., Fridlund, 1991) by a view maintaining that because emotional expressions serve an obvious communicative function and can be shown to be modified by the presence of others, the notion that emotion displays serve as symptoms of an underlying emotional state becomes obsolete. In fact, Fridlund (1991) calls a view that distinguishes between spontaneous expressions, which are elicited by an underlying emotional state, and social expressions, which respond to the social demands of the situation, romanticist.

It has long been recognized, however, that spontaneous and posed expressions are extremes on a continuum which allows and demands both social and emotional influences on the display. In fact, facial emotion displays are inherently polyvalent and may be used as emblems (Ekman, 1979), as interjections (Motley, 1993), and as signals to indicate that we understand a speaker's state (Bavelas, Black, Lemery, & Mullett, 1986). It is indeed obvious that facial expressions – like most messages – may concurrently serve several purposes and this has generally been maintained by proponents of the view that emotional facial expressions are symptoms of an underlying emotional state (e.g., Buck, 1991; Cacioppo, Bush, & Tassinary, 1992; Hess, Kappas, & Banse, 1995; see also Manstead et al., chapter 11 in this volume).

Thus, the role of facial expressions as interactional signals does not negate their role as symptoms of emotional states. Rather, emotion expressions also serve to establish and maintain aspects of relationships between interaction partners. For example, facial expressions of anger also serve to communicate high dominance and low affiliation while expressions of happiness communicate both high dominance and high affiliation (Knudson, 1996). Thus, emotion displays can be considered to serve several related purposes of which the communication of emotional states is only one.

Bühler (1934) distinguished three functions of a message: the symbolic, the symptomatic, and the appeal function. The first refers to the sign content of the message and conveys information directed at the interaction partner. The second, the symptomatic function, corresponds to a readout of the individual's state. The third function regards the possible action of the interaction partner. This model (see Figure 7.1) applies equally well to emotion displays.

For example, an expression of sadness signals that the sender has experienced an irreversible loss (Lazarus, 1991). It also suggests a specific internal state of the sender that is characterized by a specific subjective feeling state, as well as by a number of physiological and behavioral concomitants; and finally, it may serve an appeal function by motivating the observer to help or to comfort.

## Social Groups and Emotion Displays

The three different functions of emotion displays described above deserve special consideration in the framework of the current discussion. First, social group membership may influence which types of

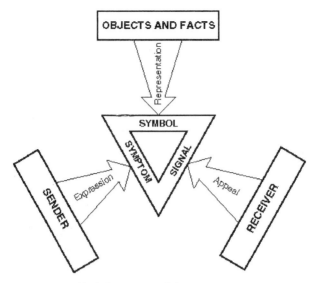

Figure 7.1. Bühler's Organon model.

events are likely to elicit a specific emotion. Social groups in the present context can be defined as members of a social category who share a common characteristic, such as men and women, members of a specific culture, members of an ingroup versus an outgroup, or people in positions of high versus low status. For example, women are more likely to react with sadness or guilt in a variety of emotion situations than men, who in turn are more likely to react with anger (see Fischer, 1993). Second, group membership influences the degree to which showing a certain emotion is appropriate to a specific context via specific display rules (see Saarni and Weber; Kupperbusch et al., chapters 4 and 2 in this volume). Third, the appeal function of certain emotion displays may vary with group membership. Specifically, certain expressive modes (e.g., crying when angry) are more permissible, and thus more likely to procure positive effects, for women than for men (Crawford, Kippax, Onyx, Gault, & Benton, 1992; see also Shields, 1987).

In sum, emotion displays in a social context serve a number of functions, each of which may to some degree depend on the real or presumed social identity of the interaction partners. Thus, knowledge of social norms regarding the display of emotions is important for selecting appropriate responses in an emotional situation (see below) as well as for interpreting the emotion displays of an interaction partner.

Consequently, the decoding of emotion displays can be based on either or both of two important sources of information: the sender's emotion displays and knowledge about the social context. However, research on these different sources of information is largely disjoint.

Regarding the first source of information, the sender's emotion displays, the facial, vocal, postural, and so forth expressions emitted by the sender can be used to draw inferences regarding the presumed emotional state of the sender using a pattern-matching approach (e.g., Buck, 1984). For example, the presence of upturned corners of the mouth and of wrinkles around the eyes can be interpreted as signaling happiness. The second source of information, the knowledge that the receiver possesses regarding both the sender and the social situation in which the interaction takes place, can take two forms. If the sender and the receiver know each other well, the receiver usually is aware of the sender's personality, beliefs, preferences, and emotional style. This knowledge permits the receiver to take the perspective of the sender and to deduce which emotional state the sender most likely is experiencing in the given situation. For example, a given expression of happiness in a very gregarious person may be interpreted as suggesting less happiness than would the same expression when shown by a person known to be very timid.

This may indeed be the most effective approach to the decoding of emotion displays in many situations (see Wiggers, 1984) and studies on emotion communication in interaction partners who know each other well, for example, in marital interactions, underline the importance of previous knowledge for emotion communication. For example, Guthrie and Noller (1988) suggest the existence of a private message system where certain emotional expressions have significance for the marital partner only.

But even when sender and receiver meet for the first time, the receiver may be able to employ stereotypical information to deduce some aspects of the sender's likely beliefs, personality, emotional style, and so forth using information on the sender's group membership. Thus, knowing that the sender is male or female or a member of a specific ethnic group may elicit knowledge regarding the display rules appropriate to the context as well as stereotypical knowledge regarding the emotional style of members of the relevant group. For example, many people share the stereotype that individuals from the northern part of a given country are less emotional than those from the southern part of the country (Pennebaker, Rimé, & Blankenship, 1996). Hence, an expression of, for example, anger, shown by a person with a northern accent may be considered to indicate a more intense emotional state than when shown by a person with a southern accent, for whom such expressions are considered to be more typical.

One aspect of social groups deserves special attention in the present context: the difference in actual or perceived power between members of different groups. This power differential has been invoked to explain why some behaviors such as the expression of anger are more allowable for members of some groups than for members of others. For example, it has been argued that many of the differences in emotion displays between men and women are due to the difference in power between these two groups (see e.g., Brody & Hall, 1993; Shields, 1987). Further, it has been suggested that certain emotion expressions such as smiling or anger displays serve to establish or maintain power differentials (e.g., Berger, Fisek, & Norman, 1989; Ridgeway & Berger, 1986; see also Henley, 1977). Also, a number of differences in cultural display rules have been suggested to be linked to differences in power structures (Markus & Kitayama, 1994). Consequently, there is some overlap in findings regarding emotion norms for some specific groups and emotion norms related to status.

In sum, emotional facial displays are polyvalent messages that can be modified by the social context of the situation. Further, the social context can be expected to modify the interpretation of a specific expression in a specific context, because context information is used as part of the process of understanding the other, allowing one to take the other's perspective in a given situation. Thus, stereotype based knowledge regarding the social group membership of the sender may be translated into decoding rules that bias the attribution of internal states to a sender. In the context of this chapter we want to emphasize, in particular, gender, culture, and social status or power, in the decoding of emotions.

In the following, we will discuss differences in emotion norms as a function of group membership. Emotion norms describe the range of acceptable behaviors for interaction partners in a particular social situation. In fact, Gallois (1994) in a recent review on emotion communication in interpersonal situations, concludes that not only are interpersonal situations involving verbal and nonverbal emotional communication, such as self-disclosure or conflict, highly rule governed but the rules are perceived as normative for the interactions. Consequently, even minor violations of emotion norms can create substantial problems for the interaction process (see also Gallois, 1993, for a discussion of this issue). Emotion norms can be considered the basis for stereotypical beliefs regarding the emotional style of members of different social groups and are an important source of information for the decoding of emotional expressions via role-taking processes.

We also present some evidence that emotion norms do, in part, translate into observable differences and hence may, within a certain range of situations, constitute valid information for the decoding of emotion displays. We will then turn to the evidence suggesting that these beliefs also influence the decoding of emotion displays. Finally, we will briefly address the converse process, that is, the inference of social group membership from emotional expressions.

## Group Membership and the Encoding of Emotional Messages

### *Culture, Emotion Norms, and Emotion Displays*

One interesting line of research regards the influence of culture on emotion norms. The notion of subjective culture (see e.g., Triandis, 1972, 1994) emphasizes elements such as shared social norms, roles, beliefs, values, communication patterns, affective styles, and so forth. Thus, cultural differences in emotion norms regarding the expression of emotions within specific types of social relationships, or to members of the ingroup versus members of outgroups, are instructive in this context. Some researchers extend the definition of culture to include gender (e.g., Tannen, 1986), and, in fact, some of the findings reported below, for example, the notion that women value emotionality more than men (Allen & Haccoun, 1976; O'Neil, Helms, Gable, David, & Wrightsman, 1986), can be understood in terms of cultural differences. However, in the context of the present chapter gender differences will be discussed separately from cultural differences.

Two lines of thinking regarding the influence of culture on emotion displays can be distinguished. On one hand, it is maintained that both emotion eliciting events and emotional feeling states are basically comparable across cultures (Wallbott & Scherer, 1986), but that the social rules regarding the adequate *display* of these states may differ

(Ekman & Friesen, 1971; Wundt, 1903; see also Kupperbusch et al., this volume). That is, it is assumed that, for example, most people would feel angry when slighted but that in some cultures or subcultures the display of this anger would be inhibited. This view is contrasted by a view that considers emotions as socially constructed and mediated by cultural knowledge. According to this view, cultures differ in how they *define* emotion-eliciting events as well as in regard to the significance of displaying a specific emotion in a specific context (see Kitayama & Markus, 1994; Wierzbicka, 1994, 1995).

There is some support for the view that basic aspects of emotion-eliciting events, or Lazarus's core relational themes (Lazarus, 1991), differ across cultures (e.g., Wierzbicka, 1995). Other evidence suggests, however, that the antecedents of emotion events are largely similar across a large number of cultures (Matsumoto, Kudoh, Scherer, & Wallbott, 1988; Mauro, Sato, & Tucker, 1992; Wallbott & Scherer, 1986). For example, Chiasson, Dubé, and Blondin (1996) found evidence that the factors contributing to happiness were largely comparable across four cultural groups from the United States, El Salvador, and Canada (English and French Canadians). Religious values and sociopolitical conditions were most important to Salvadoreans, however, whereas the North American participants emphasized hedonic factors and personal sources of power. Also, within cultures, members differ in their endorsement of the expression of a certain emotion in a certain context.

Studies on emotion norms in different cultures have generally been guided by notions regarding the influence of differences between cultures in Hofstede's (1980) four dimensions of cultural variation, specifically on the individualism versus collectivism dimension (see also, Markus & Kitayama, 1991; Triandis, 1994). For example, it has been suggested that collectivistic cultures should endorse emotion displays that foster group harmony (e.g., Matsumoto, 1991), whereas individualistic cultures may be more open to expressions of conflict (Triandis, Bontempo, Villareal, Asai, & Lucca, 1988).

Matsumoto (1990) conducted a study designed to test hypotheses regarding differences in display rules based on the difference between Americans and Japanese regarding Hofstede's individualism-collectivism and power distance dimensions. He found that American participants considered the display of disgust and sadness toward members of the outgroup, as well as of happiness in public, as more appropriate than do Japanese participants, who in turn rated the display of anger to members of the outgroup and to lower-status individuals as more appropriate. Also, W. Stephan, C. Stephan, and de Vargas (1996) report evidence that participants from Costa Rica, a collectivistic culture, expect to feel equally comfortable expressing emotions to both ingroup and outgroup members, whereas participants from the United States, an individualistic culture, expect to feel more comfortable expressing emotions to family members than to strangers.

Further, a number of studies have been concerned with the norms governing emotion expression in social relationships and have compared these rules across more or less individualistic cultures. Argyle (1986) asked subjects to rate for each of 22 types of social relationships (e.g., living together, work colleague, repairmen) to what degree each of 32 rules (e.g., "Should not use swear words in the presence of the other person") were important to this relationship. Strong similarities in rules for maintaining relationships across Hong Kong, Japan, Italy, and Britain were found. However, some differences emerged. With regard to rules for emotional expressiveness, Argyle found that Japanese subjects endorsed rules for restraining emotional expressiveness (e.g., "Should not show anger in front of the other person") for a larger number of relationship types than did members of Western cultures. Italian subjects, on the other hand, tended to endorse rules prescribing emotional expressiveness for a larger number of relationships.

K. Aune and R. Aune (1996) studied self-reports of experiencing and expressing emotions, as well as of the appropriateness of emotion expression in romantic relationships for Euro, Filipino, and Japanese Americans. Regarding the appropriateness of expressing emotions, cultural differences emerged with Japanese Americans rating the expression of emotions in romantic relationships as least appropriate, followed by Euro Americans, and Filipino Americans. They also found differences in self-reports of experiencing and expressing emotions that were consistent with the findings on the appropriateness of expressing emotions in romantic relationships for Euro, Filipino, and Japanese Americans. That such norms develop over time is illustrated by an interesting study. Cancian and Gordon (1988) used qualitative analysis to study the change in marital advice in women's magazines in the United States from 1900 to 1979. Their findings suggest that emotion norms have changed over time toward equating love with self-fulfillment and to advocate the expression of anger.

In summary, a number of studies from different research domains converge to the conclusion that norms and beliefs regarding the appropriateness of displaying emotions in social relationships differ in different cultures.


### Gender and Emotion Norms

In general, women are believed to be more emotional than men (Fischer, 1993). Numerous studies show that women are believed to show more happiness, sadness, fear, and guilt, whereas men are believed to show more anger (see Brody & Hall, 1993; Fischer, 1993 for a review). Hess, Senécal, Kirouac, Philippot, and Kleck (1997) asked subjects to read four stories for each of seven emotions and to indicate the percentage of men and women who would react with each of nine emotions to the situation described in the story. Across all six negative emotions more women than men were expected to react with sadness, shame, and guilt.

Further, women tend to value and accept emotions more than men (e.g., Allen & Haccoun, 1976; O'Neil et al., 1986; Shields, 1987). In fact, some evidence suggests that the male gender-role devalues emotional expressivity (O'Neil et al., 1986; Shields, 1987).

Also, differences regarding the appropriateness of certain expressive modes for men and women have been found. For example, crying when angry is more permissible for women than for men. In general, women are seen as more likable when expressing emotions than men (Fischer, 1993; Shields, 1987).[1] Expectations regarding differences in emotional expressivity between men and women are strong and seem to be socialized early in life as illustrated by Birnbaum (1983) who found evidence that children as young as 3 to 5 years of age report these beliefs.

Studies looking at self-reported expressiveness are largely consistent with findings on beliefs (see Fischer, 1993; Brody & Hall, 1993). As Wagner, Buck, and Winterbotham (1993) demonstrated, however, actual differences in emotional expressivity are dependent on the particular emotional stimulus, on the nature of the activity the sender is engaged in, as well as on the interpersonal situation. For example, there is some evidence that men smile more and that women express

---

[1] However, Labott, Martin, Eason, and Berkey (1991) found that a man crying while watching a sad movie was evaluated more positively than a nonemotional man, while the reverse was the case for a crying woman.

more signs of anger (Brody, 1993, cited in Brody and Hall, 1993) in mixed sex interactions than in same sex interactions. Similarly, Halberstadt and Saitta (1987), who studied smiling as a sign of low dominance, compared frequency of smiling in men and women both in media portrayals and from observations in public settings and found fewer sex differences in the latter condition. They conclude that actual differences in smiling between men and women may be rarer than previously believed. Also, based on an extensive review of the literature, Cupach and Canary (1995) conclude that whereas some consistent sex differences can be observed in conflict situations, for example, women are more likely to cry when angry, men's and women's reactions to conflict are largely similar and contingent on situational aspects.

In sum, strong beliefs regarding emotional behaviors in men and women have been documented. These beliefs are widely shared and socialized at a young age. However, actual differences between men and women may be much less pronounced and more dependent on other situational factors.

## Status and Emotion Norms

Nonverbal behavior is important in the establishment and maintenance of dominance (e.g., Henley, 1977; 1995). Some of the differences in emotion norms related to group membership have been tied to power differences. Some researchers (e.g., Shields, 1987) suggest that gender differences in emotion norms are based on power differentials and that the difference of acceptability of emotion displays for men and women reflects power differentials. For example, it has been suggested that men, like higher-status individuals in general, tend to be more likely to touch women, who are generally of lower status, than vice versa (Henley, 1995), whereas touching by women is often interpreted as sexual attraction. On the other hand, Hall and Veccia (1990) found little evidence for systematic differences in touch initiation; however, men touch women with their hands more than vice versa.

Further, some researchers suggest that the demand/withdrawal pattern observed in marital conflict situations, where a wife's demands are responded to with withdrawal by the husband (Kelley et al., 1978), can be explained in terms of the power differential between men and women. That is, husbands who tend to have more power may withdraw because they are reluctant to change this situation. In fact, Christensen and Heavey (1990) found evidence for more with-drawal by husbands when their wife wanted change and more with-drawal by wives when their husband wanted change.

A number of nonverbal behaviors have been associated with status. For example, lower-status individuals tend to initiate touch to a lesser degree and to receive more touch, show less visual dominance, and smile more (see, e.g., Henley, 1995, for a review). In this context, it has been suggested that anger displays may serve to establish or maintain power differentials. For example, Berger, Fisek, and Norman (1989) suggest that the presence of diffuse (aspects such as sex, age, or eth-nicity) or specific status characteristics in a situation creates expectan-cies regarding the acceptable behavior of the interaction partners. Ex-pressions of anger are more legitimate and are less negatively perceived when exhibited by high dominant interaction partners than when exhibited by low dominant interaction partners. In cases where status is ambiguous, for example when a low-status diffuse status cue such as female gender is combined with a high-status specific status cue such as being a medical doctor, dominance behaviors are less legitimate. Thus, an anger display by a female medical doctor should be less acceptable than an anger display by a male medical doctor.

This suggests that gender and status should interact to produce different emotion norms for high-status men than for high-status women. This indeed seems to be the case. For example, Coats and Feldman (1996) found that high-status men tend to be more expressive of anger than low-status men, whereas high-status women tend to be more expressive of happiness than low-status women.

Smiling has also been associated with status (see also LaFrance and Hecht, chapter 3 in this volume). Specifically, it has been proposed that lower-status individuals should smile more as a sign of appease-ment. Again, this hypothesis has been confirmed for men but not for women. Specifically, Deutsch (1990) found that higher-status men smile less than lower-status men, but higher-status women smile more to lower-status men and do not show differences in smiling to other groups. Similar findings were reported by Dovidio, Brown, Heltman, Ellyson, and Keating (1988), who found that subordinate men smile more, whereas no difference was found for women.

The findings presented above suggest that elements of social rela-tionships, such as intimacy, hierarchical status, and gender composi-tion, are associated with strong beliefs regarding the appropriate ex-pression of emotions by members of different groups in specific social situations. From the theoretical perspective advanced above, we expect that decoders would tend to employ knowledge regarding the appropriateness of certain emotion displays in social situations for the decoding of emotional expressions, especially in situations were the expressions are ambiguous or difficult to identify. This question will be addressed in the following section.

## Recognition of Emotion Displays

Research on the recognition of emotions from facial expressions has a long history (see Ekman, 1973). Typically, recognition of facial expressions is measured using a free-viewing judgment task for which the participant is required to indicate the appropriate emotion label by choosing a verbal response from a fixed list. Expressions are considered to be accurately recognized if the label chosen by the subjects corresponds to the label of the state that the target person aimed to express. Reviews of studies using this approach conclude that, in general, for at least some emotions such as happiness, anger, sadness, fear, disgust, contempt, and surprise, high levels of recognition accuracy are observed (e.g., Fridlund, Ekman, & Oster, 1987; Izard, 1994). Research on the development of emotion recognition ability shows that children at the age of 5 to 6 show decoding accuracies comparable to those of young adults for expressions of anger and at age 9 to 10 for anger, happiness, disgust, and surprise (Gosselin, Roberge, & Lavallée, 1995).[2]

Regarding the decoding of vocal emotion displays, reviews of the literature suggest accuracy rates that are about four to five times the rate expected by chance for emotions such as anger, fear, disgust, sadness, and happiness (see Pittam & Scherer, 1993). Interestingly, Tartter (1980; Tartter & Braun, 1994) could show that some facial expressions can be "heard," that is, the changes in the upper vocal tract caused by facial expressions such as smiling and frowning influence speech production in a reliable way and are interpreted correctly by listeners.

Social group membership should provide important information

---

[2] One should note that the majority of studies in this domain used very intense, highly prototypical facial expressions as stimulus material. These expressions are less likely to demand that the decoder take recourse to knowledge about social groups when decoding.

for the use of emotion norms when taking the perspective of the other – a key element of empathy (e.g., Hoffman, 1984) – to deduce their likely emotional state in a given situation.[3] In the following we want to summarize the limited literature concerning the influence of decoding rules on the attribution of emotions. The literature on this issue does not form a coherent body. Most of the relevant evidence stems from research on the influence of cultural norms on the attribution of emotional states. Further, the notion that status influences the decoding of emotional messages has been studied for both encoder and decoder status. This line of research overlaps with research on the effects of decoder gender on the decoding of emotional expressions, based on the notion that women are generally in positions of less power. Finally, some recent speculations on the importance of a multiculturalist approach to psychological intervention are of relevance in this context.

## Cultural Norms and the Decoding of Emotion Displays

As mentioned above, a common emotion norm in Asian countries regards the endorsement of restricted emotion expression in most social relationships. In this context, Markham and Wang (1996) point to the importance of the consistency of learning experiences. In a society that restricts the range of acceptable behaviors, more consistent learning experiences are available. This may facilitate children's ability to decode prototypical emotion expressions like those used in emotion research. In effect, in such a situation, knowledge of acceptable emotion displays eliminates choices and renders the task easier. Consistent with this view, Markham and Wang (1996) found Chinese children to be better at decoding emotional expressions of six basic emotions than Australian children, especially for a task in which children were required to either give a label or describe a situation that would elicit the emotion expression. They note that the more consistent Chinese

---

[3] The attitude that the decoder holds toward the sender's social group may also bias the decoding process. For example, there is evidence that facial expressions of people who are liked by the encoder are more accurately decoded. Gallois and Challan (1986) found that Anglo Australian subjects decoded expressions of Italian men less well than those of Anglo Australian or British men when they had access to the sound track that revealed the Italian accent. When judgments were based on the face alone, decoding of Italian men's emotion displays improved. Gallois and Challan suggest, based on the commonly held negative stereotypes regarding this group, that individuals pay less attention to the emotion displays of disliked people.

socialization practices should reduce the range of emotion interpretations for a situation compared to the range of Australian children, thus allowing a dominant correct decision to be made more easily.

The influence of rules for restricted emotion expression on the decoding of emotion displays is illustrated by a study showing that Japanese participants attribute lower intensity to expressions by both Japanese and Caucasian senders (Matsumoto & Ekman, 1989). Matsumoto and Ekman conclude that the dominant display rules lead the Japanese subjects to discount the intensity of emotion displays. Similar findings were reported by Ekman et al. (1987). In this study emotion recognition rates for facial emotion displays across cultures were high; however, some cultural differences were found. In particular, Asians rated the facial expressions of happiness, fear, and surprise shown by the non-Asian stimulus persons as less intense than did the non-Asian subjects. Also, looking at how Japanese and Australian subjects perceive each other, Pittam, Gallois, Iwawaki, and Kroonenberg (1995) found that while the same dimensional structure explained both Japanese and Australian subjects' concepts of emotion expression for eight emotions, generally, both Japanese and Australian subjects rated Japanese as less emotionally expressive.

The studies reported above focused on the intensity of the emotion attributed to the emotion display. Studies looking at decoding accuracy also found evidence for influences of culture-specific display rules. In an interesting study MacAndrew (1986) presented emotional facial expressions tachistoscopically to American and Malaysian subjects and recognition thresholds were measured. In this study, the ability to recognize anger was strongly affected by the culture and the sex of the respondents. Specifically, Malaysians required considerably longer exposure times to accurately recognize anger, a finding that the authors attribute to the strong display rules against the showing of anger in the Malaysian culture. Similarly, Matsumoto (1992) found Japanese subjects to be less accurate in recognizing anger than American subjects.

Russell, Suzuki, and Ishida (1993) compared judgments by Canadian, Greek, and Japanese participants of expressions by Caucasian actors of seven basic emotions using a free-labeling task. While ratings were largely similar across cultures, agreement on the modal response was found for 17 of the 21 sets of ratings, although some interesting differences emerged. For example, Japanese subjects were markedly less accurate in decoding fear (14% accurate versus 62% and 87% for the Canadian and Greek samples respectively). Also, Japanese incorrect responses for the happy expression suggest a wider range of interpretation of smiles than found for Greek or Canadian participants.

Comparing accuracy to decode displays by members of one's own culture versus displays by members of another culture, Shimoda, Argyle, and Ricci-Bitti (1978) found that English and Italian subjects were more accurate in decoding each other's emotion displays than in decoding the emotion displays of Japanese encoders. Also, Kilbride and Yarczower (1983) found both Zambian and American subjects to be more accurate when decoding the expressions of members from their own culture.

The studies reported above operationalize cultures as countries. However, Matsumoto (1993) pointed to the need to assess cultural differences within a country. As part of a larger study, he considered differences in decoding among members of different ethnic groups in the United States. He found, for example, that African Americans perceive greater intensity when judging emotions.

Regarding Franco and Anglo Canadians in Quebec, Hess, Senécal, and Kirouac (1996) found evidence suggesting that the perceived membership in one or the other linguistic group influenced the attribution of emotions to expressions of disgust, anger, and happiness by Franco Canadians. A somewhat different line of study investigated the influence of the perceived cultural membership of an individual on first impressions regarding emotional dispositions. In this context, research has focused on the question whether (visible or audible) differences between the encoder's and the decoder's culture influence decoding accuracy. A study focusing on the perception of emotions from vocal stimuli found that the emotions decoded from utterances by English and Russian speakers were affected by the presence of the Russian accent (Holden & Hogan, 1993). In particular, they found that English speakers tended to rate speech with a Russian accent as more angry, arrogant, and critical while no corresponding biases for Russian speakers' ratings of English accented speak was found. Senécal, Kirouac, and Hess (1997) presented short vignettes describing either an Anglo or a Franco Canadian man or women to subjects and asked them to rate the described person regarding a number of characteristics. The adjectives employed were taken from the PANAS (Watson, Clark & Tellegen, 1988) and the State-Trait Anger Expression Inventory (Spielberger, 1988). Subjects rated Francophone protagonists as showing more habitual positive affect than Anglophone protagonists.

Such biases may have important consequences in interpersonal relationships. With view to the work of therapists in a multicultural environment, it has been pointed out that lack of knowledge regarding emotion norms for members of different cultures may lead to problems in the interpretation of the affect displayed by the client on the part of the therapist. Brunel (1989) argues that therapists find it more difficult to be empathic toward members of another group, be it another ethnic group or even just a member of the opposite sex. Specifically, Brunel hypothesizes that therapists misconstrue nonverbal signals or are unable to put themselves in the place of a member of a different culture because they cannot appreciate the importance of certain events in their cultural framework and lack the cultural background knowledge regarding specific emotion norms (see also C. Hall, 1997, for a similar view regarding psychological interventions in general). However, very little research has been conducted to assess these notions.

In sum, decoding rules have been shown to influence both the intensity of emotion ratings as well as decoding accuracy. Specifically, culture-specific display rules have been shown to bias the decoding of certain emotions in certain cultures. Further, the dispositional emotionality of members of different cultural groups is evaluated differently.

*Gender*

The influence of gender on emotion recognition has been studied with regard to both encoder and decoder gender. Since the research on decoder gender largely overlaps with research on decoder status these two issues will be discussed together in the section on status.

Looking at the influence of gender stereotypes on the decoding of emotions in situations in which sender and receiver do not know each other, Hess, Blairy, and Kleck (1998) found evidence that emotional expressions are judged to express an emotion more or less intensely depending on whether the sender is a man or a woman. Specifically, male senders' expressions of disgust and sadness were judged to indicate more anger and sadness and were better recognized than were female senders' expressions of these emotions; for expressions of joy the reverse was found. Similarly, Senécal, Hess, and Kleck (1996), using drawings, found evidence that the same emotional facial expression is interpreted differently when presented with a male versus a female face outline. Also, in the study reported above, Senécal et al. (1997) found that subjects rated the female protagonists as showing more habitual negative affect. Further, it has been suggested that women's tendency to cry when angry may lead men to misinterpret the woman's anger as depression or helplessness, which in turn may lead to condescending behavior, which then further increases the woman's anger (Crawford et al., 1992).

That these biases may be socialized early is suggested by a study by Haugh, Hoffman, and Cowan (1980) showing that children 3 years of age are more likely to consider the same infant to be angry (mad) when it is labeled a boy and to be fearful (scared) when it is labeled a girl.

In sum, the available evidence suggests that differences in the interpretation of facial expressions shown by men and women may be traced to gender-based expectations of which emotion is appropriate for which gender.

### Status

The influence of status on the decoding of emotion displays has been studied both with regard to encoder and decoder status. The basic hypothesis regarding encoder status is that the display of negative affect is more appropriate for high-status encoders while low-status encoders should show more smiling. Regarding decoder status it is presumed that individuals with low power are more dependent on others and should therefore be more attentive to their emotion displays. They also obtain more advantages from correctly inferring the emotional state of high-status individuals. Some of this research overlaps with research on gender differences, since women are presumed to be generally in positions of less power.

*Encoder Status.* Most studies investigating the interpretation of nonverbal behaviors in function of the encoder status have focused on sex differences. An important line of study focuses on touch. Generally, as mentioned above, initiation of touch is more permissible for high-status than for low-status individuals. Major and Heslin (1982) summarize the literature on this issue to show that touching is viewed as more appropriate when the toucher is of higher status. However, men tend to react more negatively while women may react more positively when the toucher is of equal or ambiguous status. Similarly Storrs and Kleinke (1990) found that the status of the toucher influenced men's but not women's evaluations of the toucher.

*Decoder Status.* A number of researchers have suggested that lower-status individuals should be better decoders because of the control that higher-status individuals can exert on them. For example, it has been argued that women's higher decoding accuracy (Hall, 1978; Briton & Hall, 1995) may be explained by women's lower status. In two experiments Snodgrass (1985, 1992) assigned individuals to either a dominant (teacher/boss) or a subordinate (student/employee) role and found that status influenced decoding accuracy such that "teachers" were less accurate than "students." These findings were partially confirmed by Hall and Halberstadt (1994) who found that subordinate women employees were better decoders of a female encoder but not of a male encoder.

*Social Judgments and Decoded Affect*

Finally, not only is social group membership likely to affect the decoding of affective emotion displays but emotion displays in turn serve to communicate group membership. This issue has been most clearly addressed in the case of dominance. Social dominance influences both the encoding and the decoding of emotional expressions. Contrariwise, emotion displays serve to signal dominance. For example, Knudson (1996) found that observers inferred high dominance and high affiliation from happy faces, high dominance and low affiliation from angry faces, and low dominance from fearful faces. These findings were recently confirmed and extended by Hess, Blairy, and Kleck (1998), who found that the degree to which dominance and affiliation are inferred from different emotion displays is moderated by the sex of the expressor as well as by the ethnic origin of the expressor (Japanese or Caucasian). Similarly, a series of studies by Keating and colleagues (Keating, 1985; Keating & Bai, 1986; Keating, Mazur, & Segall, 1977) show that smiling faces are rated as less dominant than nonsmiling faces.

Looking at a different type of social group attribution, Heise (1989) suggests that lively emotion displays may moderate stigmatization based on deviant conduct. Similarly, a study by LaFrance and Hecht

(1995) suggests that individuals who smile are perceived as more trustworthy and may thus receive more leniency when committing a transgression.

More generally, higher emotional expressivity has been associated with more positive evaluations. For example, Riggio and Friedman (1986) found that men who scored higher on measures of nonverbal skill and extroversion showed more fluid expressive behavior and made better impressions on judges, whereas women who scored higher on a measure of nonverbal skill showed more facial expressiveness and created more favorable first impressions.

## Summary and Conclusions

The body of research presented above suggests that group membership has an influence on the decoding of emotion displays. These findings are clearest with regard to the influence of cultural norms and gender-specific emotion norms that bias the recognition of specific emotions in specific contexts or by members of a specific group. Specifically, these norms have been shown to bias the *intensity* of the underlying state that is attributed to a certain emotion display. Emotion norms may lead members of a culture to ascribe less intensity to displays of culturally disapproved emotion displays and to lead members of the same culture to ascribe different levels of intensity to similar emotion displays shown by men and women.

This bias may lead to failures to decode certain displays correctly, especially those of medium to low intensity. This is of specific concern since most everyday emotion expressions tend to be relatively weak and ambiguous (Motley & Camden, 1988), unlike the situation in studies on emotion recognition in which often very intense, prototypical expressions are employed as stimulus material. If social group membership influences in particular the decoding of such less intense expressions, this may have consequences for the efficacy of emotion communication between members of different social groups.

This may be of even more concern in the multicultural context of today's world. It has been argued that subordinate levels of emotion, characterized by differences in intensity, would be more likely to be culture specific. For example, different levels of fear, such as alarm, anxiety, and dread, may be more likely to reflect cultural differences (e.g., Shaver, Wu, & Schwarz, 1992; see Izard, 1994). Thus, members of different cultural groups may experience more pronounced difficulties in emotion communication as is suggested by studies using intense emotion displays as stimulus material.

Future research on these issues should address two questions in particular. First, does the influence of emotion-relevant stereotypes for members of particular groups extend to situations where the interaction partners know each other? Findings by Gaelick, Bodenhausen, and Wyer (1985) regarding the different interpretation of neutral facial expressions by men and women would suggest that it might. But more extensive research looking at a wider range of expressions in relationships not characterized by marital distress is clearly needed.

Second, the question arises whether the observed differences in the perceived intensity of emotion expression across social groups translate into differences in the attribution of emotional states (e.g., displeasure vs. irritation vs. animosity vs. anger), as well as into differences in the attribution of intentions to the sender.

## References

Allen, J. G., & Haccoun, D. M. (1976). Sex differences in emotionality: A multidimensional approach. *Human Relations, 29*, 711–722.

Argyle, M. (1986). Rules for social relationships in four cultures. *Australian Journal of Psychology, 38*, 309–318.

Aune, K. S., & Aune, R. K. (1996). Cultural differences in the self-reported experience and expression of emotions in relationships. *Journal of Cross-Cultural Psychology, 27*, 67–81.

Banse, R., & Scherer, K. R. (1996). Acoustic profiles in vocal emotion expression. *Journal of Personality and Social Psychology, 70*, 614–636.

Bavelas, J. B., Black, A., Lemery, C. R., & Mullett, J. (1986). "I show how you feel": Motor mimicry as a communicative act. *Journal of Personality and Social Psychology, 50*(2), 322–329.

Berger, J., Fisek, M. H., & Norman, R. Z. (1989). The evolution of status expectations: A theoretical extension. In J. Berger, M. Zelditch, Jr., & B. Anderson (Eds.), *Sociological theories in progress*. London: Sage.

Birnbaum, D. W. (1983). Preschoolers' stereotypes about sex differences in emotionality: A reaffirmation. *Journal of Genetic Psychology, 143*, 139–140.

Briton, N. J., & Hall, J. A. (1995). Gender-based expectancies and observer judgments of smiling. *Journal of Nonverbal Behavior, 19*, 49–65.

Brody, L. R., & Hall, J. A. (1993). Gender and emotion. In M. Lewis & J. M. Haviland (Eds.), *Handbook of emotions* (pp. 447–460). New York: Guilford Press.

Brunel, M. L. (1989). L'empathie en counseling interculturel. *Santé Mentale au Québec, 14*, 81–94.

Buck, R. (1984). *The communication of emotion*. New York: Guilford Press.

Buck, R. (1991). Social functions in facial display and communication: A reply to Chovil and others. *Journal of Nonverbal Behavior, 15*, 155–161.

Bühler, K. (1934). *Sprachtheorie*. Jena: Fischer.

Cacioppo, J. T., Bush, L. K., & Tassinary, L. G. (1992). Microexpressive facial actions as a function of affective stimuli: Replication and extension. *Personality and Social Psychology Bulletin, 18*, 515–526.

Cacioppo, J. T., Petty, R. E., Losch, M. E., & Kim, H. S. (1986). Electromyographic activity over facial muscle regions can discriminate the valence and intensity of affective reactions. *Journal of Personality and Social Psychology, 50*, 260–268.

Cancian, F. M., & Gordon, S. L. (1988). Changing emotion norms in marriage: Love and anger in U.S. women's magazines since 1900. *Gender and Society, 2*, 308–342.

Chevalier-Skolnikoff, S. (1973). Facial expression of emotion in nonhuman primates. In P. Ekman (Ed.), *Darwin and facial expression* (pp. 11–83). New York: Academic Press.

Chiasson, N., Dubé, L., & Blondin, J. P. (1996). Happiness: A look at the folk psychology of four cultural groups. *Journal of Cross-Cultural Psychology, 6*, 673–691.

Christensen, A., & Heavey, C. L. (1990). Gender and social structure in the demand/withdrawal pattern of marital conflict. *Journal of Personality and Social Psychology, 59*, 73–81.

Coats, E. J., and Feldman, R. S. (1996). Gender differences in nonverbal correlates of social status. *Personality and Social Psychology Bulletin*.

Crawford, J., Kippax, S., Onyx, J., Gault, U., & Benton, P. (1992). *Emotion and gender: Constructing meaning from memory*. London: Sage.

Cupach, W. R., & Canary, D. J. (1995). Managing conflict and anger: Investigating the sex stereotype hypothesis. In P. J. Kalbfleisch & M. J. Cody (Eds.), *Gender, power, and communication in human relationships* (pp. 233–252). Hillsdale, NJ: Lawrence Erlbaum.

Darwin, C. (1872/1965). *The expression of the emotions in man and animals*. Chicago: The University of Chicago Press. (Originally published, 1872)

Deutsch, F. M. (1990). Status, sex, and smiling: The effect of role on smiling in men and women. *Personality and Social Psychology Bulletin, 16*, 531–540.

Dovidio, J. F., Brown, C. E., Heltman, K., Ellyson, S. L., & Keating, C. F. (1988). Power displays between women and men in discussion of gender-linked tasks: A multichannel study. *Journal of Personality and Social Psychology, 55*, 580–587.

Ekman, P. (1973). *Darwin and facial expression: A century of research in review*. New York: Academic Press.

Ekman, P. (1979). About brows: Emotional and conversational signs. In K. F. M. von Cranach, W. Lepenies, & D. Ploog (Eds.), *Human ethology* (pp. 169–249). Cambridge: Cambridge University Press.

Ekman, P. (1984). Expression and the nature of emotion. In K. R. Scherer & P. Ekman (Eds.), *Approaches to emotion* (pp. 319–344). Hillsdale, NJ: Lawrence Erlbaum.

Ekman, P., & Friesen, W. V. (1971). Constants across cultures in the face and emotion. *Journal of Personality and Social Psychology, 17*, 124–129.

Ekman, P., Friesen, W. V., O'Sullivan, M., Chan, A., Diacoyanni-Tarlatzis, I., Heider, K., Krause, R., LeCompte, W. A., Pitcairn, T., Ricci-Bitti, P. E., Scherer, K., Tomita, M., & Tzavaras, A. (1987). Universals and cultural differences in the judgments of facial expressions of emotion. *Journal of Personality and Social Psychology, 53*(4), 712–717.

Fischer, A. (1993). Sex differences in emotionality: Fact or stereotype? *Feminism & Psychology, 3*, 303–318.

Fridlund, A. J. (1991). The sociality of solitary smiling: Potentiation by an implicit audience. *Journal of Personality and Social Psychology, 60*, 229–240.

Fridlund, A. J., Ekman, P., & Oster, H. (1987). Facial expressions of emotion: Review of the literature, 1970–1983. In A. W. Siegman & S. Feldstein (Eds.), *Nonverbal behavior and communication* (pp. 143–224). Hillsdale, N.J.: Lawrence Erlbaum.

Frijda, N. (1986). *The emotions*. Cambridge: Cambridge University Press.

Frijda, N. H., Kuipers, P., & ter Shure, E. (1989). Relations among emotion appraisal and emotional action readiness. *Journal of Personality and Social Psychology, 57*, 212–228.

Frijda, N. H., & Mesquita, B. (1994). The social roles and functions of emotions. In S. Kitayama & H. R. Markus (Eds.), *Emotion and culture* (pp. 51–87). Washington, DC: American Psychological Association.

Gaelick, L., Bodenhausen, G. V., & Wyer, R. S. (1985). Emotional communication in close relationships. *Journal of Personality and Social Psychology, 49*, 1246–1265.

Gallois, C. (1993). The language and communication of emotion. *American Behavioral Scientist, 36*, 309–338.

Gallois, C. (1994). Group membership, social rules, and power: A social psychological perspective on emotional communication. *Journal of Pragmatics, 22*, 301–324.

Gallois, C., & Challan, V. J. (1986). Decoding emotional messages: Influence of ethnicity, sex, message type, and channel. *Journal of Personality and Social Psychology, 51*, 755–762.

Gosselin, P., Roberge, P., & Lavallée, M. F. (1995). Le développement de la reconnaissance des expressions faciales émotionnelles du répertoire humain. *Enfance, 4*, 379–396.

Guthrie, D. M., & Noller, P. (1988). Spouses' perception of one another in emotional situations. In P. Noller & M. A. Fitzpatrick (Eds.), *Perspectives on marital interaction* (pp. 153–181). Clevedon and Philadelphia: Multilingual Matters.

Halberstadt, A. G., & Saitta, M. B. (1987). Gender, nonverbal behavior, and perceived dominance: A test of the theory. *Journal of Personality and Social Psychology, 53*, 257–272.

Hall, C. C. I. (1997). Cultural malpractice: The growing obsolescence of psychology with the changing U.S. population. *American Psychologist, 52*, 642–651.

Hall, J. A. (1978). Gender effect in decoding nonverbal cues. *Psychological Bulletin, 85*, 845–857.

Hall, J. A., & Halberstadt, A. G. (1994). "Subordination" and sensitivity to nonverbal cues: A study of married working women. *Sex Roles, 31*, 149–165.

Hall, J. A., & Veccia, E. M. (1990). More "touching" observations: New insights on men, women, and interpersonal touch. *Journal of Personality and Social Psychology, 59*, 1155–1162.

Haugh, S. S., Hoffman, C. D., & Cowan, G. (1980). The eye of the very young beholder: Sex typing of infants by young children. *Child Development, 51*, 598–600.

Heise, D. R. (1989). Effects of emotion displays on social identification. *Social Psychology Quarterly, 52*, 10–21.

Henley, N. M. (1977). *Body politics: Power, sex, and nonverbal communication.* New York: Prentice Hall.

Henley, N. M. (1995). Body politics revisited: What do we know today? In P. J. Kalbfleisch & M. J. Cody (Eds.), *Gender, power, and communication in human relationships* (pp. 27–61). Hillsdale, NJ: Lawrence Erlbaum.

Hess, U., Blairy, S., & Kleck, R. E. (1998). The influence of expression intensity, gender, and ethnicity on judgments of dominance and affiliation. Manuscript submitted for publication.

Hess, U., Blairy, S., & Kleck, R. E. (1998). The relationship between the intensity of emotional facial expressions and observers' decoding. *Journal of Nonverbal Behavior, 21*, 241–257.

Hess, U., Kappas, A., & Banse, R. (1995). The intensity of facial expressions is determined by underlying affective state and social situation. *Journal of Personality and Social Psychology, 69*, 280–288.

Hess, U., Senécal, S., & Kirouac, G. (1996). *Recognizing emotional facial expressions: Does perceived sociolinguistic group make a difference?* Poster presented at the 26th International Congress of Psychology, Montreal, 16–21 August.

Hess, U., Senécal, S., Kirouac, G., Philippot, P., Kleck, R. E. (1997). Guilty women and angry men: Gender stereotypes regarding the expression of emotions. Manuscript submitted for publication.

Hoffman, M. L. (1984). Interaction of affect and cognition on empathy. In C. E. Izard, J. Kagan, & R. B. Zajonc (Eds.), *Emotion, cognition, and behavior* (pp. 103–131). Cambridge: Cambridge University Press.

Hofstede, G. (1980). *Culture's consequences.* Berverly Hills, CA: Sage.

Holden, K. T., & Hogan, J. T. (1993). The emotive impact of foreign intonation: An experiment in switching English and Russian intonation. *Language and Speech, 36*, 67–88.

Itakura, S. (1994). Differentiated responses to different human conditions in chimpanzees. *Perceptual and Motor Skills, 79*, 1288–1290.

Izard, C. E. (1994). Innate and universal facial expressions: Evidence from developmental and cross-cultural research. *Psychological Bulletin, 115*, 288–299.

Kelley, H. G., Cunningham, J. D., Grisham, J. A., Lefebre, L. M., Sink, C. R., & Yablon, G. (1978). Sex differences in comments made during conflict within close heterosexual pairs. *Sex Roles, 4*, 473–492.

Kilbride, J. E. & Yarczower, M. (1983). Ethnic bias in the recognition of facial expressions. *Journal of Nonverbal Behavior, 8,* 27–41.

Kitayama, S., & Markus, H. R. (1994). Introduction to cultural psychology and emotion research. In S. Kitayama & H. R. Markus (Eds.), *Emotion and culture: Empirical studies of mutual influence* (pp. 1–22). Washington, DC: American Psychological Association.

Keating, C. F. (1985). Human dominance signals: The primate in us. In S. L. E. & J. F. Dovidio (Eds.), *Power, dominance, and nonverbal communication* (pp. 89–108). New York: Springer Verlag.

Keating, C. F., & Bai, D. L. (1986). Children's attributions of social dominance from facial cues. *Child Development, 57,* 1269–1276.

Keating, C. F., Mazur, A., & Segall, M. H. (1977). Facial gestures which influence the perception of status. *Sociometry, 40,* 374–378.

Knudson, B. (1996). Facial expressions of emotion influence interpersonal trait inferences. *Journal of Nonverbal Behavior, 20,* 165–182.

Labott, S. M., Martin, R. B., Eason, P. S., & Berkey, E. Y. (1991). Social reactions to the expression of emotion. *Cognition and Emotion, 5,* 397–419.

LaFrance, M., & Hecht, M. A. (1995). Why smiles generate leniency. *Personality and Social Psychology Bulletin, 21,* 207–214.

Lazarus, R. R. (1991). *Emotion and adaptation.* New York: Oxford University Press.

Linnankoski, I., Laasko, M. L., & Leinonen, L. (1994). Recognition of emotions in macaque vocalizations by children and adults. *Language and Communication, 14,* 183–192.

MacAndrew, F. T. (1986). A cross-cultural study of recognition thresholds for facial expressions of emotion. *Journal of Cross-Cultural Psychology, 17,* 211–224.

MacKinnon, N. J., & Keating, L. J. (1989). The structure of emotions: Canada-United States comparisons. *Social Psychology Quarterly, 52,* 70–83.

Major, B., & Heslin, R. (1982). Perceptions of cross-sex and same-sex nonreciprocal touch: It is better to give than to receive. *Journal of Nonverbal Behavior, 6,* 148–162.

Markham, R., & Wang, L. (1996). Recognition of emotion by Chinese and Australian children. *Journal of Cross-Cultural Psychology, 27,* 616–643.

Markus, H. R., & Kitayama, S. (1991). Culture and the self: Implications for cognition, emotion, and motivation. *Psychological Review, 98,* 224–253.

Markus, H. R., & Kitayama, S. (1994). The cultural construction of self and emotion: Implications for social behavior. In S. Kitayama & H. R. Markus (Eds.), *Emotion and culture: Empirical studies of mutual influence.* Washington, DC: American Psychological Association.

Matsumoto, D. (1990). Cultural similarities and differences in display rules. *Motivation and Emotion, 14,* 195–214.

Matsumoto, D. (1991). Cultural influences on facial expressions of emotions. *Southern Communication Journal, 56,* 128–137.

Matsumoto, D. (1992). American-Japanese differences in the recognition of universal facial expressions. *Journal of Cross-Cultural Psychology, 23,* 72–84.

Matsumoto, D. (1993). Ethnic differences in affect intensity, emotion judgments, display rule attitudes, and self-reported emotional expression in an American sample. *Motivation and Emotion, 17*, 107–123.

Matsumoto, D., & Ekman, P. (1989). American-Japanese differences in intensity ratings of facial expressions of emotion. *Motivation and Emotion, 13*, 143–157.

Matsumoto, D., Kudoh, T., Scherer, K. R., & Wallbott, H. (1988). Antecedents of and reactions to emotions in the United States and Japan. *Journal of Cross-Cultural Psychology, 19*, 267–286.

Mauro, R., Sato, K., & Tucker, J. (1992). The role of appraisal in human emotions: A cross-cultural study. *Journal of Personality and Social Psychology, 62*, 301–317.

Motley, M. T. (1993). Facial affect and verbal context in conversation: Facial expression as interjection. *Human Communication Research, 20*, 3–40.

Motley, M. T., & Camden, C. T. (1988). Facial expression of emotion: A comparison of posed expressions versus spontaneous expressions in an interpersonal communications setting. *Western Journal of Speech Communication, 52*, 1–22.

O'Neil, J. M., Helms, B. J., Gable, R. K., David, L., & Wrightsman, L. S. (1986). Gender-role conflict scale: College men's fear of femininity. *Sex Roles, 14*, 335–350.

Pennebaker, J. W., Rimé, B., & Blankenship, V. E. (1996). Stereotypes of emotional expressiveness of northerners and southerners: A cross-cultural test of Montesquieu's hypothesis. *Journal of Personality and Social Psychology, 70*, 372–380.

Pittam, J., Gallois, C., Iwawaki, S., & Kroonenberg, P. (1995). Australian and Japanese concepts of expressive behavior. *Journal of Cross-Cultural Psychology, 26*, 451–473.

Pittam, J., & Scherer, K. R. (1993). Vocal expression and communication of emotion. In M. Lewis and J. M. Haviland (Eds.), *Handbook of emotions* (pp. 185–198). New York: Guilford Press.

Pope, L. K., & Smith, C. A. (1994). On the distinct meanings of smiles and frowns. *Cognition and Emotion, 8*, 65–72.

Redican, W. K. (1982). An evolutionary perspective on human facial displays. In P. Ekman (Ed.), *Emotion in the human face* (pp. 212–280). Elmsford, NY: Pergamon.

Ridgeway, C. L., & Berger, J. (1986). Expectations, legitimation, and dominance behavior in task groups. *American Sociological Review, 51*, 603–617.

Riggio, R. E., & Friedman, H. S. (1986). Impression formation: The role of expressive behavior. *Journal of Personality and Social Psychology, 50*, 421–427.

Rosenberg, E. L., & Ekman, P. (1994). Coherence between expressive and experiential systems in emotion. *Cognition and Emotion, 8*, 201–229.

Russell, J. A., Suzuki, N., & Ishida, N. (1993). Canadian, Greek, and Japanese freely produced emotion labels for facial expressions. *Motivation and Emotion, 17*, 337–351.

Senécal, S., Hess, U., & Kleck, R. E. (1996). *The influence of gender stereotypes on the decoding of emotional facial expressions.* Poster presented at the 26th International Congress of Psychology, Montreal, 16–21 August.

Senécal, S., Kirouac, G., Hess, U. (1997). Differences in stereotypes regarding trait emotional states for Franco and Anglo Canadian men and women. Unpublished manuscript. University of Quebec at Montreal.

Shaver, P. R., Wu, S., & Schwarz, J. C. (1992). Cross-cultural similarities and differences in emotion and its representation: A prototype approach. In M. S. Clark (Ed.), *Emotion: Review of Personality and Social Psychology*, Vol. 13 (pp. 175–212). Newbury Park, CA: Sage.

Shields, A. S. (1987). Women, men, and the dilemma of emotion. In P. Shaver & C. Hendrick (Eds.), *Sex and gender* (pp. 229–250) Newbury Park, CA: Sage.

Shimoda, K., Argyle, M., Ricci-Bitti, P. (1978). The intercultural recognition of emotional expressions by three national racial groups: English, Italian, and Japanese. *European Journal of Social Psychology, 8*, 169–179.

Snodgrass, S. E. (1985). Women's intuition: The effect of subordinate role on interpersonal sensitivity. *Journal of Personality and Social Psychology, 49*, 146–155.

Snodgrass, S. E. (1992). Further effects of role versus gender on interpersonal sensitivity. *Journal of Personality and Social Psychology, 62*, 154–158.

Spielberger, C. D. (1988). State-Trait Anger Expression Inventory Revised Research Edition. Odessa, FL: Psychological Assessment Resources.

Steimer-Krause, E., Krause, R., & Wagner, G. (1990). Interaction regulations used by schizophrenic and psychosomatic patients: Studies on facial behavior in dyadic interactions. *Psychiatry, 53*, 209–228.

Stephan, W. G., Stephan, C. W., de Vargas, M. C. (1996). Emotional expression in Costa Rica and the United States. *Journal of Cross-Cultural Psychology, 27*, 147–160.

Storrs, D., & Kleinke, C. L. (1990). Evaluation of high and equal status touchers. *Journal of Nonverbal Behavior, 14*, 87–95.

Tannen, D. (1986). *That's not what I meant!* New York: Ballantine.

Tartter, V. C. (1980). Happy talk: perceptual and acoustic effects of smiling on speech. *Perception and Psychophysics, 27*, 24–27.

Tartter, V. C., & Braun, D. (1994). Hearing smiles and frowns in normal and whisper registers. *Journal of the Acoustical Society of America, 96*, 2101–2107.

Triandis, H. C. (1972). *The analysis of subjective culture.* New York: Wiley.

Triandis, H. C. (1994). Cultural syndromes and emotion. In S. Kitayama & H. R. Markus (Eds.), *Emotion and culture: Empirical studies of mutual influence* (pp. 285–306). Washington, DC: American Psychological Association.

Triandis, H. C., Bontempo, R., Villareal, M. J., Asai, M., & Lucca, N. (1988). Individualism and collectivism: Cross-cultural perspectives on self-ingroup relationships. *Journal of Personality and Social Psychology, 54*, 323–338.

Wagner, H. L., Buck, R., & Winterbotham, M. (1993). Communication of specific emotions: Gender differences in sending accuracy and communication measures. *Journal of Nonverbal Behavior, 17*(1), 29–53.

Wallbott, H. G., & Scherer, K. R. (1986). How universal and specific is emotional experience? Evidence from 27 countries on five continents. *Social Science Information, 25*, 763–795.

Watson, D., Clark, L. C., & Tellegen, A. (1988). Development and validation of brief measures of positive and negative affect: The PANAS scale. *Journal of Personality and Social Psychology, 54*, 1063–1070.

Wierzbicka, A. (1994). Emotion, language, and cultural scripts. In S. Kitayama & H. R. Markus (Eds.), *Emotion and culture: Empirical studies of mutual influence* Washington, DC: American Psychological Association.

Wierzbicka, A. (1995). The relevance of language to the study of emotions. *Psychological Inquiry, 6*, 248–252.

Wiggers, M. (1984). *Emotion recognition in children and adults*. Dissertation, University of Nijmegen.

Wundt, W. (1903). *Grundzüge der physiologischen Psychologie*. Leipzig: Wilhelm Engelmann.

PART III

# Immediate Social Factors During Interaction

# 8. Mimicry

## Facts and Fiction

URSULA HESS, PIERRE PHILIPPOT, AND
SYLVIE BLAIRY

## Objectives

"A path leads from identification by way of imitation [mimicry] to empathy, that is, to the comprehension of the mechanism by means of which we are enabled to take up any attitude at all towards another mental life." This statement by Freud (1921, p. 110) illustrates one of the many functions that mimicry has been purported to fulfill. In fact, mimicry has been suggested to do much more. Like a magic potion, it has been ubiquitously claimed as an early cognitive tool, as a path to empathy, as a means of understanding other selves, as a process fostering social coordination, and as a psychotherapeutic instrument.

Thus, few aspects of social interaction have been left untouched by speculations on this process. The present chapter attempts to reunite the manifold literatures on this topic and to try to separate fact and fiction.

## Introduction

The role of mimicry in social interactions has been most vociferously sustained by clinical psychologists from different schools who have stressed for a long time the importance of mimicry, that is, the imitation of an interaction partner's posture, facial expression, or speech characteristics, in the therapeutic process. Specifically, mimicry has been proposed as an important aspect of empathy: either, in a psycho-

Preparation of this chapter was supported in part by a grant from the FCAR to the first author and by the Fonda National de la Recherche Scientifique Belgique (8.4514.92 & 1.5.041.94F) to the second author. We would like to thank the volume editors for helpful suggestions on a draft of this chapter.

analytic tradition starting with Freud (1921), as a means of *knowing* another's inner state or as a means of *communicating* understanding and acceptance (Rogers, 1975; Bavelas, Black, Lemery, & Mullett, 1986; Bavelas, Black, Chovil, & Lemery, 1988). The psychoanalytic tradition of understanding the relationship of mimicry and empathy is based on the works of Lipps (1907; see Masson, 1985, pp. 324–325) on the understanding of other selves with which Freud was familiar. Specifically, Lipps proposed that mimicry leads – via a feedback process – to shared affect, which in turn facilitates emotion recognition. The notion that mimicry is related to the establishment of rapport and communicates acceptance can be traced to the work of Scheflen (1964) who studied congruent body posture in psychotherapeutic sessions.

Although these assumptions found wide acceptance, are frequently referred to in publications on the role of empathy on the therapeutic process (e.g., Haase & Tepper, 1972), and even provide a grounding element for some therapeutic approaches such as dance therapy (e.g., Schmais & Schmais, 1983), little empirical evidence regarding the role of mimicry in emotion recognition (does mimicry facilitate the understanding of others' internal states?), its role in the communication of understanding (does the mimicked other feel understood?), or even the existence of the phenomenon as such (do people mimic?) has been systematically accumulated. In this chapter, we will present the literature on mimicry and its role in emotion communication. Before going on to a summary of the literature, however, we would like to present a model of emotion communication and outline the proposed role of mimicry in its context with the goal of showing how the different proposed roles of mimicry can be embedded in the context of nonverbal communication.

## Theoretical Background

### Motor Mimicry, Congruence, Mirroring, and Imitation

The term *mimicry* has been employed to describe a variety of behaviors. These include the imitation of specific behaviors such as wincing when observing the pain of others (Bavelas et al., 1986; Bavelas et al., 1988), increased forearm muscle tension when watching arm wrestling (Berger & Hadley, 1975), imitation of gestures or sign language (Berger, Carli, Hammersla, Karshmer, & Sanchez, 1979), or imitation of a model's facial expressions (Hess, Philippot, & Blairy, 1998; Lanzetta &

Englis, 1989; McHugo, Lanzetta, Sullivan, Masters, & Englis, 1985; Vaughan & Lanzetta, 1980, Wallbott, 1991). Further, a number of other nonverbal behaviors have been associated with mimicry, such as the adoption of congruent postures (Scheflen, 1964) or speech accommodation (e.g., Giles & Smith, 1979).

On a conceptual level, mimicry has been assigned a number of different roles. In this context we can distinguish two major functions: first, mimicry as a means of understanding others, and second, mimicry as a process involved in the synchronization of interactions.

Regarding the first aspect, mimicry has been described as a reflexive, mainly unconscious process that entrains emotional contagion, affective empathy, or simply as an additional means of understanding the emotional reactions of others (e.g., Hatfield, Cacioppo, & Rapson, 1993; Lipps, 1907).

Regarding the role of mimicry in the synchronization of interactions, the adoption of congruent nonverbal behavior has been reported to lead to increased rapport (Rogers, 1957; Scheflen, 1964), mutual liking (Cappella, 1993), or at least more positive impressions of the person who imitates (Bates, 1975; Manusov, 1993). Further, it has been suggested that mimicry may increase coherence between interaction partners by making them more similar to one another (Gump & Kulik, 1997; Markovsky & Berger, 1983; see also Cappella, 1993). Also, from a developmental perspective, imitation has been considered as a means by which children achieve social coordination (Eckerman, Davis, & Didow, 1989) or social identity (Meltzhoff & Moore, 1992, 1994).

Thus mimicry has been implicated in the decoding of affective states, in the communication of empathy, in social coordination, as well as in aspects of person perception. Given this heterogeneity of the purported roles of mimicry in the communication of affect, it seems necessary to situate mimicry in the larger context of emotion communication and to delineate its alleged functions in the context of dyadic interactions.

## The Dyadic Lens Model

The present model is based on a framework for thinking about judgment processes that has been adapted to the communication of emotions (Brunswik, 1956; Kappas, 1991; Scherer, 1978). Figure 8.1 shows the processes involved in nonverbal communication. One should note that in this model sender and receiver labels are used for referential

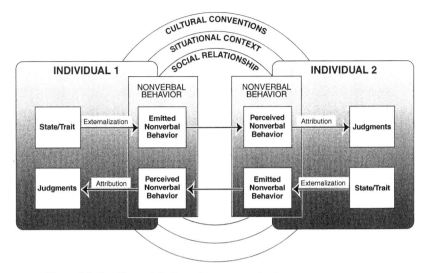

Figure 8.1. Dyadic model of emotion communication.

convenience only. In fact, both interaction partners fulfill both roles at all times. According to this model, when the sender experiences an emotional state (e.g., happiness) this state is signaled by a number of nonverbal cues (externalization: e.g., turning up of the corners of the mouth, wrinkles around the corners of the eyes). This emitted nonverbal behavior is potentially available to the receiver. The perceived nonverbal behavior is the basis for the receiver's attributions regarding the sender's state (attribution). However, some emitted behaviors may not be transmitted (e.g., a very faint smile) and thus become unavailable to the receiver. Further, the receiver may perceive the emitted cues but attribute a different internal state to the sender (e.g., smiling as a reflection of cruelty or schadenfreude). Both – the link between the sender's state and the distal indicator cues and the link between the proximal percepts and the observer's judgments – may be influenced by elements of the social and cultural context of the interaction. Thus, the model allows for the presence of display rules (see chapter 4) as well as rules guiding the decoding of emotional signals (see chapter 7).

Figure 8.2 shows the process involved in the different accounts of mimicry for one individual. Specifically, the model acknowledges feedback processes in the dyad by adding both an inter- and an intrapersonal feedback process. Interpersonal feedback takes the form of

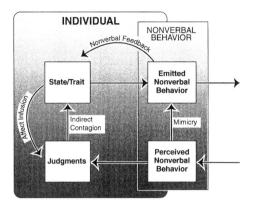

Figure 8.2. Processes involved in different accounts of mimicry.

an influence of the sender's expressive displays on the receiver's expressive displays (mimicry). Intrapersonal feedback takes the form of an influence of an individual's expressive displays on his or her own affective state (nonverbal feedback). This feedback may be from facial, postural, vocal, and even respiratory expressive behavior (Bourgeois, Couture, Herrera, Blairy, Hess, & Philippot, 1995; Hatfield, Hsee, Costello, Weisman, & Denney, 1995; Manstead, 1988; Matsumoto, 1987; Stepper, & Strack, 1993; see also Capella, 1993).

According to Lipps (1907) and others in the same tradition (see below) emotional contagion is mediated by mimicry which via nonverbal feedback influences the internal state of the individual. Another possible path for contagion has been implied by Gump and Kulik (1997) who suggest a social comparison process. This process implies that the individual first attributes a specific internal state to the interaction partner and that these judgments then influence the internal state of the individual (indirect contagion). Finally a more generalized influence of the individual's own affective state on their judgment of the interaction partner's state has been included. This process has been referred to as affect infusion (e.g., Forgas, 1995).

Figure 8.3 presents an attempt to classify the different functional roles that have been attributed to mimicry and imitation and to locate the processes implied for these functions. Specifically, mimicry has been described as a path toward empathy (Hoffman, 1984) as well as a means to express empathy (Bavelas et al., 1986; Bavelas et al., 1988; Rogers, 1975); it has been implicated in the development (Eckerman et al., 1989) and expression of social coordination (Gump & Kulik,

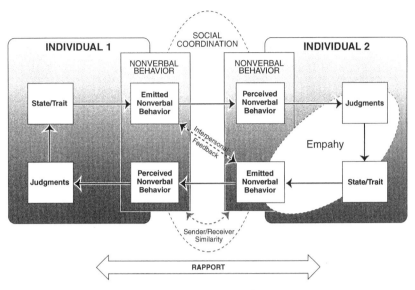

Figure 8.3. The functional roles of mimicry and imitation.

1997; Markovsky & Berger, 1983). Finally, the combination of inter- and intrapersonal feedback as well as the communication aspect of mimicry can be subsumed into the process of establishing rapport between interaction partners.

## Review of Previous Literature

As mentioned above, mimicry and imitation have been studied in a variety of contexts and from different theoretical perspectives. These different roles are purported to recruit one or several of the processes illustrated in Figures 8.1 and 8.2. One should note that these different functions of mimicry are not mutually exclusive and that they can be – and most likely are – activated simultaneously. Further, some of the roles of mimicry have been considered basic elements of others, as is the case, for example, in Lipps's model. In the following review of the literature we will highlight the role of mimicry for these psychological processes.

The review of the literature will be structured according to the theoretical perspective from which mimicry and imitation have been studied. The majority of studies on mimicry and imitation can be situated in the clinical, developmental, and social psychological domains. In the following, research from these three domains will be discussed in more detail.

## Developmental Approaches to Mimicry

The role of mimicry in the development of empathy and in the establishment of social coordination are two issues that have been addressed by developmental research on mimicry and imitation. In addition, mimicry has been suggested to function as a "primitive motor code," which might be a primary cognitive medium for learning about other people during early development.

### Mimicry as a Primitive Motor Code

Imitation, including facial expression imitation, as a primitive cognitive tool has been an enduring topic in developmental psychology (Piaget, 1959), and it is now well established that even newborns and very young infants are able to imitate facial movements to which they are exposed (for a review, see Meltzoff & Moore, 1994). Meltzoff and Moore (1994) studied nonverbal imitation in 6-week-old infants. These infants were not only able to imitate a series of facial actions when observing a model, but they also could reproduce these movement patterns after a delay of 24 hours when reexposed to the model, who then showed a neutral face. Thus, infants use imitation to reidentify and communicate with the persons they see before them. According to Meltzoff and Moore, the presence of this pattern of early imitation is not only a marker of the infant's representational capacity, but constitutes in itself "an important engine in infants' developing understanding of persons" (Meltzoff & Moore, 1994, p. 95). In this sense, imitation is a primary tool for social cognition. In an extension of the Piagetian notion that infants come to know things through acting on them, infants can be said to learn about people by imitating them. As Meltzoff and Moore (1994) put it, "Imitation is to understanding people as physical manipulation is to understanding things" (p. 96). This primitive process may be paralleled in adult learning in the type of social learning processes that have been described by Berger and colleagues (see below).

In sum, Meltzhoff and Moore assign to mimicry an important role in the process of learning to identify and understand people, a basic element in social development and in the development of empathy.

However, mimicry has been assigned an even more fundamental role in the development of empathy by Hoffman (1984), which will be discussed in the next section.

## Mimicry and the Development of Empathy

Hoffman (1984) proposes five different modes of empathic affect arousal, which enter at different stages in development. Motor mimicry, which is present from birth, is one of these modes. In an argument similar to Lipps's (1907), Hoffman proposes that an individual A automatically and for the most part unconsciously imitates individual B's affect display. Via afferent feedback of internal kinesthetic cues, individual A then experiences the same internal state as individual B and, consequently, the same type of affect. According to Hoffman, this empathic process requires few cognitive capacities. Also, Hoffman agrees with Meltzoff and Moore's (1994) proposal that imitation is a tool for person identification, which he labels "person permanence." Little empirical evidence has been accumulated for these notions; however, some indirect evidence can be gleaned from a study by Chrisholm and Strayer (1995).

This study is situated within an approach employing facial expressions as a measure of empathy in children (e.g., Eisenberg, 1989, Eisenberg & Fabes, 1990). Specifically, Chrisholm and Strayer (1995) showed 10-year-old girls videotaped scenes in which a girl of the same age is experiencing an emotion. Post-viewing interviews assessed the match (empathy) between the children's self-reported emotional state and the emotional state of the girl in the video. In addition, the children's faces were unobtrusively videotaped while they watched the scenes. An analysis of the facial responses showed that the more empathic the children were, the more likely they were to exhibit a facial expression congruent with the emotional state of the stimulus character. Inasmuch as the stimulus characters always showed emotional facial expressions that were congruent with their emotional state, this finding can be interpreted as suggestive that the more empathic children also showed more mimicry.

In sum, Hoffman views mimicry as a first path leading to empathy, a path that is active from birth. He also acknowledges other paths to empathy, which enter later in development, but maintains that mimicry remains one means of achieving empathy in adulthood.

*Mimicry and Social Coordination*

In a longitudinal study, Eckerman, Davis and Didow (1989) observed dyads of infants at 16, 20, 24, 28, and 32 months of age to assess developmental changes in social coordination. Specifically, they studied those behaviors "by which toddlers relate their own actions thematically to the specifics of their social partners' actions so as to create sustained, coordinated action on a common topic" (p. 440). The observations were made in a playroom and both vocalization and nonverbal behaviors were recorded. With age, a marked increase in acts coordinated with those of a peer was observed. Most of this developmental change was accounted for by imitation of the peer's nonverbal actions, whereas the use of words to direct the peer in a coordinated way, while increasing with age, remained infrequent. The authors interpreted these results as evidence for the notion that imitating another's nonverbal actions is a core behavioral strategy for achieving social coordination during the developmental period preceding reliance on verbal communication.

Eckerman et al.'s finding accentuates the role of mimicry in children's active attempts to regulate their environments. Similarly, mimicry, or at least nonverbal imitation, has been suggested as a means by which children can shape their environment and regulate the type of reinforcements they receive. To investigate this notion, Bates (1975) asked adults, who were placed in the role of basketball coaches, to evaluate children, who were instructed to either imitate or not imitate the adult during the training session. The coaches' judgments were more positive and they provided the children with more positive reinforcements when the latter were imitating them. Thus, nonverbal imitation can be used in the early states of development to *actively* influence the social environment as regards both peers and adults.

In sum, although empirical evidence is scarce, nonverbal imitation seems to play an important role in the early stages of social coordination before language is acquired. While a number of studies on adult dyads (see below) suggest that this function is maintained to some degree, no study has, to our knowledge, investigated the development of this function of mimicry from infancy to adulthood. Finally, imitation also seems to be instrumental in the way children, and possibly infants, manage to shape and modulate their environment.

*Summary and Conclusions*

The literature on the developmental role of mimicry shows that facial mimicry can be observed very early in infants' lives – in the hours following birth. Mimicry and imitation have been implicated in the development of social coordination, in learning about people, and in the development of empathy. Even though these notions have been well elaborated theoretically, only limited empirical evidence is available. Clearly, this area demands further research. The two notions best supported by the limited empirical evidence are that mimicry is instrumental in person identification and in social coordination, while the role of mimicry for the development of empathy, although theoretically appealing, has not been studied directly.

## Clinical Approaches to Mimicry

Like a good fairy, mimicry was present at the cradle of psychotherapy. Freud considered mimicry a key process in the understanding of and identification with others. Since then, clinical scholars of many orientations have attributed to mimicry a role in the psychotherapeutic process.

Mimicry has been suggested to play three major roles in the psychotherapeutic process. First, mimicry has been proposed as a tool for therapists to foster their understanding of their clients. From this perspective, mimicry is an active process to attain empathy, that is, an understanding of the client's feelings and perspective. While he is certainly not the only proponent of this perspective, Rogers (1957) is certainly the scholar who is most identified with it. Second, therapists' mimicry of their clients' nonverbal behavior has been suggested to positively influence the clients' evaluation of both the therapist and the therapeutical relationship. Finally, the use of body movements, including mimicry, has been advocated by some to yield beneficial mental health effects. We will now turn to a more detailed presentation of these three aspects.

*Therapist's Mimicry as a Means for Understanding the Client*

Forty years ago, Carl Rogers (1957) identified empathy as one of the crucial elements in psychotherapy. By empathy, he referred to (a) the therapist's accurate understanding of the client's inner world "as if" it was his or her own, and (b) the communication of this understanding to the client. Nonverbal behaviors have been proposed to mediate both aspects in important ways. For example, Haase and Tepper (1972) observed that "nonverbal components . . . accounted for slightly more than twice as much variance in the judged level of empathy as [*sic*] did the verbal message" (p. 421). Among these nonverbal behaviors, the therapist's mimicry of the client's nonverbal behavior has been recommended as a technique to enhance empathy as conceptualized by Rogers. For instance, Ivey, Ivey, and Simek-Downing (1987) encourage counselors-in-training to imitate a client's nonverbal behavior – a process they call "movement symmetry" to "get back on track" when lost or to improve their understanding of the client.

Despite the clinical lore that mimicry fosters empathy, very little research on the effectiveness of this approach has been conducted (Bänninger-Huber & Steiner, 1992). The literature on this subject consists mostly of naturalistic observational studies, which show that "postural congruence," a pattern in which the client's and therapist's arm, leg, and head are in mirror-imaged positions (Charny, 1966; Condon & Ogston, 1966; Scheflen, 1964), characterizes rapport between client and therapist. Scheflen (1972) defines postural congruence between counselors and clients as an index of empathy. However, no study has directly investigated whether therapists' mirroring or mimicking does indeed increase the accuracy of their perception of the client's feeling. Regarding the communication of empathy by the therapist, several studies manipulated therapists' mimicry or mirroring and assessed the clients' perception of the therapists' understanding. These studies will be reviewed in the next section.

Hsee, Hatfield, and Chemtob (1992) addressed the relationship between mimicry and empathy in a simulation of a therapist–patient interaction by showing subjects a videotaped excerpt of a stimulus person. The stimulus person reported verbally to be either sad or happy and showed either a happy or a sad facial expression. While subjects' rating of the stimulus person's mood was mostly determined by the verbal message, the subjects' own mood was influenced equally by the verbal report and the facial expression of the stimulus person. Hsee et al. suggest that a therapist's emotions (i.e., their contagion based empathy) might similarly be determined in part by a facial mimicry process, whereas the therapist's assessment of the client's affective state might be based more on the verbal message.

In sum, no empirical evidence can be found for the clinical lore that empathy (possibly mediated by mimicry) increases the accuracy of therapists' perception of their clients' affective state. However, there is some indication that mimicry of a client's facial expression may affect the therapist's mood. Yet, the stronger effects of mimicry in the clinical setting may be those affecting the client and not the therapist. These effects are reviewed in the next section.

### Therapist's Mimicry and Clients' Perceptions

Contrary to the "objective" consequences of mimicking in the thera-peutic process, much work has been devoted to the "subjective" con-sequences of mimicking. This research can be organized along two lines. First, a series of studies investigated the effects of therapists' mimicking on evaluations by the client. A second series of studies addressed the influence of mimicry on the global perception of the therapist–client relation, that is, the impression of having "rapport."

*Clients' Evaluation of the Therapist.* A number of nonverbal behaviors by the therapist have been reported to influence the client's evaluation of the therapist (e.g., Harper, Wiens, & Matarasso, 1978). Specifically, eye contact, forward body lean, smiling, nodding, and direct body orientation positively affect judgments of warmth, empathy, and gen-uineness (for a review, see Harper et al., 1978). In this context, congru-ent body movements and mirror imaged posture have been found to be positively related to perceptions of affiliation and to increase verbal disclosure (Cappella, 1981). Further, a number of studies (see below) show that individuals who imitate others are evaluated more posi-tively by the imitated person (Bates, 1975; Manusov, 1993).

It is thus reasonable to propose that therapists who mimic their clients should also be evaluated more positively. Maurer and Tindall (1983) found support for this notion in a study manipulating the postural congruence of counselors who interviewed adolescents to discuss career plans. The adolescents' ratings of the counselors' em-pathy revealed that counselors who mirrored the posture of the ado-lescents were judged to be more empathic. Similarly, in two experi-ments by Navarre (1981, 1982), subjects were interviewed by an individual who either did or did not adopt a congruent posture. Again, the interviewer was rated more positively when adopting a congruent posture than when adopting an incongruent posture.

In sum, the generally positive effect of mimicry on evaluations can also be observed in clinical settings. The next section discusses studies showing that this positive effect is not limited to the person of the therapist but also applies to the therapeutic relationship as a whole.

## Mimicry and Rapport

One predictor of positive psychotherapy outcome is the quality of the relationship between client and therapist. At its most holistic level, this quality has been described as a feeling of rapport or relatedness (e.g. Charny, 1966). Bernieri (1988) illustrates the notion of rapport as follows: "High states of rapport are often associated with descriptive terms such as harmonious, smooth, 'in tune with,' or 'on the same wavelength.' Likewise, states of low rapport are often associated with terms such as awkward, 'out of sync,' or 'not getting it together'" (p. 121). Some studies suggest that mimicry fosters the feeling of rapport.

In an in-depth analysis of a filmed psychotherapy session, Charny (1966) observed that the vocal content of the interaction was consistently more positive, interpersonal, specific, and bound to the therapeutic situation when the therapist mimicked the client, that is, adopted a congruent posture. However, when the therapist did not mimic the client, the vocal content was more self-oriented, negational, and nonspecific, and tended to be self-contradictory and nonreferenced. Charny concluded that mimicry was a behavioral indicator of rapport. Similar findings have been reported by Scheflen (1964), who found that the occurrence of congruent body postures in psychotherapy groups coincides with shared ideological positions, and by Condon and Ogston (1966), who noted that the congruent timing of posture shifts was associated with interactional synchrony.

More detailed analyses of the relationship between rapport and mimicry have been conducted outside of the clinical realm. For instance, in a series of studies, Bernieri and collaborators (Babad, Bernieri, & Rosenthal, 1989; Bernieri, 1988) analyzed videotapes of young couples in interaction. They found that the couples whose movements showed the most synchrony also felt the most emotional rapport with each other. In a more recent study, Bernieri, Gilles, Davis, and Grahe (1996) studied indices of rapport in 50 dyads in either a cooperative or an adversarial discussion. In both conditions, interactional synchrony was found to be an important predictor of self-reports of rapport.

Similarly, LaFrance and Broadbent (1976), who studied students in a classroom situation, found that students who mirrored the teacher's body and arm posture also reported feeling more rapport and involvement in the class, an observation that was replicated in a subsequent study (LaFrance, 1979). In another study, however, LaFrance and Ickes (1981) observed that posture mirroring during a first encounter in a waiting room produced self-consciousness and an impression of constraint and awkwardness in the mimicked individual. This finding may be explained by Cappella's (1981) conclusions regarding the importance of timing relational behaviors appropriately. He also suggests that behaviors that signal intimacy may be perceived negatively when they seem situationally inappropriate. It is possible that during a first encounter mimicry implies an inappropriate level of intimacy or that the mimicked behaviors in LaFrance and Ickes's study were not well timed in the framework of the interaction and therefore negatively perceived.

In sum, the available evidence, based, however, mainly on correlational studies, suggests that certain types of mimicry, in particular postural congruence, are markers of rapport during an interaction. Yet, the mere production of this type of mimicry does not suffice to produce a feeling of rapport. The study of LaFrance and Ickes (1981) illustrates that it may even have the opposite effect. As noted by Davis (1985, p. 70), "Simple recommendations to mirror the posture of a client are missing some other component(s) that inhere in the processes of rapport or empathy."

### Mimicry as a Healing Process

A number of therapeutic techniques include the client's imitation of the therapist or the reverse. Dance therapy is the technique that refers the most directly to mimicry (Schmais & Schmais, 1983). Dance therapy deals with what a person feels, and how and when these feelings are psychically and physically processed. In the more specific context of psychoanalytic dance therapy, Siegel (1995) claims that therapists interpret movements by mirroring unfinished movement phrases and by offering new ways of adaptation and interpersonal communication in a nonverbal manner. She proposed the concept of somatic countertransference, that is, the dance therapist uses mirroring to convey acceptance, neutrality, or empathy as a means toward positive therapeutic outcomes. From this perspective, Schmais and Schmais (1983) observed that dance therapy students who were good at mirroring movement also had better nonverbal observational abilities than those who were not skilled at mirroring movement. However, the clinical effectiveness of mimicry as a healing technique is yet to be established, and the available evidence is merely anecdotal.

### Summary and Conclusion

Despite the clinical lore regarding the importance of therapists' mimicry for an empathic understanding of their patients, very little research has been systematically conducted on this subject, and most of this research has been correlational in nature. Moreover, the available evidence suggests that this lore is not founded empirically. There is no evidence that mimicking increases the accuracy of the therapist's assessment of the patient's affective state. However, there is some evidence that mimicry affects the therapist's affective state, that is, produces affective contagion.

One of the reasons this lore has proved so persistent, despite the lack of supportive evidence, might be that a certain type of mimicry by the therapist seems to positively influence the patient's evaluations and to foster a climate of positive rapport during therapeutic sessions. Yet, parameters that are optimal to yield this positive aura are still to be defined and, clearly, more research in this domain is needed.

An intriguing fact in considering this literature is that it mostly investigates postural mimicry, neglecting facial mimicry. However, it has been largely established that facial expressions convey much more information about one's inner state than posture (Ekman & Friesen, 1969). Future research in this area might benefit by focusing more on faces.

## Social Approaches to Mimicry

In the domain of social psychology, mimicry and imitation have been studied in a number of different contexts and from a number of different theoretical perspectives. First, a number of studies have addressed the question of whether adults do in fact mimic facial or other nonverbal displays. In this context, the question of whether exposure to emotional facial expressions is associated with emotional contagion has also been of interest.

A second line of research has linked mimicry to affective empathy, emotion recognition, and emotional contagion. These three processes were first linked by Lipps (1907). In this context, the notion that mimicry may actually serve to communicate empathy rather than be a process underlying empathy has also been advanced (Bavelas et al., 1986; Bavelas et al., 1988). Finally, some researchers have addressed the role of mimicry and imitation in the context of social coordination (Gump & Kulik, 1997; Markovsky & Berger, 1983; Sullins, 1991) and person perception (Bates, 1975; Capella, 1993; Manusov, 1993).

## Facial and Nonverbal Mimicry in Adults

The question of whether adults show congruent facial expressions to the facial displays of others has been addressed in a series of studies by Dimberg (1982, 1988; Dimberg & Lundqvist, 1988).[1] In these studies, subjects saw a series of angry and happy facial expressions. In general, subjects showed an increase in EMG activity over the zygomaticus major site (the muscle that turns the corners of the mouth up in smiling) when looking at happy expressions and an increase in EMG activity over the corrugator supercilii site (the muscle that pulls the eyebrows together and down in frowning) when watching angry faces. That is, subjects smiled at smiling faces and frowned at frowning faces. In addition, Dimberg and Lundqvist (1988) found that subjects reported more fear when looking at angry faces and more happiness when looking at happy faces. These findings were replicated and extended by Lundqvist (1995), who studied subjects' facial reactions to emotional expressions of sadness, happiness, fear, anger, surprise, and disgust. Lundqvist found that subjects' facial EMG activity over different muscle sites was largely congruent with the facial expressions they observed.

Berger and Hadley (1975) approached the question of whether subjects mimic the behaviors they observe from a social learning perspective. They wanted to investigate whether subjects mimic the behavior of a model and whether such mimicry can be conditioned to external events. They found clear evidence that subjects show an increase in EMG activity in the lip region when observing a person stutter,

---

[1] It is important to note, that Dimberg (e.g., Dimberg, 1990) does not employ the term *mimicry* but rather refers to facial reactions to facial expressions – an appellation that does not presume a specific cause, such as the one proposed by Lipps (1907), and is more open to other explanations.

whereas they show an increase in forearm muscle activity when they watch a model arm wrestling. Only limited support for the notion that mimicry can be conditioned to external events was found.

Similarly, Vaughn and Lanzetta found that participants who observed a confederate who seemingly winces after receiving an electric shock in the acquisition phase of a vicarious conditioning paradigm show facial EMG responses congruent with wincing as well as skin conductance responses (Vaughn & Lanzetta, 1980, 1981). Vaughn and Lanzetta interpret the increases in skin conductance as a sign of empathic arousal.

Further, Vaughn and Lanzetta (1981) found that the skin conductance response was larger when participants were instructed to amplify their facial reactions than when participants were instructed to just observe the model or to inhibit their facial reactions. Vaughn and Lanzetta's (1981) approach was based on considerations regarding the facial feedback hypothesis, which stipulates that an individual's facial behavior influences her internal state. Specifically, increases in expressiveness have been shown to be accompanied by increases in experienced emotional state (for reviews, see, e.g., Manstead, 1988; Matsumoto, 1987).

A similar approach was chosen by Bush, Barr, McHugo, and Lanzetta (1989), as well as Laird, Alibozak, Davainis, Deignan, Fontanella, Hong, Levy, and Pacheco (1994). Bush et al. (1989) showed subjects videotaped comedy routines that contained dubbed-in close-ups of people smiling either under instructions to not move the face at all or under no facial instructions. Subjects who were free to move their faces showed more facial EMG activity congruent with smiling at dub points and reported more amusement than subjects who were not free to move their faces. Laird et al. (1994) advanced and found support for the notion that individuals who are more prone to facial feedback effects are also more likely to both mimic and show emotional contagion.

Thus, a series of studies using a variety of paradigms found evidence that adults tend to mimic the nonverbal behaviors they observe. As mentioned above, a number of authors (e.g., Hatfield et al., 1993; Hoffman, 1984; Lipps, 1907) suggest that mimicry is an automatic, reflex-like response to the observed nonverbal display. This notion is put in doubt, however, by a number of studies showing that the tendency to mimic a confederate's display could be influenced by the situational context.

*Situational Influences on Adult's Mimicry.* A series of studies by Lanzetta and colleagues investigated the conditions under which participants show "counterempathy," that is, a response opposite to the one shown by the model. In this context, Lanzetta and Englis (1989) found that participants who believed themselves to be in cooperation with a confederate showed mimicry, that is, increased skin conductance and wincing in response to wincing by the confederate. However, participants who believed themselves to be in competition showed a counterempathic response; that is, they showed increased skin conductance and wincing in response to smiles by the confederate. The notion of counterempathy was also central to two studies by McHugo et al. (1985) and McHugo, Lanzetta, and Bush (1991). McHugo et al. (1985) showed participants news excerpts showing then-president Reagan. Following each excerpt, participants indicated their subjective feeling state; during the presentation of the excerpt the participants' facial reactions were measured using facial EMG. Participants with neutral or positive attitudes toward Reagan reported more warmth and less fear in response to Reagan's displays of happiness/reassurance and more fear and less warmth in response to Reagan's displays of fear/ evasion and of anger/threat. Participants who held negative attitudes toward Reagan reported low levels of warmth and high levels of fear to all displays. In this study, all participants, regardless of their political attitude, showed facial displays congruent with mimicry. However, a different pattern emerged in a study by McHugo et al. (1991). In this study, participants saw excerpts showing both then-president Reagan and a well-known opponent of Reagan, Senator Hart, in order to enhance the saliency of the observers' political attitudes; further, the study included both strong and weak displays of happiness/ reassurance. In this latter study, political attitude modulated facial responses to strong but not to weak displays of happiness/reassurance by Reagan. Reagan opponents reacted to strong but not to weak displays of happiness/reassurance by Reagan with less zygomaticus major activity (indicative of smiling) and more corrugator supercilii activity (indicative of frowning) than did Reagan supporters (for a review of these studies see also McHugo & Smith, 1996).

We (Hess, Philippot, & Blairy, 1998) also posed the question regarding the circumstances under which participants are likely to mimic. This study suggests that whether or not individuals show congruent facial expressions depends on the specific task they have to perform. Specifically, participants who had the task of assessing the genuineness of an emotional expression did not show mimicry whereas participants who had the task of assessing the emotion portrayed showed mimicry. In this context, we could also show that not all congruent expressions can be considered to be mimicry. Rather, some congruent nonverbal behaviors may be due to time-locked but independent processes. Following this logic, frowning that occurs in response to cognitive load may appear as a congruent facial expression to angry faces (which are usually difficult to decode). However, this type of congruent expression would not qualify as mimicry.

In sum, a growing body of studies from different theoretical backgrounds, using different manipulations and experimental tasks, agree that adults tend to show congruent facial expressions to the expressive displays of others. However, studies by Lanzetta and Englis (1989) and McHugo and collaborators (McHugo et al., 1985; McHugo et al., 1991) as well as by Hess et al., show that the presence of this effect depends on aspects of the situation such as the nature of the task the participants are engaged in or participants' attitude toward the model.

## Mimicry, Empathy, and Emotion Recognition

Lipps (1907) suggested that the observation of emotion displays leads to mimicry, which in turn elicits a congruent emotional state in the observer. Lipps proposed a model according to which individuals tend to imitate the emotional displays of their interaction partners. These imitated behaviors elicit – via a feedback process – corresponding emotional states. The observers relate their own feeling state to their knowledge about emotional experiences and attribute the emotional state to the interaction partner. In summary, imitation leads to shared affect, which facilitates emotion recognition. This notion has more recently been taken up by Hatfield, Cacioppo, and Rapson (1993), who define "primitive contagion" as "the tendency to automatically mimic and synchronize expressions, vocalizations, postures, and movements with those of another person and, consequently, to converge emotionally" (pp. 153–154). Congruent with Hatfield et al.'s notions, Hsee, Hatfield, and Chemtob (1992) found evidence for emotional contagion, in a study in which they asked subjects to judge a videotaped target person's emotional state (see above). However, they did not assess the subject's own facial expressions.

Wallbott (1991), in an attempt to test Lipps's hypothesis, filmed participants while they were judging the emotions shown in a series of photographs. Two weeks later the participants were shown the video recordings of their own facial expressions and asked to judge which emotion they had decoded. Above chance congruence between these judgments was found. These findings suggest that individuals who accurately decode others' nonverbal displays emit nonverbal cues regarding the decoded nonverbal behavior. Further, they are able to later accurately decode these cues. However, this study, while highly suggestive, offers only indirect evidence for Lipps's hypothesis.

Blairy, Herrera, and Hess (in press) took a more direct approach to test Lipps's hypothesis. We asked participants to either mimic a stimulus person's facial expressions or to show a specific, incongruent, facial expression while decoding a series of expressions of anger, happiness, disgust, fear, and sadness. According to Lipps's theory, mimicry should be associated with better emotion recognition scores. However, the results showed no difference between participants who mimicked and participants who showed the incongruent expressions. Further, no relationship between the level of naturally occurring mimicry and decoding accuracy emerged in a correlational study without specific mimicry instructions.

Bavelas et al. (1986, 1988) propose a rather different account of the role of mimicry in empathic processes. Specifically, they submit that mimicry does not serve to initiate an empathic process but rather to communicate empathy. In two series of studies they present evidence that observers' mimicry of behaviors such as wincing in pain or body canting is only present when the sender is facing the observer and can be viewed by him or her. Further, they could show that naive judges consider an observer's congruent behavior a sign of empathy.

In sum, while the individual elements of Lipps's theory can be shown to occur in emotion communication, the mediational link between mimicry and decoding accuracy proposed by Lipps has not been supported. However, mimicry is *perceived* as an index of empathy and mutual understanding.

*Social Coordination in Adult Dyads*

A number of studies have investigated the notion that mimicry and contagion may serve to increase behavioral convergence between interaction partners. Thus, the imitation of an interaction partner's nonverbal behavior leads to greater behavioral similarity. The notion that crowd behavior with its high level of behavioral homogeneity (LeBon,

1895) may be in parts entrained by mimicry has been proposed by Markovsky and Berger (1983). They interpreted their finding that crowd noise increases mimicry to arm wrestling as evidence in favor of this hypothesis.

Sullins (1991), as well as Gump and Kulik (1997), formulated a related hypothesis. Specifically, they considered the possibility that social comparison processes, which tend to result in behavioral convergence, are linked to mimicry and contagion. Sullins (1991) found evidence that low expressive individuals who were asked under a pretext to spend time sitting opposite a high expressive individual converged emotionally toward the more expressive person's mood. However, this was the case only when both individuals were expecting to perform the same task later on and thus were relevant comparison partners. Similarly, Gump and Kulik (1997) found that subjects mimic each other or a confederate more when they perceive themselves to be in a similar rather than a dissimilar situation and more when under threat. Gump and Kulik (1997) also found evidence for more emotional contagion when subjects were in similar rather than dissimilar situations. Interestingly, a mediational analysis did not suggest that contagion was mediated by mimicry, thus creating doubt regarding another mediational process proposed in the Lipps model.

Finally, some evidence for the notion that mimicry may serve to increase concordance among interaction partners was presented by Cappella (1993). He looked at transition frequencies for smiling behavior by two interaction partners (both smile, only A smiles, only B smiles, neither smiles) and found that the exchange of smiles seems to be initiated by one interaction partner, imitated by the other, and then ceased by one or the other.

In sum, consistent evidence from studies using different methodologies suggests that mimicry enhances social coordination and may play an important role in social comparison processes. In fact, mimicry is both facilitated by perceived similarity between observer and target and seems to increase similarity further.

*Mimicry, Imitation, and Person Perception*

A further role of mimicry has been suggested in the context of person perception. Specifically it has been suggested that mimicking another person's displays may make us more attractive to that person. Cappella (1993) reports findings that suggest that mimicry of an interaction partner's smiling behavior leads to more liking by the interaction partner even after controlling for other factors such as the relationship with the interaction partner or gaze behavior. Similarly, Bates (1975) found that adult subjects who had been imitated by a child were significantly more positive when rating the child than subjects who had not been imitated. However, this effect vanishes when the adult is aware that the child had been instructed to imitate. These findings were replicated by Manusov (1993). A complementary finding was reported by LaVoie and Adams (1978) who found that a model's warmth in interpersonal style was associated with the degree of imitation of the model's nonverbal behavior.

*Summary and Conclusions*

In summary, there is consistent evidence that adults mimic the nonverbal displays of others in many situations. Additional evidence is found for emotional contagion. However, adults' tendency to mimic a model is influenced by situational factors, such as participants' experimental task, their attitudes toward the model, or the relevance of the model as a comparison partner.

While mimicry has been related to empathy, little evidence exists for the notion that mimicry is a basic element of affective empathy. However, evidence that mimicry may serve to communicate empathy, to enhance similarity between interaction partners, and to increase liking of interaction partners is more consistently found. These latter processes are important factors in the establishment of rapport – a concept related to empathy.

## Conclusions

We started this chapter with a quote from Freud underlining the importance of mimicry for an empathic process that presupposes two major functions of mimicry. First, via the imitation–affect induction process proposed by Lipps, mimicry enhances one's understanding of the affective state of an interaction partner. Second, mimicry communicates this understanding. Consequently, we posed three questions: (a) do people mimic? (b) does the mimicked other feel understood? and (c) does mimicry facilitate the understanding of others' internal states? These questions have been addressed by research from different domains of psychology, most notably, from the domains of developmental, clinical, and social psychology. The first two questions find ready answers in the literature. However, regarding the third question the issue is more complicated.

## Do People Mimic?

Regarding the first question, evidence from studies on both adults and infants suggests strongly that in general people show nonverbal displays that are congruent with the displays they observe, and that these displays often represent mimicry. However, two points of caution are suggested. First, not all congruent nonverbal displays may be mimicry. Second, whether people mimic or not may depend on situational factors.

## Does the Mimicked Other Feel Understood?

Regarding this question, congruent evidence from both social psychological and psychotherapy research emerged. The available evidence clearly favors the notion that mimicry communicates empathy and also fosters feelings of rapport between interaction partners. While this is one of the clearest findings in the present body of literature, two points of caution emerging from the present review of the literature need to be advanced, before giving the recommendation to employ mimicry as a tool for signaling empathy. The first concerns the timing of mimicry with regard to the microtiming during a specific interaction, and the second concerns the issue of when in the establishment of a relationship mimicry may be appropriate. Behaviors that are presented voluntarily and do not respect interactional sequences may do more harm than good. Similarly, when employed too early in a relationship, mimicry may signal an inappropriate level of intimacy and thus be negatively perceived.

## Does Mimicry Facilitate the Understanding of Others' Internal States?

The notion that mimicry facilitates understanding of others' emotional states is based on a model which assumes that mimicry leads to contagion, which in turn fosters decoding accuracy (Lipps, 1907). Regarding the different elements of this model, evidence exists not only for the notion that people mimic (see above) but also for the notion that people experience contagion (Sullins, 1991; Hsee et al., 1992;

Blairy, Herrera, & Hess, in press; Hess & Blairy, 1996). However, only a very few studies have assessed the hypothesis that mimicry mediates decoding accuracy. These studies could not find correlations between level of mimicry and decoding accuracy (Blairy, Herrera, & Hess, in press). Further, other research (Gump and Kulik, 1997) failed to find evidence for a mediation of contagion effects through mimicry.

In fact, given the better documented contagion effects (see also Hatfield et al., 1993), one could speculate that the link between contagion and decoding accuracy should vary according to the nature of the contagion-induced emotion. Specifically, based on the AIM model proposed by Forgas (see, e.g., Forgas, 1995) we suggest that affect-infusion effects may modulate this link. Affect infusion refers to the notion that an individual's affective state influences social judgments. While a detailed discussion of this theory exceeds the framework of this paper, suffice it to note the AIM model predicts that contagion of positive emotion leads to a decrease in decoding accuracy, whereas contagion of sadness leads to an increase in decoding accuracy.

## What Does Mimicry Do?

So what are the effects of mimicry? Based on the review of the literature reported above, the strongest effects of mimicry are those that pertain to the social relationship between interaction partners. Specifically, individuals who mimic each other tend to behave in similar ways, experience more similar feeling states, experience rapport, and perceive each other more positively.

In fact, these effects of mimicry may underlie mimicry's purported role in therapeutic success and in the development of empathy.

With regard to the notion that mimicry leads to empathy and prosocial behavior as expressed by Hoffman (1984), mimicry may indeed have this effect, but based on the increase in similarity between interaction partners procured by mimicry and not by the affect induction process proposed by Hoffman. Specifically, mimicry makes us more similar to others and empathy and prosocial behavior have been found to be fostered by similarity between interaction partners (see, e.g., Krebs & Miller, 1985). Thus mimicry may lead to empathy and prosocial behavior via the associated increase in similarity and not via an increase in understanding of the other's state.

With regard to the positive effects of mimicry on the therapeutical process, which were invoked in the introduction, the role of mimicry is likely to be important but not for the reasons assumed by Freud and later by many others. Mimicry does not enhance a therapist's empathy. However, mimicry has a positive effect on rapport and on the feeling of understanding in the client. These two processes may then lead to more verbal disclosure by the client (see Capella, 1981) and thus exert a positive influence on the therapeutic process.

In sum, mimicry may in fact be a magic potion that wields a positive influence on social relationships as well as on therapeutic processes, but mimicry may have this effect because it makes us more similar to our interaction partner, and thus makes the other seem more attractive, more positive, and more worthy of help, and not because it makes us more empathic.

## References

Babad, E., Bernieri, F., & Rosenthal, R. (1989). Nonverbal communication and leakage in the behavior of biased and unbiased teachers. *Journal of Personality and Social Psychology, 56,* 89–94.

Bänninger-Huber, E., & Steiner, F. (1992). Identifying microsequences: A new methodological approach to the analysis of affective regulatory processes. In M. Leuzinger-Bohleber, H. Schneider, & R. Pfeifer (Eds.), *Two butterflies on my head: Psychoanalysis in the interdisciplinary scientific dialogue* (pp. 257–276). Heidelberg: Springer.

Bates, J. E. (1975). Effects of a child's imitation versus nonimitation on adults' verbal and nonverbal positivity. *Journal of Personality and Social Psychology, 31,* 840–851.

Bavelas, J. B., Black, A., Chovil, N., & Lemery, C. R. (1988). Form and function in motor mimicry: Topographic evidence that the primary function is communicative. *Human Communication Research, 14,* 275–299.

Bavelas, J. B., Black, A., Lemery, C. R., & Mullett, J. (1986). "I show how you feel": Motor mimicry as a communicative act. *Journal of Personality and Social Psychology, 50,* 322–329.

Berger, S. M., & Hadley, S. W. (1975). Some effects of a model's performance on an observer's electromyographic activity. *American Journal of Psychology, 88,* 263–276.

Berger, S. M., Carli, L. L., Hammersla, K. S., Karshmer, J. F., & Sanchez, M. E. (1979). Motoric and symbolic mediation in observational learning. *Journal of Personality and Social Psychology, 37,* 735–746.

Bernieri, F. (1988). Coordinated movement and rapport in teacher-student interactions. *Journal of Nonverbal Behavior, 12,* 120–138.

Bernieri, F., Gilles, J. S., Davis, J. M., & Grahe, J. E. (1996). Dyad rapport and the accuracy of its judgment across situations: A lens model analysis. *Journal of Personality and Social Psychology, 71,* 110–129.

Blairy, S., Herrera, P., & Hess, U. (in prep.). *Mimicry and the judgment of emotional facial expressions.* University of Quebec at Montreal.

Bourgeois, P., Couture, J., Herrera, P., Blairy, S., Hess, U., & Philippot, P. (1995). *Induction des émotions par rétroaction faciale et respiratoire.* Poster presented at the 18th annual meeting of the Société Quebecoise pour la Recherche en Psychologie, Ottawa, 27–29 october.

Brunswik, E. (1956). *Perception and the representative design of psychological experiments.* Berkeley and Los Angeles, CA: University of California Press.

Bush, L. K., Barr, C. L., McHugo, G. J., & Lanzetta, J. T. (1989). The effects of facial control and facial mimicry on subjective reactions to comedy routines. *Motivation and Emotion, 13,* 31–52.

Cappella, J. N. (1981). Mutual influence in expressive behavior: Adult-adult and infant-adult dyadic interaction. *Psychological Bulletin, 89,* 101–132.

Cappella, J. N. (1993). The facial feedback hypothesis in human interaction: Review and speculation. Special Issue: Emotional communication, culture, and power. *Journal of Language and Social Psychology, 12,* 13–29.

Charny, J. E. (1966). Psychosomatic manifestations of rapport in psychotherapy. *Psychosomatic Medicine, 28,* 305–315.

Chrisholm, K., & Strayer, J. (1995). Verbal and facial measures of children's emotion and empathy. *Journal of Experimental Child Psychology, 59,* 299–316.

Condon, W. S., & Ogston, W. D. (1966). Sound film analysis of normal and pathological behavior patterns. *Journal of Nervous and Mental Diseases, 143,* 338–457.

Davis, M. R. (1985). Perceptual and affective reverberation components. In A. P. Goldstein & G. Y. Michaels (Eds.), *Empathy: Development, training, and consequences* (pp. 62–108). Hillsdale, NJ: Lawrence Erlbaum.

Dimberg, U. (1982). Facial expressions. *Psychophysiology, 19*(6), 643–647.

Dimberg, U. (1988). Facial expressions and emotional reactions: A psychobiological analysis of human social behavior. In H. L. Wagner (Ed.), *Social psychophysiology and emotion: Theory and clinical applications* (pp. 131–150). Chichester: Wiley & Sons, Ltd.

Dimberg, U. (1990). Facial electromyography and emotional reactions. *Psychophysiology, 27,* 481–494.

Dimberg, U., & Lundqvist, O. (1988). Facial reactions to facial expressions: Sex differences. *Psychophysiology, 25,* 442–443.

Eckerman, C. O., Davis, C. C., & Didow, S. M. (1989). Toddlers' emerging ways of achieving social coordinations with a peer. *Child Development, 60,* 440–453.

Eisenberg, N. (1989). Empathy and sympathy. In U. Clark (Ed.), *Child development today and tomorrow* (pp. 137–154). San Francisco, CA: Jossey-Bass Inc.

Eisenberg, N., & Fabes, R. A. (1990). Empathy: Conceptualization, measurement, and relation to prosocial behavior. *Motivation and Emotion, 14,* 131–149.

Ekman, P., & Friesen, W. V. (1969). Nonverbal leakage and cues to deception. *Psychiatry, 32,* 88–105.

Forgas, J. P. (1995). Mood and judgment: The Affect Infusion Model (AIM). *Psychological Bulletin, 117,* 39–66.

Freud, S. (1955). Group psychology and the analysis of the ego. In J. Strachey (Ed. and Trans.), *The standard edition of the complete psychological works of*

*Sigmund Freud* (Vol. 18). London: Hogarth Press. (Original work published 1921)

Giles, H., & Smith, P. M. (1979). Accommodation theory: Optimal levels of convergence. In H. Giles & R. N. St. Clair (Eds.), *Language and social psychology*, (pp. 45–56). Oxford: Blackwell.

Gump, B. B., & Kulik, J. A. (1997). Stress, affiliation, and emotional contagion. *Journal of Personality and Social Psychology, 72*, 305–319.

Haase, R. F., & Tepper, D. T., Jr. (1972). *Nonverbal components of empathic communication. Journal of Counseling Psychology, 19*, 417–424.

Harper, R., Wiens, A., & Matarasso, J. (1978). Nonverbal communication: The state of the art. New York: Wiley.

Hatfield, E., Cacioppo, J. T., & Rapson, R. L. (1993). *Emotional contagion*. Madison, WI: C. W. Brown.

Hatfield, E., Hsee, C. K., Costello, J., Weisman, M. S., & Denney, C. (1995). The impact of vocal feedback on emotional experience and expression. *Journal of Social Behavior and Personality, 10*, 293–312.

Hess, U., & Blairy, S. (1996). Does watching happy expression make us happy? Facial mimicry and emotional contagion to dynamic emotional facial expressions. *Psychophysiology, 33,* 545 (Abstract).

Hess, U., Philippot, P., & Blairy, S. (1998). Facial reactions to emotional facial expressions: Affect or cognition? *Cognition and Emotion, 12*, 509–532.

Hoffman, M. L. (1984). Interaction of affect and cognition on empathy. In C. E. Izard, J. Kagan, & R. B. Zajonc (Eds.), *Emotion, cognition, and behavior* (pp. 103–131). Cambridge: Cambridge University Press.

Hsee, C. K., Hatfield, E., & Chemtob, C. (1992). Assessments of the emotional states of others: Conscious judgments versus emotional contagion. *Journal of Social and Clinical Psychology, 11*, 119–128.

Ivey, A. E., Ivey, M. B., & Simek-Downing, L. (1987). *Counseling and psychotherapy: Integrating skills, theory, and practice*. Englewood Cliffs, NJ: Prentice-Hall.

Kappas, A. (1991). The illusion of the neutral observer: On the communication of emotion. *Cahiers de linguistique française, 12*, 153–168.

Krebs, D. L., & Miller, D. T. (1985). Altruism and aggression. In G. Lindzey & E. Aronson (Eds.), *Handbook of social psychology* (pp. 1–72). New York: Random House.

LaFrance, M. (1979). Nonverbal synchrony and and rapport: Analysis by the cross-lag panel technique. *Social Psychological Quarterly, 42*, 66–70.

LaFrance, M., & Broadbent, M. (1976). Group rapport: Posture sharing as a nonverbal indicator. *Group and Organization Studies, 1*, 328–333.

LaFrance, M., & Ickes, W. (1981). Posture mirroring and interactional involvement: Sex and sex typing effects. *Journal of Nonverbal Behavior, 5*, 139–154.

Laird, J. D., Alibozak, T., Davainis, D., Deignan, K., Fontanella, K., Hong, J., Levy, B., & Pacheco, C. (1994). Individual differences in the effects of spontaneous mimicry on emotional contagion. *Motivation and Emotion, 18*, 231–247.

Lanzetta, J. T., & Englis, B. G. (1989). Expectations of cooperation and competition and their effects on observers' vicarious emotional responses. *Journal of Personality and Social Psychology, 33,* 354–370.

LaVoie, J. C., & Adams, G. R. (1978). Physical and interpersonal attractiveness of the model and imitation in adults. *The Journal of Social Psychology, 106,* 191–202.

LeBon, G. (1895). *Psychologie des foules.* Paris.

Lipps, T. (1907). Das Wissen von fremden Ichen. In T. Lipps (Ed.), *Psychologische Untersuchungen (Band 1)* (pp. 694–722). Leipzig: Engelmann.

Lundqvist, L. O. (1995). Facial EMG reactions to facial expressions: The case of facial emotional contagion? *Scandinavian Journal of Psychology, 36,* 130–141.

McHugo, G. J., Lanzetta, J. T., & Bush, L. K. (1991). The effect of attitudes on emotional reactions to expressive displays of political leaders. *Journal of Nonverbal Behavior, 15,* 19–41.

McHugo, G. J., Lanzetta, J. T., Sullivan, D. G., Masters, R. D., & Englis, B. G. (1985). Emotional reactions to a political leader's expressive displays. *Journal of Personality and Social Psychology, 49,* 1513–1529.

McHugo, G. J., & Smith, C. A. (1996). The power of faces: A review of John T. Lanzetta's research on facial expression and emotion. *Motivation and Emotion, 20,* 85–120.

Manstead, A. S. R. (1988). The role of facial movement in emotion. In H. L. Wagner (Ed.), *Social psychophysiology: Theory and clinical application* (pp. 105–129). Chichester: John Wiley and Sons, Ltd.

Manusov, V. (1993). "It depends on your perspective": Effects of stance and beliefs about intent on person perception. *Western Journal of Speech Communication, 57,* 27–41.

Markovsky, B., & Berger, S. M. (1983). Crowd noise and mimicry. *Personality and Social Psychology Bulletin, 9,* 90–96.

Masson, J. M. (Ed. and Trans.) (1985). *The complete letters of Sigmund Freud to Wilhelm Fliess, 1887–1904.* Cambridge, MA: Belknap.

Matsumoto, D. (1987). The role of facial response in the experience of emotion: More methodological problems and a meta-analysis. *Journal of Personality and Social Psychology, 52,* 759–768.

Maurer, R. I., & Tindall, J. H. (1983). Effect of postural congruence on client's perception of counselor empathy. *Journal of Counseling Psychology, 30,* 158–163.

Meltzhoff, A. N., & Moore, M. K. (1992). Early imitation within a functional framework: The importance of person identity, movement, and development. *Infant Behavior and Development, 15,* 479–505.

Meltzhoff, A. N., & Moore, M. K. (1994). Imitation, memory, and the representation of persons. *Infant Behavior and Development, 17,* 83–99.

Navarre, D. (1981). *Posture sharing in the interview dyad.* Unpublished doctoral dissertation, State University of New York at Buffalo.

Navarre, D. (1982). Posture sharing in dyadic interaction. *American Journal of Dance Therapy, 5,* 28–42.

Piaget, J. (1959). *La formation du symbole chez l'enfant : imitation, jeu et reve* (Play, dreams, and imitation in childhood). Neuchatel, Suisse: Delachaux & Niestle.

Rogers, C. R. (1957). The necessary and sufficient conditions of therapeutic personality change. *Journal of Consulting Psychology, 21,* 95–103.

Rogers, C. (1975). Empathic: An unappreciated way of being. *The Counseling Psychologist, 5,* 2–9.

Scheflen, A. (1964). The significance of posture in communication systems. *Psychiatry, 27,* 316–331.

Scheflen, A. E. (1972). *Body language and social order: Communication as behavioral control.* Englewood Cliffs, NJ: Prentice Hall.

Scherer, K. R. (1978). Personality inference from voice quality: The loud voice of extraversion. *European Journal of Social Psychology, 8,* 467–487.

Schmais, C., & Schmais, A. (1983). Reflecting emotions: The movement-mirroring test. *Journal of Nonverbal Behavior, 8,* 42–54.

Siegel, E. V. (1995). Psychoanalytic dance therapy: The bridge between psyche and soma. *American Journal of Dance Therapy, 17,* 115–128.

Stepper, S., & Strack, F. (1993). Proprioceptive determinants of affective and nonaffective feelings. *Journal of Personality and Social Psychology, 64,* 211–220.

Sullins, E. S. (1991). Emotional contagion revisited: Effects of social comparison and expressive style on mood congruence. *Personality and Social Psychology Bulletin, 17,* 166–174.

Vaughan, K. B., & Lanzetta, J. T. (1980). Vicarious instigation and conditioning of facial expressive and autonomic responses to a model's expressive displays of pain. *Journal of Personality and Social Psychology, 38,* 909–923.

Vaughan, K. B., & Lanzetta, J. T. (1981). The effect of modification of expressive displays on vicarious emotional arousal. *Journal of Experimental Social Psychology, 17,* 16–30.

Wallbott, H. G. (1991). Recognition of emotion from facial expression via imitation? Some indirect evidence for an old theory. *British Journal of Social Psychology, 30,* 207–219.

# 9. Facial Expression and Emotion

## A Situationist View

JOSÉ-MIGUEL FERNÁNDEZ-DOLS

For centuries, people – including all kinds of scholars – have been influenced by the colorful and attractive term *expression of emotion*. The term *expression* comes from the Latin word *exprimere*, meaning "to squeeze out." The etymology suggests that when we "express," we "squeeze out" our emotions.

A casual use of this term has led people to think that facial behavior "squeezes out" emotion, and some researchers have looked for "universal" prototypical facial configurations directly squeezed out of the experience of some particular "basic" emotions (e.g., Tomkins, 1962). In this view, "universal" means that these expressions of emotion are autonomous, separate entities that are internally determined. Of course, researchers concede that a situation can influence people's facial behavior, but as a kind of "noise," an epiphenomenon that merely interferes with the universal signal.

The central assumption of this approach – the existence of a small number of prototypical expressions of basic emotion – has a puzzling peculiarity: It does not fit the available empirical data about the actual facial behavior of people, or even nonhuman primates, experiencing intense emotions.

One typical example of this problem concerns the smile of happiness, which has been portrayed as the clearest example of a universal prototypical expression, with the highest ratings of recognition across different cultures. Smiles have been defined as the result of pulling the lip corners obliquely; researchers have considered that true happy smiles include also the action of orbicularis oculi pulling the skin from

The research presented in this chapter was supported by the award PS95–0042 from the Spanish DGICyT.

242

the cheeks and forehead toward the eyeball (Ekman, 1992). This expression, called the Duchenne smile, has been considered as the prototypical expression of happiness. Interestingly, the links between happiness and smiling are uncertain, both from an evolutionary and from an empirical point of view.

In evolutionary terms, the homology between human smiles and other primates' most comparable facial behavior (the "silent bared-teeth"; Van Hooff, 1972; Preuschoft, 1992) is restricted to the morphological resemblance of the two gestures. The homology provides no evidence of a necessary or sufficient link between these similar facial movements and the experience of happiness. In fact, this facial behavior is, in most of the primates, linked to affiliative contacts and situations in which animals are having a hard time, for example, trying to appease others or facing danger. In anthropomorphic terms, we can say, for example, that Tokean macaques smile when they are seeking friends and chimpanzees smile when they are afraid (Preuschoft & Van Hooff, 1995).

This uncertain state of things poses a series of interesting warnings about how to apply a limited pattern of behavioral homologies to the complexities of human psychology (see also Fridlund, 1994). The evolutionary bases of the claimed link between smiling and happiness only support a Minimal Universality hypothesis (Russell & Fernández-Dols, 1997). This hypothesis claims universality for muscular movement itself, but not for its psychological background. Hollywood moviemakers have overcome minimal universality in an unfortunate way: When they want to show chimpanzees with "happy" smiles, they give them an electric shock. The chimpanzees display the "silent bared-teeth" face and people "recognize the happiness" of their remote relatives (see Reynolds, 1981, p. 89). However, psychologists should not model themselves on Hollywood moviemakers. We should try not to propel our assumptions beyond the evidence.

This point leads us to the second source of uncertainty about a presumed universal expression of happiness. What are people's actual facial behavior when they are very happy? Over the last few years we have been trying to answer this question by recording the facial behavior of adults who are experiencing strong emotions, and particularly happiness. Each time, smiling was not found as the most characteristic expression, or it was simply not observed at all (Fernández-Dols & Ruiz-Belda, 1995a; Kraut & Johnston, 1979; Ruiz-Belda & Fernández-Dols, 1997). We found that smiling had no necessary or sufficient link with emotional experience, but that it was linked to social interaction.

This problem with the relation between happiness and smiling could be extended to other emotions and their presumed facial expressions. We have discussed these problems elsewhere (see Fernández-Dols & Ruiz-Belda, 1997), problems that raise serious questions about the empirical support of the universality of "facial expressions" (Russell & Fernández-Dols, 1997). In this paper I shall consider new aspects of "facial expressions" by focusing on a theoretical alternative to current mainstream views. In order to do so, I shall introduce a theoretical framework that has not been considered by current researchers on facial behavior and emotion: the situationist approach.

## The Situationist Approach

The situationist approach to facial expressions has been available in psychology for a considerable time. George Herbert Mead (1934) pointed out, following Wundt, that gestures are parts of a social act that serves as stimulus to other individuals' acts. These gestural interactions are not necessarily deliberate and are compared by Mead to boxers' and fencers' feints and parries. Neither Wundt nor Mead approved of Darwin's approach to facial gestures as "expressions" of emotion:

> It was easy for Wundt to show that [Darwin's] was not a legitimate point of attack on the problem of these gestures. They did not at bottom serve the function of expression of the emotions: that was not the reason why they were stimuli, but rather because they were parts of complex acts in which different forms were involved. They became the tools through which the other forms responded. . . . They are part of the organization of the social act, and highly important elements in that organization. (Mead, 1967, p. 44)

Wundt's and Mead's views provide researchers with important alternatives to current approaches. For these authors, the only feasible scientific way of describing facial gestures consists of analyzing facial expressions as a fraction of an interactive process. Emotions are only a likely psychological counterpart of facial behavior, with no necessary or sufficient relationship to the gestures themselves. What we usually mean by "facial expression" consists of interactive readiness patterns that precede consciousness. These patterns are not aimed at "expressing" – squeezing out – any content in the mind of the individual.

Psychologists were sympathetic to the situationist approach to facial behavior until the 1960s (e.g., Bruner & Tagiuri, 1954). At this time, Tomkins's interpretation of Darwin established the assumption of a restricted set of universal expressions of emotion, which still constitutes the mainstream approach to this question (e.g., Baron & Byrne, 1997).

Paradoxically, current ethologists are much closer to Mead's criticisms of Darwin and, as early as the 1970s, they developed the "expression as interaction" approach (Hinde, 1985; Smith, 1977). Ethologists portrayed facial behavior as an interactive phenomenon, whose meaning cannot be disentangled from its context. As eminent ethologist Robert Hinde (1982) has pointed out, the context is essential to the meaning of a message ("message plus context = meaning"). In this view, emotions are an important factor, but just one more factor, neither necessary nor sufficient, in facial messages. The meaning of a facial behavior is mostly understood in terms of its interactive context. Fridlund's (1994) theory is a first step toward recovering this approach to facial behavior, completely neglected in the psychology of emotion over the last twenty years (for a description of Fridlund's theory, see the chapter by Manstead, Fischer and Jakobs in this volume).

Besides the ethological approach, contemporary social psychology should also be able to provide psychologists with interesting tools for the study of facial behavior. According to situationist social psychology, founded by Kurt Lewin, behavior can be more accurately explained and predicted as a portion of a situation embedded in a dynamic tension system (Ross & Nisbett, 1991).

Approaches of Lewinian inspiration are quite rare in the study of facial expression (cf. Bavelas & Chovil, 1997). Even social psychologists' studies on this issue are usually based on theoretical models such as Ekman's (1972) and Izard's (1971), which were mostly inspired by the strongly antisituationist views of biologists such as Darwin and clinicians such as Tomkins (1962).

How can facial behavior be approached from a Lewinian standpoint? First, researchers should not be misled by the etymology of the word *expression*. The emotions cannot be simply "squeezed out" into a limited, universal, and autonomous set of expressions. Any behavior, including facial behavior, should be explained in terms of the situation in which it is observed. It is dynamic tensions between inducing and restricting factors that cause expressions. Thus, emotions are an important factor, but just one more factor, neither necessary nor sufficient, in facial behavior. Changes in facial behavior are best understood in terms of situational variables.

In the following paragraphs I shall explore this alternative line of thought and its potential for overcoming some of the limitations of studying facial behavior in terms of "universal expressions." In particular I shall argue that mainstream researchers' lack of attention to the concepts of situation and tension system (Ross & Nisbett, 1991) has led them to commit three serious errors that are probably widespread in commonsense approaches to facial behavior. (a) First, people (including psychologists) mix up different kinds of behavior under the label "expression," giving rise to *unrealistic descriptions* of this phenomenon. (b) This lack of realism misleads people's (including psychologists') interpretations of situations in which facial expressions are displayed, resulting in attributional errors. (c) Finally, unrealistic representations of expressions and expressive situations are aggravated by a widespread lack of attention to the *dynamic relationships* among the factors that cause facial behavior.

## Unrealistic Description of the Expression

The commonsense view on facial expression – whose closest scientific version is Ekman's (1972) Neurocultural Model – assumes that emotion triggers spontaneous signals easily recognized by human beings. Variation in these signals is explained as the result of following learned display rules aimed at feigning the appropriate or suppressing the inappropriate expression.

Unfortunately, while this description may fit commonsense views, it hardly fits an empirical description of facial behavior. The most apparent conceptual problem is that this model mixes up *molecular* and *molar* categories, treating them as equivalent to one another.

*Molecular* categories consist of quite specific actions (Sackett, Ruppenthal, & Gluck, 1978). A molecular category of facial behavior is an exclusive set of muscular movements (e.g., movement of the zygomaticus major). *Molar* categories combine different kinds of behavior in generic classes defined by the outcome of the actions; a molar category is an aggregate of different and interchangeable motor actions that are described under a generic label (e.g., polite smiling).

The "expressions," as alluded to in the definition of the prototypical and universal expressions of emotion, are *molecular* categories. They are described by a restricted set of muscular movements and last for a few seconds (Ekman, 1984). On the other hand, the concept of display rules requires a *molar* description of facial behavior. Display rules are defined as culturally learned rules regarding the appropriateness of showing certain expressions in certain situations, that is, establishing when people can or cannot display their "true," "spontaneous" expressions of emotion (e.g., when people feel obliged to resort to a conscious control of their facial behavior by either feigning other expressions, or attenuating, amplifying, or suppressing the "real one"). The "expressions" alluded to in this definition summarize a heterogeneous set of facial actions over periods that may last for minutes or even hours.

The accuracy of molar and molecular descriptions are not necessarily related, and cannot confirm or disconfirm one another. For example, we can say, in molar terms, that we have been reading this book for an hour, even though, in molecular terms, we could say that we have been drinking tea during a period included in this last hour.

Thus, commonsense views and the Neurocultural Model are vague in terms of how they describe expressive behavior and the causes of its variation. Variation of a molecular category of facial behavior ("expression") is not necessarily linked to the variation of a molar category of facial behavior ("expression"?). The molecular "expression" of emotion and the molar "expression" governed by display rules are different phenomena. For example, soccer fans can facially react with a frown at the very moment their team scores, but subsequently display a more complex and social facial behavior most of the time (e.g., smiles).

The lumping together of two different kinds of facial behavior (those determined by the molar strategies and those determined by molecular reactions) as a sole phenomenon ("facial expression of emotion"), has led to serious problems. Friesen's (1972) study, considered the most convincing evidence of display rules, consisted of a comparison between Japanese and American students. Their facial behavior was observed at two different times: when watching alone the third of a series of three stressful film clips, and when interacting with an interviewer while watching, for a second time, the first of the three stressful clips. Friesen concluded that the Japanese and American students displayed similar expressions in the first condition but followed different display rules in the second condition, in which the Japanese students showed fewer negative facial expressions. Irrespective of some problems about the inference of expressive homogeneity in the first condition,[1] Friesen's study mixed up, as the same kind of "expression," two very different categories of facial behavior. On one side, the students' molecular, *direct* reactions to particular stimuli from a stressful film. On the other, a short episode of molar, interactive strategies when students were talking with an interviewer while the clips were appearing on the screen.

This second, molar facial strategy was, undoubtedly, directly influenced by several important nonemotional factors, such as the interviewer's own facial behavior, students' interpretation of the situation (e.g., in terms of status), the previous interactive sequence, and students' self-presentation and impression management. It is not clear, however, that this second condition elicited any particular emotion. Even if emotions were elicited, it is not clear whether any emotional reaction in this interactive sequence was caused by the stressful films. They were more likely to have been caused by other, more salient situational factors (e.g., the interviewer himself).

For example, American students' more frequent negative expressions might be the result, not of less concealment of their emotional reactions to the film, but of using facial mimics as symbolic messages (e.g., illustrators) to the interviewer while describing the films (see Chovil, 1991). Equally, Japanese students' neutral or positive expressions might be a consequence, not of concealing their emotional reactions to the film, but of a sincere appreciation of the interviewer's concern about their current state of mind. In summary, the display rules described by Friesen in this study are not necessarily about the molecular facial reactions to a particular emotional elicitor, but rather about a later molar interactive episode only indirectly related to the prior experience of emotion.

Friesen's experiment led some psychologists to assume that any variation in the universal "expressions of emotion" was explained by

---

[1] There were several problems in the comparison between the first condition and the second condition. Students' facial behavior in the first condition was not as homogeneous as expected. For example, the most frequent facial response was "surprise" in the Americans, whereas it was "sadness" in the Japanese (see Fernández-Dols & Ruiz-Belda, 1997, for a discussion of this question). Furthermore, the second condition included two episodes, and in the first of these – which is not usually mentioned in the summaries of Friesen's study – Japanese and American students displayed similar facial behavior (Friesen, 1972).

display rules, that is, restricted to learned habits of interaction. Not surprisingly, as mentioned above, recent empirical evidence shows that this conclusion was premature. Researchers have found a wide variability in the instantaneous, molecular facial reactions of intense emotion, which cannot be explained either in terms of "display rules" or "facial expressions of emotion" (Camras, Malatesta, & Izard, 1991; Carroll & Russell, 1997; Fernández-Dols & Ruiz-Belda, 1995a; Fernández-Dols, Sánchez, Carrera, & Ruiz-Belda, 1997; Kraut & Johnston, 1979).

Lack of realism in the description of facial expressions results from the strong antisituationist stance of models such as the neurocultural one. Research on "facial expression" confuses the facial behavior linked to an instantaneous experience of emotion and the facial behavior linked to the interaction surrounding an emotional episode. The spontaneous facial behavior of people in intense emotional episodes is a complex and changeable process that does not fit the prototypical models suggested by common sense.

## Attribution Errors

The controversy between situationism and dispositionism was one of the most important psychological debates of the 1970s. Today, psychological wisdom endorses most of Mischel's (1968) skepticism about the prevalence of cross-situational dispositions and their corresponding behavioral consistencies across settings. In this vein, one of the main tasks of social psychologists has been to show that people, including researchers, underestimate situational influences, while overestimating dispositional influences (Jones & Nisbett, 1971; Ross, 1977). Laypeople and psychologists alike seem too often to be "nativists": They infer stable abilities attitudes and personality traits, and expect "consistency in behavior or outcomes across widely disparate situations and contexts" (Ross, 1977, p. 184).

Even though some authors (see Russell, 1994, 1995; cf. Ekman, 1995; Izard, 1995) have provided evidence of methodological and conceptual flaws in the recognition studies, it is clear that people (at least people from literate cultures, and at least in some conditions) are attributing particular emotions to particular faces. This pattern of attribution is called the "universal recognition of emotion," and it might be considered as another case of the "nativism" denounced by Ross.

The first evidence for this suspicion is the striking contrast between actual behavior and "universal expression." The empirical studies that have tried to describe the actual coherence between experience of emotion and facial behavior have provided ambiguous or negative results. Why, then, do people attribute particular emotions to particular faces with remarkable consistency?

The most feasible answer to this question is suggested by the above-mentioned unrealistic description of facial expressions. When people "recognize" emotions they are simply making a kind of illusory correlation. They link some emotions to some gestures that, in fact, lack any necessary or sufficient connection with the experience of emotion. Salient facial gestures and emotions are extracted from long-term interactive situations and lumped together into an ideal and unrealistically consistent representation of an "emotional expression." For example, affiliative smiling and happiness are usually observed in the same interactive situations, which leads people to believe that smiling is a sign of happiness across all kinds of situations and contexts.

Indirect evidence supporting this hypothesis comes from Carroll and Russell's (1996) study on the way in which people judge combinations of facial and contextual sources of information. Most of the researchers found (see Fernández-Dols & Carroll, 1997) that people judged combinations in terms of the facial information. Carroll and Russell reversed this trend by using prototypical "expressions of emotion" (e.g., anger) whose physical features (e.g., staring eyes, furrowed eyebrows, lips pressed tightly together) could be explained by nonemotional actions included in the situation (e.g., a person peering at a distant message and having difficulty in making a decision about it).

In the above-mentioned example, a usually labeled "expression of anger" became an "expression of puzzlement" because it was displaying physical actions that were plausible for nonemotional reasons. People could "recognize" that a "universal expression" is not necessarily related to a sole emotion. Some salient situational hints helped them to overcome the bias that leads to "recognizing" universal expressions.

Direct evidence in support of this conclusion comes from a series of studies carried out by Fernández-Dols and Russell (1992). People were given the opportunity of "unlumping" the situation by explicitly focusing their attention on two different periods: the molecular, noninteractive experience of emotion and the molar interaction that surrounds the emotion.

In the first study of this series of experiments, stimuli were 11 pairs of neutral faces and prototypical "expressions of emotion" and 11 pairs of sentences. Both sentences described the same emotional episode. In one sentence ("immediate experience") the protagonist was mentally appraising the situation. In the other ("long-term interaction"), the protagonist was communicating her experience by speaking to someone. For instance, in one condition concerning happiness, the facial expression was a smile and the pair of sentences concerned winning the lottery. In the "immediate experience" condition, the protagonist thought "We have won the prize!"; in the "long-term interaction" condition, the protagonist spoke to someone, saying "John, we have won the prize!" To emphasize the difference between the two conditions, we borrowed a convention from cartoons. The social/spoken versions of the sentences are given in Table 9.1.

Subjects were tested individually in 11 trials, each concerning one emotion. The experimenter presented each pair of photographs and corresponding pair of sentences. Subjects were asked to pair faces and

Table 9.1. *Percentage of subjects associating facial displays with a spoken, social situation (Fernández-Dols & Russell, 1992)*

| Emotion | Spoken version of sentence | Percentage |
|---|---|---|
| Happiness | "John, we have won the prize!" | 85.0 |
| | "John, our son will come back from the war tomorrow!" | 85.0 |
| Anger | "You harmed our son!" | 95.0 |
| | "Peter, you cheated me!" | 60.0 |
| | "Lionel, you have made me miss the bus!" | 80.0 |
| Sadness | "John, I miss my son so much!" | 70.0 |
| | "Sweetheart, I have not passed the exam!" | 80.0 |
| Fear | "Please, help me! There is somebody hiding in my kitchen!" | 90.0 |
| | "John, please help me! A strange man is following me!" | 95.0 |
| Disgust | "Look at this dead rat!" | 65.0 |
| | "Look at this food, it's spoiled!" | 85.0 |

Note: $N = 20$

sentences in the "most plausible" or "most natural" way. The experimenter pointed out that one sentence was thought, the other spoken, and there were no right or wrong answers.

Table 9.1 shows the percentage of subjects associating the facial display with the spoken sentence, that is, the social situation. Overall, facial expression was associated with the spoken sentence in 178 of the 220 trials (80.9%). For each type of emotion, most of the subjects (from 75% to 92.5%) placed the facial display with the spoken version of the sentence.[2] Moreover, every subject individually showed this pattern; across the 11 trials the median number of spoken sentences associated with emotion expression was 9, with a range of 6 to 11.

As we expected, subjects were able to differentiate the actual, immediate experience of emotion from the surrounding interaction. This simple manipulation allowed us to show that people do not necessarily link "expressions of emotion" to the experience of emotion ("immediate experience" condition), but rather to other actions. The usual "recognition" studies do not take into account these other actions (e.g., communicative actions). Thus, subjects are forced into making raw, large-scale correlations between facial behavior and emotion. Further research is needed to support the primary conclusion from this data: that "universal recognition of emotions" is an attributional error caused by representational heuristics and misinterpreted by psychologists' "nativist" approach to facial behavior.

### Lack of Attention to the Tension System

From a Lewinian standpoint, expressions should be the result of a tension system. Ross and Nisbett (1991) made two important observations about tension systems. The first is that a particular phenomenon is determined not only by inducing but also by restricting forces. The second observation is that many behavioral systems are in quasi-stationary equilibrium, as a result of a balance of conflicting forces. These two principles have a corollary: There is no clear proportion

---

[2] A feasible alternative interpretation of these results is that subjects' pairing occurred because the pairing of the neutral display with the spoken version seemed somehow unnatural (for example, because the pictures suggest no movement of lips). A study tested this hypothesis by asking judges to rate all possible combinations of faces and sentences. Thus, we excluded all the combinations rated as "unnatural" from the data. Results again confirmed our hypothesis, that is, "expressions" were linked to the interactive vignette.

between the magnitude of a force acting upon a system and the magnitude of its consequences. A large force may be incapable of breaking the complex balance between different small forces, while a small force can cause dramatic changes in an apparently stable system (which, in fact, is subject to important tensions in unstable equilibrium). Lewin called these forces, which can change behavior, "channel factors," since they open or close the flow of a particular behavior.

Dissonance theory (Festinger, 1957) is a prototypical example of the application of these assumptions to attitudes. An apparently petty situation (e.g., giving a short speech for a token amount of money) can change our attitudes because of tension between conflicting attitudes and behavior, or between others' and our own attitudes. Another recent example of the Lewinian approach is Steele and Aronson's (1995) research on a controversial issue (the intellectual test performances of African Americans). Steele and Aronson found that some minimal situational changes (a change in the description of the test that enhanced the risk of confirming a negative stereotype) impaired African American students' performance, altering the tension system of negative and positive forces that collide in any evaluative situation.

The concept of tension system leads to a radical reconsideration of concepts such as "expression" and "display rule." As referred to above, the "universal expression of happiness" is not actually observed in most spontaneous episodes of intense happiness (e.g., Fernández-Dols & Ruiz-Belda, 1995b), and this mismatch has also been observed for other emotions.

For example, Ruiz-Belda and Fernández-Dols (1997) carried out two field studies in which emotions were reported by 10 players in a bowling alley and 20 soccer fans watching their team. All interactive and noninteractive facial behavior immediately prior to the emotion reports was codified. Happiness predicted smiling only for episodes of interaction. The experience of anger, fear, sadness, disgust, and surprise, meanwhile, never predicted any of the expressions of basic emotion described by Ekman and Friesen (1978). Similar findings for different emotions have been reported by Camras (Camras, Malatesta, & Izard, 1991), Fernández-Dols and Ruiz-Belda (1995a), Fernández-Dols, Sánchez, Carrera, and Ruiz-Belda (1997), and Kraut and Johnston (1979).

The important thing here is that careful empirical description of facial behavior of intense emotion reveals a remarkable variety of facial behaviors. This finding suggests that true "expressions" of emotion are in fact the output of complex tension systems. Figure 9.1 shows three different kinds of "expressions of happiness" by people who obviously did not try to control or disguise their facial behavior: Olympic gold medalists when they were on the podium (Fernández-Dols & Ruiz-Belda, 1995a), winners when they realized they had won (Fernández-Dols & Ruiz-Belda, 1995b), and toreros (bullfighters) "in the flow," absorbed in their fight (García-Higuera & Fernández-Dols, 1997). The bullfighters' facial behavior is particularly striking, and

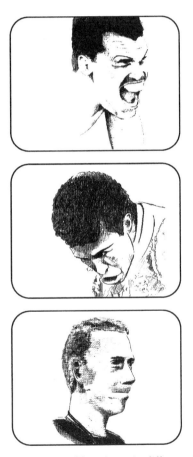

Figure 9.1. Three expressions of happiness in different situations: (from top to bottom) a swimmer at the moment in which he realizes he has won, a bullfighter "in the flow," and an Olympic gold medalist during the awards ceremony.

concerns intense emotional experience. We found this specific expression consistently linked to the moment in which the bullfighter is completely absorbed in his fight, having been successful in deceiving the animal. Bullfighters must focus all their attentional resources on the bull. They are not conscious of their facial expression, which in any case lacks relevance in bullfighting since spectators cannot see the bullfighter's face from their seats. According to toreros' reports, this is "the happiest time" in their life, a moment they would not trade for any other experience.

Actual facial behavior during periods of intense emotion is a complex and rapid succession of facial movements, and "channel factors" entrain this stream of behavior into stable facial configurations. Figure 9.2 shows one typical unstable tension system in an episode of intense happiness. An Olympic gold medalist displays, over less than one second, various facial configurations, which are entrained into a prototypical expression of happiness when she interacts with people around her. The "channel factor" of stable smiling is "mundane" interaction, not "dramatic" emotion.

With respect to "display rules," the concept of tension system leads us to abandon the mainstream approach, in which expression is substantially invariant across situations and display rules are epiphenomenal, a kind of noise that can momentarily change facial appearance but is not inherent to the expression of emotion.

If we assume that molecular facial expressions of emotion are the unstable, instantaneous, and unbidden (see Ekman, 1992) output of a tension system, display rules become a factor that could only be effective if instantaneous and automatically elicited.[3] In this case, however,

---

[3] If we are not prepared to accept that "true" facial expressions of emotion and display rules are equally instantaneous and unbidden, then the only plausible hypothesis is that conscious display rules control not the molecular expressions themselves, but other molar expressions derived from the spontaneous episode. For example, if you smile in triumph and then you discover that your friend is sad, you may try to repress further smiling. In this kind of situation, display rules would not concern the "true" instantaneous expressions of emotion themselves, but rather other facial behavior loosely related to emotions that can be observed in long-term interactive sequences.

An alternative, but even more problematic, line of reasoning would consist of assuming that display rules are unconscious. In this case, we are talking about a mysterious construct that makes the causal link between facial expression and emotion unfalsifiable: Any case in which spontaneous facial behavior does not fit the predicted prototypical expressions could be explained in terms of a cultural or idiosyncratic (unobserved) display rule.

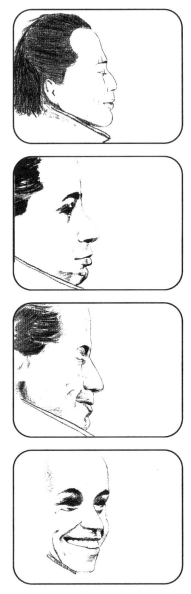

Figure 9.2. A dynamic tension system in action. An Olympic gold medalist displays, over less than one second, a large number of rapid and unstable expressions during a noninteractive stage of the ceremony. She finally displays a stable social smile (bottom) when a "channel factor," a particular social interaction, appears. (Reprinted from Fernández-Dols & Ruiz-Belda (1995b), with permission of Kluwer Academic Press.)

we would have no reason to consider instantaneous (and presumably unbidden) display rules as less "spontaneous" and "unbidden" than emotion.

Thus, "display rules" are not merely "noise" that prevents the manifestation of true "universal expressions." As mentioned above, the tension system approach assumes that a phenomenon is determined not only by inducing but also by restricting forces. Display rules can become a primary cause of facial behavior. In this way, the concept of display rule must be included in a larger framework (see the interesting concept of "display management" by Saarni and Weber in this volume) in which the relationship between facial behavior and emotion is more complex. In this view, people – even very young children – do not simply control their expression when they feel an emotion in a particular situation. People *simultaneously* control their expression and their own emotional experience in the flow of a social interaction. There is no unidirectional, causal relation between emotion and expression: The expression, the emotion, and the interactive strategies (including display rules) constitute a system that includes bidirectional causal relations. In fact, the lack of observational studies of pure display rules at work, either in children (see Saarni and Weber, in this volume) or adults (see Matsumoto, 1990, and Kupperbusch et al. in this volume), may be indicative of the empirical and logical impossibility of describing display rules as a mere filter that distorts universal, ready-to-use packages of facial expressions.

Further empirical support for the tension-system approach to facial expression comes from various sources, including the study of the development and regulation of human facial behavior.

Most of the research on the sociality of facial expression (see chapters by Wagner and Lee, and by Manstead, Fischer, and Jakobs in this volume) indirectly supports this view by endorsing the need for more complex causal hypotheses about the relationship between emotion, interaction, and facial behavior. Nevertheless, Fogel, a developmental psychologist, and his collaborators (see Fogel & Thelen, 1987; Messinger, Fogel, & Dickson, 1997) are the only authors who have explicitly and systematically endorsed an approach to expressions as outputs of dynamic systems. From this approach, "the mutual influence of facial actions with neurophysiological and interpersonal factors ... means that facial actions index interrelationships between [muscular, cerebral, neural, attentional, experiential, and interactive] relevant constituents" (Messinger et al., 1997, p. 206). For example, Messinger points out how different kinds of smiling (e.g., play smiling or Duchenne smiling) could arise, through development, as a "down-top" process: Simultaneous interaction with different "channel factors" of the environment (e.g., wincing in intense affective reactions plus smiling in social encounters) would create patterns of neural activity associated with the production and perception of certain facial configurations.

## Conclusion

A cursory approach to facial behavior and emotion from situationist social psychology suggests that researchers should:

1. Carefully describe the actual situations in which facial behavior is performed and emotions elicited. We should discriminate between the lumping together of facial behavior and emotion (i.e., the "expressions") and the real – and much more complex – relationship between these phenomena.
2. Analyze the fascinating attributional error that leads to the above-mentioned "lumping together," as a new line of inquiry within the field of attributional biases.
3. Reconsider the simplistic, linear relationships between facial behavior and emotion suggested by previous research. We should develop and test models in which facial behavior is approached as an output of a tension system of situational and affective forces.

How worthwhile is it to carry out studies from this alternative perspective? There is no categorical answer to this question. The only valid answer in science is long-term productivity. And, in terms of productivity, my guess is that the situationist approach is potentially far more productive than the "universal expression" approach.

## References

Baron, R. A., & Byrne, D. (1997). *Social Psychology* (8th ed.). Boston: Allyn and Bacon.

Bavelas, J. B., & Chovil, N. (1997). Faces in dialogue. In J. A. Russell & J. M. Fernández-Dols (Eds.), *The psychology of facial expression* (pp. 334–346). New York: Cambridge University Press.

Bruner, J. S., & Tagiuri, R. (1954). The perception of people. In G. Lindzey (Ed.), *Handbook of social psychology* (Vol. 2, pp. 634–654). Cambridge, MA: Addison-Wesley.

Camras, L. A., Malatesta, C., & Izard, C. E. (1991). The development of facial expressions in infancy. In R. S. Feldman & B. Rimé (Eds.), *Fundamentals of nonverbal behavior* (pp. 73–105). Cambridge: Cambridge University Press.

Carroll, J. M., & Russell, J. A. (1996). Do facial expressions signal specific emotions? Judging emotion from faces in context. *Journal of Personality and Social Psychology, 70,* 205–218.

Carroll, J. M., & Russell, J. A. (1997). Facial expressions in Hollywood's portrayal of emotion. *Journal of Personality and Social Psychology, 72,* 164–176.

Chovil, N. (1991). Social determinants of facial displays. *Journal of Nonverbal Behavior, 15,* 141–154.

Ekman, P. (1972). Universals and cultural differences in facial expressions of emotion. In J. K. Cole (Ed.), *Nebraska Symposium on Motivation, 1971* (Vol. 19, pp. 207–283). Lincoln, NE: University of Nebraska Press.

Ekman, P. (1984). Expression and the nature of emotion. In K. R. Scherer & P. Ekman (Eds.), *Approaches to emotion* (pp. 319–343). Hillsdale, NJ: Lawrence Erlbaum.

Ekman, P. (1992). An argument for basic emotions. *Cognition and Emotion, 6,* 169–200.

Ekman, P. (1995). Strong evidence for universals in facial expression: A reply to Russell's mistaken critique. *Psychological Bulletin, 115,* 286–287.

Ekman, P., & Friesen, W. V. (1978). *Facial Action Coding System (FACS): A technique for the measurement of facial action.* Palo Alto, CA: Consulting Psychologists Press.

Fernández-Dols, J. M., & Carroll, J. M. (1997). Is the meaning perceived in facial expression independent of its context? In J. A. Russell & J. M. Fernández-Dols (Eds.), *The psychology of facial expression* (pp. 275–294). New York: Cambridge University Press.

Fernández-Dols, J. M., & Ruiz-Belda, M. A. (1995a). Are smiles a sign of happiness?: Gold medal winners at the Olympic Games. *Journal of Personality and Social Psychology, 69,* 1113–1119.

Fernández-Dols, J. M., & Ruiz-Belda, M. A. (1995b). Expression of emotion versus expressions of emotions: Everyday conceptions about spontaneous facial behavior. In J. A. Russell, J. M. Fernández-Dols, A. S. R. Manstead, & J. C. Wellenkamp (Eds.), *Everyday conceptions of emotion* (pp. 505–522). Dordrecht, NL: Kluwer Academic Press.

Fernández-Dols, J. M., & Ruiz-Belda, M. A. (1997). Spontaneous facial behavior during intense emotional episodes: Artistic truth and optical truth. In J. A. Russell & J. M. Fernández-Dols (Eds.), *The psychology of facial expression* (pp. 255–274). New York: Cambridge University Press.

Fernández-Dols, J. M., & Russell, J. A. (1992). *Are facial displays social or emotional?* Unpublished manuscript.

Fernández-Dols, J. M., Sánchez, F., Carrera, P., & Ruiz-Belda, M. A. (1997). Are spontaneous expressions and emotions linked? An experimental test of coherence. *Journal of Nonverbal Behavior, 21,* 163–177.

Festinger, L. (1957). *A theory of cognitive dissonance.* Palo Alto, CA: Stanford University Press.

Fogel, A., & Thelen, E. (1987). Development of early expressive and communicative action: Reinterpreting the evidence from a dynamic systems perspective. *Developmental Psychology, 23,* 747–761.

Fridlund, A. J. (1994). *Human facial expression: An evolutionary view.* San Diego, CA: Academic Press.

Friesen, W. V. (1972). *Cultural differences in facial expression in a social situation: An experimental test of the concept of display rules.* Unpublished doctoral dissertation, University of California, San Francisco, CA.

García-Higuera, J. A., & Fernández-Dols, J. M. (1996). Unpublished raw data.

Hinde, R. A. (1982). *Ethology.* Glasgow, UK: Fontana.

Hinde, R. A. (1985). Expression and negotiation. In G. Zivin (Ed.), *The development of expressive behavior: Biology-environment interactions* (pp. 103–116). Orlando, FL: Academic Press.

Izard, C. E. (1971). *The face of emotion.* New York: Appleton Century Crofts.

Izard, C. E. (1995). Innate and universal facial expressions. Evidence from developmental and cross-cultural research. *Psychological Bulletin, 115,* 288–299.

Jones, E. E., & Nisbett, R. E. (1971). The actor and the observer: Divergent perceptions of the causes of behavior. In E. E. Jones, D. E. Kanouse, H. H. Kelley, R. E. Nisbett, S. Valins, & B. Weiner (Eds.), *Attribution: Perceiving the causes of behavior* (pp. 79–94). Morristown, NJ: General Learning Press.

Kraut, R. E., & Johnston, R. E. (1979). Social and emotional messages of smiling: An ethological approach. *Journal of Personality and Social Psychology, 37,* 1539–1553.

Matsumoto, D. (1990). Cultural similarities and differences in display rules. *Motivation and Emotion, 14,* 195–214.

Mead, G. H. (1967). *Mind, self, and society from the standpoint of a social behaviorist.* Chicago: The University of Chicago Press. (Original work published 1934.)

Messinger, D. S., Fogel, A., & Dickson, K. L. (1997). A dynamic systems approach to infant facial action. In J. A. Russell & J. M. Fernández-Dols (Eds.), *The psychology of facial expression* (pp. 205–226). New York: Cambridge University Press.

Mischel, W. (1968). *Personality and assessment.* New York: Wiley.

Preuschoft, S. (1992). "Laughter" and "smile" in Barbary Macaques (*Macaca sylvanus*). *Ethology, 91,* 220–236.

Preuschoft, S., & van Hooff, J. A. R. A. M. (1995). Homologizing primate facial displays: A critical review of methods. *Folia Primatologica, 65,* 121–137.

Reynolds, P. C. (1981). *On the evolution of human behavior: The argument from animals to man.* Berkeley, CA: University of California Press.

Ross, L. (1977). The intuitive psychologist and his shortcomings: Distortions in the attribution process. *Advances in Experimental Social Psychology, 10,* 174–219.

Ross, L., & Nisbett, R. E. (1991). *The person and the situation: Perspectives of social psychology.* New York: McGraw-Hill.

Ruiz-Belda, M. A., & Fernández-Dols, J. M. (1997). *Spontaneous facial expressions of discrete emotions in everyday life.* Unpublished manuscript.

Russell, J. A. (1994). Is there universal recognition of emotion from facial expression? A review of the cross-cultural studies. *Psychological Bulletin, 115,* 102–141.

Russell, J. A. (1995). Facial expressions of emotion: What lies beyond minimal universality? *Psychological Bulletin, 118,* 379–391.

Russell, J. A., & Fernández-Dols, J. M. (1997). What does a facial expression mean? In J. A. Russell & J. M. Fernández-Dols (Eds.), *The psychology of facial expression* (pp. 3–30). New York: Cambridge University Press.

Sackett, G. P., Ruppenthal, G. C., & Gluck, J. (1978). Introduction: An overview of methodological and statistical problems in observational research. In G. P. Sackett (Ed.), *Observing behavior: Data collection and analysis methods* (pp. 1–14). Baltimore, MD: University Park Press.

Smith, W. J. (1977). *The behavior of communicating: An ethological approach.* Cambridge, MA: Harvard University Press.

Steele, C. M., & Aronson, J. (1995). Stereotype threat and the intellectual test performance of African Americans. *Journal of Personality and Social Psychology, 69,* 797–811.

Tomkins, S. S. (1962). *Affect, imagery, consciousness* (Vol. 1). New York: Springer.

Van Hooff, J. A. R. A. M. (1972). A comparative approach to the phylogeny of laughter and smiling. In R. A. Hinde (Ed.), *Nonverbal communication* (pp. 209–241). Cambridge: Cambridge University Press.

# 10. Facial Behavior Alone and in the Presence of Others

HUGH WAGNER AND VICTORIA LEE

## Introduction

Most research on facial behavior has dealt with individuals in isolation from other people. Often this has been with the intention of examining the nature of "spontaneous" facial expressions, unmodified by social influences (e.g., Buck, Savin, Miller & Caul, 1972), or because the focus of interest has been to isolate the expressions of "basic" emotions (e.g., Ekman, 1989). However, as is evident from the contributions to this volume, in recent years greater attention has been paid to facial expression and nonverbal behavior in general in social situations. Perhaps the simplest form of social context is to be in the presence of a noninteracting social partner. We review a number of studies that have examined the effects of such a social context on facial behavior. It is apparent, however, that this social context is not as simple as it might seem, and the results of studies of this type of social context depend on the nature of the other person present. Almost all of these results may be accounted for by differing levels of uncertainty about the other person's role.

Next, we draw attention to two oversimplifications in research on nonverbal behavior. The one more connected with the preceding discussions is the observation that focusing on inhibition and excitation tends to conceal the fact that different social contexts tend to produce *qualitatively different* facial behavior, rather than simply inhibiting or facilitating the same behavior. The more general point is that traditional approaches examine nonverbal behavior in isolation from its interactional context. We argue that nonverbal behavior in real settings is inextricably bound up with the verbal behavior that it usually accompanies and cannot be understood without reference to that verbal communication. Finally, we describe an exploratory study illustrating one particular way in which the meaning of facial behavior depends on its verbal context.


## Being Alone versus Being in Company

Studies comparing emotional expression when people are alone or in social situations have produced conflicting results. On the one hand is a series of results suggesting that social presence *increases* expressiveness (see Table 10.1). Early work by Andrus (1946) showed that the frequency of laughter increases with increasing audience size. Young and Fry (1966) similarly showed that subjects drawn from the same introductory psychology class laughed and smiled more when listening to jokes together than when they were alone. In a series of studies, Chapman (1973; 1975) and Chapman and Wright (1976) showed that 7- and 8-year-old children smiled and laughed more at funny stories when another child from their own class was present as an audience

Table 10.1. *Studies showing facilitation by social presence*

|  | Stimuli | Relation | Others' role |
|---|---|---|---|
| Andrus (1946) | humorous | ? | coacting |
| Young & Fry (1966) | humorous | college classmates | coacting |
| Chapman (1973) | humorous | friends | observing < coacting |
| Chapman (1975) | humorous | older children | different task < same |
| Chapman & Wright (1976) | humorous | older children < classmates | observing < coacting |
| Brightman et al. (1975, 1977) | pleasant & unpleasant tastes | ? | coacting |
| Kraut & Johnston (1979) | public smiling | friends; passersby | coacting; observing interacting |
| Bainum et al. (1984) | free play | classmates | parallel < cooperative |
| Fridlund (1991) | humorous | friends | coacting |

than they did when they were alone. They laughed even more when another child was present as a fellow listener. These effects were smaller when the companions were two years older and were also smaller when the companions were listening to different materials. Brightman, Segal, Werther, and Steiner (1975; 1977) showed that facial expressions only matched evaluations of taste when subjects tried pleasant and unpleasant foods in the presence of others. Kraut and Johnston (1979) showed that smiling in a number of situations, most famously after bowling, depended on being with, or directly confronting, friends (or, in one case, passersby). Bainum, Lounsbury, and Pollio (1984) observed children in free play and found that smiling and laughing occurred more often when the children were in parallel play than when another child was nowhere near. Smiling and laughing occurred even more when children were engaged in cooperative play. Finally, Fridlund (1991) showed that subjects who viewed humorous materials in the company of friends smiled more than those who viewed them alone.

In contrast is a number of studies showing that social presence *inhibits* expressive behavior. These are summarized in Table 10.2. Friesen and Ekman (see Ekman, 1972; Friesen, 1972) showed that subjects interviewed while they viewed distressing films showed less facial expression of disgust and fear than when they were alone. (This study will be considered in greater detail in a later section.) Kleck et al. (1976) found that men were less expressive of pain when they were

Table 10.2. *Studies showing inhibition by social presence*

|  | Stimuli | Relation | Others' role |
|---|---|---|---|
| Friesen & Ekman (Ekman 1972) | distressing films | stranger | observing |
| Kleck et al. (1976) | pain | stranger |  |
| Yarzower, Kilbride et al. (1979–83); 3 papers | posing; viewing various stimuli | experimenter | observing |
| Kraut (1982) | pleasant & unpleasant odors | stranger | coacting behind screen |
| Friedman & Miller-Herringer (1991) | concealing pleasure | stranger | competing |

observed than when they were alone. Another series of studies (Kilbride & Yarczower, 1980; 1983; Yarczower, Kilbride, & Hill, 1979) showed that the presence of one or two experimenters inhibited children's expressiveness in a posing task, or in response to viewing various emotional stimuli, compared to when they were alone. Kraut (1982) placed a subject and another person (described as another subject) on either side of a gauze screen, so that they could see each other's gross movements. He found that facial expressiveness in response to pleasant and unpleasant odors was lower when another person was present than when the subject was alone. Friedman and Miller-Herringer (1991) arranged for subjects to win in a competitive situation, either alone or in the presence of the defeated confederates. The overt expression of pleasure was inhibited more in the social situation than in the nonsocial situation.

Buck, Losow, Murphy, and Costanzo (1992) have suggested that one feature distinguishing studies that show facilitation from those that show inhibition is the affective nature of the stimuli or situation, with pleasant stimuli producing facilitation, and unpleasant stimuli inhibition. However, it may be seen from Tables 10.1 and 10.2 that only two of the published studies showing inhibition used only unpleasant stimuli. Two other factors more clearly differentiate the two sets of studies. First, the *role* of the other person: Coaction usually leads to facilitation, and being observed leads to less facilitation, or to inhibition. Second, the *relationship* between the subject and his or her social partner or partners: In all but one of the studies showing facilitation in which it is possible to identify the relationship, the partner or partners were friends, or at least classmates or familiar older children. (The exception is Kraut and Johnston's observation of smiling in interaction with passersby.) In studies where the companion was an older child, the facilitation effect was reduced compared to when the companion was a classmate. On the other hand, in all of the studies showing inhibition, the partner was not a friend or acquaintance, although his or her actual role varied, often being an experimenter or observer and never directly coacting.

## Judgment Studies

In a number of studies in Manchester, we have directly examined the effect of the relationship between coacting subjects on their expressive behavior. The studies have mostly been modifications of the slide viewing paradigm introduced by Buck and his colleagues some 25 years ago (Buck et al., 1972). The main difference between the Buck and Manchester paradigms is that, while Buck's subjects were videotaped both silently viewing slides and describing their reactions to them, in Manchester we have used only silent viewing conditions. Thus, when the videotapes are shown to judges, the judges in the original paradigm viewed subjects who were, part of the time, describing their feelings into a microphone, while in Manchester the videotapes are of subjects who remain silent throughout. Overall, the inclusion of a talk period does not increase communication between subjects and judges (Wagner, MacDonald, & Manstead, 1986), although the relation of communication with other variables, such as gender and the nature of the stimulus material, may change between silent view and talk periods (Buck, Baron, & Barrette, 1982; Wagner, Buck, & Winterbotham, 1993). Other differences from the Buck paradigm have varied from study to study. In some, we have asked judges to rate the apparent feelings of subjects instead of, or in addition to, trying to identify the type of material viewed. In some, judges have made overall ratings of expressiveness. In some studies, subjects have viewed videotaped stimuli instead of still photographs.

We will be considering two types of measurement of facial behavior in this chapter. The first concerns *recognizability* (or decodability). This is typified by Buck et al.'s (1972) "accuracy measure," which is based on how well judges can identify (recognize or decode) the type of material being viewed by the subjects. Alternatively, it could be a measure of how well judges can identify (recognize or decode) the emotion shown by the subject. The second type of measure is of *expressiveness*. This is based on direct judgments of the amount or intensity of expressive behavior shown by the subject. Some measures, such as Buck et al.'s (1972) *pleasantness* measure, which is derived from the correlation between subject's and judges' ratings of the pleasantness of a stimulus or the corresponding expression, probably combine aspects of both decodability and expressiveness.

### Friends and Strangers

The first study comparing the effects of the presence of a friend or a stranger (Wagner & Smith, 1991) was typical. Seven pairs of friends and 7 pairs of strangers, all female students, were seated alongside each other facing a projection screen, beneath which was hidden a video camera. They were videotaped, without their prior knowledge, while they silently viewed 32 slides pretested to evoke in the maximum number of subjects responses of happiness, tenderness, amusement, peacefulness, puzzlement, anger, sadness, and disgust. The slides, and these emotion terms, were selected in earlier studies to represent emotion terms used freely by this subject pool (see Wagner, 1990). Subjects in the present study indicated their strongest reaction to each slide by checking the appropriate term from this list and rating the strength of the reaction. The videotapes were edited to show one subject of each pair at any time, selecting two 5-second clips of each subject viewing slides to which they responded with each emotion term. Five female judges viewed all the clips, viewing the members of each pair in different sessions. Their task was simply to check on lists of the eight emotion terms the one that best described the subject's response in each clip.

Recognizability was measured by how well judges could identify from expressions on the subjects' faces the emotion terms nominated by the subjects. Table 10.3 shows the overall percentage correct and the percentage expected to be correct by chance, based on the frequency with which the judges used each response term (see Wagner,

Table 10.3. *Mean percent correct emotion recognition*

| | Friend | | Stranger | | Sig. Of difference |
|---|---|---|---|---|---|
| | % Correct | Chance % | % Correct | Chance % | |
| Amused | 67.9[a] | 22.0 | 34.3[a] | 15.0 | $p < .01$ |
| Tender | 10.0[a] | 4.2 | 7.9 | 5.5 | $p < .05$ |
| Sad | 27.7[b] | 15.9 | 19.8 | 24.5 | $p < .05$ |
| Disgusted | 31.7[a] | 15.6 | 34.9[a] | 16.8 | |
| Angry | 13.6 | 8.4 | 11.4 | 10.2 | |
| Peaceful | 15.5 | 9.5 | 9.8 | 10.5 | |
| Happy | 5.0 | 3.8 | 3.6 | 2.9 | |
| Puzzled | 30.0 | 20.6 | 20.0 | 23.4 | |
| Overall | 23.8[a] | 12.5 | 17.5[b] | 12.5 | $p < .05$ |

[a] Percent correct significantly greater than chance, $p < .01$
[b] Percent correct significantly greater than chance, $p < .05$
*Source:* Wagner & Smith, 1991.

1993). Overall, accuracy for subjects with friends was higher than that for subjects with strangers. This was true for all individual emotions, except for disgust, and significantly so for amusement, tenderness, and sadness. Anger, peacefulness, happiness, and puzzlement were not recognized significantly better than chance by either group. The results confirm the expectation that subjects viewing stimuli in the presence of coacting friends are more expressive than those in the presence of coacting strangers. Furthermore, this is so for at least one negative emotion (sadness), as well as for positive ones (amusement and tenderness).

One weakness of this study is that it did not include a condition in which subjects were alone, so that it is not possible to conclude both that friends are facilitative *and* that strangers are inhibitive relative to being alone. In a subsequent study (Wagner, unpublished data), we did include a solitary condition. Subjects were covertly videotaped while they silently viewed a brief comedy film, a mildly aversive extract from an antivivisection film, and a neutral film about dry stone walls in Cumbria. Twenty viewed the films alone, 20 with a friend, and 20 with a stranger. Five judges were shown brief clips recorded during the pleasant and unpleasant films only, but they were told that there were three films, including a neutral one. (This was intended to reduce ceiling effects.) The judges' task was to identify which of the three types of film the subject appeared to be watching in each clip.

The type of film was significantly better identified for those watching with a friend (90% correct), than for those either alone (62.5%) or with a stranger (57.5%). However, there was no significant difference between the alone and stranger conditions. These results were the same for both pleasant and unpleasant films. So, while the presence of a friend facilitated recognizability of expression, the presence of a stranger did not inhibit it.

Buck et al. (1992, Study 2) reported a similar study with a condition in which subjects were alone. In social presence conditions, subjects took it in turns, after a silent viewing period, to describe their feelings about the four types of slide they were viewing. The slide categories were sexual, scenic, unusual, and unpleasant. Judges viewed videotapes of the subjects recorded during the silent period, and recognition was measured by the number of times the judges correctly identified the type of slide that subjects were viewing. Their overall results show that accuracy was lower for those viewing with strangers than for both those viewing alone and those viewing with friends. The expressions of those recorded with a friend were more recognizable than those of solitary subjects for sexual and unpleasant slides. Those with a stranger were less recognizable than those of solitary subjects for unpleasant and unusual slides. Thus, these results show inhibition by a stranger and facilitation by a friend, although it should be noted that only for sexual slides was recognizability of those with a friend significantly greater than those with a stranger. The effect of friend and stranger both depended on the nature of the stimulus material. We shall return to this in a later section.

### Uncertainty and Conformity

Our interpretation of these results follows suggestions made by Guerin (1986), after a review of the literature on social facilitation effects. He concluded that two factors are involved in the effects on behavior of the noninteractive and noncompetitive presence of others. First, mere presence effects occur when in the presence of another person, but only when there is *uncertainty* about the other person's behavior (or role, or intentions). Second, there is a tendency for *conformity* to public standards or norms when in the presence of another person. This effect is stronger when the other is observing the subject, and also when the other is an experimenter.

We suggest that the data described up to now concerning facilitation or inhibition of expressiveness in the presence of friends and of strangers, and also the variations in degree of facilitation depending on the details of the study, may be explained by these factors. In relation to facial behavior, uncertainty about the other person leads one to be wary of revealing much about oneself through one's reactions to stimuli, especially emotional stimuli. Uncertainty will, of course, be greater about a stranger than a friend. As in the mere presence studies reviewed by Guerin, it will be greater when the other person cannot be clearly monitored. Similarly, it will be greater when the other person is observing rather than coacting, and probably when the other person is performing a different task. Conformity will lead one to produce conventional or expected expressions or to disguise one's reactions to emotional stimuli when that is what convention dictates. Conformity effects are related to a possible evaluative role of the other person and relate to the control of social approval and disapproval. This will also be greater with strangers than with friends, especially when the stranger is an experimenter or some other authority figure. However, for children these effects will be less strong when the other person is a slightly older child than when the other is an adult, since the child subject is less likely to perceive a child one or two years his or her senior as an evaluative person. All of these effects and variations are reflected in the results we have summarized.

One prediction following from these considerations is that anything that reduces the degree of uncertainty about the stranger's role or behavior should reduce the effect. In a further study (Wagner, Gee, & Quine, 1993) we failed to find a difference between the presence of a friend and that of a stranger. This occurred, we believe, because of an accidental "manipulation." This study used a slide viewing paradigm to compare the expressiveness of subjects coviewing emotional stimuli with a friend or with a stranger. The facial expressions of those coviewing with a stranger were just as well recognized as those of subjects coviewing with a friend, and recognition was comparable to that for subjects recorded with friends in the Wagner and Smith (1991) study described earlier. To streamline the running of the study, the students running the subjects decided to get them to fill in questionnaires in the same room, while waiting for 10 to 15 minutes to take part in the viewing stage of the experiment. The pairs of strangers were similarly aged students, and many pairs were observed to have been talking when the experimenter entered the room before they coacted in the experimental task. These factors resulted in a reduction in the uncertainty of the other's behavior and consequently a smaller stranger effect.

The same thing seems to have happened in a study by Hess, Banse, and Kappas (1995), which we shall describe in more detail in the next section. Two conditions of this study allowed the comparison of the amount of smiling by subjects viewing comedy films with a friend or with a stranger. The data showed no significant difference between those viewing with friends and those viewing with strangers. However, before this part of the study, subjects and their partners (friends or strangers) had spent about 30 minutes together collaborating on writing a text to be presented in front of a camera. Hess et al. recognized that this might affect the relationship between the strangers, but believed such an effect would be minimal because "a 30-min interaction cannot provide the same information that friends who frequently have known each other for years have about each other" (p. 282). Our point is that strangers do not need this much information. Enough information to reduce uncertainty is all that is required to reduce the inhibitory effect of strangers, and this is certainly available in a 30-min collaborative task.

While these arguments are, we believe, consistent with all of the published data, they are, nonetheless, post hoc explanations. To confirm that variations in uncertainty underlie the differential effects of social presence, direct experimental tests are required, independently manipulating and assessing uncertainty. To our knowledge, no studies of this nature have been published.

## Real and Implicit Audiences

It is clear from the results presented up to now that, even when alone, people continue to produce facial displays that can, albeit to a limited degree, be used by observers to identify the person's reported feelings or the type of stimulus being viewed. Those who emphasize the emotionally expressive function of facial behavior have argued that, under solitary conditions, we come closest to being able to observe the spontaneous "read-out" of emotion. Ekman (1984) was quite clear about this: "In private, when no display rules to mask expression were operative, we saw the biologically based, evolved, universal facial expressions of emotion" (p. 321). Although Buck (1984) argued that "pure" spontaneous communication is possible, he nevertheless was cautious about whether or not we can actually observe it: "When a sender is alone ... he or she should feel little pressure to present a proper image to others, any emotional expression under such circumstances should be more likely to reflect an actual motivational/emotional state. Even under these circumstances, however, processes of 'inhibition' may alter tendencies toward spontaneous expression" (p. 20). That is, Buck left open the possibility that a solitary individual would still operate under constraints imposed by socialization.

Both Ekman and Buck, it seems, underestimate the true sociality of the experimental situation used in many studies of "spontaneous" or solitary expression. Some years ago we (Wagner et al., 1986) pointed out that Buck's slide viewing paradigm is actually quite a social situation. As we described earlier, subjects talk about their feelings into a visible microphone and rate their response orally. Usually an experimenter is in an adjacent control room whose door is left ajar. In our less social version of the paradigm, overall recognition accuracy (60% better than chance) was comparable with that in other studies of "spontaneous" communication (ranging from 56% to 70% above chance). Wagner et al. (1993) directly compared communication in silent and talking periods within a slide viewing paradigm. Generally, accuracy was actually better in the silent period than in the talk period.

These findings are entirely consistent with the arguments advanced in the previous section, since the person (the experimenter) with whom the subjects were interacting was a stranger (in the case of Wagner et al., 1993, an older man from a different culture). Making the situation more overtly social, by having subjects talk about their feelings, would be expected to enhance the inhibitory effect of the stranger, reducing the subjects' expression of their feelings.

Fridlund (1994) took this further. (See also the chapter by Manstead, Fischer, and Jakobs in this volume.) He argued that there are five ways in which sociality is indicated apart from the physical presence of others:

1. *We often treat ourselves as interactants.* For example, we talk to ourselves and produce facial expressions when doing so.
2. *We often act as if others are present when they are not.* Sometimes we do this to rehearse what we will say (and the faces we will pull) when we next meet a person, or we do it inadvertently when we believe another person is present.
3. *We often imagine that others are present when they are not.* For example, we daydream about what would happen if we were to meet a particular person, or we remember things that happened when we were with others.
4. *We often forecast interaction and deploy displays appropriately.* We may, for example, scowl on entering a room to indicate to others that we do not wish to interact with them, or, conversely, smile to indicate our willingness to do so.
5. *We often treat nonhumans and animate and inanimate objects as interactants.* This is obvious in the case of owners talking to pets, gardeners to plants, and children to toys.

In the following discussion, we will focus on the second of these proposals, that we act as if others are present even when they are not.

Fridlund (1991) argued that this process operates in experimental situations so that, quite apart from the experimenter, subjects may take into the ostensibly solitary situation an implicit companion, such as a friend. For example, subjects viewing an amusing film might think "my friend would enjoy this," and would thereby put themselves into a social situation. Fridlund conducted a study intended to demonstrate this process taking place, by varying the likelihood of this happening. His study had four experimental conditions, in each of which subjects watched an amusing film while electromyographic (EMG) activity was recorded from over the zygomaticus major muscle. In one group, each subject came to the laboratory alone and viewed the film alone. In each of the other three conditions the subject came to the laboratory with a friend. In one condition, the subject and the friend viewed the film together in the same room. In another condition, the subject and friend were separated, the friend apparently going to a different room to view the same film simultaneously. In the last condition, the friend went to a different room to perform some completely unrelated task. Thus, the four conditions varied in sociality, from the most social (physical presence), through viewing with an implicit friend, then viewing with an absent friend doing something unrelated, and finally solitary viewing. The expectation was that the amount of smiling (measured by the EMG) that subjects displayed would decrease in parallel with this order of decreasing sociality.

The results did not exactly support this expectation but, in a sense, went further. Those who believed that their friend was viewing the same film in another room showed *just as much* smiling as those whose friend was physically present, and both of these groups smiled more than those who came alone. No other differences were significant. None of the groups differed from any other in self-reported happiness, so differences in response to the films could not account for these effects. Thus, smiling was enhanced just as much by an implicit friend as by a physically present friend.

Hess et al. (1995) conducted a study intended to replicate and extend that of Fridlund. They did not use an alone condition, but half of the subjects came to the experiment with a friend, and half were paired with a stranger. In addition, to examine more closely the effect of the intensity of the evoked response, subjects viewed two films pretested to evoke different intensities of amusement. Those with strangers showed a medium amount of smiling, which was not affected by either the sociality of the situation (physical presence, separate viewing the same films, or separate doing a different task) nor by how amusing the film was. For friends, smiling was significantly greater for the more amusing film. Also for friends, there was a nearly significant effect of sociality, with physical presence producing the most smiling, and separate/different task the least. Hess et al. argued that the finding of an effect of stimulus intensity is inconsistent with Fridlund's view, which they described as predicting that only sociality would affect smiling. However, if facial behavior is about communication, it must be affected by what is to be communicated (its type or its intensity) as well as by sociality. That is, if people use facial behavior to signal to a friend that they find a film amusing, we would expect them to use it, also, to signal *how* amusing they find the film.

One thing that neither of these studies, nor the studies described by Manstead et al. in this volume, have examined is the subjects' perceptions and experience of the situation. In particular, if subjects are displaying to their friends in the separate viewing situation, then on postexperimental inquiry they should report that they thought about their friends. Subjects who do not report thinking about their friends should show no facilitation of expression. In conditions when subjects are separated from a stranger there is no reason to expect them to think of the stranger as an implicit audience. They would, therefore, not report thinking about the stranger, and would not show an implicit audience effect. We are currently working on studies to investigate these matters.

### Beyond Facilitation and Inhibition

So far, all the data discussed have concerned the facilitation or inhibition of particular, or recognizable, facial expressions. However, only a very narrow view of the role of facial expression in social interaction would predict that facilitation and inhibition are all that would occur. As Hess et al. (1995) put it: "Assessing the intensity of facial displays as a means of assessing sociality may not be the most adequate procedure" (p. 286). Rather, facial behavior is seen by proponents of the "Emotions View," as well as by its opponents, as important *aspects of social interaction*. Both proponents (e.g., Ekman & Friesen, 1969) and opponents (Chovil, reported in Fridlund, 1994) have provided descriptions of these paralinguistic and other functions of facial behaviors. These behaviors include movements that may be homomorphic with what are usually described as "facial expressions of emotion."

In the present context, the import of this is that being in the presence of a stranger would not necessarily simply inhibit facial expressiveness. Neither should we expect the effects to be uniform across different types of stimuli and tasks. This is well illustrated in the study by Buck et al. (1992) described earlier. The only significant difference between those viewing with friends and those with strangers was in response to *sexual* slides (mostly Playboy-type pin-ups). Concern about the evaluative role of the other person, and uncertainty about that person's response, would probably be greater when one is viewing the sexual stimuli than other stimuli, so this is exactly the difference we would expect. Indeed, facial behavior, in particular smiles and eye gaze, has been shown to be central to the interpersonal communication of the intimacy of a relationship and is dependent on the intimacy of the topic (Argyle & Dean, 1965). We would, therefore, expect to observe reduced levels of nonverbal behavior while talking to a relative stranger about an intimate topic.

In our study summarized in Table 10.3, the categories most similar to those used by Buck et al. were disgust (unpleasant slides), peacefulness (scenic), and puzzled (unusual). We did not include a category equivalent to the sexual one. The lack of difference for the three similar categories is just as was found by Buck et al. The significant differences we observed for amusement, tenderness, and sadness might be explicable by the same sort of argument. In each case, responding overtly to stimuli expected to arouse these emotions might be thought to be revealing to a stranger, indicating frivolity in the case of humorous stimuli or weakness in the other two cases.

In social situations, particularly those with a stranger, we should expect a variety of behaviors to be produced that do not relate in a one-to-one way to the type of stimulus. Ekman and Friesen (1969) distinguished *emblems, manipulators, illustrators,* and *regulators,* each of which might be used differently in social situations involving friends and those involving strangers. Thus, the presence of a stranger might produce facial signals of a conventional or polite nature, unrelated in any obvious way to the stimulus, rather than simply inhibiting the production of stimulus-related expressions.

One excellent example of this is the Japanese–American study of Friesen and Ekman (Ekman, 1972; Friesen, 1972). The study is, of course, usually cited as an example of the operation of a cultural display rule, namely, a Japanese display rule to mask negative affect with a smile in the presence of another person. This interpretation has recently been questioned by Fridlund (1994). We do not want to go into this issue here. Rather, we want to draw attention to a different aspect of these data, one that is similar in the two cultural groups studied, namely, that the presence of another person produces *variation* in facial behavior.

This study had three stages. First, 25 Japanese and 25 American students viewed distressing films alone. In this condition, subjects in both cultural groups showed a large number of facial expressions classified as "negative" and very few "positive" expressions. Next, each subject was formally interviewed by a member of their own culture (a graduate student). In this situation, the majority of both American (22 subjects) and Japanese (24 subjects) showed positive, or a mixture of positive and negative, facial expressions. Only one subject in each group showed only negative affect. There was no significant difference between the groups. Finally, the interview continued while the subject viewed again the most unpleasant scenes from the last film he had seen. Under these conditions, about the same number of Japanese subjects (22) continued to produce positive, or positive and negative, expressions, but fewer American subjects (14) did so. Two Japanese and 4 American subjects showed only negative expressions. This time, the Japanese showed significantly more positive expressions than did the Americans. What is interesting about these data in the present context is the similarity, rather than the difference, between the Japanese and American subjects' behavior in the presence of the interviewer. In both cultural groups, the presence of a stranger, probably seen as of higher status, who was interviewing them, resulted in a *decrease* in facial expressions of a type we might call "appropriate" to the stimulus material and an *increase* in expressions that are "inappropriate" to the stimuli, predominately smiles.

So, people may react to the presence of a stranger by producing more facial signals not directly related to the stimulus. However, these signals are not necessarily restricted to the "masking" expressions described by Ekman (1972) as one of the four ways in which display rules can modify the appearance of emotional facial expressions. They may include any of the other classes of facial signal appropriate to the individual and the situation, such as Ekman and Friesen's (1969) emblems, manipulators, and illustrators, as well as intentional deception.

Judgment based experimental paradigms such as those we have concentrated on up to this point, taken together with paradigms based on facial measurement, are the main source of the information we have about facial behavior. These paradigms have become standard ones because of the nature of the research questions that have been asked about facial behavior (see Wagner, 1997). To the extent that the questions that have been asked are meaningful, interesting, and important, then these methods may be valid and useful. However, one implication of the type of result to which we have just drawn attention is that, irrespective of the position we adopt in relation to the behavioral ecology and emotional expression views of facial behavior, facial behavior clearly does much more than express or comment on emotional responses. What is more, it is essential to focus on variation in *type* of behavior, as well as its intensity.

We believe that it is essential now to examine the functions of facial signals in relation not only to experienced emotion, but to the personal and social demands on the individual, and of the interaction of which the individual is part. In short, nonverbal behavior should not be treated as an independent channel of expression or communication, but as a form of behavior that cannot be properly understood unless examined together with the verbal communication with which it is inextricably bound. As Wierzbicka (1995) put it: "In order to understand human communicative behavior, we need an integrated description of verbal and nonverbal communication" (p. 247).

## Nonverbal Behavior in Its Verbal Context

In Manchester, we are interested in the processes involved in communicating past emotional events in a nontherapeutic setting. We are currently exploring the application of an integrated approach to the study of nonverbal and verbal communication in such a situation. One study has involved videotaping, unobtrusively, 54 subjects talking about a positive and a negative emotional experience. The results to be presented here consist of a microanalysis of one female subject talking to a researcher about an event which evoked powerful negative emotion. (For a full account, see Lee & Beattie, 1998.)

The incident the subject described happened while she was working as a care assistant and nurse's aide in an American hospital. She had been asked to transfer a patient from his wheelchair to the bed. What should have been a relatively simple and smooth operation, however, did not go according to plan. The patient tried to walk by himself, fell, cracked two ribs, subsequently punctured his lung, and two weeks later died. The focus of the analysis was on how this person actively constructed her account of the incident, including her emotional feelings about the event. Further, the ways in which the description performed social functions such as offering attributions, blamings, and justifications were examined. The analysis used techniques derived from both discourse analysis (Edwards & Potter, 1992) and

conversation analysis (Sacks, 1992). However, not only did the research examine *what* was said but also *how* it was said. Thus, it not
only considered the content of the talk but also examined the ways in
which accompanying nonverbal behavior, specifically Duchenne
smiles, non-Duchenne smiles, and eye gaze, were organized around
certain rhetorical constructs within the talk.

Conversation analytic work on the relationship between verbal and
nonverbal behavior has focused on interactional management and has
been concerned with how verbal and nonverbal behavior may be
organized to accomplish certain interactional ends (see Beattie, 1983).
Nonverbal behavior has been conspicuously absent from research in
discourse analysis, which is surprising given that it can completely
alter the meaning or reading of any utterance. The statement "I hate
you" said with a particular intonation and with certain accompanying
nonverbal behavior (smile, eye gaze, etc.) changes dramatically the
underlying meaning, and from a discourse analytic perspective, the
action orientation of the utterance. Lee and Beattie present a discourse
analytic focus on the action orientation of talk, but in addition an
analysis of the accompanying nonverbal behavior and some interpretation of how these behaviors are functioning with respect to talk. The
question asked was: How can nonverbal behavior be used to affect
the overall action orientation of the utterance?

Three broad predictions were examined. First, when the speech is
positive, the nonverbal behavior will also be positive (e.g., more
smiles); that is, the two channels of communication operate together
for effective communication. The second is the antithesis of the first:
That the two channels operate in opposition, so that when talk is very
negative, speakers offset this negativity with positive nonverbal behavior. The third position is that there is no overall consistent relationship between verbal and nonverbal behavior, but that nonverbal behavior is merely used to mark important transitions within and
between turns (Goodwin, 1981; Kendon, 1967).

This person's account of her negative emotional event was not
uniformly negative. Rather, the talk included positive and negative
features that were organized together into rhetorical constructs known
as contrastive pairs (Atkinson, 1984). A contrastive pair consists of
two consecutive items or parts of discourse, which contrast with one
another in some way. They have been shown to be important in
various types of persuasive communication (see Beattie, 1988) and are
believed to be a common element in a wider variety of emotional

accounts. The contrastive pairs identified in this person's speech are shown in Figures 10.1–10.4. The figures also show how Duchenne smiles, non-Duchenne smiles, and eye gaze are organized within the contrastive pairs.

In order to examine the function of nonverbal behavior, the duration of the different forms of nonverbal behavior were collapsed across all four contrastive pairs (see Table 10.4). Much more smiling, specifically Duchenne smiling, occurred during the negative parts of these contrastive pairs than during the positive. Of a total of 18.3 seconds of Duchenne smiling in these sequences, 69.9% occurred during the negative and 30.1% during the positive statements. There was less non-Duchenne smiling, and it occurred equally in positive and negative parts of the contrasts. It is also clear that most smiling was accompanied by eye gaze, but, while this was particularly true of Duchenne smiling, it did not depend on whether the smiling occurred during positive or negative statements. Thus, 68.8% of Duchenne smiling was accompanied by gaze, and 55.8% of non-Duchenne smiling was so accompanied. At the same time, we can see that most gaze occurred during smiles. During negative statements, 84% of gaze accompanied smiles, and during positive statements, 56.8% accompanied smiles.

These results support the second prediction: Duchenne smiles and eye gaze operated to offset or ameliorate the verbal message. However, this was not the only function of nonverbal behavior in this

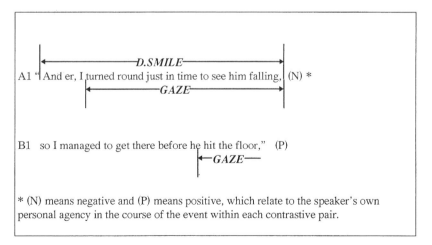

Figure 10.1. Organization of Duchenne and non-Duchenne smiles and eye gaze, within the first contrastive pair. (After Lee and Beattie, 1998.)

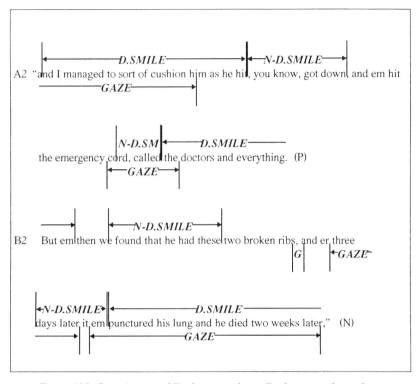

Figure 10.2. Organization of Duchenne and non-Duchenne smiles and eye gaze, within the second contrastive pair. (After Lee and Beattie, 1998.)

discourse. Duchenne smiles in particular, and eye gaze to a lesser extent, terminated at the exact juncture between the negative and positive components of the contrastive pairs, thus operating to highlight the transition between the two parts of the contrast, as suggested by the third prediction.

It is possible that the speaker smiled more within the most negative parts of her talk in order to construct herself as a good and trustworthy person and thus ameliorate judgments of possible wrongdoing (see also LaFrance & Hecht, 1995). It is important to note, however, that in the present study it was the Duchenne smile that occurred primarily within the negative parts of the contrastive pairs, whereas non-Duchenne smiles occurred far less frequently and approximately equally often within negative and positive parts. Ekman (1989) posited that the Duchenne smile, the "smile of enjoyment," accompanies experienced positive emotions such as happiness, pleasure, or enjoy-

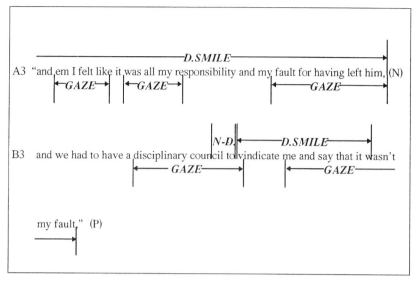

Figure 10.3. Organization of Duchenne and non-Duchenne smiles and eye gaze, within the third contrastive pair. (After Lee and Beattie, 1998.)

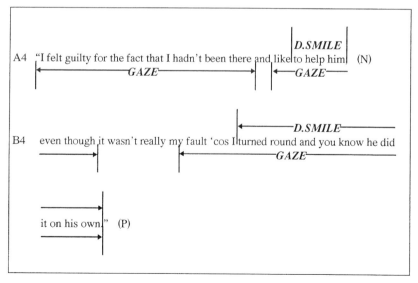

Figure 10.4. Organization of Duchenne and non-Duchenne smiles and eye gaze, within the fourth contrastive pair. (After Lee and Beattie, 1998.)

Table 10.4. *Durations (seconds) of smiles and gaze in different parts of contrastive pairs*

| | Positive | | | Negative | | | Grand total |
|---|---|---|---|---|---|---|---|
| | Total | With gaze | No gaze | Total | With gaze | No Gaze | |
| Duchenne smiles | 5.5 | 3.6 | 1.9 | 12.8 | 9.0 | 3.8 | 18.3 |
| Non-Duchenne smiles | 2.3 | 1.4 | 0.9 | 2.9 | 1.5 | 1.4 | 5.2 |
| No smiles | 9.2 | 3.8 | 5.4 | 4.3 | 2.0 | 2.3 | 13.5 |
| TOTAL | 17.0 | 8.8 | 8.2 | 20.0 | 12.5 | 7.5 | 37.0 |

*Source:* Lee & Beattie (1998).

ment. Ekman, Davidson, and Friesen (1990) stated that "Duchenne smiles are the signal for *any* positive emotions, such as ... *relief*" (p. 350, emphasis added). Relief is one possible emotional response for a person describing a situation such as this one: A negative experience that she appeared to have resolved. The occurrence of Duchenne smiles would then be understandable. But would we expect relief, or any other positive emotion, to be experienced during the more negative aspects of the account rather than during the more positive parts?

As well as showing more Duchenne smiles while talking about the most negative parts of the event, the speaker also showed more eye gaze. Argyle and Cook (1976) stated that "a number of studies have found that people who look more are seen as more truthful or credible" (p. 91) and that, in general, "research supports the proposition that people who look more (and with longer glances) create a more favourable impression and are liked more" (p. 91). Thus, this speaker could have been using increased eye gaze as part of her self-construction as a credible person. However, Rutter and Stephenson (1979) argued that the function of gaze is primarily to collect information about others rather than to communicate affect. According to this view, this speaker could have been using increased levels of eye gaze during the recounting of the worst parts of the event in order to monitor the effect that such talk had on the interviewer.

We might ask how else the subject could have behaved nonverbally. She could have recounted these parts of the trauma still smiling but with gaze averted. Although smiling could have led to a positive self-presentation, the averted gaze would diminish this effect. Alternatively, she could have recounted these parts of the event with a neutral or even sad face, possibly with gaze averted. Such nonverbal behavior might lead to a rather different interpretation of the speaker's thoughts and feelings about the incident and subsequent blame for it. For example, nonsmiling and averted gaze might portray that the speaker found it difficult to talk about the event as it still troubled her or that she was indeed to blame for the incident.

We believe that the speaker was using both verbal and nonverbal behavior in ways that presented herself as a good and credible person. Even though as a result of *what* she said she could have come across negatively, *how* she said it (i.e., the way it was constructed in terms of verbal and nonverbal behavior) intimated that she and the situation were not that bad. This study highlights the need to examine how the nonverbal and verbal systems of communication interact in social situations. If nonverbal behavior had been analyzed on its own, we might have concluded, from the high levels of positive nonverbal behavior, that the subject was experiencing positive emotion.

This single case analysis informs us of the functions that nonverbal behavior appears to be performing for one individual. We do, of course, have to consider the question of generalizability. To what extent do the conclusions apply to other individuals describing the same type of event or to people describing different sorts of event, perhaps in different situations? One thing the case study has done is pose a number of questions and generate a number of hypotheses. For example, does the use of smiling and eye gaze shown by this person occur as a result of an individual's having resolved the issues raised by a traumatic event? Under what circumstances would we find concordance between the affective valence of nonverbal and verbal behavior? The type of analysis described here is, of course, extremely time consuming. We are currently adapting this approach to examine how nonverbal behavior relates to the function of the discourse in all the talk recorded in this study.

## Conclusions

As we have pointed out, most studies of facial expression have used highly constrained laboratory situations such as those described in the earlier sections of this chapter. These studies have been very informative about a number of theoretical issues that are relevant to noninteracting persons. However, there has been a tendency, explicit or implicit, to generalize the results of such research to less constrained, more social situations. This has led to the general assumption that the main function of facial expressions in social, interactive situations is to express emotional feelings. We have argued that, in order to understand nonverbal behavior in social situations, it is necessary to study that behavior *together with* its verbal context. As we have shown, such an integrated approach can lead to different interpretations of the functions of facial expressions. This kind of approach is essential if we are to study communicative behavior in social situations.

## References

Andrus, T. D. (1946). A study of laugh patterns in the theatre. *Speech Monographs, 13*, 114.

Argyle, M., & Cook, M. (1976). *Gaze and mutual gaze*. Cambridge: Cambridge University Press.

Argyle, M., & Dean, J. (1965). Eye-contact, distance, and affiliation. *Sociometry, 28*, 289–304.

Atkinson, J. M. (1984). *Our masters' voice: The language and body language of politics*. London: Methuen.

Bainum, C. K., Lounsbury, K. R., & Pollio, H. R. (1984). The development of laughing and smiling in nursery school children. *Child Development, 55*, 1946–1957.

Beattie, G. (1983). *Talk: An analysis of speech and nonverbal behaviour in conversation*. Milton Keynes: Open University Press.

Beattie, G. (1988). *All talk: Why it's important to watch your words and everything you say*. London: Weidenfeld and Nicolson.

Brightman, V., Segal, A., Werther, P., & Steiner, J. (1975). Ethologic study of facial expressions in response to taste stimuli. *Journal of Dental Research, 54*, L141.

Brightman, V., Segal, A., Werther, P., & Steiner, J. (1977). Facial expression and hedonic response to taste stimuli. *Journal of Dental Research, 56*, B161.

Buck, R. (1984). *The communication of emotion*. New York: Guilford.

Buck, R., Baron, R, & Barrette, D. (1982). Temporal organization of spontaneous emotional expression: A segmentation analysis. *Journal of Personality and Social Psychology, 42*, 506–517.

Buck, R., Losow, J. I., Murphy, M., & Costanzo, P. (1992). Social facilitation and inhibition of emotional expression and communication. *Journal of Personality and Social Psychology, 63*, 962–968.

Buck, R. W., Savin, V. J., Miller, R. E., & Caul, W. F. (1972). Communication of affect through facial expressions in humans. *Journal of Personality and Social Psychology, 23*, 362–371.

Chapman, A. J. (1973). Social facilitation of laughter in children. *Journal of Experimental Social Psychology, 9*, 528–541.

Chapman, A. J. (1975). Humorous laughter in children. *Journal of Personality and Social Psychology, 31*, 42–49.

Chapman, A. J., & Wright, D. S. (1976). Social enhancement of laughter: an experimental analysis of some companion variables. *Journal of Experimental Child Psychology, 21*, 201–218.

Edwards, D., & Potter, J. (1992). *Discursive psychology*. London: Sage.

Ekman, P. (1972). Universals and cultural differences in facial expressions of emotion. In J. K. Cole (Ed.), *Nebraska symposium on motivation, 1971* (pp. 207–283). Lincoln, NE: University of Nebraska Press.

Ekman, P. (1984). Expression and the nature of emotion. In K. Scherer & P. Ekman (Eds.), *Approaches to emotion* (pp. 319–343). Hillsdale, NJ: Lawrence Erlbaum.

Ekman, P. (1989). The argument and evidence about universals in facial expressions of emotion. In H. Wagner & A. Manstead (Eds.), *Handbook of social psychophysiology* (pp. 143–164). London: John Wiley, Ltd.

Ekman, P., Davidson, R. J., & Friesen, W. V. (1990). The Duchenne smile: Emotional expression and brain physiology II. *Journal of Personality and Social Psychology, 58* (2), 342–353.

Ekman, P., & Friesen, W. V. (1969). The repertoire of nonverbal behavior: Categories, origins, usage, and coding. *Semiotica, 1*, 49–98.

Fridlund, A. J. (1991). Sociality of solitary smiling: Potentiation by an implicit audience. *Journal of Personality and Social Psychology, 60*, 229–240.

Fridlund, A. J. (1994). *Human facial expression: An evolutionary view*. New York: Academic Press.

Friedman, H. S., & Miller-Herringer, T. (1991). Nonverbal display of emotion in public and in private: Self-monitoring, personality, and expressive cues. *Journal of Personality and Social Psychology, 61*, 766–775.

Friesen, W. V. (1972). *Cultural differences in facial expressions in a social situation: An experimental test of the concept of display rules.* Unpublished doctoral dissertation, University of California, San Francisco.

Goodwin, C. (1981). *Conversational organization: Interaction between speakers and hearers*. New York: Academic Press.

Guerin, B. (1986). Mere presence effects in humans: A review. *Journal of Experimental Social Psychology, 22*, 38–77.

Hess, U., Banse, R., & Kappas, A. (1995). The intensity of facial expression is determined by underlying affective state and social situation. *Journal of Personality and Social Psychology, 69*, 280–288.

Kendon, A. (1967). Some functions of gaze direction in social interaction. *Acta Psychologica, 26* (1), 1–47.

Kilbride, J. E., & Yarczower, M. (1980). Recognition and imitation of facial expressions: A cross-cultural comparison between Zambia and the United States. *Journal of Cross-Cultural Psychology, 11*, 281–296.

Kilbride, J. E., & Yarczower, M. (1983). Ethnic bias in the recognition of facial expressions. *Journal of Nonverbal Behavior, 8*, 27–41.

Kleck, R. E., Vaughan, R. C., Cartwright-Smith, J., Vaughan, K. B., Colby, C. Z.,

& Lanzetta, J. T. (1976). Effects of being observed on expressive, subjective, and physiological responses to pain stimuli. *Journal of Personality and Social Psychology, 34,* 1211–1218.

Kraut, R. E. (1982). Social presence, facial feedback, and emotion. *Journal of Personality and Social Psychology, 42,* 853–863.

Kraut, R. E., & Johnston, R. (1979). Social and emotional messages of smiling: An ethological approach. *Journal of Personality and Social Psychology, 37,* 1539–1553.

LaFrance, M., & Hecht, M. A. (1995). Why smiles generate leniency. *Personality and Social Psychology Bulletin, 21* (3), 207–214.

Lee, V., & Beattie, G. (1998). The rhetorical organisation of verbal and nonverbal behaviour in emotion talk. *Semiotica, 120,* 39–92.

Rutter, D. R., & Stephenson, G. M. (1979). The functions of looking: effects of friendship in gaze. *British Journal of Social and Clinical Psychology, 18,* 203–205.

Sacks, H. (1992). *Lectures on conversation*, Vols. 1 and 2. Edited by G. Jefferson. Oxford: Basil Blackwell.

Wagner, H. L. (1990). The spontaneous facial expression of differential positive and negative emotions. *Motivation and Emotion, 14,* 27–43.

Wagner, H. L. (1993). On measuring performance in category judgment studies of nonverbal behavior. *Journal of Nonverbal Behavior, 17,* 3–28.

Wagner, H. L. (1997). Methods for the study of facial behavior. In J. Russell & J. M. Fernández-Dols (Eds.), *The psychology of facial expression* (pp. 31–54). New York: Cambridge University Press.

Wagner, H. L., Buck, R., & Winterbotham, M. (1993). Communication of specific emotions: Gender differences in sending accuracy and communication measures. *Journal of Nonverbal Behavior, 17,* 29–53.

Wagner, H. L., Gee, R., & Quine, D. (1993). Understanding the effects of friends' and strangers' presence on facial expression. Unpublished manuscript, University of Manchester.

Wagner, H. L., MacDonald, C. J., & Manstead, A. S. R. (1986). Communication of individual emotions by spontaneous facial expressions. *Journal of Personality and Social Psychology, 50,* 737–743.

Wagner, H. L., & Smith, J. (1991). Facial expressions in the presence of friends and strangers. *Journal of Nonverbal Behavior, 15,* 201–214.

Wierzbicka, A. (1995). Kisses, handshakes, bows: The semantics of nonverbal communication. *Semiotica, 103,* 207–252.

Yarczower, M., Kilbride, J. E., & Hill, L. A. (1979). Imitation and inhibition of facial expressions. *Developmental Psychology, 15,* 453–454.

Young, R. D., & Fry, M. (1966). Some are laughing; some are not – why? *Psychological Reports, 18,* 747–754.

# 11. The Social and Emotional Functions of Facial Displays

ANTONY S. R. MANSTEAD, AGNETA H. FISCHER, AND
ESTHER B. JAKOBS

## Introduction

A widely accepted psychological account of the relationship between emotion and facial displays is that the latter are expressive of the former. The function of facial movement is therefore to communicate one's internal state. The modern version of this view can be traced to Charles Darwin (1872), whose thesis was that facial displays have been shaped by evolutionary forces. More specifically, Darwin argued that facial behavior associated with emotion can be understood in terms of three general principles. The most important of these, the principle of "serviceable associated habits," holds that facial actions during emotion reflect movements that were once functional for the organism. An often-cited example is that the raising of eyebrows thought to be characteristic of certain emotional states, such as surprise, serves to increase visual input. Darwin argued that the originally functional value of these movements resulted in their being repetitively executed, and therefore habitual, and (through a Lamarkian process) heritable. Darwin also suggested that these movements come to have communicative value, such that facial movements associated with emotion provide conspecifics with information about the individual's internal state. This, in turn, is informative about how the individual is likely to act.

The present chapter addresses precisely the same issues as those that concerned Darwin: What is it that is expressed by the face during emotion? Are these facial actions expressive of an underlying emotional state? Alternatively, are these facial actions functional in a more social sense, in that they are signals to conspecifics about action dispositions or intentions? Theorists and researchers who have been influenced by Darwin have tended to accept the assumption that a particular pattern of facial activity is expressive of a particular emotional state. According to this perspective, facial behavior associated with emotion is (other things being equal) expressive of that emotion. We will refer to this position as the *emotional expression* view.

An alternative position, the *behavioral ecology* view, dispenses with the central role played by emotion. Interestingly, this view also rests on evolutionary principles. The difference is that it treats facial behavior as a "display," that is, as a signal to conspecifics of the individual's intentions. The essence of the argument is that it is functional for organisms to know each other's intentions, in the sense that this increases their chances of survival. Thus a signaling system that enables these intentions to be broadcast and received would be naturally selected.

Both perspectives on the relationship between facial actions and emotion acknowledge the communicative functions of facial actions.[1] According to the first position, the communicative function of facial movement derives from the fact that it expresses an internal emotional state. According to the second position, the communicative function of facial movement is primary: The facial movements we associate with emotional episodes have evolved because they signal our social motives and intentions to others. In the remainder of this chapter we examine theoretical arguments and empirical evidence for each point of view and we will conclude by proposing an integration of these theoretical perspectives.

## The Emotional Expression View

*Theoretical Positions*

Darwin's ideas concerning facial expression were rekindled in the 1960s by the publication of two volumes by Tomkins (1962, 1963) in

---

[1] The emotional expression view, in particular, draws a distinction between "involuntary" and "voluntary" expressions, arguing that certain facial movements are spontaneous and expressive of an emotional state, while others are deliberate and serve social-communicative purposes. This theoretical distinction, while interesting in its own right, will not be further discussed in the present chapter. No one seriously questions the idea that people are able voluntarily to "pose" facial movements and that such posed movements may have no relationship with subjective emotion. Thus the contested theoretical ground does not involve those facial movements, sometimes called "emblems" (see Ekman & Friesen, 1969), which are consciously employed for social signaling purposes.

which he offered a theoretical rationale for conducting research on the face as a means of understanding emotion and personality. According to this analysis, facial action is a key component in a coordinated pattern of activity that constitutes emotion. The essence of the argument is that emotions are adaptive responses that have a strong genetic component. At the core of this adaptive response system lies a prewired set of connections between subjective feeling states and facial movements; together, these form what is sometimes referred to as an "affect program."

Almost as important as the provision of a theoretical rationale for studying the face was the publication of a study by Tomkins and McCarter (1964) in which they showed that carefully selected photographs of facial expressions elicited high levels of agreement among observers who were asked to judge what kind of emotions were depicted in the photographs. Although photographs had been used by previous researchers (including Darwin), Tomkins and McCarter were among the first to develop a systematic experimental procedure yielding evidence consistent with the notion of a facial affect program. If the link between subjective emotion and facial expression is innate, then adult judges (who would have been exposed to thousands of instances of expression of emotion) should have little difficulty in identifying what is being expressed.

Izard's (e.g., 1991) *differential emotions theory* is a development of Tomkins's ideas. Three aspects of emotion are distinguished: neural, neuromuscular/expressive, and experiential. At the neuromuscular/ expressive level, according to Izard, "emotion is primarily facial activity and facial patterning" (1991, p. 42). The pivotal role played by facial and (to a lesser extent) bodily responses is clear from the following: "When neurochemical activity, via innate programs, produces patterned facial and bodily activities, and the feedback from these activities is transformed into conscious form, the result is an emotion feeling/experience that is both a motivating and meaningful cue-producing experience" (1991, p. 42). Differential emotions theory identifies 10 so-called fundamental emotions that, according to Izard, (a) have specific neural substrates, specific configurations of facial movements, and distinct subjective feeling states; (b) are derived from evolutionary processes; and (c) have organizing and motivational properties that serve adaptive functions. The 10 emotions in question are interest, enjoyment, surprise, sadness, anger, disgust, contempt, fear, shame, and shyness. Ekman's (e.g., 1972) *neurocultural theory* shares many features with differential emotions theory, although it is more specific concerning the conditions under which the link between basic emotions and their associated facial expression can be disturbed or distorted. In Ekman's case there are seven basic emotions: fear, surprise, anger, disgust, sadness/distress, happiness, and (added subsequently) contempt.

One implication of Ekman's and Izard's theories is that there should be a close correlation between subjective emotion and facial activity. According to Izard, subjective emotion is determined by feedback from facial movements; according to Ekman, both subjective emotion and facial movements are outputs of a central affect program. An example of a study investigating the relationship between subjective emotion and facial action is that of Ekman, Friesen, and Ancoli (1980). Participants were shown two types of film. One was intended to elicit positive affect and consisted of three short film clips; the other was intended to elicit negative affect and consisted of one, longer clip. Facial reactions to these film clips were covertly recorded and later scored using the Facial Action Coding System (FACS; Ekman & Friesen, 1978). Various parameters of facial activity (e.g., intensity and length of specific "action units" or AUs) were then compared with self-reported emotional reactions to the clips. Several of the findings suggest a relationship between emotional feelings as reported by the participants and their facial activity as measured by FACS. For example, those participants who never showed any activity of the lip corner puller (AU12, the action produced by contracting the zygomaticus major, which would colloquially be called a "smile") reported themselves as having felt less happy than did those who did show lip corner puller activity. Further, self-reported disgust in response to the negative film was found to be significantly correlated with both the total number of negative facial actions shown and the total duration of these actions.

A study by Gosselin, Kirouac, and Doré (1995) also provides support for the relationship between particular emotions and facial displays. Actors were asked to portray six emotions (happiness, anger, fear, sadness, surprise, and disgust) after having read and interpreted short scenarios that were pretested to elicit these emotions. The actors were unaware of the fact that facial expression was the main focus of the study. Their faces were videotaped and subsequently scored using FACS. The action units predicted by Ekman and Friesen (1978, 1982) to be prototypical for each of the six emotions occurred significantly more often when portraying the emotion in question than did unpredicted action units. Next, participants were asked to judge the emotional category to which each videotaped facial display would belong. The judges' recognition accuracy exceeded chance in all cases.

Less supportive of the notion that there is a close relationship between feelings and facial activity are the results of a study by Fernández-Dols, Sánchez, Carrera, and Ruiz-Belda (1997). Participants viewed film excerpts (one neutral, one intended to elicit negative emotion). Facial behavior during the film viewing was covertly video-recorded and scored using FACS, and subjective emotion was assessed by means of self-reports. Thirty-five participants reported experiencing one or more specific emotions during the final 8-second sequence of the negative movie excerpt; 14 of these reported disgust, 11 reported surprise, 2 reported fear, 7 reported disgust and surprise, and 1 reported disgust, sadness, and fear. The emotions were rated on a 10-point intensity scale, and the mean ratings suggest that the experienced emotions were quite intense: 7.6 for disgust, 6.7 for surprise, and 8.0 for fear. Only 2 of the 35 participants were scored as exhibiting the FACS codes that would be expected, given their self-reported emotions and Ekman and Friesen's (1978) predictions concerning the relation of facial actions to emotion. Thirteen participants maintained neutral expressions during the 8-second film sequence. The 20 remaining participants made facial movements that were inconsistent with their self-reported emotion.

A possible explanation for the discrepancy between the results of Gosselin et al. (1995) and those of Fernández-Dols and associates (1997) is that the facial displays in the former study were acted out rather than spontaneous. A study directly comparing judgments of spontaneous and posed expressions (Motley & Camden, 1988) confirmed that recognition accuracy is much better in the case of the posed expressions. Posed displays are presumably more easily recognized than spontaneous faces because they are more prototypical; that is, because they are better *exemplars* of how anger, fear, and so on, are displayed in the face. Spontaneous faces are generally less clear-cut because everyday emotional stimuli are typically less intense and less unambiguous than the carefully preselected stimuli typically used in laboratory experiments (see also Russell, 1994).

A second implication of differential emotions and neurocultural theory is that stimuli that elicit fundamental emotions are likely to be universal ("Threat of a real danger causes fear in all people" [Izard, 1991, p. 50]), and that exposure to such a stimulus therefore creates the impulse to engage in the associated pattern of facial activity, even if this impulse is controlled or inhibited. For each of the basic emotions, argues Ekman (e.g., 1984) there are distinctive universal facial expressions that can be traced phylogenetically. This means that when the relevant facial affect program is stimulated, efferent impulses for the relevant pattern of facial actions will be produced. Whether or not these impulses are translated into a visible facial expression depends on a number of factors, the most important of which are "display rules" (Ekman & Friesen, 1969; see also Kupperbusch et al., chapter 2 in this volume).

Thus, although there may be some cross-cultural variation in facial displays due to the presence of culturally variable display rules, for those emotions that are specified as "fundamental" or "basic," there should be some fundamental cross-cultural universality in the way that these emotions are (a) expressed and (b) recognized. The universality of expression prediction derives straightforwardly from the assumption that the patterned facial activity associated with these emotions reflects the operation of an innate facial affect program. The universality of recognition prediction is less straightforward. One reason for making this prediction is a simple extension of the universality of expression argument: If there is such consistency in the way in which at least certain emotions are expressed, it should be relatively simple to learn the association between emotion and expression. A more complex basis for this prediction depends on extending the notion of adaptive value from the single organism to the dyad or social group. A facial pattern may originally have been adaptive for the individual, in the sense that it increased the organism's visual field or enhanced visual acuity, but it may later have come to be adaptive for conspecifics, in the sense that it helped them to find food, avoid predators, or to predict the behavior of the individual who displays the facial activity. However, this adaptive value could not be gained unless conspecifics had the capacity to detect and recognize these facial displays.

Both the prediction that the way in which emotions are displayed in the face is universal and the prediction that the way in which facial expressions of emotion are recognized by others is universal have been subjected to empirical tests. Most convincing for the universalist position would be evidence concerning universals in the way in which emotions are expressed in the face, but there is surprisingly little research on this issue. This is probably partly due to the fact that it is even harder to investigate this question than it is to conduct research on the universality of recognition. One study investigating universality of expression was reported by Ekman (1972; see also Friesen, 1972). The participants were Japanese and American students. They were shown two types of film, one a travelogue and the other known to evoke negative emotions such as fear and disgust. Their facial reactions to these films were covertly recorded and scored using the Facial Affect Scoring Technique (FAST; Ekman, Friesen, & Tomkins, 1971). There was a high degree of consistency in the Japanese and American participants' facial responses to the negative film, with similar movements occurring at similar moments. While this study goes some way to showing that persons who live in different cultures engage in the same facial actions in response to the same stimulus, it also has some important limitations. First, the relationship between subjective emotion and facial activity is unclear; second, the range of emotions aroused by the negative film was limited, and third, the two cultures concerned are not visually isolated from each other. To our knowledge there are no studies examining universality of expression across visually isolated cultures.

There is more evidence relating to the universality of recognition prediction. A widely cited study is the one reported by Ekman and Friesen (1971). The participants were members of the South Fore tribe living in the highlands of New Guinea. They were shown photographs of Caucasian faces depicting facial displays that had been judged by members of Western, literate cultures to be good exemplars of six emotions. These faces were associated with the same emotions by members of a remote, preliterate culture who had had little contact with Westerners. Ekman and Friesen (1971) also briefly report another study in which Fore participants were asked to pose the faces they associated with certain emotional settings; these expressions were videotaped and shown to U.S. college students, who "accurately" judged the intended emotion. Ekman and Friesen use this evidence to reject the argument that the Fore participants in their main study were able to choose the correct photograph because they had learned to recognize the way in which Westerners express emotions. Ekman and Friesen reason that it is unlikely that this learning would enable them to pose the "Western" expression, as well as recognize it in others. The one aspect of the findings that did not support the investigators' hypothesis – the failure of Fore adults to discriminate fear from surprise, when fear was the target emotion – was explained by Ekman and Friesen as reflecting the fact that in Fore culture fearful events tend also to be surprising. Interestingly, the American judges could not distinguish between the New Guinean expressions of fear and surprise.

The evidence for the universality of emotion expression and recognition has generally been assumed to be fairly strong. Currently, however, there are deep differences of opinion regarding the strength of support provided by the studies for the universalist predictions (see Russell, 1994, 1995; Ekman, 1994). One of the major criticisms is that the facial movements that serve as stimuli in most of these studies are posed and static rather than spontaneous and dynamic, leaving open the question of whether the facial movements that would normally be exhibited by people from non-Western countries in the course of their social interactions would also be readily interpretable by Westerners. Although this is not the appropriate place in which to review all the arguments concerning this research (see Russell, 1994; reactions from Ekman, 1994, and Izard, 1994; rejoinder by Russell, 1995; and Kupperbusch et al., in this volume), it can be concluded with some safety that the degree of emotion recognition exhibited by such participants is (a) less than one would expect on the basis of a straight universality argument, but (b) greater than one would expect if there were no systematic connection between facial activity and emotional state. In short, the evidence is consistent with what Russell (1995) describes as a "minimal universality" position, whereby the degree of agreement exhibited by observers who are asked to infer the emotional state of another person on the basis of facial actions is greater than chance, and these inferences are moreover often quite accurate.

The evidence in relation to the two basic assumptions of the emotional expression view generally seems at least consistent with the notion that facial movements are expressive of underlying emotional states. The problem, for present purposes, is that the evidence is so indirect. As noted earlier, one could infer that the greater-than-chance agreement between judges, coupled with the greater-than-chance accuracy in labeling the state associated with a pattern of facial movement, arises from an underlying consistency in the way that emotional states are expressed in the face. This consistency would facilitate the learning of the association between facial movements and emotions; however, because this association presumably needs to be learned through experience, and because of the large cultural and individual variations both in ecology and in emotion lexicons, both the agreement across and within cultures and the level of accuracy of judgments is far from perfect.

## The Behavioral Ecology View

A radical challenge to the emotional expression view has been offered by Fridlund (1991, 1992, 1994) who rejects the notion that there is a direct relationship between emotion and facial expressions, let alone the idea that facial expressions are *caused* by underlying emotional states. Instead, he advances a *behavioral ecology* view in which he systematically undermines the role played by emotion. Fridlund's critique of what he calls the "emotion view" of human facial displays (what we referred to above as the emotional expression view) has stimulated debate concerning the role played by social contextual factors in the production of and functions served by facial displays (see Fernández-Dols, chapter 9 in this volume, for a detailed discussion of the social-communicative function of facial displays). Below we summarize Fridlund's principal arguments.

### The Relationship between Emotions and Facial Displays

Fridlund's basic argument is that there is no theoretical or unambiguous empirical evidence to sustain the idea that emotions play a causal role in facial expressions: "Adults are certainly considered to 'have emotions,' but the relation of adult display to emotion, as usually defined, is adventitious" (Fridlund, 1994, p. 135). The concept of emotion expression, and specifically of display rules, is seen by Fridlund as a typical product of a two-factor model, as proposed by Ekman (e.g., 1972, 1982; Ekman & Friesen, 1982), Izard (e.g., 1977, 1991) and others. This model is based on a dichotomy between a genetically based facial affect program, on the one hand, and internalized social conventions concerning emotion expressions, on the other. It assumes that emotions are innate and that they automatically give rise to expressions, in the form of facial displays, except when they are consciously regulated in social situations where people wish to hide or transform their "true" emotions. As a consequence of this reasoning, a distinction is made between "felt" or authentic faces, and false or social faces. In contrast, Fridlund claims that people may show a huge variety of facial displays, which are not restricted to a certain number of basic emotions. In the behavioral ecology view, therefore, "there are neither fundamental emotions nor fundamental expressions of them" (Fridlund, 1994, p. 139), but rather facial displays are specific to intent and context.

A further argument against the importance of emotions is that facial displays depend on the context in which they occur rather than on the underlying emotional state presumably experienced by the individual. For example, we may smile when feeling happy, but also when feeling moved, afraid, uncertain, or ashamed. We may cry when feeling sad, but also when feeling intensely happy, angry, jealous, or moved. Smiling should therefore not be seen as an expression of happiness, but rather as a display signifying one's readiness to affiliate, to continue the current interaction, or to display empathy with another person. Similarly, one *may* cry when one is feeling sad; however, the function of crying is not to express the sadness, but rather to display one's need for comfort, or one's sense of ultimate helplessness. A smiling or crying face (or indeed any other facial display) can thus be associated with a variety of emotions. Thus, there is no one-to-one relationship between a basic emotion and a prototypical face. Whether a particular face co-occurs with a particular emotion depends on the nature of the social interaction and not on the intensity of the felt emotion.

This argument has received some experimental support (Fernández-Dols & Ruiz-Belda, 1995; Fridlund, 1991; Wagner and Lee, chapter 10 in this volume). In Fridlund's (1991) study participants were randomly assigned to view pleasant film clips in one of four different social conditions: alone; alone, but in the belief that the same-sex friend with whom they had arrived at the lab was engaged in a different task in a nearby room; alone, but in the belief that the friend was viewing the same film in a nearby room; or together with the friend. Self-reports of emotion and measures of EMG activity (zygomaticus major and corrugator supercilii) were obtained. The amount of facial activity – mainly smiling – was found to covary with the context in which the film was viewed but not with self-reported emotion. Fernández-Dols and Ruiz-Belda (1995) reported similar results in their study of facial displays of gold medal winners at the Olympic games. They found that social context predicted the amount of facial display, in the sense that medalists smiled more during the "interactive stage" in the award ceremony (i.e., when waving to the crowd and receiving applause) than during the noninteractive stages (i.e., when waiting behind the podium, or listening to the national anthem). In contrast to this variation in smiling as a function of social context, medalists rated their happiness as similarly intense across all stages of the ceremony. Wagner and Lee (in this volume) studied nonverbal behavior during verbal communication. Their analysis of the facial behavior of a woman talking about a negative emotional event reveals that much smiling occurred during the negative parts of the conversation. Wagner and Lee point out that if the verbal context were to be ignored, one would be led to conclude that the speaker was experiencing positive emotion.

A final theoretical argument Fridlund advances in rejecting emotions as determinants of facial displays is that there are no valid criteria in order to judge whether someone is or is not "having an emotion." No consensus on how to define emotion has ever been reached, he argues. Self-reports are not to be trusted and behavioral measures can only be used to infer emotion indirectly. Furthermore, if emotion is inferred from facial activity, emotion cannot then be used to explain this facial activity. Bringing emotion into the picture simply diminishes the chances of arriving at a good explanation of facial displays, according to Fridlund.

## Facial Displays as Social Signals

If facial displays are not expressive of underlying emotional states, what functions *do* they serve? According to the behavioral ecology view, such displays are basically social tools. They serve to communicate social motives, and they are driven by social intents. Our faces signal motives such as the readiness to play, affiliate, appease, attack, submit, or continue current interaction; the recruitment of comfort; conflict about whether or not to attack; and the declaration of superiority or of neutrality. Faces are not "readouts" of inner states – or even readouts of social intents – but rather are a means of social communication. Thus, one cries when one wants comfort, one smiles when one wants to play or affiliate, and one displays a fearful face when one wants to be rescued. "Displays are declarations that signify our trajectory in a given social interaction, that is, what we will do in the current situation, or what we would like the other to do" (Fridlund, 1994, p. 130).

Fridlund distances his own view from early ethological accounts, which tended to treat behavioral displays as static, fixed action patterns, thereby ignoring the role of observers in the formalization of behavior. The focus of such research was on the sender, not on the receiver, resulting in a one-sided view of social interaction. Instead, he quotes ethological evidence that the vigilance for the displays of others is important in the evolution of behavioral displays. Neocortical and paleocortical cells in humans and nonhumans, for example, have been shown to be responsive to photographs of the faces of conspecifics, even at young ages. Further evidence comes from research on vervet monkeys and shows that the identity of the recipient is important: These monkeys react to calls made by ingroup members but not to those of outgroup members. Thus, the occurrence of social signals should not be studied independently of the vigilance for signals, the comprehension of these signals, the identity of the interactant, and the context of the interaction.

There is also empirical evidence for the interactive nature of human facial displays. Fernández-Dols and Ruiz-Belda's (1995) study of gold medal winners at the Olympic games and Fridlund's (1991) experiment, described above, clearly testify to the importance of social interaction in human facial displays. Further, in a series of observational studies, Kraut and Johnston (1979) found that people smiled more when interacting with others, as compared to when they were alone, irrespective of the positivity or negativity of the circumstances. For example, bowlers at a bowling alley hardly smiled at all when facing the pins, even when scoring a "spare" or a "strike," but they did do so after turning around to face their friends in the waiting pit. Another relevant study is the one reported by Chovil (1991), who showed that when participants listened to "close call" stories under different social conditions (e.g., over the telephone or face-to-face), their facial displays (mainly wincing and grimacing) increased as a function of how "social" the situation was. All these studies provide indirect support for Fridlund's argument: The sociality of the situation gives rise to certain social motives (e.g., to affiliate or to give comfort, or to help) that determine the type of facial activity that is displayed.

Also consistent with the behavioral ecology view are studies showing that the identity of the interactant (e.g., friend vs. stranger) influences facial displays. The assumption is that people have different social motives when interacting with a friend, a colleague, or a complete stranger. Wagner and Smith (1991) found that friends who are in the same room, rating their emotions in response to a series of slides, show more facial displays than strangers performing the same task. Friends may be assumed to have a motive to support each other, at least in their thoughts (they were not allowed to talk), whereas strangers would probably have a greater motive for keeping distant.

*Implicit and Explicit Sociality*

The fact that people make faces when alone could be seen as inconsistent with the behavioral ecology view. If no one else is present, social motives should not be engaged, and as a consequence there should be no facial display. However, drawing on other social approaches (e.g., Vygotsky, 1962; Wertsch, 1985), Fridlund argues that a "truly alone" condition does not exist, because there is no inner or private self: We are *always* influenced by our social environment. We may be physically alone, but we are never mentally so: We treat ourselves as interactants, we act as if others are present, we imagine that others are present, we anticipate interaction, or we treat nonhumans or objects as interactants. This, according to Fridlund, explains why people show facial displays even when they are alone: These situations are *implicitly* social.

Studies of "implicit sociality" show that alone subjects smile more or less, depending upon the specific context. For example, in the Fridlund (1991) experiment, described earlier, participants smiled more when they believed that their friend was watching the same film clip in a nearby room, compared to when they were alone. Support for implicit audience effects was also found in affective imagery studies (Fridlund, Kenworthy, & Jaffey, 1992; Fridlund, et al., 1990). When asked to imagine situations that they enjoyed, but in which they were either alone (low social), or with others (high social), participants exhibited more facial EMG activity during the high social situations (Fridlund et al., 1990). In order to control for type of imaginary situations, participants in Fridlund et al.'s (1992) study were presented with "high social" and "low social" situations for each of four emotions: happiness, anger, fear, and sadness. Imaginary audience effects were found for all four emotion categories: "High social" happy situations increased lip and cheek activity, "high social" fear situations led to increments in activity in the brow and lip sites, "high social" anger situations attenuated overall facial activity, and "high social" sad situations showed an increase in activity in forehead and brow sites.

Chovil's (1991) findings suggest that sociality is not present or absent but is rather a matter of degree. Some of her participants judged how situations differed with respect to sociality. The following rank-order was found, ranging from least to most social: (1) Listening to another person's voice, previously recorded on audiotape; (2) listening to another person seated behind a partition; (3) listening to another, physically absent person over the telephone; and (4) listening to another person in a face-to-face setting. As described earlier, subjects' facial activity increased monotonically with the sociality of the situation.

According to Fridlund, then, because emotional situations are more often than not social in nature, the variations in facial display found in previous studies are due not to differences in emotionality, but rather to differences in sociality. For example, vignettes, slides, or videos intended to elicit strong emotions may in fact have been quite social in content, depicting persons or interactions between persons. In other words, emotionality and sociality may have been confounded in many studies investigating the effect of emotions on facial displays.

*Problems with the Behavioral Ecology View*

Fridlund has raised some important issues and rightly stresses the social functions of facial displays. However, there are problems with his behavioral ecology view and also with his reinterpretation of previous studies. Because some of these have already been discussed elsewhere (see Buck, 1994; Frijda, 1995; Hess, Banse, & Kappas, 1995) and because this is not the appropriate place to enter into detailed discussion of the rights and wrongs of Fridlund's critiques of previous research, we will limit ourselves here to an analysis of the theoretical and empirical arguments for the role of emotions versus social contexts in influencing facial displays.

*Social versus Emotional Determinants of Facial Displays*

The first question to be considered is whether emotions need to be expelled from an explanatory framework of facial displays. According to Fridlund the evidence for a causal, one-to-one relationship between emotions and facial displays is poor. However, while it needs to be acknowledged that the empirical support is not overwhelming, the evidence is not inconsistent with the idea that emotions do play a role in facial displays. For example, in the previously described study by

Ekman, Friesen, and Ancoli (1980), participants who never smiled reported themselves as feeling less happy than those who did. Further, in the studies by Gosselin et al. (1995) and Wagner, MacDonald, and Manstead (1986), judges were able to recognize different emotions from facial displays. These studies suggest that the relationship between emotion and facial display is not an incidental one, even if it is far from perfect.

Fridlund's primary rationale for rejecting the role of emotions in facial displays seems to be theoretical: The emotion expression view clearly argues that emotions are neurologically based states. As a consequence, if they are not, as Fridlund asserts, there is no theoretical reason why they should be related to facial displays. However, in our view, emotions do not have to be "basic" or part of a prewired affective program in order to play a role in producing facial activity. Facial displays can be seen as one of the multiple components by which the emotion process can be characterized (e.g., Frijda, 1986; Scherer, 1984). From such a perspective, emotions can be conceived of as processes that are elicited in reaction to an emotional situation. In many contemporary theories of emotion, the emergence of different components of the emotion, including facial displays, is assumed to result from appraisal, reappraisal, and regulation processes. In this context it should be emphasized that it is not only the emotional stimulus per se that is appraised but also its social context. For example, if someone encounters a stranger on the street in the middle of the night, any tendency to appraise this situation as threatening would be modified by the knowledge that one is in the company of a male friend, or that one has just successfully completed training in self-defense. Further, while one person may try to suppress his or her fear in such situations, another may scream in order to get help. Whether facial displays will occur, and which ones will be shown, is not an entirely automatic process either, but is very likely to depend upon a range of appraisal and regulation processes.

Given our assumption that emotion does play a role in many facial displays, albeit for social or cognitive reasons rather than biological ones, a second question that needs to be addressed is whether it is possible to determine the relative roles of social and emotional factors in the occurrence of facial displays. One of the issues in this debate is the alleged confounding of emotional and social factors (e.g. Buck, 1991; Chovil & Fridlund, 1991). Buck (1991), for example, argues that the presumed effects of sociality found in the studies of Fridlund and others are actually effects of variations in emotion intensity, whereas Fridlund claims the opposite to be the case. In other words, the question is whether social factors and emotional factors can be disentangled, and if so, whether or not emotions reflect changes in social contexts.

In an attempt to investigate the relationship between social context and emotion, we (Jakobs, Manstead, & Fischer, 1996) conducted a vignette study in which we systematically varied social context while holding the emotional event constant. Subjects were presented with vignettes that were pretested to elicit anger, fear, sadness, happiness, being moved, or disgust. Sociality was varied by framing the situations in one of three ways: The protagonist was described as being alone, in the presence of a stranger, or in the presence of a friend. Respondents were asked to imagine themselves in the described situation and to report their emotions. The results showed that anger was the only emotion that varied as a function of the social context manipulation. This led us to the conclusion that emotion does not necessarily reflect the type of social context in which it occurs, and that how influential the context is may depend on the emotion in question. A closer inspection of individual vignettes even suggests that the specific situation affects the intensity and type of self-reported emotions, presumably because the same social context (e.g., being with a friend) may generate different types of social motives in relation to different events. For example, in two of the four fear vignettes, self-reported fear decreased significantly as a result of being in the company of either a friend or a stranger. What these two vignettes had in common was that the presence of a friend or even a stranger could reasonably be considered to be reassuring or comforting (for example, when one is trying to find a night bus in a strange city, and suddenly realizes that somebody is following him or her). This would presumably diminish the social motive to ask for help, and it would also decrease the appraisal of threat. In the other two fear vignettes, however, the presence of others would not have made any difference to the amount of threat to which the protagonist was exposed (e.g., when crossing an intersection in one's car, and noticing that a large truck is approaching from the left at high speed). Here self-reported fear did not vary as a function of the social context manipulation.

In conclusion, the results of this study show that changes in social context do *not* always affect one's feelings. However, they also suggest that the intensity and type of self-reported *emotion* is influenced if the presence of the other person could somehow make a difference, for example, because his or her (anticipated) actions or mere presence is either comforting, disturbing, reassuring, annoying, and so on. Sociality and self-reported emotion should therefore not be regarded as indistinguishable or as completely interdependent, but rather as theoretically and empirically separate factors that have partly autonomous dynamics.

The role of sociality and emotionality as independent determinants of *facial displays* was investigated by Hess and colleagues (1995). They partly replicated Fridlund's (1991) experiment, but they added two factors: the intensity of the stimulus material (low or high), and the identity of the other person (friend or stranger). It was found that social context effects were only present when the other was a friend, and that stimulus intensity explained more of the variance in facial displays than did differences in social context. Similar results were obtained in one of our own experiments (Jakobs, Manstead, & Fischer, in press). In a modified and extended replication of Fridlund's (1991) study, we created five different social contexts in which humorous films were viewed: (1) alone; (2) with a friend in a nearby room doing an irrelevant task; (3) with a friend in the same room doing an irrelevant task; (4) with a friend in a nearby room, viewing the same films; and (5) with a friend in the same room, viewing the same films together. Like Hess et al. (1995), we also varied the intensity of the stimulus. Participants viewed two film clips that had been pretested to elicit either a moderate or a strong degree of amusement. Otherwise the nature of the films was very similar: Eddie Murphy played the major character in both, and they depicted similar types and degrees of social interaction. Participants' facial displays were unobtrusively videotaped and subsequently analyzed using FACS. After viewing the films, participants rated their feelings during the film clips.

Stimulus intensity had a marked impact on facial activity. More smiling (in terms of both AU12 [lip corner puller] and AU6 [cheek raiser]) occurred during the strong clip, compared to the moderate one. There was also a significant increase in smiling across the five social contexts, which were assumed to increase in level of sociality (see Figure 11.1), although this social context effect was significant only in the case of the stronger clip. This effect was also only found for the AU12 (lip corner puller) scores, which is interesting given that AU6 is generally deemed to be the marker of "Duchenne," or enjoyment, smiles. Moreover, the impact of context was limited to the

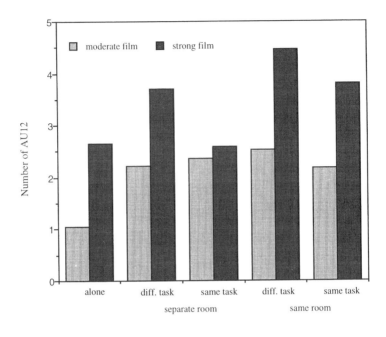

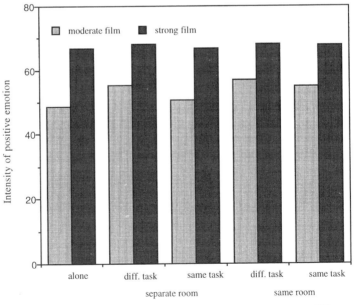

Figure 11.1. *Top*: Number of facial displays (AU12) in reaction to different film clips in different social contexts. *Bottom*: Intensity of positive emotion in reaction to different film clips in different social contexts.

physical presence versus absence of others: Whether the friend was engaged in the same or a different task made no difference to the amount of smiling. Overall, the intensity of the emotional stimulus had a stronger effect on facial displays than did social context.

We also found a relationship between subjective emotion and facial displays. When the emotional self-reports of people who smiled while viewing the films were compared to those of people who did not smile, the former were found to report more positive emotions than the latter. Furthermore, facial activity measures were correlated with self-reported positive emotion, and these correlations were stronger in those conditions involving less sociality; for example, all correlations between self-report and facial display were significant in the alone condition, whereas only a few were significant in the coviewing condition.

This pattern of correlations is not easy to reconcile with the behavioral ecology view. By contrast, it poses fewer problems for the emotional expression view. When a person is alone, social factors presumably play a smaller role than when others are present, and facial behavior is less constrained by these social considerations. In this context, therefore, smiling should be more likely to reflect the person's affective state. The more social a situation is, the stronger the social demands will be, resulting in a poorer relationship between smiling and subjective experience (cf. Buck, 1984; Ekman, 1973).

We interpret these findings as showing that both emotional and social contextual factors can determine facial activity, and as supporting the suggestion that the emotion expression view and the behavioral ecology view are *not* mutually exclusive. It is possible to influence smiling via manipulation of sociality, but also via manipulation of emotion intensity. Moreover, both our own research and the Hess et al. (1995) study show that the effects of sociality are typically weaker than are those of stimulus intensity.

In a further experiment (Jakobs, Manstead, & Fischer, 1998), we used sad film clips rather than happy ones. Smiling may be an exceptional case, given the intuitive obviousness of the fact that smiles frequently serve both social (politeness, appeasement) and emotional (happiness, love, amusement) functions. This is less self-evidently the case for certain negative displays, such as "sad" faces: Although sad faces clearly can serve social purposes, such as eliciting sympathy or comfort from others, they do not do this as a matter of social convention in the same way that a smile routinely signals a greeting between people who know each other. Thus a demonstration of sociality effects on sad faces would provide more compelling support for the behavioral ecology view. We created five viewing conditions: (1) alone; (2) with a stranger in a nearby room watching the same films; (3) with a friend in a nearby room watching the same films; (4) with a stranger in the same room, watching the same films; and (5) with a friend in the same room, together watching the same films. Participants viewed two clips that pretesting showed to be moderate or strong with respect to the degree of self-reported sadness they elicited. Unobtrusively recorded videotapes of participants' faces were analyzed using FACS, and participants rated their subjective emotions in a questionnaire.

Linear trend analyses demonstrated an increase in smiling (AU12, lip corner puller; AU6, cheek raiser) over the five experimental conditions, but also a decrease in fear (AU1, inner brow raiser; AU2, outer brow raiser; AU4, brow lowerer; and AU5, upper lid raiser) and sadness displays (AU1, inner brow raiser; AU4, brow lowerer; AU15, lip corner depressor) (see Figure 11.2). Stimulus intensity also influenced sad displays, with more displays occurring during the stronger excerpt. With respect to subjective emotion, social context affected positive emotions, such that participants felt happier when someone else (friend or stranger) was physically present, and stimulus intensity affected sadness, such that the stronger excerpt elicited greater sadness.

Unlike the findings with respect to smiling, there was no evidence, in the sense of significant positive correlations, of a positive relationship between emotions and facial displays. These results are in line with the behavioral ecology view. However, the finding that the alone situation evoked more sadness displays than did any of the four social contexts is difficult to explain on the basis of the behavioral ecology view. From this perspective it would be predicted that the motive to seek comfort or, in this experiment, to communicate one's negative feelings, would be stronger in contexts in which one's friend is implicitly or explicitly present. Instead, the observed difference between the alone condition and the social conditions seems to be consistent with the operation of a display rule stating that one should suppress one's sadness in situations where others are present.

Overall, the results of both the study of Hess et al. (1995) and our own studies do not support Fridlund's claim that facial displays can be explained without any reference to emotion. Whether a relationship exists and how strong it is depends upon the emotional stimulus, the

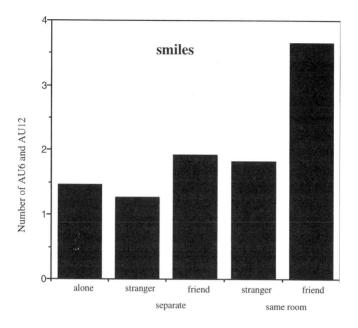

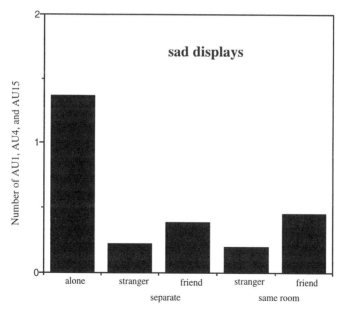

Figure 11.2. *Top*: Number of AU6 and AU12 in different social contexts in response to sadness-evoking film clips. *Bottom*: Number of AU1, AU4, and AU15 in different social contexts in response to sadness-evoking film clips.

type of emotion, and the social context. In the case of positive stimuli, we found that emotions were related to facial displays in the sense that more facial displays were shown when more intense emotions were experienced. In the case of sadness-evoking stimuli, however, we did not find a strong relationship between negative emotions and facial displays.

## Conclusion

Where does the present analysis of the debate between these two allegedly opposing views on facial displays leave us? We agree with Fridlund and others (e.g., Ortony & Turner, 1990; Russell, 1994) that the empirical evidence for a neurologically based isomorphic relationship between a set of "basic emotions" and a particular configuration of facial displays is poor. This seems to have fueled Fridlund's main objection against the emotion expression view, namely, that emotions bear no systematic relationship with facial displays. However, to assert that not all facial displays can be traced back to an emotional state does not lead automatically to the conclusion that emotions should be expelled altogether from an explanatory framework. This much is even implied in the list of social motives cited by Fridlund (1994, p. 129), many of which can be classified as unambiguously emotional in the sense that they are typically reactions to emotional stimuli. For example, the motives to recruit succor, to attack, to submit, and to wish to be rescued are ones that normally arise in emotional situations. While not all social motives have their basis in an acute emotional episode, the majority can hardly be imagined independently of accompanying emotions.

Both the theoretical arguments and the empirical evidence for asserting that emotions are simply by-products of ongoing social interaction, and that facial displays are generated only by the social motives aroused during this interaction, strike us as weak. Above we presented evidence that facial activity is related to subjective emotional states; while it does not necessarily follow that there is an isomorphic relation between a given emotional state and a particular configuration of facial activity, there is at least some evidence that particular configurations of facial activity typically accompany particular emotions. On the other hand, there is not much direct evidence of the relationship between social motives and facial displays. Fridlund's argument that emotions are not well defined and hard to measure is, quite apart from being questionable, equally applicable to his own concept of social motives.

Thus, given our assumptions that (a) during emotional episodes faces are likely to communicate (aspects of) our emotional life, and (b) social motives are an integral part of being emotional, the question that needs to be addressed is "which are the major factors that determine facial displays in particular contexts?" So far, the idea of social motives playing a crucial role in facial displays has received only indirect support. For example, the fact that people smile more in social situations than when they are alone can be explained in ways other than the account offered by the behavioral ecology view: For example, they may enjoy the situation more, simply because it is more pleasant to share one's enjoyment with others, or they might be "infected" by the smiling of others.

On the basis of our own studies we suggest that the following contextual factors are important. First, the *intensity* of the emotional stimulus not only determines whether a recognizable facial display will occur (see Wagner et al., 1986), but also whether the presence of other persons matters (Jakobs, Manstead, & Fischer, in press). If one only shows a faint smile, one is unlikely to smile more in the implicit or explicit company of a friend; however, if something is really funny, the kind of social situation in which one finds oneself does make a difference. This suggests that the intensity of the stimulus influences one's social motives. Second, the *type of emotion* affects not only what one wants to express emotionally, but also what one wants to communicate socially. Anger entails a tendency to attack, pride a wish to tell everyone, love a longing to be with another person, shame an inclination to withdraw, and so on. The accompanying faces may jointly reflect emotional action tendencies and social motives (cf. Frijda & Tcherkassof, 1997). Third, there may be differences between *facial displays* with respect to the types of functions they serve in various contexts and the social motives that elicit them. Smiling serves different functions, emotional as well as social. However, our study of sad faces suggests that these facial displays may primarily signal a motive to be comforted (one component of sadness), but on the other hand may be neutralized or even substituted (at least in social contexts) in order to save one's face. Fourth, one's *social role* in the situation affects the emotions one is most likely to feel and the social motives one has.

This not only implies the presence or absence of another person, but also one's affective and/or status relationship with the other person, the identity of the other person, and one's task in that situation.

Although advocates of the two perspectives reviewed here disagree fundamentally with each other on a number of important issues, we do not believe that there are solid empirical or theoretical grounds for claiming that facial displays are determined solely either by social or by emotional factors. It seems fruitless to regard the two views as mutually exclusive. Instead, we argue that facial actions serve both emotional and social functions. Our own and others' studies of the determinants of facial movements have shown that variations in both social context and emotion can result in changes in facial activity. Facial displays are seemingly determined by a complex of factors that arise from the emotional and social context in which they occur. Emotion may be one such factor, a cultural display rule another, a social motive to communicate still another. We assume that faces are not reflections of basic emotions, but rather the bearers of information about someone's psychological status to one or more others. This psychological status should not be conceived of as a single state, that is, as a single (basic) emotion, or as a single social motive, but rather as a blend of emotions, intentions to act, and motives to communicate, each of which may have a bearing on the face displayed. Process models of emotion, such as those proposed by Scherer (1984) and by Frijda (1986), accord well with this assumption, in that they acknowledge multiple components, the unfolding of emotion over time, and the continuous operation of regulatory forces on these components. Thus, although we agree with Fridlund in concluding that the empirical evidence and theoretical arguments for a limited set of basic emotions are weak, we do not regard this as a reason to discard the concept of emotion as a key determinant of facial displays.

## References

Buck, R. (1984). *The communication of emotion.* New York: Guilford Press.

Buck, R. (1991). Social factors in facial display and communication: A reply to Chovil and others. *Journal of Nonverbal Behavior, 15,* 155–161.

Buck, R. (1994). Social and emotional functions in facial expression and communication: The readout hypothesis. *Biological Psychology, 38,* 95–115.

Chovil, N. (1991). Social determinants of facial displays. *Journal of Nonverbal Behavior, 15,* 141–154.

Chovil, N., & Fridlund, A. J. (1991). Why emotionality cannot equal sociality: Reply to Buck. *Journal of Nonverbal Behavior, 15,* 163–168.

Darwin, C. R. (1872). *Expression of the emotions in man and animals*. London: Albemarle.

Ekman, P. (1972). Universals and cultural differences in facial expression of emotion. In J. Cole (Ed.), *Nebraska symposium on motivation* (Vol. 19, pp. 207–283). Lincoln, NE: University of Nebraska Press.

Ekman, P. (1973). *Darwin and facial expression: A century of research in review*. San Diego, CA: Academic Press.

Ekman, P. (Ed.) (1982). *Emotions in the human face*. New York: Cambridge University Press.

Ekman, P. (1984). Expression and the nature of emotion. In P. Ekman & K. Scherer (Eds.), *Approaches to emotion* (pp. 319–343). Hillsdale, NJ: Lawrence Erlbaum.

Ekman, P. (1994). Strong evidence for universals in facial expressions: A reply to Russell's mistaken critique. *Psychological Bulletin, 115*, 268–287.

Ekman, P., & Friesen, W. V. (1969). The repertoire of nonverbal behavior: Categories, origins, usage, and coding. *Semiotica, 1*, 49–98.

Ekman, P., & Friesen, W. V. (1971). Constants across cultures in the face and emotion. *Journal of Personality and Social Psychology, 17*, 124–129.

Ekman, P., & Friesen, W. V. (1978). *The Facial Action Coding System*. Palo Alto, CA: Consulting Psychologists Press.

Ekman, P., & Friesen, W. V. (1982). Felt, false, and miserable smiles. *Journal of Nonverbal Behavior, 6*, 238–252.

Ekman, P., Friesen, W. V., & Ancoli, S. (1980). Facial signs of emotional experience. *Journal of Personality and Social Psychology, 39*, 1125–1134.

Ekman, P. Friesen, W. V., & Tomkins, S. S. (1971). Facial Affect Scoring Technique (FAST): A first validity study. *Semiotica, 3*, 37–58.

Fernández-Dols, J. M., & Ruiz-Belda, M. A. (1995). Are smiles a sign of happiness? Gold medal winners at the Olympic games. *Journal of Personality and Social Psychology, 69*, 1113–1119.

Fernández-Dols, J. M., Sánchez, F., Carrera, P., & Ruiz-Belda, M. A. (1997). Are spontaneous expressions and emotions linked? *Journal of Nonverbal Behavior, 23*, 163–177.

Fridlund, A. J. (1991). Sociality of solitary smiling: Potentiation by an implicit audience. *Journal of Personality and Social Psychology, 60*, 229–240.

Fridlund, A. J. (1992). The behavioral ecology and sociality of human faces. In M. S. Clark (Ed.), *Review of Personality and Social Psychology*, Vol. 13 (pp. 90–121). Newbury Park, CA: Sage.

Fridlund, A. J. (1994). *Human facial expression: An evolutionary view*. New York: Academic Press.

Fridlund, A. J., Kenworthy, K. G., & Jaffey, A. K. (1992). Audience effects in affective imagery: Replication and extension to dysphoric imagery. *Journal of Nonverbal Behavior, 16*, 191–211.

Fridlund, A. J., Sabini, J. P., Hedlund, L. E., Schaut, J. A., Shenker, J. I., & Knauer, M. J. (1990). Audience effects on solitary faces during imagery: Displaying to the people in your head. *Journal of Nonverbal Behavior, 14*, 113–137.

Friesen, W. V. (1972). *Cultural differences in facial expressions in a social situation:*

*An experimental test of the concept of display rules.* Unpublished doctoral dissertation, University of California, San Francisco.

Frijda, N. H. (1986). *The emotions.* Cambridge: Cambridge University Press.

Frijda, N. H. (1995). Expression, emotion, neither, or both? A review of "Human facial expression: An evolutionary view" by A. J. Fridlund. *Cognition and Emotion, 9* (6), 617–637.

Frijda, N. H., & Tcherkassof, A. (1997). Facial expression and modes of action readiness. In J. A. Russell & J. M. Fernández-Dols (Eds.), *The psychology of facial expression* (pp. 78–102). New York: Cambridge University Press.

Gosselin, P., Kirouac, G., & Doré, F. Y. (1995). Components and recognition of facial expression in the communication of emotion by actors. *Journal of Personality and Social Psychology, 68,* 83–96.

Hess, U., Banse, R., & Kappas, A. (1995). The intensity of facial expression is determined by underlying affective state and social situation. *Journal of Personality and Social Psychology, 69,* 280–288.

Izard, C. E. (1977). *Human emotions.* New York: Plenum.

Izard, C. E. (1991). *The psychology of emotions.* New York: Plenum.

Izard, C. E. (1994). Innate and universal facial expressions: Evidence from developmental and cross-cultural research. *Psychological Bulletin, 115,* 288–299.

Jakobs, E., Manstead, A. S. R., & Fischer, A. H. (1996). Social context effects on emotional experience. *Journal of Nonverbal Behavior, 20,* 123–143.

Jakobs, E., Manstead, A. S. R., & Fischer, A. H. (1998). Sociality effects on negative facial displays: Physical presence and relation with the other. Manuscript submitted for publication.

Jakobs, E., Manstead, A. S. R., & Fischer, A. H. (in press). Social motives and subjective feelings as determinants of facial displays: The case of smiling. *Personality and Social Psychology Bulletin.*

Kraut, R. E., & Johnston, R. E. (1979). Social and emotional messages of smiling: An ethological approach. *Journal of Personality and Social Psychology, 37,* 1539–1553.

Motley, M. T., & Camden, C. T. (1988). Facial expression of emotion: A comparison of posed expressions versus spontaneous expressions in an interpersonal communication setting. *Western Journal of Speech Communication, 52,* 1–22.

Ortony, A., & Turner, T. J. (1990). What's basic about basic emotions? *Psychological Review, 97,* 315–331.

Russell, J. A. (1994). Is there universal recognition of emotion from facial expression? A review of cross-cultural studies. *Psychological Bulletin, 115,* 102–141.

Russell, J. A. (1995). Facial expressions of emotion: What lies beyond minimal universality? *Psychological Bulletin, 118,* 379–391.

Scherer, K. R. (1984). Emotion as a multicomponent process: A model and some cross-cultural data. In P. Shaver (Ed.), *Review of personality and social psychology* (Vol. 5, pp. 37–63). Beverly Hills, CA: Sage.

Tomkins, S. S. (1962). *Affect, imagery, consciousness. Vol. 1, The positive affects.* New York: Springer.

Tomkins, S. S. (1963). *Affect, imagery, consciousness. Vol. 2, The negative affects.* New York: Springer.

Tomkins, S. S., & McCarter, R. (1964). What and where are the primary affects? Some evidence for a theory. *Perceptual and Motor Skills, 18,* 119–158.

Vygotsky, L. S. (1962). *Thought and language.* Cambridge, MA: MIT Press.

Wagner, H. L., MacDonald, C. J., & Manstead, A. S. R. (1986). Communication of individual emotions by spontaneous facial expressions. *Journal of Personality and Social Psychology, 50,* 737–743.

Wagner, H. L., & Smith, J. (1991). Facial expression in the presence of friends and strangers. *Journal of Nonverbal Behavior, 15,* 201–215.

Wertsch, J. (1985). *Vygotsky and the social formation of mind.* Cambridge, MA: Harvard University Press.

# PART IV

# The Role of Nonverbal Behavior in the Facilitation of Social Interaction

# 12. The Evolution of a Parallel Process Model of Nonverbal Communication

MILES L. PATTERSON

The study of nonverbal communication is central to an understanding of social interaction. Among the more important issues in this research is determining how patterns of nonverbal communication develop over the course of interaction. That is, how do we explain the give-and-take of nonverbal communication as people make adjustments to one another? The purpose of this chapter is to discuss the evolution of one approach – the parallel process model of nonverbal communication (Patterson, 1995) – through theoretical developments emerging independently in the areas of nonverbal exchange and social cognition.

Because my own work has been a part of this evolution, I will provide a kind of a personal perspective on the changing theoretical landscape. The first section of this chapter focuses on theories that attempt to explain nonverbal exchange, that is, the sequential adjustments partners make in their nonverbal involvement with one another. Early theories regarding these patterns of nonverbal exchange were characterized by reactive explanations for these sequential adjustments in interaction.

## Theories of Nonverbal Exchange

### Reactive Theories

The reactive approach attempts to explain one person's nonverbal intimacy or involvement (e.g., distance, gaze, touch, expressiveness) as the product of, or reaction to, the partner's preceding behavior. Presumably, reactions to a partner's behavioral change are mediated by covert processing that, in turn, determines the behavioral adjustment. For example, if Mary approaches Tom closely and touches him as she starts to talk, Tom's covert processing of Mary's behavior determines his behavioral response. The first attempt at explaining these nonverbal adjustments was equilibrium theory (Argyle & Dean, 1965).

*Equilibrium Theory.* My acquaintance with equilibrium theory dates back to the fall of 1966 when I started to review the research on space in social interaction, preliminary to my dissertation proposal. Although I found the work of Hall (1959, 1963, 1966) and Sommer (1959, 1961, 1962) on the structure and meaning of space interesting, Argyle and Dean's (1965) article was unique because it described a simple, yet elegant, theory accounting for dynamic changes in nonverbal behavior between interactants.

Equilibrium theory proposed that interactants' behavioral intimacy or involvement was expressed in terms of distance, gaze, smiling, and other related cues. This involvement was, however, constrained by the intimacy of the partners' relationship. Equilibrium was achieved when the overall level of nonverbal involvement was comfortable or appropriate for a dyad, that is, consistent with their relationship intimacy. This equilibrium point was different for every relationship. So, for example, the behavioral involvement of good friends would be greater than that of mere acquaintances. More important, however, was the predicted adjustment when the equilibrium was disturbed. Specifically, when a deviation from a comfortable or appropriate level of behavioral involvement occurred, behavioral adjustments by one partner (or both of them) would compensate for the inappropriate involvement.

Because several different behaviors contributed to the overall involvement level, adjustments might be made in any one behavior or in combinations of different behaviors. For example, suppose an inappropriately close approach and touch initiated by one person produced disequilibrium (and its resulting discomfort) in the partner. The partner might turn away and decrease gaze in an attempt to compensate for the close approach and touch. In a complementary fashion, if the initial approach were not close enough, a compensatory adjustment might increase involvement through a more directly facing orientation and increased gaze.

The results of experiments by Argyle and Dean (1965) and two field studies of spatial invasion (Felipe & Sommer, 1966) provided early support for equilibrium theory. The compensatory adjustments reported in these articles were reactions that immediately followed close approaches by a confederate. As I read about this, I wondered if there might also be residual effects of disequilibrium on a subsequent inter-action. That is, if individuals were placed in uncomfortably close ar-rangements, would compensation carry over to a second interaction? Consequently, my dissertation research examined the effects of a close seating arrangement in an initial interaction on subjects' approach distance in a second interaction (Patterson, 1968). Alas, what seemed to be a good idea in the abstract was not supported in the laboratory. Of course, in another sense there was residual compensation – I did receive my degree.

A number of other studies in the late 1960s and early 1970s did find clear support for equilibrium theory (see reviews by Cappella, 1981; Patterson, 1973). There were, however, a few instances where in-creased involvement by one person led to a similar reaction from the partner, that is, reciprocation, not compensation (e.g., Breed, 1972; Jourard & Friedman, 1970). Sometime after the review paper on equi-librium theory (Patterson, 1973), I reexamined the empirical research. Virtually all of the research through the early 1970s that supported equilibrium theory engaged a confederate-stranger who approached too closely, gazed too much, or touched unsuspecting subjects. These studies were typically conducted in laboratories, libraries, and other public settings where the subjects had little control over their environ-ment. Given these circumstances, it is not surprising that the subjects might avoid (i.e., compensate) by leaving, turning away, reducing gaze, or in some other fashion, decreasing involvement with the in-truder. But was this characteristic of interactions that involve friends or family members (or even friendly family members) in their own homes and territories? Of course, this question was difficult to answer empirically because experimental research rarely examined people in close relationships on their own turf.

Nevertheless, it was unlikely that compensation was the only re-sponse to increased nonverbal intimacy. If it were, we wouldn't be around here to speculate about it. Of course, sexual intimacy is only one example of the way that increased involvement by one person is matched or reciprocated by a partner. The attachment between par-ents and children, the shared intimacy of good friends, and occasions of both celebration and grief are examples of how we often reciprocate the initiation of a partner's increased involvement. So, how can we explain contrasting patterns of nonverbal involvement, that is, both compensation and reciprocation? Three different models enlisted affect as the primary mediator of changing patterns of nonverbal involvement.

*Affect-Based Models.* What kinds of processes might mediate contrasting behavioral adjustments to a change in a partner's nonverbal involvement? An important clue was the result, from a number of studies, that linked physiological arousal to close approaches and/or increased gaze (e.g., Kleinke & Pohlen, 1971; McBride, King, & James, 1965; Nichols & Champness, 1971). If adjustments in a partner's nonverbal involvement were sufficiently large to increase in arousal, then the labeling of this arousal might mediate subsequent nonverbal adjustments (Patterson, 1976). In effect, this was a modification of the arousal and labeling processes in Schachter's (1964) two-factor theory of emotions.

It seemed to me, however, that changes in a partner's nonverbal involvement might also decrease arousal. For example, a comforting touch when a person is fearful would probably lower arousal level, as would the departure of someone who is disliked. Thus, rather than considering only increases in arousal as Schachter did, both increases and decreases in arousal might serve as a signal alerting the individual to changes in the social environment (Mandler, 1975). In such a case, a much broader range of interactions might be covered.

With the mediating processes in place, the predicted behavioral adjustments in the arousal-labeling model were straightforward. If the arousal change–labeling process resulted in negative affect (e.g., fear or anxiety), compensation was predicted (Patterson, 1976). This was consistent with Argyle and Dean's (1965) suggestion that anxiety was a likely result of excessive proximity or gaze. Furthermore, compensatory adjustments (e.g., turning away) should reduce the negative affect and allow a person greater comfort and control in the situation. If the arousal change-labeling process resulted in positive affect (e.g., liking or love), reciprocation was predicted (Patterson, 1976). Such a reaction would be characteristic of a response to a good friend or a lover. Finally, if the partner's change in nonverbal involvement was not great enough to produce a change in arousal, then there would be no change in affect and no motivation for a behavioral adjustment.

Although the arousal model of nonverbal exchange was an improvement over equilibrium theory, I had no illusions about it being the final word on the topic – and it wasn't. A year after it was published, Ellsworth (1977) offered a particularly insightful criticism of the mediating mechanism in the arousal model. She suggested that it would be a luxury to sit back and try to understand one's own feelings as you are interacting with another person. Instead, a person's cognitions would be focused on trying to understand the meaning of the change in a partner's behavior (Ellsworth, 1977). In addition, the model made much more sense in predicting behavioral adjustments following *increased* involvement (e.g., close approach, touch, gaze) than in predicting adjustments following *decreased* involvement (e.g., moving away, decreasing gaze). For example, according to the model, if Tom moves away from Mary and Mary experiences negative affect, she will compensate and try to increase involvement. Well, that's possible, but Mary may also feel hurt and angry (negative affect), tell Tom to get lost, and move farther away from him (i.e., reciprocate his initial move).

The mediating role of affect was also emphasized in two later models (Burgoon, 1978; Cappella & Greene, 1982). Both of these theories emphasized an initial discrepancy process that compared the partner's actual involvement level to an expected level of involvement. Unlike the arousal-labeling model, where the cognitive component was a self-attribution process, the cognitive component (i.e., the discrepancy evaluation) in these two theories was a more or less automatic comparison between the expected and actual level of involvement. This comparison process was important because as the discrepancy increased, so did the level of arousal. The specific role of the arousal-affect link was, however, very different in the two theories.

In Burgoon's (1978) expectancy-violation model, the valence of the affect was a product of the reward value of the partner. Thus, an unexpectedly high involvement by a rewarding partner (e.g., an attractive or high-status individual) was likely to be experienced positively, whereas the same behavior by a nonrewarding partner was likely to be experienced negatively. Like the arousal-labeling model, positive affect produced reciprocation and negative affect produced compensation.

According to Cappella and Greene (1982), the labeling process in the arousal model was too slow and unwieldy to account for the rapid adjustments that people often make in the course of interaction. So they proposed that the critical mediating processes in reacting to a partner were driven by arousal. The initial stage engaged a discrepancy evaluation, that is, a comparison between the expected and actual level of involvement of the partner. This model proposed that, as the discrepancy between the expected and actual involvement levels increased, arousal also increases. Arousal, in turn, determines the valence and intensity of affect. Moderate levels of arousal produce the most positive affect and lead to reciprocation, whereas high levels of arousal produce negative affect and lead to compensation.

The models described here engage different mediating mechanisms in explaining patterns of nonverbal exchange, but they all share two important commonalities. First, they are all reactive in nature. That is, they try to explain an individual's reactive adjustments to a partner's initial behavior in terms of specific mediating processes. As a result, these theories do not consider the origin of particular exchanges, but only conditional, reactive adjustments to a prior pattern of behavior. In addition, some patterns of nonverbal exchange are not strictly reactive anyway. For example, in some sequences, like greetings and departures, individuals follow a common script. That is, partners act on shared expectancies about the behavioral sequence, rather than simply "reacting" to each other's behavior.

Second, all of the models are affect driven. That is, behavioral adjustments are primarily a product of the affect resulting from the partner's preceding behavior. Although the theories propose different mechanisms for generating affect, they all predict similar adjustments once the affect is present. Specifically, positive affect leads to reciprocation of the partner's behavior change and negative affect leads to compensation. A simple affect-driven mediating process cannot, however, account for occasions when people manage their behavior to create a particular impression, in spite of their feelings. For example, a student might try ingratiation (a close approach, high level of gaze, smiling, and a liberal dose of compliments) on a disliked professor in an attempt to get a break on a grade or extra time on an overdue assignment.

In summary, it seems clear that the affect-based models offer more comprehensive explanations of nonverbal exchange than that proposed by equilibrium theory. Nevertheless, these models also have substantial limitations. They do not address the initiation of interaction sequences and they cannot account for occasions when people act in a fashion that is inconsistent with their underlying affect. The functional model was an attempt to address these issues in a broader theoretical framework.

*Functional Model*

The functional model of nonverbal exchange (Patterson, 1982, 1983, 1991) emphasizes how different functions of interaction might alter the dynamics of nonverbal exchange. The distinction between affect-driven behavior and managed or deliberate behavior is particularly important in this model. Spontaneous patterns might be explained by processes like those described in the affect-based models, but managed patterns would follow a different course. That is, managed patterns might well be inconsistent with the individual's affective reaction toward a partner.

The functional model is also different from the earlier theories in providing an explicit recognition of the role of factors such as culture, gender, and personality in shaping the specific nonverbal expression of different functions. Figure 12.1 illustrates how the component processes of the model relate to one another. First, the combination of the genetic and environmental determinants constrains the range of communication options available to individuals. At a general level, we all share some common tendencies that have been selected over the course of evolution. On this common foundation, culture, gender, and personality affect our choice of social situations and the relationships we develop with others in those settings.

The combined influence of the antecedent factors also affects the course of interaction, first, through the preinteraction mediators. That is, specific behavioral predispositions, arousal reactions, and cognitive-affective expectancies are primed and likely to be activated in the interaction. For example, an individual who is socially anxious (i.e., a personality factor) is likely to (1) keep a greater distance from others, gaze less, and initiate fewer comments; (2) experience increased physiological arousal; and (3) have more negative self-focused thoughts and expectancies than someone who is not anxious (Patterson & Ritts, 1997). In turn, these mediating behavioral, physiological, and cognitive processes affect an individual's perceived function of the interaction and level of nonverbal involvement.

An example of contrasting functions might be useful at this point. The anticipation and development of a casual conversation with a friend would be clearly different from a job interview. In the former situation, people are typically relaxed and unconcerned about how to "act." Consequently, nonverbal involvement would be substantially

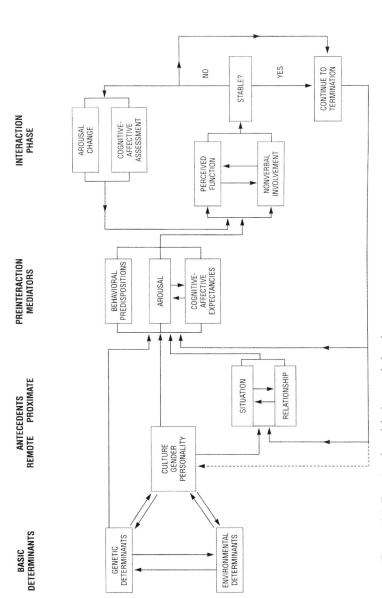

Figure 12.1. Functional model of nonverbal exchange.

determined by affect. In contrast, in the interview, the nonverbal re-actions would be more closely managed and monitored. Specific patterns of nonverbal involvement would be determined by impression management goals and not by affective reactions to the interviewer. Consequently, patterns of nonverbal involvement may develop independently from interpersonal affect. Even here, however, the particular course of these two interactions would also be shaped by the culture, gender, and personality of the actor and partner.

In the interaction phase of this model, patterns of compensation and reciprocation are no longer the simple result of a change in affect (as predicted by the affect-based models), but also the product of strategic patterns initiated independently from affect. Consequently, simple predictions of behavioral adjustments were no longer possible. Instead, the critical outcome measure in the model is the relative stability of the pattern of nonverbal exchange. In general, to the extent that interaction partners have comparable preferences for nonverbal involvement and share similar perceptions of the function of the interaction, their patterns of nonverbal exchange will tend to be relatively stable and predictable.

In contrast, if their preferred levels of involvement and their perceptions of the interaction are different, their patterns of nonverbal exchange will tend to be unstable. In the right side of Figure 12.1, instability leads to arousal change and a cognitive-affective assessment. If the resulting behavioral adjustments and/or changes in the perceived function are adequate, the interaction will move toward greater stability. If stability is not achieved, the individual is likely to cycle through the arousal-assessment-adjustment sequence again. There is, of course, a limit to the amount of instability people will endure. At some point, continued failure to achieve some sort of stability will lead to ending the interaction. Finally, when the interaction ends, the feedback links leading from the termination outcome identify the residual effects of the interaction on components and processes affecting subsequent interactions.

The functional model is an attempt at a more comprehensive explanation of nonverbal exchange that could address the limitations of earlier theories. That is, instead of merely focusing on reactive adjustments, this model proposes that different functions might find their expression in the *initiation* of specific patterns of nonverbal involvement. Once initiated, scripted patterns might run their course with only minor adjustments required in adapting to a partner's specific reactions. In addition, specific influence functions, like impression management or deception, are often expressed independently of an individual's underlying affect. Thus, according to the functional model, behavior is not consistently related to a person's underlying affect. Nevertheless, there is a cost in attempting to be more comprehensive. Specifically, the functional model does not generate the kinds of specific predictions that clearly followed from the earlier theories.[1]

There is, however, another more pervasive limitation of the functional model and the other theories that preceded it. They all attempt to explain how one aspect of nonverbal communication (i.e., nonverbal involvement) is initiated or encoded, but they failed to provide an explanation for the continuous reception or decoding of nonverbal communication. That is, how do we process the nonverbal input from ourselves and others and how does this processing affect the encoding of nonverbal behavior?

### Whither Social Cognition?

The primary focus of the theories described up to this point was to explain and predict patterns of nonverbal exchange. Among the cognitive processes enlisted as mediating mechanisms by these theories were expectancies, emotional labeling, scripts, and attributions. In the various theories, these processes were engaged in an episodic fashion as the proximate determinants of nonverbal patterns. But, because cognitive processes, like patterns of behavior, are continuously engaged, it is necessary to consider the broader, dynamic relationship between cognitions and behavior.

Two specific issues reflecting this dynamic relationship merit attention here. First, cognitions not only affect behavior, but behavior also affects cognitions (Bem, 1972). In addition, it is often necessary to evaluate the utility of our behavior toward others. For example, we might wonder if we've impressed a new acquaintance or if the boss believes the excuse for being late. Thus, our cognitions about our partners are constrained by our own goal-directed behavior. The second issue provides the foundation for the new parallel process model of nonverbal communication. It is simply the assumption that there are finite limits to the cognitive resources of individuals. Thus, the

---

[1] A recent book by Burgoon, Stern, and Dillman (1995) provides a comparative review of these different theories of nonverbal exchange.

attention and effort invested in one area (e.g., behavior management) will not be available for use in another area (e.g., judging the truthfulness of a partner). Before it is possible to integrate these cognitive processes into a more comprehensive model of nonverbal communication, it is necessary to see how these processes operate in making sense of our social worlds.

*Perceiving Others*

Person perception has long been a popular topic in social psychology. It is not my intention to review such an extensive field in this chapter but, rather, to get a sense of the different kinds of processes involved in forming impressions of others. One way of classifying these processes is in terms of the kind of stimulus information that different theories emphasize. A number of theories focus on the way that the *appearance and physical characteristics* of individuals are processed in making inferences about others (e.g., Anderson, 1981; Brewer, 1988; Fiske & Neuberg, 1990; Smith & Zarate, 1992; Wyer & Srull, 1986).

Most of these theories propose that the processing of information occurs through either category-based or integration mechanisms. Category-based, or top-down, processing occurs when the physical characteristics or appearance of a target person cue useful social categories. For example, there are usually a number of redundant nonverbal cues, like a person's figure, facial appearance, voice, hair style, and clothing that reliably indicate the sex of an individual. In a similar fashion, other combinations of appearance cues lead to automatic category judgments about race and age. Once we categorize a person, then additional impressions are quickly formed.

Some automatic judgments may also be the result of specific, conditional rules developed over time. For example, Smith (1990) suggests that automatic judgments are the result of cumulative experiences in the processing of social information. That is, we learn that if a particular cue or behavior is present, then a broader judgment is defensible. Often these "if-then" conditional judgments occur outside of awareness (Smith, 1990).

In contrast, the integration mechanism, or bottom-up processing, starts with the identification of specific attributes and then combines them, leading to an overall judgment. The fictional detective Sherlock Holmes was a master at these kinds of judgments. That is, he noticed and integrated apparently unrelated pieces of information, such as the accent, clothing, gait, and physical disabilities, to determine that his client was a dock worker or a military officer. Usually, the categorization process is primary because it is virtually automatic and engages a minimum of cognitive effort. Because integration is more cognitively demanding, it is typically initiated only when categorization does not provide a satisfactory solution or when there is reason to validate the initial judgments.

Other theories focus on the way that *behavioral information* is used in making trait attributions. For example, Trope (1986) proposed that causal inferences about behavior required two stages, with behavior identification first, followed by a second, higher order process of trait attribution. This two-stage process is characteristic of the typical correspondent inference. For example, you might be introduced to someone who gives you an enthusiastic handshake and a broad smile, and gazes steadily while expressing verbal interest in what you have to say. In the first stage, identifying this pattern of behavior as friendly is an automatic process. This is quickly followed, in the second stage, by a characterization that this is a friendly person.

Gilbert and his colleagues added a third, conditional stage in which perceivers might correct trait attributions when there was evidence for a possible environmental cause for the behavior (Gilbert, Pelham, & Krull, 1988). This third stage could be activated only when there were sufficient cognitive resources to consider a possible correction. If the perceiver's resources were otherwise occupied (e.g., with self-presentational concerns), it is unlikely that the correction stage would be completed.

Whether perceivers focus on appearance or on behavior, the first two approaches describe judgments that result from social inference. In contrast, a third approach assumes that judgments are the product of the direct perception of *affordances* (Gibson, 1979). Social affordances are the pragmatic relational information present in the target person's appearance and movements. This information suggests what the target person can do for the perceiver or what the perceiver can do to the target person (McArthur & Baron, 1983).

An example of such direct perception is the reaction of adults to the baby faces of infants. That is, the characteristic facial features of an infant – large eyes, small, rounded chin, and a disproportionately large forehead – lead to positive, nurturant reactions (Berry & McArthur, 1985, 1986). Presumably, such judgments were selected for their adaptive value in relating to infants who are dependent on the nurturance of others. Furthermore, adults with baby faces are also seen as more warm, open, and less responsible than adults with dominant-looking faces.

In summary, these three approaches emphasize different types of information, often nonverbal in nature, and relatively distinct mechanisms for processing the information. As a result, these different perspectives on perceiving others are more complementary than competing explanations of person perception. That is, each process may be engaged for distinct kinds of stimuli under different circumstances. Finally, the processes described here vary in terms of their cognitive complexity. That is, some processes are automatic (e.g., categorization and perception of affordances) and others (e.g., integration and correction) are more cognitively demanding.

*Self-Perception*

The majority of theory and research in social cognition deals with how we select and process information about others. But there is much more to social cognition than just the direct perception of others. First, judgments about ourselves are important in the course of interaction. Self-perception theory (Bem, 1972) proposes that we often come to understand ourselves the same way we come to understand others. That is, we observe our own behavior and then we make an attribution about ourselves, especially when prior feelings or judgments are not particularly strong. For example, an individual might "notice" that she is smiling, gazing, and talking a great deal with a new acquaintance and conclude that she really likes this person. In such a case, one's own nonverbal behavior may be an especially important source of information about the self.

To the extent that self-perception is the result of inferential processes, then inferences about the self may be constrained by available cognitive resources, just as inferences about others are. Not all judgments about the self, however, are a product of social inference. Facial feedback theory (Buck, 1980) proposes that emotional experience is the product of feedback from facial muscle movement. According to facial feedback theory, spontaneous changes in facial expressions precede and determine an individual's feeling state. The critical feedback here is neural, not cognitive, and, consequently, when (and if) these reactions develop, they are automatic.

*Metaperception*

Sometimes the most important judgments about others involve assessing how they feel about us, or metaperception. If you're trying to impress someone or sell something, it is more important to know what the other person thinks about you and your message than it is to make trait attributions about the person. Results from our laboratory suggest that metaperception may be affected by the application of cognitive resources, just as the direct perception can be (Patterson, Churchill, Farag, & Borden, 1991/1992). Specifically, we found that subjects who had a less demanding impression management task (compared to those who had a more demanding task) were more accurate in judging how their partners thought of them. Presumably, subjects' attention to managing their own behavior decreased attention and/or effort in judging their partners.

How might metaperspective judgments develop? A commonsense view would suggest that, in attending to the verbal and nonverbal reactions of our partners, we are able to infer their judgments about us. Although this kind of process may happen, Kenny and DePaulo (1993) suggest two other processes that are mediated by self-perception. Specifically, metaperspective accuracy may result from either a self-judgment or a direct observation process. With the self-judgment process, individuals form self-perceptions and then assume that others view them as they view themselves. With the direct observation process, individuals "observe" their own behavior and then try to judge how others are likely to view them on the basis of that behavior (Kenny & DePaulo, 1993).

*Action Schemas*

Although there was some reference to scripts and expectancies in the discussion of the functional model, the role of action schemas on the cognitive side of interaction deserves closer attention. Because action schemas are cognitive mechanisms that directly relate to the behavioral side of interaction, they play a central role in an integrated model of nonverbal communication. In general, action schemas can provide a means for actors to understand their own behavior and to anticipate and monitor the sequence of events in an interaction. First, action identification theory proposes that individuals identify their actions in a variety of ways from low-level descriptions of how the action is performed to high-level descriptions of the purpose of the action (Vallacher & Wegner, 1987). Actions tend to be identified at a higher level as long as the action can be maintained.

A good example is that of impression management. "Making a good impression" might describe the high-level identification, that is, the purpose in managing one's behavior in meeting someone important. A low-level identification of the same sequence might focus on specific behavioral components, such as approaching the partner at a moderately close distance, maintaining a high level of gaze, smiling and nodding in response to the partner's comments, and directing the conversation to the partner's interests. When individuals are skilled in a particular activity, their performance will tend to be better when they have a high-level action identification. In contrast, when individuals are less skilled in an activity, their performance will tend to be better with a low-level action identification (Vallacher & Wegner, 1987).

Sometimes our action schemas are focused on the sequence of events in a particular setting. Scripts (Abelson, 1981; Schank & Abelson, 1977) and memory organization packets (MOPs) (Kellerman & Lim, 1990; Schank, 1982) are similar constructs that refer to the sequential ordering of actions. To the extent that scripts or MOPs work effectively, a minimum of cognitive resources is invested in behavior management, leaving more for evaluating the partner and the message content.

*Summary*

From this brief review, it is clear that cognitive processes in interaction cover a wide range of concerns relating to the partner, the self, and the interaction. Furthermore, different processes vary in the demands that they put on available cognitive resources. Some processes are automatic and operate even when cognitive resources are extremely limited, whereas other processes can only be activated when resources are plentiful. Finally, it should also be emphasized that social cognitions are typically driven by pragmatic concerns about the ongoing interaction (Fiske, 1992). In other words, our thoughts are guided by the need to act.

**An Overview of the Parallel Process Model**

Theoretical analyses of interaction and communication have, for the most part, treated acting and thinking as processes that might be explained independent of one another. Such a strategy is convenient, and even defensible, because interactions are extremely complex events. Nevertheless, it is clear from the discussion here, that the "divide and conquer" approach misrepresents our common experience in relating to others. Instead, by recognizing that social behavior and social cognition are parallel processes that affect one another, it is possible to develop a theoretical framework that captures some of the dynamic interdependence of action and thought.

The basic assumption underlying this parallel process approach is that interactants are simultaneously engaged in interdependent social behavior and social cognition. That is, individuals are encoding dispositions, feelings, intentions, or other information into verbal and behavioral expression while, at the same time, decoding the verbal and nonverbal behavior of their partners *and* monitoring and experiencing their own behavior. Such an agenda seems truly remarkable, and it is, but there are some features that make it more manageable. Specifically, some of the behavioral and cognitive processes operate automatically and minimize the opportunity for system overload. Consistent with my earlier model (Patterson, 1982, 1983), the functional basis for nonverbal communication is emphasized. That is, patterns of cognition and interactive behavior may be seen as adaptive reactions to the social environment. A basic concern is making explicit the parameters that define the scope of the parallel process model.

### Parameters of the Model

First, the approach described here is primarily an individualistic one. That is, it emphasizes the development of and relationship between the behavioral and cognitive processes of one person in relating to a partner. Nevertheless, the model is also relevant for the emergence of dyadic patterns. For example, the rapport resulting from increased contact and attachment between partners may be seen in their increased behavioral coordination (Bernieri & Rosenthal, 1991; Tickle-Degnen & Rosenthal, 1990). The issue of shared or coordinated social cognitions is one that has recently been gaining attention (see for example Nye & Brower, 1996) and is certainly relevant for this model.

A second, related concern involves the level of analysis of specific behaviors. There are two issues that are relevant here: (1) individually defined versus dyadically defined behaviors, and (2) component behaviors versus patterns of behaviors. Some behaviors, like facial expression, posture, gestures, or vocal cues, can be adequately described without specific reference to a partner. Other behaviors, like mutual gaze, interpersonal distance, or touch, necessarily require the presence and/or action of another person. Although it is important to recognize the operational differences between these two types of behaviors, both types are interactive and an appropriate focus for the present model. The issue of component cues and behaviors versus patterns of behavior is one that has been addressed frequently in the past (e.g., Argyle & Dean, 1965; Cappella, 1981; Mehrabian, 1969; Patterson, 1976, 1983). The emphasis in this model is on the encoding and decoding of patterns of behavior, especially in terms of nonverbal involvement (Patterson, 1982, 1983) and behavioral coordination (Bernieri & Rosenthal, 1991) between interactants.

Third, although the model is an attempt to explain the dynamic relationship between the behavioral and cognitive processes involved in nonverbal communication, the constraints imposed by verbal communication are also recognized. Specifically, it is assumed that a common pool of cognitive resources serves all communication demands. Thus, the priority of and the relative cognitive demands on the verbal and nonverbal channels will necessarily affect how the behavioral and cognitive processes of nonverbal communication develop. For example, if the verbal side of the interaction has a high priority and demands great attention and effort to manage well, then the more demanding behavioral and social judgment processes of nonverbal communication are more likely to suffer than are the automatic ones. Even though the specifics of verbal communication are not addressed, the cognitive demands associated with the verbal channel are part of the larger picture of how people process nonverbal communication.

## Structure of the Parallel Process Model

The details of the parallel process model have been discussed elsewhere (Patterson, 1995), so in the remainder of this chapter, I will, first, briefly describe the structure of the model and then discuss the dynamic interdependence of the social judgment and behavioral processes. The parallel process model is composed of four related components, including: (1) determinants, (2) the social environment, (3) cognitive-affective mediators, and (4) social judgment and behavioral processes (see Figure 12.2).

*Determinants and Social Environment.* Among the factors that have received the greatest attention as determinants of nonverbal communi-

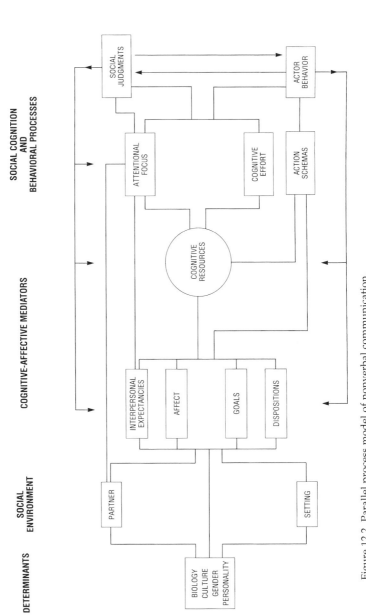

Figure 12.2. Parallel process model of nonverbal communication.

cation are *biology, culture, gender,* and *personality.* There is an extensive literature on how these factors affect nonverbal communication (for example, see Burgoon, Buller, & Woodall, 1989; Fridlund, 1994; E. T. Hall, 1966; J. A. Hall, 1984; Patterson, 1991; Russell, 1994). More specifically, the effects of the determinants may be seen in the selection of social environments and in the operation of the cognitive-affective mediators. The critical aspects of the social environment are the *interaction partners* and the *setting* itself. First, partners are important because we have different expectancies for different partners and, consequently, adjust our behavior to accommodate those differences. Nevertheless, we also seek out others who are more, rather than less, similar to ourselves (Byrne, 1971). Next, because (1) the determinants affect the choice of settings (self-selection) and (2) the settings themselves appeal to specific segments of the population (setting selection), people in any given setting will be more homogeneous than will those in a random sampling of the population (Wicker, 1979). This increased similarity across interactants and the complementary self- and setting selection pressures should make nonverbal communication more predictable and facilitate the activation of the automatic behavioral and cognitive processes.

*Cognitive-Affective Mediators.* The cognitive and affective mediators develop from the combined influence of the determinants and the social environment. That is, biology, culture, gender, and personality contribute to patterns of group and individual differences that affect both the choice of the social environment and the activation of the cognitive and affective mediators – dispositions, goals, affect, interpersonal expectancies, and cognitive resources. Each of these mediators can, in turn, influence the other mediators. *Dispositions* refer to actor states precipitated in a specific social environment. The more obvious dispositions are related to the actor's personality characteristics, but dispositions may be precipitated by the partner, the setting, or other mediators. An example of a disposition that is particularly important in communication is social anxiety.

*Goals* may be described as the cognitive representations of desired states for which people strive (Berger, Knowlton, & Abrahams, 1996). The plans that people generate to achieve goals in interaction directly shape the cognitive and behavioral processes of nonverbal communication. For example, if I have a goal of getting a new acquaintance to like me, the behavioral tactics in my plan are likely to include being especially friendly and attentive to this person. The focus of my cognitions is likely to be very specific also. A metaperspective (e.g., what does she think about me?) will be more important than a direct perspective in judging the partner (e.g., what kind of a person is she?). In addition, I will be more concerned about carefully monitoring my own behavior (self-perception). Thus, specific goals affect the investment of cognitive resources, as reflected in the type of information noticed and the depth of processing this information. Finally, it should be emphasized that the central role of goals is consistent with a broader functional approach to nonverbal communication (Patterson, 1983, 1991).

*Affect* in interactions is a product of the individual's momentary dispositions and goals, relationship to the partner, and the setting constraints. Of course, affect can be directly influenced by the behavior of the partner, as the reactive theories of nonverbal exchange all described (e.g., Argyle & Dean, 1965; Burgoon, 1978; Cappella & Greene, 1982; Patterson, 1976). Research on person perception also indicates that affect is important in forming judgments of others (e.g., Higgins & Sorrentino, 1990; Isen, 1984). Reviews by Watson and Clark (1984) and Alloy and Abramson (1988) suggest that negative affect is related to increased accuracy in social judgments, but there are exceptions to this "depressive realism" effect (Campbell & Fehr, 1990).

*Interpersonal expectancies* are particularly salient in the link between behavioral and social judgment processes in nonverbal communication. First, expectancies about a partner's behavior provide the comparison against which we judge their actual behavior (Burgoon, 1978; Cappella & Greene, 1982). Second, expectations about a partner can determine, indirectly, the very behavior that the perceiver later judges, that is, a self-fulfilling prophecy (Rosenthal, 1966, 1974). When self-fulfilling prophecies result in the behavior expected of the partner, actors are typically unaware of the influence of their own behavior on their partner (see Gilbert & Jones, 1986) and, consequently, are more likely to make correspondent dispositional inferences about their partners, that is, fundamental attribution error. Nevertheless, Jussim (1991) cautions that some effects that look like self-fulfilling prophecies are really accurate perceptions of social reality. Because subtle appearance or behavioral cues can reflect underlying dispositions, the perception of such cues represents accuracy in judgment, not a self-fulfilling prophecy (see also Ambady & Rosenthal, 1992).

*Cognitive resources* refers to the total cognitive capacity available for attending to, processing, and managing both the cognitive and the behavioral processes. Obviously, resources may often be invested in concerns not related to the interaction, such as worries about health, finances, or personal relationships. Even when resources are concentrated substantially on the immediate social situation, they can be variously distributed toward the self, the partner, the setting, or the topic of conversation. The specific distribution of available resources can be an important determinant of the outcome of interaction processes. Nevertheless, because some cognitive and behavioral processes are automatic in nature, it is *not* the case that investing more resources in a particular process necessarily improves the quality of judgments or actions.

*Social Judgment and Behavioral Processes.* Both our thoughts and actions in social settings require varying amounts of *attention* and *cognitive effort*. Depending on the availability of cognitive resources and the priority of specific judgments and actions, the application of those resources can vary widely. For example, impressions of a partner's attractiveness are likely to be automatic as long as there is, at least, some attention to the partner. Thus, such a judgment will require no cognitive effort and little or no cognitive resources. In a similar fashion, *action schemas*, such as a script about making a good impression, engage a minimum of cognitive resources.

In contrast, some judgments involve the weighing of complex and/or inconsistent information and, consequently, require much greater attention and effort. Similarly, difficult strategic patterns of behavior and unsuccessful attempts at influence may necessitate greater cognitive effort in behavior management. From a functional perspective, it is assumed that, to the extent that current judgment and behavioral processes meet interpersonal goals, there is little incentive to invest more effort in considering other options.

## Dynamics of Parallel Processes

Although most research on interaction and communication tacitly recognizes the interdependence of social cognition and social behavior, there is little in the way of theory to explain how this interdependence may operate. The parallel process model is an attempt at delineating the relationship between social judgment and social behavior in nonverbal communication. The model assumes a functional approach to interaction, that is, the social judgment and behavioral processes complement one another in the service of adaptive interpersonal goals. Thus, neither process can be completely understood without simultaneous consideration of the other process.

But just how does the dynamic relationship between the social judgment and behavioral processes affect nonverbal communication? Instead of trying to discuss the broad relationships in the model, which can be found elsewhere (e.g., Patterson, 1995, 1996), I'll address the role of two specific cognitive mediators – dispositions and goals – in shaping the interdependence of the parallel processes.

*Dispositions*

Individual dispositions are initially the product of the determinants and the social environment, but they can also be influenced by the other cognitive-affective mediators. Dispositions can have a direct effect on both attention and the distribution of available cognitive resources. A particularly salient disposition in nonverbal communication is that of social anxiety. Although the chronic experience of social anxiety may be seen as a personality characteristic, most people experience social anxiety on occasion in difficult social situations.

Social anxiety is characterized by (1) increased physiological arousal, (2) negative, self-focused cognitions, and (3) avoidant behaviors, such as decreased verbal and nonverbal involvement with others (Patterson & Ritts, 1997). In terms of the model, this means that relatively more cognitive resources are focused on both negative self-evaluations and behavior management and fewer resources directly on the partner. Not surprisingly, when attention is directed toward oneself rather than one's partner, accuracy in judging the partner's reactions decreases (Tromsdorff & John, 1992). Furthermore, attention to the partner is more likely to be in the form of a metaperspective (i.e., what does he think of me?) than a direct perspective (i.e., what kind of person is he?).

The difficulties of anxious individuals are not, however, merely a product of attention and misplaced resources. The behavior of socially anxious individuals, especially the reduction in gaze, also affects the parallel judgment processes. Specifically, as people look less at their partners, they have less visual information from which they can form impressions. Overall, avoidant behavior and its resulting reduction in partner information, combined with excessive self-focused attention, place socially anxious individuals at a distinct disadvantage in relating to others.

It should be emphasized that social anxiety is also precipitated by situational factors. When the stakes in an interaction increase, such as when the interaction is an important job interview or meeting a very important person, most people experience situational social anxiety. A very practical problem involves the way that social anxiety may contribute to difficulties in interacting with members of outgroups. For example, sometimes majority group members are unsure about how to handle interactions with minority outgroups. Even well-meaning, unprejudiced individuals may experience social anxiety in interacting with outgroup members (e.g., members of a different race or minorities or homosexuals) because they are concerned about not saying or doing something that would offend them. But the accompanying anxious behavior, such as decreased gaze and verbal reticence, may be perceived by outgroup individuals as indicative of prejudiced feelings (Devine, Evett, & Vasquez-Suson, 1996). Furthermore, the ingroup individual's dilemma is exacerbated by knowing that the anxious behavior may be seen as indicative of prejudice. That is, such knowledge probably makes it even more difficult to behave in a friendly, relaxed fashion.

Other dispositions also affect the selective application of cognitive resources in behavioral and social judgment processes. For example, high self-monitoring individuals (Snyder, 1974) attend carefully to behavior management in dealing with others, but if their routines are scripted, the drain on cognitive resources will be minimal. Need for cognition (Cacioppo & Petty, 1982) is another dispositional factor that may affect how people apply their cognitive resources to parallel processes in interaction. High need for cognition people might be expected to have an advantage in the more demanding, controlled processing of information about others, but does such a disposition tend to undercut the utility of generally accurate automatic judgments? That is, might high need for cognition individuals think too much about automatic judgments?

*Goals*

Interpersonal goals are particularly important in the distribution of cognitive resources and the interdependence of social judgment and behavioral processes. In fact, one metagoal, proposed by Berger (1995), is that of efficiency. That is, because people can devote extensive cognitive resources in a plan and its execution, a pervasive concern is simply attaining a goal in an efficient manner. A second metagoal is that of using socially appropriate means to reach specific goals (Berger, 1995). Thus, most people are concerned about not offending others in achieving what they want, whether it is simply information or a substantial favor. Of course, the most efficient means of achieving a social goal is not necessarily the most appropriate.

Metagoals identify broad, general constraints in dealing with others that affect the availability of cognitive resources, but specific goals determine the immediate distribution of resources to social judgment and behavioral processes. A good example might be the case of the employment interview. First, the interviewer would typically be much less concerned about impression management than the applicant would. As a result, the interviewer can invest more cognitive resources in her primary goal, that is, gathering information about and forming an accurate, direct impression of the applicant. In contrast, the applicant is primarily concerned about impression management and is, probably, minimally concerned about forming an accurate, direct impression of the interviewer. But a goal of impression management necessarily requires the adoption of a metaperspective to evaluate the merits of the impression management tactics. Thus, the applicant will be sensitive to any evaluative reactions that the interviewer might signal.

Because the applicant usually has much more at stake than the interviewer does, applicants will typically experience more social anxiety than do interviewers. In turn, this may complicate the demands of impression management, especially if the applicant does not possess an effective "make a good impression" script. There are, of course, exceptions to this scenario. Sometimes, very desirable applicants may be highly recruited and the leverage shifts from the interviewer to the applicant. In such a case, the interviewer may be focused on impression management and the applicant on judging the interviewer and the company.

One circumstance that is particularly relevant for the distribution of cognitive resources is the recognition that a specific goal has not been met. That is, when a goal is blocked, people usually make some adjustments in their plans and/or tactics. For example, the common response to being unsuccessful in communicating geographic directions was simply to increase vocal intensity (Berger & diBattista, 1992,

1993). There were, however, some results suggesting that people who had longer speech onset latencies in their second attempt at giving directions made more abstract corrections.

Sometimes a simple change in tactics may develop even before any difficulty in communication is even apparent. Recently, as I was coming into the office, I was approached by an individual with a heavy foreign accent who asked me where a particular room was in my building. Without thinking about it (that's the point of this example), I gave the rather simple directions, but in an overloud voice. I doubt that this made the directions clearer. He was too polite to tell me that he was only lost, not deaf.

Although people are inclined to make less cognitively demanding corrections following goal blocking, there are circumstances that result in greater effort. For example, individuals who are highly motivated to achieve their goals are likely to initiate more cognitively demanding plans to reach those goals or, at least, initiate such alterations earlier in the correction sequence (Berger, Knowlton, & Abrahams, 1996). The actual demand on available resources and the likelihood of success in achieving the goals with specific behavioral adjustments depends on how well learned and how effective the routines are. Corrections consisting of scripted sequences, high-level action identification, and MOPs should conserve cognitive resources for other interpersonal demands.

Finally, it is important to appreciate that not only do social judgments serve later behavioral strategies, but behavioral strategies may also be initiated to test social judgments. Sometimes individuals selectively seek and weigh information to make as strong a case as possible for a preordained judgment (Baumeister & Newman, 1994). In contrast to the notion of an "intuitive scientist" who tries to form accurate impressions of others, the "intuitive lawyer" tries to find information that supports predetermined conclusions about others (Baumeister & Newman, 1994). Thus, in an interaction context, intuitive lawyers would manage their behavior toward a partner to precipitate a reaction that supports their initial preferred judgment. To the extent that an individual operates as an intuitive lawyer, greater cognitive resources may be required for selective attention to and processing of partner information.

A similar, but less biased, strategy may involve attempts at diagnosing a partner's attitudes or preferences. For example, in dating relationships, one person might escalate behavioral intimacy to determine the partner's readiness for a sexual relationship. An alternate tactic might be "playing hard to get" as a means of testing a partner's interest and commitment. In a similar fashion, a salesperson might describe a possible "deal" in order to determine the customer's interest in buying a particular product. In these instances, the actor initiates a kind of "trial balloon" in order to obtain a very practical, focused evaluation of a partner's sentiments about a course of action.

In summary, the plans initiated to achieve particular goals can determine where and how cognitive resources are invested in communication. Furthermore, the interdependence of social judgment and behavioral processes is reflected in more than their sharing of a common pool of resources. The utility of specific behavioral tactics depends on simultaneous social judgments (e.g., metaperception) and, in turn, social judgments may be tested by specific behavioral tactics.

## Conclusions

In the past, theoretical analyses of the behavioral and person perception components of interaction have employed contrasting perspectives that isolate the two processes. In this chapter, these two perspectives were examined in the evolution of theory on the behavioral and cognitive components in nonverbal communication. The parallel process model presented here provides one means for integrating behavioral and social cognition processes into a common, functionally based system of nonverbal communication. That is, the individual is an interactant simultaneously engaged in adaptive behavioral (encoding) and social cognition (decoding) processes.

Because behavioral and social cognition processes complement one another, a change in expectancies, affect, goals, or dispositions can lead to a new balance in the attention and cognitive effort invested in these parallel processes. For example, successful self-presentation requires an investment of cognitive resources not only in behavior management but also in the metaperspective judgments of the partner. That is, the metaperspective judgments constitute the means to evaluate the efficacy of the impression management attempt.

In this model, the distribution of cognitive resources for behavioral and person perception processes is especially important. Behavior that is (1) more automatic (e.g., guided by action schemas) and (2) shaped by more positive dispositions (e.g., low social anxiousness) typically engages a smaller claim on cognitive resources than behavior that is (1) less automatic and (2) shaped by more negative, self-focused dispositions (e.g., high social anxiousness). On the person perception side, automatic judgments produced by appearance, nonverbal cues, and vocal cues require a minimum of cognitive resources. In contrast, the processing of verbal input and the necessity of adjusting initial inferences require a larger investment of cognitive resources (Gilbert et al., 1988).

Although the behavioral and person perception processes draw on a common pool of cognitive resources, the effects of limited resources are selective and not necessarily negative. In fact, it is likely that increased attention to automatic or scripted behavioral sequences reduces their effectiveness (Vallacher & Wegner, 1987). In a similar fashion, the application of cognitive resources to otherwise effective automatic judgments can reduce accuracy (Wilson & Schooler, 1991).

Finally, it is probably fair to say that the primary strength of the parallel process model lies in its integrative perspective on nonverbal communication. The particular components of the model and their relationships to one another are matters for empirical testing, but the *approach* of this model seems less in question. That is, attention to the dynamic interdependence of parallel encoding and decoding processes will promote the ecological validity of research and contribute to a better understanding of nonverbal communication.

### References

Abelson, R. P. (1981). The psychological status of the script concept. *American Psychologist, 36*, 715–729.

Alloy, L. B., & Abramson, L. Y. (1988). Depressive realism: Four theoretical perspectives. In L. B. Alloy (Ed.), *Cognitive processes in depression*. New York: Guilford Press.

Ambady, N., & Rosenthal, R. (1992). Thin slices of behavior as predictors of interpersonal consequences: A meta-analysis. *Psychological Bulletin, 111*, 256–274.

Anderson, N. H. (1981). *Foundations of information integration theory*. New York: Academic Press.

Argyle, M., & Dean, J. (1965). Eye-contact, distance, and affiliation. *Sociometry, 28*, 289–304.

Baumeister, R. F., & Newman, L. S. (1994). Self-regulation of cognitive processes. *Personality and Social Psychology Bulletin, 20*, 5–19.

Bem, D. J. (1972). Self-perception theory. In L. Berkowitz (Ed.), *Advances in experimental social psychology* (Vol. 6, pp. 1–62). New York: Academic Press.

Berger, C. B. (1995). A plan-based approach to strategic communication. In D. E. Hewes (Ed.), *The cognitive bases of interpersonal communication* (pp. 141–179). Hillsdale, NJ: Lawrence Erlbaum.

Berger, C. B., & diBattista, P. (1992, November). *Adapting plans to failed communication goals*. Paper presented at the annual meeting of the Speech Communication Association, Chicago.

Berger, C. B., & DiBattista, P. (1993). Communication failure and plan adaptation: If at first you don't succeed, say it louder and slower. *Communication Monographs, 60,* 220–238.

Berger, C. B., Knowlton, S. W., & Abrahams, M. F. (1996). The hierarchy principle in strategic communication. *Communication Theory, 6,* 111–142.

Bernieri, F. & Rosenthal, R. (1991). Coordinated movement in human interaction. In R. S. Feldman & B. Rimé (Eds.), *Fundamentals of nonverbal behavior* (pp. 410–431). New York: Cambridge University Press.

Berry, D. S., & McArthur, L. Z. (1985). Some components and consequences of a babyface. *Journal of Personality and Social Psychology, 48,* 312–323.

Berry, D. S., & McArthur, L. Z. (1986). Perceiving character in faces: The impact of age-related craniofacial changes on social perception. *Psychological Bulletin, 100,* 3–18.

Breed, G. (1972). The effect of intimacy: Reciprocity or retreat? *British Journal of Social and Clinical Psychology, 11,* 135–142.

Brewer, M. B. (1988). A dual process model of impression formation. In T. K. Srull & R. S. Wyer, Jr. (Eds.), *Advances in social cognition* (Vol. 1, pp. 1–36). Hillsdale, NJ: Lawrence Erlbaum.

Buck, R. (1980). Nonverbal behavior and the theory of emotion: The facial feedback hypothesis. *Journal of Personality and Social Psychology, 38,* 811–824.

Burgoon, J. K. (1978). A communication model of personal space violations: Explication and an initial test. *Human Communication Research, 4,* 129–142.

Burgoon, J. K., Buller, D. B., & Woodall, W. G. (1989). *Nonverbal communication: The unspoken dialogue.* New York: Harper & Row.

Burgoon, J. K., Stern, L. A., & Dillman, L. (1995). *Interpersonal adaptation: Dyadic interaction patterns.* Cambridge: Cambridge University Press.

Byrne, D. (1971). *The attraction paradigm.* New York: Academic Press.

Cacioppo, J. T., & Petty, R. E. (1982). The need for cognition. *Journal of Personality and Social Psychology, 42,* 116–131.

Campbell, J. D., & Fehr, B. (1990). Self-esteem and perceptions of conveyed impressions: Is negative affectivity associated with greater realism? *Journal of Personality and Social Psychology, 58,* 122–133.

Cappella, J. N. (1981). Mutual influence in expressive behavior: Adult-adult and infant-adult dyadic interaction. *Psychological Bulletin, 89,* 101–132.

Cappella, J. N., & Greene, J. O. (1982). A discrepancy-arousal explanation of mutual influence in expressive behavior for adult-adult and infant-infant dyadic interaction. *Communication Monographs, 49,* 89–114.

Devine, P. G., Evett, S. R., & Vasquez-Suson, K. A. (1996). Exploring the interpersonal dynamics of intergroup contact. In R. M. Sorrentino & E. T. Higgins (Eds.), *Handbook of motivation and cognition: The interpersonal context* (Vol. 3, pp. 423–464). New York: Guilford.

Ellsworth, P. C. (1977, September). *Some question about the role of arousal in the interpretation of direct gaze.* Paper presented at the annual convention of the American Psychological Association Convention. San Francisco, CA.

Felipe, N. J., & Sommer, R. (1966). Invasions of personal space. *Social Problems, 14,* 206–214.

Fiske, S. T. (1992). Thinking is for doing: Portraits of social cognition from daguerreotype to laserphoto. *Journal of Personality and Social Psychology, 63,* 877–889.

Fiske, S. T., & Neuberg, S. L. (1990). A continuum of impression formation, from category-based to individuating processes: Influences of information and motivation on attention interpretation. In M. P. Zanna (Ed.), *Advances in experimental social psychology* (Vol. 23, pp. 1–74). New York: Academic Press.

Fridlund, A. J. (1994). *Human facial expression: An evolutionary view.* San Diego, CA: Academic Press.

Gibson, J. J. (1979). *The ecological approach to visual perception.* Boston, MA: Houghton-Mifflin.

Gilbert, D. T., & Jones, E. E. (1986). Perceiver-induced constraint: Interpretations of self-generated reality. *Journal of Personality and Social Psychology, 50,* 269–280.

Gilbert, D. T., & Krull, D. S. (1988). Seeing less and knowing more: The benefits of perceptual ignorance. *Journal of Personality and Social Psychology, 54,* 193–202.

Gilbert, D. T., Pelham, B. W., & Krull, D. S. (1988). On cognitive busyness: when person perceivers meet persons perceived. *Journal of Personality and Social Psychology, 54,* 733–740.

Hall, E. T. (1959). *The silent language.* Garden City, NY: Doubleday.

Hall, E. T. (1963). A system for the notation of proxemic behavior. *American Anthropologist, 65,* 1003–1026.

Hall, E. T. (1966). *The hidden dimension.* Garden City, NY: Doubleday, 1966.

Hall, J. A. (1984). *Nonverbal sex differences: Communication accuracy and expressive style.* Baltimore, MD: Johns Hopkins University.

Higgins, E. T., & Sorrentino, R. M. (Eds.). (1990). *Handbook of motivation and cognition: Foundations of social behavior* (Vol. 2). New York: Guilford Press.

Isen, A. M. (1984). Toward understanding the role of affect in cognition. In R. S. Wyer, Jr., & T. K. Srull (Eds.), *Handbook of social cognition* (Vol. 3, pp. 179–236). Hillsdale, NJ: Lawrence Erlbaum.

Jourard, S. M., & Friedman, R. (1970). Experimenter-subject "distance" and self-disclosure. *Journal of Personality and Social Psychology, 15,* 278–282.

Jussim, L. (1991). Social perception and social reality: A reflection-construction model. *Psychological Review, 98,* 54–73.

Kellerman, K., & Lim, T. (1990). The conversation MOP: III. Timing of scenes in discourse. *Journal of Personality and Social Psychology, 59,* 1163–1179.

Kenny, D. A., & DePaulo, B. M. (1993). Do people know how others view them? An empirical and theoretical account. *Psychological Bulletin, 114,* 145–161.

Kleinke, C. L., & Pohlen, P. D. (1971). Affective and emotional responses as a function of the other person's gaze and cooperativeness in a two-person game. *Journal of Personality and Social Psychology, 17,* 308–313.

Mandler, G. (1975). *Mind and emotion.* New York: Wiley.

McArthur, L. Z., & Baron, R. M. (1983). Toward an ecological theory of social perception. *Psychological Review, 90,* 215–247.

McBride, G., King, M. C., James, J. W. (1965). Social proximity effects of galvanic skin responses in adult humans. *Journal of Psychology, 61,* 153–157.

Mehrabian, A. (1969). Some referents and measures of nonverbal behavior. *Behavior Research Methods and Instrumentation, 1,* 203–207.

Nichols, K. A., & Champness, B. G. (1971). Eye gaze and the GSR. *Journal of Experimental Social Psychology, 7,* 623–626.

Nye, J. L., & Brower, A. M. (Eds.) (1996). *What's social about social cognition?* Thousand Oaks, CA: Sage.

Patterson, M. L. (1968). *Social space and social interaction.* Unpublished doctoral dissertation, Northwestern University.

Patterson, M. L. (1973). Compensation in nonverbal immediacy behaviors: A review. *Sociometry, 36,* 237–252.

Patterson, M. L. (1976). An arousal model of interpersonal intimacy. *Psychological Review, 83,* 235–245.

Patterson, M. L. (1982). A sequential functional model of nonverbal exchange. *Psychological Review, 89,* 231–249.

Patterson, M. L. (1983). *Nonverbal behavior: A functional perspective.* New York: Springer-Verlag.

Patterson, M. L. (1991). A functional approach to nonverbal exchange. In R. S. Feldman & B. Rimé (Eds.), *Fundamentals of nonverbal behavior* (pp. 458–495). New York: Cambridge University Press.

Patterson, M. L. (1995). A parallel process model of nonverbal communication. *Journal of Nonverbal Behavior, 19,* 3–29.

Patterson, M. L. (1996) Social behavior and social cognition: A parallel process approach. In J. L. Nye & A. M. Brower (Eds.), *What's social about social cognition?* (pp. 87–105). Thousand Oaks, CA: Sage.

Patterson, M. L., Churchill, M. E., Farag, F., & Borden, E. (1991/1992) Impression management, cognitive demand, and interpersonal sensitivity. *Current Psychology, 10,* 263–271.

Patterson, M. L., & Ritts, V. (1997). Social and communicative anxiety: A review and meta-analysis. In B. R. Burleson (Ed.), *Communication Yearbook 20* (pp. 262–303). Thousand Oaks, CA: Sage.

Rosenthal, R. (1966). *Experimenter effects in behavioral research.* New York: Appleton-Century-Crofts.

Rosenthal, R. (1974). *On the social psychology of the self-fulfilling prophecy: Further evidence for pygmalion effects and their mediating mechanisms.* New York: M.S.S. Information Corporation Modular Publication.

Russell, J. A. (1994). Is there a universal recognition of emotion from facial expression? A review of the cross-cultural studies. *Psychological Bulletin, 115,* 102–141.

Schachter, S. (1964). The interaction of cognitive and physiological determinants of emotional state. In L. Berkowitz (Ed.), *Advances in experimental social psychology* (Vol. 1, pp. 49–80). New York: Academic Press.

Schank, R. C. (1982). *Dynamic memory: A theory of reminding and learning in computers and people.* Cambridge: Cambridge University Press.

Schank, R. C., & Abelson, R. P. (1977). *Scripts, plans, goals, and understanding: An inquiry into human knowledge structures.* Hillsdale, NJ: Lawrence Erlbaum.

Smith, E. R. (1990). Content and process specificity in the effects of prior experiences. In T. K. Srull & R. S. Wyer, Jr. (Eds.), *Advances in social cognition* (Vol. 3, pp. 1–59). Hillsdale, NJ: Lawrence Erlbaum.

Smith, E. R., & Zarate, M. A. (1992). Exemplar-based model of social judgment. *Psychological Review, 99,* 3–21.

Snyder, M. (1974). Self-monitoring of expressive behavior. *Journal of Personality and Social Psychology, 30,* 526–537.

Sommer, R. (1959). Studies in personal space. *Sociometry, 22,* 247–260.

Sommer, R. (1961). Leadership and group geography. *Sociometry, 24,* 99–110.

Sommer, R. (1962). The distance for comfortable conversation: A further study. *Sociometry, 25,* 111–116.

Tickle-Degnen, L., & Rosenthal, R. (1990). The nature of rapport and its correlates. *Psychological Inquiry, 1,* 285–293.

Tromsdorff, G., & John, G. (1992). Decoding affective communication in intimate relationships. *European Journal of Social Psychology, 22,* 41–54.

Trope, Y. (1986). Identification and inferential processes in dispositional attribution. *Psychological Review, 93,* 239–257.

Vallacher, R. R., & Wegner, D. M. (1987). What do people think they're doing? Action identification and human behavior. *Psychological Review, 94,* 3–15.

Watson, D., & Clark, L. A. (1984). Negative affectivity: The disposition to experience aversive emotional states. *Psychological Bulletin, 96,* 465–498.

Wicker, A. W. (1979). *An introduction to ecological psychology.* Monterey, CA: Brooks/Cole.

Wilson, T. D., & Schooler, J. W. (1991). Thinking too much: Introspection can reduce the quality of preferences and decisions. *Journal of Personality and Social Psychology, 60,* 181–192.

Wyer, R. S., Jr., & Srull, T. K. (1986). Human cognition in its social context. *Psychological Review, 93,* 322–359.

# 13. Conflict Issues and Conflict Strategies as Contexts for Nonverbal Behavior in Close Relationships

JUDITH A. FEENEY, PATRICIA NOLLER,
GRANIA SHEEHAN, AND CANDIDA PETERSON

In this chapter, we report three studies of close relationships where the focus is on nonverbal behavior during conflict, and where context is an important variable. The first study compares nonverbal behavior in response to different types of conflict issues: those involving a concrete topic and those involving the actual relationship between the members of the couple. In addition, this study assesses relationship satisfaction as a context for nonverbal behavior. The second study looks at the nonverbal behavior related to demanding and withdrawing in marital interaction. The contextual variables are relationship satisfaction and whose issue (husband's or wife's) is being discussed. In the third study, the way in which conflict is dealt with in the family (that is, the strategies couples report for either marital or parent–child conflict) provides the context. Links between this context and adolescent siblings' perceptions of each other's nonverbal behaviors are explored.

*Relationship Satisfaction as a Context*

How conflict is dealt with in close relationships is seen as a critical determinant of relationship satisfaction (Noller & Fitzpatrick, 1990, 1993). Partners may use constructive or destructive strategies, and the nonverbal behaviors used are likely to vary with the type of strategy, the type of conflict, and the level of investment in the issue.

Observational studies have shown that distressed couples use more negative communication behaviors, such as criticizing, commanding, and complaining, and fewer positive communication behaviors such as agreeing, assenting, and approving. In addition, distressed couples exchange more punishments and fewer rewards than do satisfied cou-

348

ples, and they are more likely to react to negative relational events in a way that escalates the conflict (Noller & Fitzpatrick, 1990; Schaap, Buunk, & Kerkstra, 1988).

Distressed marriages are characterized by an emotional climate that involves more negative affect and more reciprocity of negative affect. These findings have been replicated across different cultures, including the United States ( Margolin, 1981; Notarius & Johnson, 1982), the Netherlands (Schaap et al., 1988), Germany (Revenstorf, Vogel, Wegener, Hahlweg, & Schindler, 1980), and Australia (Noller, 1984). How the context of relationship satisfaction influences nonverbal responses is addressed in the first two studies reported in this chapter.

*Type of Conflict Issue as Context*

Conflicts in close relationships can be divided into those that are about content issues and those that are about the nature of the relationship itself (Noller & Fitzpatrick, 1993). According to some writers (e.g., Greenberg & Johnson, 1986; Jacobson & Margolin, 1979), conflict about the nature of the relationship is most likely to occur when spouses or other family members differ in their preferences for closeness and autonomy, with one partner wanting more intimacy and more time spent together, and the other wanting more privacy and independence.

In a classic study of relationship conflict, Raush, Barry, Hertel, and Swain (1974) had spouses engage in two different types of conflict, one about content issues and one involving closeness and distance in the relationship. Interactions that centered on content issues tended to be much less heated and to be resolved more easily. In the relationship-based scenes, there was less cognitive communication behavior (defined as neutral acts, suggestions, and rational arguments), fewer attempts to resolve the conflict, and more rejection and coercion.

Raush and his colleagues also found differences between discordant and other couples in the relationship-based scenes. In one of these interactions, the husband was instructed to act in a cold and distant manner toward his partner, and the wife was told to try and reconcile; in the other scene, the roles of husband and wife were reversed. Discordant couples engaged in less cognitive behavior, especially when asked to act distant. In addition, more coercive behaviors were employed by both discordant husbands and wives when asked to act distant, and by discordant husbands when asked to try to reestablish closeness. These issues of distance and closeness are directly relevant to the first study described here, in which a modified version of Raush et al.'s (1974) methodology was employed.

### Investment in the Issue as a Context

An important pattern of behavior during conflict is the demand-withdraw pattern of interaction, where one partner (the demander) pressures for discussion of an issue and for change in the partner's behavior, while the other partner (the withdrawer) avoids discussion of the issue by disengaging or withdrawing from the discussion. There is empirical evidence that the demand-withdraw pattern is affected by both relationship satisfaction and gender. The pattern is more common in couples low in relationship satisfaction, and women tend to be more often in the demanding role and men in the withdrawing role, independent of relationship satisfaction (Christensen, 1988; Christensen & Heavey, 1990; Heavey, Layne, & Christensen, 1993).

Christensen and Heavey (1990) tested the possibility that who demands and who withdraws from a conflict interaction may be related to who has most investment in the issue. They compared an individual differences perspective, which asserts that basic differences between men and women dictate their conflict behavior, and a social structure perspective, which asserts that individual conflict behavior will depend on the nature of the conflict and the spouse's goals in that conflict. Spouses engaged in two conflict interactions, one in which the wife wanted change and one in which the husband wanted change. The individual differences perspective predicts that spouses would behave consistently as demanders or withdrawers across the two issues, whereas the social structure perspective predicts that spouses' behavior would depend on the issue under discussion, with individuals being more demanding when they themselves wanted change and more withdrawing when the partner wanted change.

Observational measures of demanding and withdrawing (Christensen & Heavey, 1990; Heavey et al., 1993) showed differences in spouse behavior across the two interactions, but did not completely support the social structure perspective. For wives' issues, wife demand/husband withdraw was much more likely than husband demand/wife withdraw. For husbands' issues, however, the two patterns were equally likely to occur. In other words, the most common pattern was wife demand/husband withdraw, which was particularly likely to occur when the wife's issue was being discussed. In the second study reported here, we look at the nonverbal correlates of demand/withdraw and the extent to which the nonverbal behavior related to this pattern was affected by the contextual variables of whose issue was being discussed, relationship satisfaction, and gender.

## Family Conflict Patterns as Context

As well as engaging in observational research to explore the demand-withdraw pattern, Christensen (1988) has developed a self-report measure, the Communication Patterns Questionnaire, which includes items to measure demand-withdraw and other responses to conflict. This measure is used in the third study reported here to assess the climate of marital and parent–child conflict present in families with adolescents.

In a number of studies, marital conflict has emerged as a more important predictor than marital satisfaction of behavior problems in the offspring (Grych & Fincham, 1990). Frequent unresolved conflict between spouses, and high levels of violence and coercion in the marital relationship, have also been found to predict poor quality relationships among the siblings in a family (Volling & Belsky, 1992).

It is difficult, however, to pinpoint the causal basis for correlational findings of this kind. It is possible that hostile, poorly resolved marital conflict undermines children's adjustment in a direct manner by producing stress in the offspring as they witness parental arguments, and by exposing them to models of hostility and aggression that carry over into their dealings with siblings and peers. Alternatively, maladaptive marital conflict patterns may have an indirect effect on children's adjustment by undermining the quality of the parent–child relationship. When a husband and wife find themselves enmeshed in coercive or avoidant styles of marital conflict, they may lack the motivation, skills, or confidence to forge close and harmonious relationships with their children.

As noted by Grych and Fincham (1990), another limitation of much of the existing literature on marital conflict and child problems results from the fact that the bulk of previous studies have not drawn a clear distinction between constructive and destructive marital conflict patterns. For this reason, in the study to be reported, our goal was to link the conflict strategies used by parents during marital and parent–child conflict, and parents' and children's perceptions of each other's behavior during interaction.

In exploring the implications of marital and parent–child conflict, it is common to think that any given family provides an identical context for all its members. Research has, however, highlighted the fact that the family context is by no means unitary. For example, offspring experience the family in very different ways from their parents (Callan & Noller, 1986; Noller & Callan, 1988).

Further, the family context may manifest itself differently, even to family members from the same generation. Mothers report more conflict than fathers do in interactions with their adolescent sons and daughters (Montemayor, 1982; Vuchinich, 1987). The higher frequency of conflict in the family context, as perceived by the mother, does not necessarily reflect poorer relationship quality, however. Rather, the higher level of conflict with mothers seems to be linked with greater intimacy and more frequent self-disclosure between adolescent offspring and their mothers, as well as with mothers' more consistent and effective involvement in negotiating disagreements toward mutually acceptable solutions (Vuchinich, 1987).

In the third study reported here, we explore the link between marital and parent–child conflict and family members' perceptions of one another's behavior. Given the finding that mothers and fathers differ in their reports of parent–child conflict, a specific issue that we wanted to examine was whether mothers' or fathers' reports of family conflict were more strongly related to perceptions of family members' nonverbal behavior.

*Nonverbal Behavior in Conflict Interactions*

Conflicts between intimate partners tend to be very emotional events, particularly in the case of high-conflict interactions in distressed relationships (Gottman & Levenson, 1988). During conflict interactions, anger and distress are likely to be expressed both verbally and nonverbally. In other words, conflict between relationship partners produces emotional responses that tend to be reflected in behavior, and especially in nonverbal behavior. In fact, some researchers have seen the link between emotion and nonverbal behavior in close relationships as so strong that they have virtually equated the two constructs;

for example, Gottman (1979, p. 79) has defined affect as "nonverbal behaviors of the speaker during message transmission."

Although we do not agree that emotion can be reduced to a set of observable behaviors, there is evidence that relationship partners' attempts to control or inhibit their emotions are likely to result in nonverbal leakage, especially when the emotion is strong (Levenson, 1994). Hence, we take the perspective that emotional processes occurring during conflict interactions tend to be reflected in nonverbal behavior, either intentionally or unintentionally.

Patterson (1983, chapter 12 in this volume) uses the concept of nonverbal involvement to describe a set of nonverbal behaviors central to social interactions. Relevant nonverbal behaviors are gaze, facial expressiveness (such as smiling), gestures, and head nods. Patterson suggested that high levels of nonverbal involvement would be indicated by increased gaze, more facial expressiveness, more gestures, and more head nods. These high-involvement nonverbal behaviors are likely to be critical in conflict interactions, given that they express an individual partner's willingness to engage in attempts to resolve the conflict. By contrast, low-involvement behaviors, such as head down, head turn away, and lack of gaze, reflect a tendency to avoid dealing with relationship issues. The implications of avoiding versus engaging in conflict are central to theorizing about marital conflict, but remain a source of controversy (Fitzpatrick, 1988; Roloff & Cloven, 1990).

Research has shown that during marital conflict, nonverbal behaviors are just as important as verbal behaviors in predicting how persuasive a message is and how satisfied partners are with the interaction (Gottman, Markman, & Notarius, 1977; Newton & Burgoon, 1990). Satisfaction with communication has been linked with nonverbal behaviors tapping physical involvement, and satisfaction with the relationship has been linked with nonverbal behaviors such as gestures, self adaptors, and behaviors expressing a willingness to cooperate (Newton & Burgoon, 1990).

In their study of interactions between couples in established relationships, Newton and Burgoon (1990) also identified nonverbal correlates of verbal tactics used during conflict between intimates. For example, verbal blaming, threatening, and accusations were associated with indirect orientation, animated gestures, and loud vocal tone. Verbal behaviors involving partners invalidating one another were associated with frequent and animated gestures, forward lean, head shake, loud vocal tone, and fast vocal rate. By contrast, verbal support and reinforcement of the partner were associated with direct orientation, physical involvement and cooperation, and vocal involvement and submissiveness. These researchers did not explore the nonverbal correlates of conflict avoidance or withdrawal, an issue that will be explored in detail in the second study reported in this chapter.

Consistent with the findings of Newton and Burgoon (1990), Lochman and Allen (1981) reported reliable links between verbal and nonverbal behaviors for dating couples during conflict interactions. There is some controversy, however, about the extent to which couples interpret specific nonverbal behaviors during conflict in the same way. Lochman and Allen (1981) reported that subjects rarely based their perceptions of either their own or their partner's behavior on the actual rates of nonverbal behaviors. Reduced eye contact, particularly, was affected by the immediate context, being variously interpreted as disapproval, lower interpersonal power, or reduced intimacy.

Further, relationship satisfaction seems to affect the way in which nonverbal behaviors are perceived. In a study of romantic partners, Manusov (1990) reported that as satisfaction decreased, negative nonverbal behaviors were seen as more intentional, stable, and controllable, whereas positive behaviors were seen as more external, unstable, and specific. These findings are consistent with a large body of literature that shows that unhappy couples tend to interpret their partners' behavior in ways that are detrimental to the relationship (Fincham & Bradbury, 1988).

### *A Study with Type of Conflict Issue as the Primary Context*

This study used three standardized interaction scenes involving explicit conflicts of interest between partners, based on the work of Raush et al. (1974). (More detail about this study is found in Feeney 1998.) One of these scenes involved a concrete issue, specifically the use of leisure time spent together. The other two scenes involved the relationship between the partners more directly and focused on conflict over closeness and distance. These latter two scenes are more likely to be seen as threatening the security of the relationship and are likely to be dealt with differently, depending on the level of relationship satisfaction experienced by the partners.

Seventy-two long-term dating couples took part in the study. They ranged in age from 17 to 37 years, and the length of their current dating relationships ranged from 12 to 77 months. Before taking part in the interaction scenes, couples independently completed a measure of relationship satisfaction, the Quality Marriage Index (Norton, 1983). This measure contains six items which assess the quality of the dyadic relationship.

In the scene involving the concrete issue (leisure scene), a conflict of interests was set up by asking each partner to advocate pursuing a different leisure activity, to be undertaken in a period of time that the couple had previously agreed to spend together. In the scenes involving issues of closeness and distance, males and females were primed to act in particular ways. Specifically, in one of these scenes, the male was instructed to act in a cold and distant manner toward his partner. Following the procedures used by Raush et al. (1974), this distancing behavior was primed by asking the male to focus on some incident or some quality about his partner that would disturb him intensely. In the same scene, the female partner was instructed to attempt to reestablish closeness with her partner. The other scene involving issues of closeness and distance was a reciprocal of the first, with the female instructed to act cold and distant and the male instructed to try to reestablish closeness. The three scenes were enacted in counterbalanced order, and each interaction was videotaped for five minutes.

An independent observer recorded the occurrence of 15 nonverbal behaviors related to approach and avoidance tendencies, based on the work of Simpson, Rholes, and Nelligan (1992): touching partner's body, touching partner's face, placing arm or hand on partner's shoulder, hugging, kissing, holding hands, resisting contact, leaning toward partner, leaning away from partner, moving toward partner, moving away from partner, turning head or body toward partner, turning head or body away from partner, smiling, and eye contact. A second observer rated a sample of 30 videotapes for these behaviors, and correlations assessing interrater reliability ranged from .79 to .97.

Most of these behaviors were recorded using frequency counts (that is, the number of separate occurrences of each behavior in each scene). However, frequency counts were not appropriate for assessing three behaviors: turning toward partner, turning away from partner, and eye contact. Some subjects, for example, gazed at their partners almost continuously, and the low score for eye contact, which a count of separate occurrences would yield, would not reflect the true extent of this behavior. For this reason, these three behaviors were recorded using global rating scales ranging from 1 = very infrequent to 6 = very frequent. Behaviors recorded using frequency counts were later recoded as 6-point scales, based on their frequency distributions, to make them comparable in scale with those recorded as global ratings.

Principal-components factor analysis of the ratings of nonverbal behavior revealed two major factors that accounted for 32% of the variance. The first factor, labeled touch, was defined by five behaviors: touching partner's body, touching partner's arm, touching partner's face, hugging, and kissing. The second factor was a bipolar factor with positive factor loadings on turning away, moving away, and leaning away from partner, and negative loadings on eye contact and moving toward the partner. This factor was labeled avoidance. Scores on the factors of touch and avoidance were obtained by summing the ratings on the relevant behaviors.

To assess the links between relationship satisfaction and nonverbal behavior, correlations were calculated between scores for self and partner on the Quality Marriage Index and the touch and avoidance factors, separately for each gender and for each interaction scene. For the leisure scene, none of the eight correlations was statistically significant. In other words, there were no links between relationship satisfaction and the use of touching or avoiding behavior, for either men or women.

For the scene in which males were instructed to act cold and distant, there was a negative relation between males' avoidance and both males' and females' relationship satisfaction ($r = -.36$, and $-.29$, respectively). That is, in couples in which either partner reported high relationship satisfaction, men engaged in less avoiding behavior than occurred in other couples.

For the reciprocal scene, in which females were asked to act cold and distant, there was a similar negative relation between females' avoidance and both males' and females' relationship satisfaction ($r = -.26$, and $-.23$, respectively). Again, in couples in which either partner reported high relationship satisfaction, women engaged in less avoiding behavior. Together, these results indicate that even when individuals were primed to act in a cold and distant manner toward their partners, those in more satisfying relationships were less likely to engage in avoidant behaviors such as turning and moving away from partner, and a lack of eye contact.

In the female-distant scene, there was also a negative relation between males' relationship satisfaction and their avoidance ($r = -.24$), and a positive relation between females' relationship satisfaction and males' touching behavior ($r = .24$). These results indicate that when men were primed to reestablish closeness with their cold and distant partners, those in more satisfying relationships were less likely to engage in avoidant behaviors and more likely to touch their partners in positive ways.

These findings highlight the importance of the context, in terms of the type of issue that couples are dealing with, in determining how differences in relationship satisfaction are played out in nonverbal behavior. It seems that when issues involve concrete goal conflicts, happy and unhappy couples engage in similar patterns of nonverbal behavior. In contrast, when issues of psychological closeness and distance are at stake, the nonverbal behavior of happy and unhappy couples is more divergent.

The most consistent link with relationship satisfaction was for avoidance. In particular, unhappy couples engaged in higher levels of avoidance as a way of expressing their negativity and disaffection. Of course, a certain level of avoidant behavior is to be expected when individuals are asked to act in a distant manner; the important point to note is that couples with higher levels of satisfaction used fewer avoidant behaviors. Such behaviors as physical distancing and failure to establish eye contact are likely to be perceived negatively by the partner and to interfere with successful resolution of serious conflicts.

In interactions in which individuals were primed to reestablish closeness with their partners, links between relationship satisfaction and nonverbal behavior were restricted to males. Males who reported higher satisfaction engaged in less avoidance, and males whose partners reported higher satisfaction engaged in more use of positive touching. The gender-specific nature of these results is consistent with Gottman's claim that men are more likely to be the reconcilers in close relationships, except in situations where conflict levels are very high (Gottman & Levenson, 1988). In addition, Noller (1984) reported that males' communication behavior was more central to relationship satisfaction than that of females.

## A Study with Investment in the Issue as the Primary Context

The goal of this second study was to explore the links between global ratings of demanding and withdrawing in the conflict interactions of married couples and particular nonverbal behaviors. We were also interested in whether the frequency of particular nonverbal behaviors was affected by who has most investment in the issue (that is, who wants change), the gender of the person doing the demanding and withdrawing, and the marital adjustment level of the couple. These questions arise from the research and theorizing of Christensen and his colleagues (Christensen & Heavey, 1990; Heavey et al., 1993) on the contextual factors affecting demanding and withdrawing in husbands and wives.

We were interested in the actual nonverbal behaviors used by partners during demanding and withdrawing phases of conflict interactions. We wanted to know which nonverbal behaviors are engaged in by those rated as high in demanding or high in withdrawing. Further, as theorized by Christensen and his colleagues, we were interested in whether there was any evidence that the frequency of nonverbal behaviors related to demanding and withdrawing differs, depending on whether the wife's issue or the husband's issue is being discussed, and whether husbands or wives are doing the demanding or withdrawing. In addition, given that the demand/withdraw pattern of interaction is more common in couples low in marital satisfaction (Christensen, 1988; Noller & White, 1990), we expected differences between happy and unhappy couples in their nonverbal behavior. In line with Patterson's (1983, 1997; chapter 12 in this volume) suggestion, mentioned earlier, that high levels of nonverbal involvement would be indicated by increased gaze, more facial expressiveness, more gestures, and more head nods, we would expect demanding behavior to be high in nonverbal involvement, and withdrawing behavior to be low in involvement.

The sample included 29 couples recruited for earlier studies by Christensen and Heavey (1990) and Heavey et al. (1993). All of the couples had at least one child. Relationship satisfaction was assessed using Spanier's (1976) Dyadic Adjustment Scale, with 19 of the couples being high in relationship satisfaction ($M = 115$), and the other 10 couples being low in relationship satisfaction ($M = 86.5$). (See Noller, Christensen, & Heavey, under revision, for more detail.)

Two conflict interactions were videotaped for each couple, one in which the topic discussed was primarily experienced as an issue by the wife, and one in which the topic was primarily experienced as an issue by the husband. Issues to be discussed by the couple were decided on the basis of a questionnaire completed by each partner separately. In addition, issues were videotaped in counterbalanced order.

The interactions were rated for demanding and withdrawing behavior on 9-point scales. To assess demanding behavior, interactions were rated on three dimensions: discussion (tries to discuss the problem, is engaged and involved in the topic at hand), blames (blames, accuses, or criticizes the partner), and pressures for change (requests, demands, nags, or otherwise pressures for change in the partner). To assess withdrawing behavior, two scales were used: avoidance (avoids discussing the problem; e.g., hesitates, changes topic, diverts attention, or delays discussion), and withdraws (withdraws, becomes silent, or refuses to discuss the topic). Four observational variables were created for each interaction: husband-demand, husband-withdraw, wife-demand, and wife-withdraw scores were created separately for the husband's issue ($M$ = 15.1, 5.6, 13.6, 4.7 respectively) and the wife's issue ($M$ = 11.8, 5.8, 16.8, 4.5 respectively; note that demand is on a scale from 3 to 27, whereas withdraw is on a scale from 2 to 19). Coefficient alphas were computed for the demand subscale (four alphas, with a mean of .69) across the three ratings, and for the withdraw subscale (four alphas, with a mean of .77) across the two ratings.

The interactions were also coded for the presence of nonverbal behaviors seen as particularly relevant to assessing nonverbal involvement in the context of conflict interaction in marriage. Behaviors coded were gaze, open smile (smile showing upper teeth), closed smile (smile with lips closed), head up, head down, head nod, head turn, forward lean, open gestures (any gesture [movement of hand] where the open hands extend beyond the edges of the body), and closed gestures (any gesture where hands are folded across the body). Reliabilities were calculated and ranged from .81 to .41.

Previous research has indicated that spouses are more likely to be demanding when their own issue is being discussed and more likely to be withdrawing when their partner's issue is being discussed. For this reason, we focused on whether nonverbal behaviors related to high involvement were correlated with demand ratings when a spouse's own issue was being discussed, and whether behaviors associated with low involvement were correlated with withdraw ratings on the partner's issue. Separately for husbands' issues and wives' issues, we correlated outsider ratings of husbands' and wives' demanding and withdrawing behaviors with the frequency with which a particular nonverbal behavior occurred (assessed as the number of 15-second segments in which the behavior was coded as present).

On wives' issues, wives who were engaging in demanding behavior were less likely than other wives or husbands to use the closed smile. In addition, husbands who were engaging in withdrawing behavior used less gaze and fewer open gestures, and more head down and head turn. On husbands' issues, there were no links between husbands' demanding behavior and any of the nonverbal behaviors coded. Wives' withdrawal behavior, on the other hand, was related to their use of head down.

These results seem to provide more support for the proposition that withdrawal is related to low involvement than for the proposition that demanding is related to high involvement. Demanding may be carried more by the vocal channel, an assertion that is supported by the finding that the negativity of messages tends to be carried by the vocal channel, rather than by the verbal or visual channels (Noller, 1985). On the other hand, husbands' withdrawal from discussion of their wives' issues seems to be clearly defined by low-involvement behaviors such as lack of gaze, head down, and head turn.

It also seems clear that what might be called the classic demand/ withdraw pattern is more likely on the wife's issue, as shown by Christensen and Heavey (1990). The lack of effects for the husband's issue is likely to reflect the finding that wife demand/husband withdraw occurs more frequently on the wife's issue, with no clear pattern for the husband's issue.

To further explore the links between these nonverbal involvement behaviors and contextual variables, we conducted ANOVAs using relationship satisfaction, gender, and issue as the independent variables. The dependent variables for these analyses were the nonverbal behaviors that were correlated with demanding or withdrawing.

We first considered the high-involvement behaviors of gaze and open gestures. There was more gaze and more open gesturing on wives' issues than on husbands' issues. For open gestures, wives were also more likely to use open gestures on their own issues than on their husbands' issues. On the other hand, open gestures were used more by high-satisfaction spouses on husbands' issues than on wives' issues.

In other words, there seemed to be more high-involvement behaviors on wives' issues than on husbands' issues, and wives were more likely to use open gestures on their own issues than on their husbands' issues. These results imply more openness to information and suggestion on these issues. The finding that spouses high in satisfaction were more likely to use open gestures on the husband's issue suggests more willingness by these couples to deal with these issues in a frank and open manner.

With regard to low-involvement behaviors, wives were more likely to use head down on their own issue than on the husband's issue. In addition, spouses low in relationship satisfaction were more likely than high-satisfaction spouses to use head down. Head turn was used more by both genders on wives' issues than on husbands' issues. In other words, both high-involvement and low-involvement behaviors are occurring more on wives' issues, with wives as well as husbands using these low-involvement behaviors at some point in the interaction. Perhaps even demanding wives eventually respond to husbands' withdrawal by displaying withdrawal behaviors themselves.

## A Study with Family Conflict Patterns as the Primary Context

In the studies reported so far, we have focused on nonverbal behavior in the context of relationship conflict, using dating and married couples. In the third study, we focus on marital and parent–child conflict as contexts for the nonverbal behavior of family members. In particular, we were interested in whether adolescents' perceptions of each other's behavior depended on whether conflict is dealt with constructively or destructively in their families.

In an earlier self-report study of patterns of family interaction, we reported that there were links between ways of dealing with marital and parent–child conflict, links between ways of dealing with parent–child and sibling conflict, but no links between ways of dealing with marital and sibling conflict (Noller, Feeney, Peterson, & Sheehan, 1995). These results suggest that children learn their conflict patterns, not by direct modeling of their parents' conflict behaviors, but through their own conflict interactions with their parents (who seem to behave similarly in their conflicts with their children as they do with each other). We termed this process *interaction-based transmission*. In line with our earlier comments about the link between conflict and emotional arousal, it is likely that emotional experience is central to this process. Specifically, conflict patterns that are generally considered destructive involve either negative high-involvement behaviors (e.g., coercive behaviors) or low-involvement behaviors (e.g., withdrawal), both of which may result from attempts to deal with strong emotion.

In this third study we used families with adolescent twins. (This study has previously been reported in a conference paper by Noller, Feeney, Peterson, & Sheehan, 1996.) Both monozygotic (25 families) and dizygotic twins (43 families) were included, and both same-sex (48 families) and mixed-sex twins (20 families). Twins ranged in age from 12 to 17, with a mean age of 14.03 years. We used twins to control, at least in part, for differences in age and birth order normally present between siblings.

Family conflict was assessed using a revised version of the Communication Patterns Questionnaire (CPQ; Christensen, 1988; Christensen & Sullaway, 1984). The CPQ is a self-report measure that assesses the extent to which dyads use various interaction strategies during conflict. In addition to Christensen's marital version of the questionnaire, we designed a parent-child version of the scale with similar items. Items describe the role of each participant in a particular conflict pattern (e.g., husband threatens/wife backs down; mutual withdrawal). Participants rated each item on a 9-point scale, from 1 = very unlikely to 9 = very likely. Noller and White (1990) assessed the factor structure of the marital scale and found four factors: mutuality, coercion, destructive process (including such items as demand/withdraw and pressure/resist), and postconflict distress. In the present study, rather than the destructive process factor, we used Christensen's (1988) demand/withdraw factor, because this factor was more stable across the different relationships (that is, marital and parent–child). In addition, the demand-withdraw scale fits more clearly with the other work being discussed in this chapter.

The twins were videotaped while discussing together their experience of being twins, including whether it was possible for parents of twins to always treat both twins the same, and whether that was the best way for parents to behave. After this 5-minute interaction, the videotape was replayed, and the twins independently rated the middle three minutes, assessing themselves and their co-twin on each of four global rating scales, similar to those used by Callan and Noller (1986): calm-anxious, unfriendly-friendly, loving-rejecting, controlling-democratic.

The interactions were also coded by independent observers, using more specific behavioral ratings. Based on previous literature, the specific behavioral ratings were divided into three subsets: conversational management and support (nonsupportive verbal, supportive verbal, directive, asks questions, answers questions, dominance), nonverbal behaviors (kinesic expressiveness, unpleasant facial animation, pleasant facial animation, posture, proxemic attentiveness, random physical activity), and vocalic behaviors (vocal pleasantness, vocal unpleasantness, vocal intensity, vocal expressiveness, vocal fluency). See Table 13.1 for the operational definitions of these behaviors.

The specific behaviors were rated on 5-point scales with a value of 1 given when the behavior was frequent and consistent, and a value of 5 given when no behavior indicative of the particular dimension was coded. Each behavioral scale was accompanied by a detailed information sheet, defining the behavior of interest and outlining the particular behavioral cues that comprised the dimension, as well as frequency, intensity, consistency, and the combination of cues that defined each point on the scale.

We examined the patterns of correlations between the global rating scales (of outsider and twins) and the specific behavioral scales (outsider only) in order to be able to describe the global ratings in behavioral terms. These correlations are summarized in Table 13.2. The links between the global ratings and specific behaviors are theoretically meaningful and suggest high validity of both sets of ratings.

To assess the links between family conflict and twins' perceptions of each other's behavior, we related CPQ ratings to ratings from the videotaped interaction. To do this, we conducted canonical correlation analyses relating the CPQ ratings of marital and parent–child conflict to the global ratings made by the twins in assessing each other's behavior. There were no links between marital conflict and twins' perceptions of each other's behavior. There were links between fathers' reports of parent–child conflict and twins' ratings of one another, but no links between mothers' reports and twins' ratings.

Specifically, when fathers rated their conflict with their first-born twin as high in demand/withdraw, first-born twins rated second-born twins as more anxious, more rejecting, and more involved in their interaction. In terms of the behaviors associated with the dimensions of anxiety and rejection, these twins were seeing their co-twins in generally negative terms, as being less supportive, more directive, engaging in less pleasant facial expression and voice tone, being less fluent, and asking fewer questions.

Similarly, when fathers rated their conflict with their second-born twin as high in coercion and postconflict distress and low in mutuality, second-born twins rated first-born twins as less friendly in their interaction. In behavioral terms, these twins were seeing their co-twin

Table 13.1. *Operational definitions of the conversational content, nonverbal and verbal behavioral codes*

| Behavioral code | Definition | Example |
|---|---|---|
| *Conversational content* | | |
| Nonsupportive verbal | Conversational content that communicates opposition to someone else through antagonism or disagreement, or through active avoidance | Sarcasm, blame, disapproval |
| Supportive verbal | Conversational content that communicates solidarity with someone else through support, agreement, and appreciation | Expresses concern, agreement, commonality |
| *Conversational management* | | |
| Instruction | Conversational content involving directive or instructive statements | Requests to engage in particular behavior or to change behavior |
| Asks questions | Conversational content through which a person asks for information or expression of opinion | Request for clarification or confirmation of what has been said |
| Answers questions | Conversational content through which a person responds to a question asked | Gives opinions, expresses feelings, repeats, clarifies, confirms |
| Conversational dominance | Conversational content where a person controls and directs the course of the conversation | Changing topic, directing back to topic, interrupting |
| *Nonverbal behavior* | | |
| Expressiveness | Kinesic expressiveness through facial animation, gesturing, body and head movements | Head nods, use of emblem and illustrator gestures |

*(continued)*

| Behavioral code | Definition | Example |
| --- | --- | --- |
| *Nonverbal behavior* | | |
| Unpleasant facial animation | Facial animation communicating opposition to someone else through disagreement or antagonism, or to make fun of the other person | Glaring, smirking, rolling eyes |
| Pleasant facial animation | Facial animation intended to communicate closeness, friendliness, approval and concern | Smiling, laughter, expressions of concern |
| Posture | Postural tension through openness, symmetry and rigidity in posture | Folding arms, body rigid, legs and shoulders symmetrical |
| Proxemic attentiveness | Behavior that communicates close interpersonal and conversational distance through direction of orientation and proximity | Leaning forward, touching, direct body and facial orientation |
| Random physical activity | Use of self- and object-adaptor behaviors, postural shifts, random trunk, limb, and head movements | Playing with hair, rocking and twisting in chair, foot tapping |
| *Vocalic behavior* | | |
| Vocal pleasantness | Pleasant and warm speech | Variable intonation, rhythm, and resonance |
| Vocal unpleasantness | Unpleasant and cold speech | Abruptness in speech, harsh tone, accusatory intonation |
| Vocal intensity | Intensity in amplitude, tempo, and pitch | Loud speech, fast speech |
| Vocal expressiveness | Variation in pitch, tempo, and amplitude | Pitch variety, tempo variety, variety in amplitude |
| Vocal fluency | Clarity of articulation | Decrements in speech, breaks, or silences; disjointed, jerky speech |

Table 13.2. *Summary of relations between specific behaviors and outsider's and twins' global ratings*

| Global rating scale | Links with outsider's global ratings | Links with twins' global ratings |
| --- | --- | --- |
| Anxious-calm | higher anxiety linked with: less support more directives | higher anxiety linked with: more nonsupport less facial pleasantness less vocalic pleasantness less vocal fluency less asking of questions more unpleasant facial animation |
| Friendly-unfriendly | more friendliness linked with: more support more pleasant vocalics less unpleasant vocalics less facial animation | more friendliness linked with: more support fewer directives more vocal fluency |
| Rejecting-loving | more rejection linked with: more directives less support less pleasant vocalics | more rejection linked with: more directives less support less pleasant vocalics |
| Democratic-controlling | more democratic linked with: less unpleasant vocalics less unpleasant animation more asking of questions more support less nonsupport | more democratic linked with: less unpleasant vocalics |

as less supportive, as using a less pleasant voice tone and more unpleasant facial expressions.

The lack of links between conflict patterns in the marital relationship and the twins' perceptions of one another's behaviors is consistent with the self-report study mentioned earlier (Noller et al., 1995). It seems that adolescents' perceptions of one another are affected more by the parent–child relationship than the marital relationship, although, in the earlier study, we found strong links between communication in the marital and parent–child relationships, suggesting that parents behave similarly in conflict situations with one another and with their children.

With regard to parent–child conflict, there were strong links between the fathers' reports of parent–child conflict and twins' perceptions of each other's behavior. In families where fathers reported destructive patterns of parent–child conflict, adolescent twins viewed each other's behavior more negatively. In this context, it is interesting to note that in this same study, fathers' reports of both marital and parent–child conflict were also linked with their perceptions of their adolescents' behavior during a conflict interaction involving both parents and the twins (Noller, et al., 1996). Perhaps these negative perceptions of siblings are influenced by attitudes and behaviors of parents, or at least of fathers, in a similar way to that by which conflict patterns are transmitted across generations (Noller et al., 1995).

## General Discussion

In each of the studies, nonverbal behavior was clearly affected by the context in which the interaction occurred. In the first study, nonverbal behavior was jointly influenced by the type of conflict issue and relationship satisfaction, with differences between satisfied and dissatisfied couples occurring only on relationship based issues. In that study, the most consistent link with relationship satisfaction was for avoidance behavior, when partners were primed to act cold and distant. Unhappy couples used more avoidance behaviors in this context. When asked to reestablish closeness, satisfied husbands used less avoidance than other husbands, and husbands of satisfied wives were more likely to touch their partners in positive ways. In terms of our perspective on nonverbal behavior as being indicative of emotional processes, these findings suggest that the emotions aroused for dissatisfied couples by the relationship based issue were dealt with by avoidance of the partner, while those aroused for satisfied couples were more likely to be dealt with by approaching the partner, particularly for husbands.

Avoidance (or low-involvement behavior) was also very important in the second study. Behaviors such as lack of gaze, head down, and head turn were most clearly linked to ratings of withdrawal, although only for the wife's issue. In addition, the only main effect of satisfaction was that spouses low in relationship satisfaction used more head down than those high in satisfaction. These findings suggest that withdrawal is more common in low-satisfaction couples and on wives' issues, and they raise the question of the function of withdrawal from conflict, particularly by men. For example, Noller (1993) and Christensen and Heavey (1990) have suggested that avoidance may be used by husbands in this context to exert power and to maintain the status quo. The fact that husbands are more likely to withdraw from discussing wives' issues supports this proposition. An alternative explanation, as suggested by Gottman and Levenson (1988), is that they withdraw to control their high levels of emotional arousal.

High-involvement behaviors were not clearly linked to ratings of demanding. As noted earlier, it is possible that demanding behaviors include categories other than the visual behaviors coded in this study; vocalics (voice tone) and verbal behaviors may be relevant here. Such a claim is supported by the findings from the third study, in which vocalics and verbal behaviors were related to ratings of anxious versus calm, friendly versus unfriendly, and loving versus rejecting, with unpleasant vocalics and unsupportive and directive behavior being clearly related to the negative poles of these scales.

It is important to note that the "type of issue" variable was operationalized quite differently in the first and second studies. In the first study, type of issue referred to whether a specific problem or the relationship itself was being discussed. In the second study, the focus was on who was most concerned about the issue and therefore was likely to be more invested in getting it resolved. In the first study, it was clear that there were more differences between satisfied and dissatisfied spouses in their nonverbal behaviors when the issue concerned the relationship itself. In the second study, it was clear that, on wives' issues, men rated as withdrawing displayed a cluster of nonverbal behaviors easily identified as low involvement. Findings were not so clear on husbands' issues or for wives' behavior.

The third study points to the effects of conflict behaviors in the family, beyond the immediate context of the conflict interaction. What this study shows is that the ways in which conflicts are dealt with in the family, particularly between fathers and children, have a pervasive effect on family relationships, even affecting relationships between siblings. In addition, it seems likely that these effects are transmitted nonverbally, particularly through unpleasant vocalics (anxious, unfriendly, rejecting, controlling), less facial pleasantness (anxious, unfriendly), unpleasant facial animation (unfriendly), and nonsupportive behaviors. These findings suggest that fathers who use unfriendly and nonsupportive behaviors in dealing with their conflicts with their children, are likely to affect not only their relationships *with* their children, but also the relationships *between* their children, which tend to be more hostile.

Given the importance of avoidance in the first two studies, it is interesting to note that when fathers reported demand-withdraw behavior in their interactions with their first-born children, the siblings were more likely to perceive each other in negative ways. It is possible that the children interact with each other in emotion-laden conflict situations in similar ways to how their fathers interact with them, and that these destructive patterns create the high levels of hostility (Noller et al., 1995). It is also possible that the siblings' hostility is an emotional reaction to the way each of them behaves in interaction with the father.

These three studies, taken together, indicate the importance of nonverbal communication in family relations. What these studies also show, as do other studies reported in this volume, is that nonverbal behavior is affected by the context in which the interaction occurs. The contexts we compared included the level of satisfaction in the couple relationship, the type of conflict issue being discussed, the level of investment in the issue, and the ways in which conflict is typically handled in the family. These studies point clearly to the need to take context into account when studying nonverbal behavior in the family.

## References

Callan, V. J., & Noller, P. (1986). Perceptions of communication in families with adolescents. *Journal of Marriage and the Family, 48,* 813–820.

Christensen, A. (1988). Dysfunctional interaction patterns in couples. In P. Noller & M. A. Fitzpatrick (Eds.), *Perspectives on marital interaction* (pp. 31–52). Clevedon and Philadelphia: Multilingual Matters.

Christensen, A., & Heavey, C. L. (1990). Gender, power, and marital conflict. *Journal of Personality and Social Psychology, 59,* 73–85.

Christensen, A., & Sullaway, M. (1984). The Communication Patterns Questionnaire. Available from the authors at Department of Psychology, University of California, Los Angeles, CA 90024.

Feeney, J. A. (1998). Adult attachment and relationship-centered anxiety: Responses to physical and emotional distancing. In W. S. Rholes and J. A. Simpson (Eds.), *Attachment theory and close relationships* (pp. 189–218). NY: Guilford.

Fincham, F. D., & Bradbury, T. N. (1988). The impact of attributions in marriage: An experimental analysis. *Journal of Social and Personal Relationships, 7,* 122–130.

Fitzpatrick, M. A. (1988). *Between husbands and wives.* Newbury Park, CA: Sage.

Gottman, J. M. (1979). *Marital interaction: Empirical investigations.* New York: Academic Press.

Gottman, J. M., & Levenson, R. W. (1988). The social psychophysiology of marriage. In P. Noller & M. A. Fitzpatrick (Eds.), *Perspectives on marital interaction* (pp. 181–200). Clevedon & Philadelphia: Multilingual Matters.

Gottman, J. M., Markman, H., & Notarius, C. I. (1977). The topography of marital conflict: A sequential analysis of verbal and nonverbal behavior. *Journal of Marriage and the Family, 39,* 461–477.

Greenberg, L., & Johnson, S. M. (1986). Emotionally focused couples' therapy. In N. S. Jacobson & A. S. Gurman (Eds.), *The clinical handbook of marital therapy.* New York: Guilford.

Grych, J. H., & Fincham, F. D. (1990). Marital conflict and children's adjustment: A cognitive-contextual framework. *Psychological Bulletin, 108,* 267–290.

Heavey, C. L., Layne, C., & Christensen, A. (1993). Gender and conflict structure in marital interaction: A replication and extension. *Journal of Consulting and Clinical Psychology, 61,* 16–27.

Jacobson, N. S., & Margolin, G. (1979). *Marital therapy: Strategies based on social learning and behavior exchange principles.* New York: Brunner-Mazel.

Levenson, R. W. (1994). Emotional control: Variations and consequences. In P. Ekman & R. J. Davidson, *The nature of emotion: Fundamental questions* (pp. 273–279). New York: Oxford University Press.

Lochman, J. E., & Allen, G. (1981). Nonverbal communication of couples in conflict. *Journal of Research in Personality, 15,* 253–269.

Manusov, V. (1990). An application of attribution principles to nonverbal behavior in romantic dyads. *Communication Monographs, 57,* 104–118.

Margolin, G. (1981). Behavior change in happy and unhappy couples: A family life cycle perspective. *Behavioral Assessment, 11,* 101–118.

Montemayor, R. (1982). The relationship between parent-adolescent conflict and the amount of time adolescents spend alone and with parents. *Child Development, 53,* 1512–1519.

Newton, D. A., & Burgoon, J. K. (1990). Nonverbal conflict behaviors: Functions, strategies, and tactics. In D. D. Cahn (Ed.), *Intimates in conflict: A communication perspective* (pp. 77–104). Hillsdale, NJ: Lawrence Erlbaum.

Noller, P. (1984). *Nonverbal communication and marital interaction.* Oxford: Pergamon Press.

Noller, P. (1985). Negative communications in marriage. *Journal of Social and Personal Relationships, 2,* 289–301.

Noller, P. (1993). Gender and emotional communication in marriage: Different cultures or differential social power. *Journal of Language and Social Psychology, 12,* 92–112.

Noller, P., & Callan, V. J. (1988). Understanding parent–adolescent interactions: Perceptions of family members and outsiders. *Developmental Psychology, 24,* 707–714.

Noller, P., Christensen, A., & Heavey, C. L. (under revision). Nonverbal behavior and the demand-withdraw pattern of marital interaction. Available from Department of Psychology, University of Queensland, 4072, Australia.

Noller, P., & Fitzpatrick, M. A. (1990). Marital communication in the Eighties. *Journal of Marriage and the Family, 52,* 832–843.

Noller, P., & Fitzpatrick, M. A. (1993). *Communication in family relationships.* Englewood Cliffs, NJ: Prentice Hall.

Noller, P., Feeney, J. A., Peterson, C., & Sheehan, G. (1995). Learning conflict patterns in the family: Links between marital, parental, and sibling relationships. In T. Socha & G. Stamp (Eds.), *Parents, children, and communication: Frontiers of theory and research* (pp. 273–298). Hillsdale, N.J.: Lawrence Erlbaum.

Noller, P., Feeney, J. A., Peterson, C. A., & Sheehan, G. (1996, Montreal). Marital conflict interaction and its implications for parent–adolescent relationships. Paper presented at the International Congress of Psychology, Montreal.

Noller, P., & White, A. (1990). The validity of the Communication Patterns Questionnaire. *Psychological Assessment: A Journal of Consulting and Clinical Psychology, 2,* 478–482.

Norton, R. (1983). Measuring marital quality: A critical look at the dependent variable. *Journal of Marriage and the Family, 45,* 141–151.

Notarius, C. I., & Johnson, J. S. (1982). Emotional expression in husbands and wives. *Journal of Marriage and the Family, 44,* 483–489.

Patterson, M. L. (1983). *Nonverbal behavior: A functional perspective.* New York: Springer-Verlag.

Raush, H. L., Barry, W. A., Hertel, R. K., & Swain, M. A. (1974). *Communication, conflict, and marriage.* San Francisco, CA: Jossey-Bass.

Revenstorf, D., Vogel, B., Wegener, C., Hahlweg, K., & Schindler, L. (1980). Escalation phenomena in interaction sequences: An empirical comparison of distressed and nondistressed couples. *Behavior Analysis and Modification, 2,* 97–116.

Roloff, M., & Cloven, D. (1990). The chilling effect in interpersonal relationships. In D. Cahn (Ed.), *Intimates in conflict* (pp. 49–76). Hillsdale, NJ: Lawrence Erlbaum.

Schaap, C., Buunk, A. P., & Kerkstra, A. (1988). Marital conflict resolution. In P. Noller & M. A. Fitzpatrick (Eds.), *Perspectives on marital interaction* (pp. 203–244). Clevedon & Philadelphia: Multilingual Matters.

Simpson, J. A., Rholes, W. A., Nelligan, J. S. (1992). Support seeking and support giving within couples in an anxiety-provoking situation: The role of attachment styles. *Journal of Personality and Social Psychology, 62,* 434–446.

Spanier, G. B. (1976). Measuring dyadic adjustment: New scales for assessing the quality of marriage and similar dyads. *Journal of Marriage and the Family, 44,* 709–720.

Volling, B. L., & Belsky, J. (1992). The contribution of mother–child and father–child relationships to the quality of sibling interaction: A longitudinal study. *Child Development, 63,* 1209–1222.

Vuchinich, S. (1987). Starting and stopping spontaneous family conflicts. *Journal of Marriage and the Family, 49,* 591–601.

# 14. Love's Best Habit

## Deception in the Context of Relationships

D. ERIC ANDERSON, MATTHEW E. ANSFIELD, AND
BELLA M. DePAULO

> When my love swears that she is made of truth,
> I do believe her, though I know she lies,
> That she might think me some untutor'd youth,
> Unlearned in the world's false subtilties.
> Thus vainly thinking that she thinks me young,
> Although she knows my days are past the best,
> Simply I credit her false-speaking tongue;
> On both sides thus is simple truth suppress'd.
> But wherefore says she not she is unjust?
> And wherefore say not I that I am old?
> O, love's best habit is in seeming trust,
> And age in love loves not t' have years told.
> Therefore I lie with her, and she with me,
> And in our faults by lies we flattered be.
>
> William Shakespeare, Sonnet 138

When Shakespeare penned these lines, he captured some issues about deception that continue to intrigue laypersons and scholars to this day. One of the primary concerns, particularly about deception within the context of a close relationship, is whether one can truly know when one's romantic partner or friend is lying. A hypothesis that is both comforting and intuitively appealing is that we are most accurate at detecting the deception of the people with whom we spend the most time, such as our best friends, romantic partners, and family members, because we have the most exposure to their idiosyncratic verbal and nonverbal cues to deceit as well as their ordinary, truthful behavior. This hypothesis rests on several assumptions, however. First of all, there is an assumption that there *are* idiosyncratic cues to deceit (as compared to nomothetic cues that would be equally evident to people inside and outside of relationships). Second is the assumption that people can learn cues to deception that may be idiosyncratic to particular individuals. Further, there is an assumption that deception occurs frequently enough to make the learning of idiosyncratic cues a practical possibility. Feedback, too, may be essential: If a person suspects a partner of lying but never learns for sure if the suspicion was justified, then the partner's verbal and nonverbal behavior during the episode cannot serve as definitive evidence of a particular style of lying. Finally, the hypothesis positing a link between familiarity and accuracy assumes that cues to deception that have already been learned will be noticed at the time of a new deception.

Shakespeare's sonnet also suggests that while the speaker knows that his love is lying, he believes her nonetheless. This is a curious paradox, but one that is completely understandable if one looks to the motives of the target of the deception. Perhaps all of the nonverbal cues to deception are present, yet the man chooses to overlook them for the sake of the relationship, or to preserve his image of his love as a truthful person. Therefore, he essentially gives her the benefit of the doubt even though, at some level, he recognizes the deceit.

In this chapter, we will review the available research on deception and deception detection in the context of close relationships. We will examine the various motivations, both of the liar and of the target of deception, that may improve or undermine accuracy at detecting deception. In addition, we will explore why deception may occur in relationships, and how it may, at times, help preserve a relationship when the truth might threaten it.

## Importance

The telling and detecting of lies has been the topic of hundreds of publications; the importance of this area of research needs no further comment. But why might it be important to study the *social context* of deception? First of all, it is possible that the rates of deception differ in different kinds of relationships, with important implications. Central to this issue is the question of whether people tell more or fewer lies to those they care about most, such as a best friend or romantic partner, compared to those they care about less, such as casual acquaintances or strangers. We might expect to find that people are most honest with their close relationship partners. After all, honesty, openness, and trust are the hallmarks of close relationships and are in part what make them stand out from other relationships. Alternatively, however, we might just as easily hypothesize that people are least honest with those whom they care about the most. Millar and Tesser (1988) hold that lies are told to people whose expectations the liars have violated. If, for example, a young boy realizes that his mother thinks he can do no wrong, but he actually does engage in bad behavior, he might lie in order to cover that behavior. Close relationship partners are especially likely to have such positive behavioral expectations, and so they are most likely to be the targets of lies told to meet or exceed those expectations.

If fewer lies are told to close relationship partners than to casual acquaintances, then an assumption of truthfulness in the context of close relationships may be appropriate and may contribute to the harmoniousness of the relationships. If instead, lies are more common in closer relationships, then it is possible that accuracy at detecting lies will also be greater in those relationships because of the more frequent opportunities for learning the relevant cues. A second reason why the social context of deception may be important is that lies told in different kinds of relationships may spring from very different motivations and may even have their own characteristic cues. The repercussions of deceit may also differ in different kinds of relationships. Lies about affairs, for instance, may be much more consequential in the context of long-standing marriages than newly developing dating relationships. The people we care about the most may have the potential to hurt us the most, especially if their lies go undetected.

Liars who are caught in their lies risk scorn and stigma; the risk is even greater when the targets of the lies are close relationship partners than when they are acquaintances or strangers (Maier & Lavrakas, 1976). The consequences of lies told to close relationship partners may also reverberate more widely. Members of a relationship dyad (e.g., friends, spouses) share networks of friends. Therefore, when trust is violated, it may not be only the target of the lie who vilifies the liar. Other network members may help carry the grudge. Because the consequences of deception within relationships may be more severe, liars may be more motivated to get away with their lies to their relational partners than their lies to strangers.

## Deception and Nonverbal Behavior

*You can't hide your lyin' eyes*
*And your smile is a thin disguise*
The Eagles, "Lyin' Eyes"

Much research has focused on the nonverbal behaviors that accompany deception, and there is ample evidence that people behave differently when they are lying than they do when they are telling the truth (DePaulo & Friedman, in press; DePaulo, Stone, & Lassiter, 1985a; Zuckerman, DePaulo, & Rosenthal, 1981). These differences in behavior may alert targets of deception that a lie is being perpetrated upon them. Liars, in general, speak less fluently than truth tellers; their tales are filled with hesitations, grammatical errors, and um's and er's. They often sound like they are trying to distance themselves from their own stories. Compared to those who are about to tell the truth, people who are about to lie take more time to plan. This is not always advantageous to the liars, as their lies can end up sounding more rehearsed than their truths. People's duplicitous tales are often shorter than their truthful ones and spoken in a higher pitch. They may also include more irrelevant information, overly generalized comments, and negative statements. Fabrications often seem less internally consistent than truthful renderings of actual facts and feelings.

There are also some visual cues to deceit. "Lying eyes," for example, are blinking eyes with dilated pupils, and lying limbs are those that fidget, tap, and scratch.

The set of cues that are accurate, reliable indicators of deception does not overlap perfectly with the set of cues that people *think* are accurate and reliable indicators of deception. For example, although parents frequently admonish children to "look them in the eyes" as a test of truthfulness, gaze avoidance is only a reliable cue to deception when liars are not Machiavellian (manipulative) sorts. Other folkloric cues to deception, such as increased latency of response, slower rate of speech, increased postural shifts, and lack of smiling also do not reliably discriminate between truths and lies (DePaulo, Stone, & Lassiter, 1985a).

The differing patterns of gazing for people who differ in Machiavellianism is just one example of a more general precautionary note about cues to deceit: They may differ for different kinds of people.

Situational factors can be important, too. For example, lies told in contexts in which people are highly motivated to escape detection may differ systematically from those told in less consequential settings (DePaulo & Kirkendol, 1989). Even happenstance can undermine the reliability of nomothetic cues to deceit. For example, although people blink more often when lying than when telling the truth, the frequent blinking of a person who just started wearing contact lenses may have little to do with deceit.

It is possible that within a specific relationship, both nomothetic and idiographic cues will be important. A father, for example, may show many of the same cues to deceit that people generally show. In addition, he may have his own personal style of lying. Even more specifically, he may have a special way of lying to his children that is different from the way he lies to strangers. He may also distinguish among his children, for example, by lying in different ways to his sons than to his daughters. He may even lie in particular ways to a particular son or a particular daughter.

The evidence pertinent to the specificity of cues to deceit is sparse and sometimes merely suggestive. For example, in a study of whether people can be trained to detect deception more successfully if they receive feedback on the accuracy of their guesses (Zuckerman, Koestner, & Alton, 1984), it was reported that feedback did improve accuracy – but the improvement was specific to the persons whose truths and lies were being judged. By watching a particular person lying and telling the truth, and receiving feedback each time as to whether that person really was lying or telling the truth, trainees became better at detecting the deceit of that particular person. However, they were not any better at detecting the deceit of a different person. The study therefore provides suggestive evidence that different people lie in their own characteristic ways. It also indicates that with systematic feedback, accuracy at recognizing such idiosyncrasies can be improved.

With regard to relationship specific idiosyncrasies, we know of just one study (Buller & Aune, 1987) of the cues that might characterize lies told to people in different relationship categories. As we will discuss in more detail later, the study showed that people lie in more stereotypical ways when their targets are strangers than when they are intimates.

It seems, then, that people trying to detect the deception of a close relationship partner may need to focus particularly on idiosyncratic cues to deception. But how simple is it to note these cues? Based on other research on nonverbal behavior and empathic accuracy in close relationships, the answer to that question may be, "not simple at all."

## Perception of Nonverbal Behavior in Close Relationships

*Going through security*
*I held her for so long*
*She finally looked at me in love*
*And she was gone*

Crosby, Stills, and Nash, "Just a Song Before I Go"

Even if a relational partner is not trying to deceive, it can be a difficult task to know what that person is thinking or feeling. The difficulty is not just a matter of whether the telltale cues are present and clear. Motivational factors are important, too. For example, the sadness on a wife's face when her husband says "I love you" may be so threatening to the relationship that the husband may be motivated to interpret the sadness as some other emotion. Simpson, Ickes, and Blackstone (1995) found evidence for such a self-protective function in the empathic decoding of close relationship partners. The greater the threat to the relationship, the lower the empathic accuracy. This "motivated inaccuracy" resulted in levels of empathic accuracy that were even lower than those reported in studies involving total strangers.

Other mechanisms besides the self-protective motivational one may also be useful in explaining the inaccuracy. For example, perceptions of close relationship partners may be influenced more by theories about those partners than by their actual behavior. The theories might be based on personal experiences with the partner. They can also follow from more general person perception processes, such as assumed similarity, in which a person assumes that another (in this case, a relational partner) shares his or her current emotional state (Thomas & Fletcher, 1997). Since close relationship partners generally select on similarity, assumptions of similar feelings should be more accurate for relational partners than for randomly selected strangers, leading to what appears to be greater insight into the other person's feelings. In fact, this is only coincidental, and the actual insight is into one's own feelings, rather than the true feelings of one's partner. Thomas, Fletcher, and Lange (1997) found that people involved in relationships for shorter lengths of time have greater shared cognitive focus (they think about the same things at the same time), and consequently greater empathic accuracy than those involved for longer periods of time.

Perhaps as relationships develop, partners no longer do the work of interpreting behavioral cues and rely on theories about their partners, based on experience, motivated biases, or assumed similarity. In these ways, theory driven judgments about close relational partners may short-circuit a search for diagnostic behavioral cues emitted in the situation. The search for specific cues is cognitively taxing, so if there are shortcuts that yield results that are somewhat accurate ("good enough"), relational partners may feel that there is little reason to engage in more effortful processing.

## Incidence of Deception

> *Honesty, is such a lonely word,*
> *Everyone is so untrue.*
> *Honesty is hardly ever heard,*
> *And mostly what I need from you.*
> Billy Joel, "Honesty"

Lying is a fact of daily life. On the average, people tell at least one lie a day, and one lie in every five of their social interactions. Over the course of a week, they also lie to at least 30 % of the people in their lives with whom they interact. These are the conclusions of a pair of studies reported by DePaulo, Kashy, and their colleagues (DePaulo & Kashy, 1998; DePaulo, Kashy, Kirkendol, Wyer, & Epstein, 1996; Kashy & DePaulo, 1997), in which college students and people from the community kept diaries every day for a week of all of their social interactions and all of the lies that they told during those interactions. Nontrivial rates of lying have also been reported by others (e.g., Camden, Motley, & Wilson, 1984; Turner, Edgley, & Olmstead, 1975).

The telling of a lie may involve a deliberate decision that results from a mental calculus of risks and benefits. In the context of close personal relationships, the most important risks may be the risks to the relationship. In deciding whether to lie, people need to weigh the risks to the relationship posed by the lie itself against the risks of revealing the information that they are tempted to hide with a lie (Feeley, 1997).

Honesty and openness are coveted qualities of personal relationships. Opportunities to confide in others and to be trusted, in turn, with their confidences provide some of the most potent satisfactions that personal relationships have to offer. Similarly, the possibility of simply being oneself with a minimum of artifice or pretense is deeply gratifying. An early literature overstated the importance of complete candor in relationships, and we do not intend to resurrect that error. Though we acknowledge the need for self-disclosure in order to progress to deeper stages of intimacy (Altman & Taylor, 1973), we also recognize, as have many before us (e.g., Bochner, 1982; Parks, 1982), the impracticality, impossibility, and undesirability of total disclosure. That caveat aside, we maintain that relatively high levels of openness and honesty are in large part what make close personal relationships feel close.

## Types of Lies

The little lies that people tell in their everyday lives can violate the cherished ideals of close personal relationships. When people feel that they cannot tell each other how they really performed at school or at work, and when they too often fear that they cannot safely express their true feelings and opinions, the relationship is unlikely to feel like a close one. In these examples, the fact of the lie (e.g., that the relationship partner would not admit to a mistake on an assignment) is more threatening to the relationship than the information covered by the lie (in this case, the mistake itself). We expect, then, that in the domain of everyday lies, people will tell fewer lies (per social interaction) to the people in their lives to whom they feel closest.

The DePaulo and Kashy (1998) diary studies showed just that. Overall, the closer the relationship, the lower the rate of lying within that relationship. For example, when only nonromantic and nonfamily categories are considered (i.e., best friends, friends, acquaintances, and strangers), the lowest rate of lying occurs in conversations with best friends, while the highest rate occurs with strangers. Closeness also predicts lower rates of everyday lying when all relationship partners are considered. So, closeness does provide some insulation from the little lies of everyday life, but those in close relationships are still deceived by their partners at times.

Serious lies, however, are most often told to cover serious transgressions and deep betrayals of trust, such as romantic infidelities. In these instances, the information covered by the lie may be more threatening to the relationship than the lie itself (McCornack & Levine, 1990a), and therefore telling the lie may be the strategy of choice.

Autobiographical studies of serious lies support this prediction: When describing the most serious lie they ever told to someone else, or the most serious lie anyone ever told to them, people overwhelmingly report that the teller and the target of these lies were close relationship partners (DePaulo, Ansfield, Kirkendol, & Boden, 1997).

*Lies and Closeness*

In accounting for the relatively low rate of lying to close relationship partners in the realm of everyday lies, we have focused so far on emotional closeness. But the feeling of closeness is only one kind of closeness. Also important is the extent of interaction with the other person – that is, "behaving close" rather than "feeling close" (see Aron, Aron, & Smollan, 1992; Berscheid, Snyder, & Omoto, 1989; Miller, Mongeau, & Sleight, 1986). People in relationships can engage in many activities together without feeling close, and they might subjectively "feel" close even though they are not engaging in activities together. For instance, two people could work together extensively on a project without developing feelings of closeness. Likewise, college friends may be geographically separated after graduation, yet still maintain the feelings of closeness in their friendship.

Along with extensive interaction (behaving close) comes not only greater opportunity to experience and note the idiosyncratic cues to deception, but also practical impediments to the telling of successful lies. People who interact with us extensively get to know more and more about us, and that limits the topics that are ripe for lies. We can, for example, try to impress strangers at a cocktail party with stories of our dazzling typing speed, but we cannot even attempt that lie with co-workers who have witnessed our hunt-and-peck technique. We could attempt other kinds of lies with people we see often, but we may be deterred by the effort it would take to maintain the lie over countless, ongoing interactions. A third deterrent is lowered expectations for success. If we think that the people who interact with us most often and most extensively are less likely to be fooled by our lies, we may be less likely to try to fool them. There is evidence that people do in fact believe that those closest to us are most adept at detecting our deception (Feeley, 1997). This may fuel the confidence people have in their ability to detect the lies of their close relationship partners.

Exactly what makes close others "close" is also, at times, a problematic question. Although feeling close and behaving close are theoretically separable, empirically they are joined (Aron et al., 1992). Relationships characterized by extensive interactions are usually also characterized by feelings of closeness. We think that people will tell fewer lies (per social interaction) to the people in their lives with whom they interact more frequently and to the people they have known for longer periods of time because these are the people with whom they share the closest emotional bonds. Despite the practical considerations that could lower the rate of lying to partners with whom we are behaviorally interdependent, it is the emotional deterrents that will be most powerful. This is, in fact, what DePaulo and Kashy (1998) found in their diary studies of everyday lies. Emotional closeness, frequency of interacting, and duration of the relationship, considered individually, each predicted a lower rate of lying. However, when all three were considered simultaneously, only emotional closeness remained significant.

## Motivations for Deception

> *Did you do it for love?*
> *Did you do it for money?*
> *Did you do it for spite?*
> *Did you think you had to, honey?*
> The Eagles, "The Long Run"

Lies are told for a variety of reasons. Self-serving lies follow from motivations such as avoiding punishment and blame ("No, I didn't take the last cookie"), conveying desired impressions of ourselves ("Me? Oh, sure, I've been to the opera"), instrumental considerations ("Of course I'll clean up my room if you give me money for concert tickets"), and privacy needs ("That phone call? It was from . . . my mother"). All of these examples, and others (e.g., DePaulo et al., 1996; see also chapter 4 by Saarni & Weber, in this volume), illustrate lies that are told to protect or enhance oneself, or to get one's way.

Very different, motivationally, from self-serving lies are altruistic ones. Altruistic lies are told to protect other people, or to help them feel better or get their way. "You look great," "You did the right thing," "What a wonderful dinner," "I'm sure you will do fine," "I, too, would love to just have a quiet weekend at home," and "I agree with you completely" are all examples of altruistic lies. Altruistic liars hide their own feelings and opinions, and sometimes sacrifice their own preferences and desires, in order to please their partners. In the domain of everyday lying (to all interaction partners, including strangers), altruistic lies are the exceptions. Self-serving lies occur at a rate of about twice that of altruistic ones. But is this the way things work in close personal relationships?

The short answer is "no." The closer one is to a relational partner, the fewer lies one tells, and relatively more of those lies are altruistic. This is an important consideration if there are differences in behavior when telling altruistic as opposed to self-serving lies, especially if these differences make one type of lie harder to detect. Liars probably know that their lie will be perceived as more reprehensible and less justified when it benefits themselves rather than others. We might expect, then, that self-serving liars will be more motivated to get away with their lies, since the risks are higher for them. Therefore, when people tell self-serving lies they may, theoretically, feel and look more anxious and guilty than when they tell altruistic lies. This is just how perceivers expect liars to act (DePaulo, Stone, & Lassiter, 1985a). Therefore, the tellers of self-serving lies may be more likely to be labeled as liars than the tellers of altruistic lies.

There is another important reason why the tellers of altruistic lies may be more likely to get away with their lies, and that is because they are telling others exactly what they want to hear. In contrast, many self-serving lies imply damaging information about the partner, the relationship, or even the self if they are found out. Therefore, the targets of self-serving lies may be motivated to let potential lies lie. This motivation may be especially great when the relationship is especially important. If, in fact, people in close relationships are particularly motivated to believe altruistic lies and to remain oblivious to self-centered ones, then their many experiences with each other's styles of communicating may come to naught. They could be equalled, or even outdone, by total strangers in the accuracy with which they detect their partner's lies.

## Deception Detection

> *Lie to me, I promise I'll believe . . .*
> *Lie to me, but please don't leave.*
> Sheryl Crow, "Strong Enough"

Deception detection is not an easy business. This is evident from the results of laboratory studies in which participants (senders) typically communicate truthfully half of the time and lie the other half of the time, and targets (judges) attempt to determine whether each communication was a truth or a lie. In such studies, we would expect targets to be correct 50% of the time by chance alone. Across many different studies using many different kinds of paradigms (mostly involving strangers), accuracy at recognizing truths and lies is typically around 53% to 58% and rarely better than 65% (DePaulo, Stone, & Lassiter, 1985a; Kraut, 1980).

As people become more familiar with each other they may develop a sense of each other's "baseline" for communicating truthfully (e.g., Miller et al., 1986). This knowledge of what a person is "like" ordinarily can serve as a comparison for judging behavior that seems unusual and might therefore be attributed to deception. Those without a relational history must rely upon characteristics of the communication itself (coherence, content, plausibility) or cultural theories about what cues reliably indicate deception, rather than a portfolio of cues specific to the person learned over the course of many interactions.

A pure form of the "familiarity" hypothesis has been tested in a number of studies in which participants watch, a varying number of times, the exact same truthful baseline segment communicated by a stranger. They then are shown truthful and deceptive test segments from the same stranger, and are asked to identify them as truthful or deceptive. In these studies, accuracy at the test segments indeed improves linearly up to a certain number of repetitions of the baseline truthful segment (about four), then decreases with further repetitions (Bauchner, Brandt, & Miller, 1977; Brandt, Miller, & Hocking, 1980a, 1980b, 1982; Feeley, deTurck, & Young, 1995). Although this kind of familiarity is very different from what might accrue over the course of naturally occurring relationships, the research does at least suggest that familiarity effects could be important.

Outside of the lab, familiarity is also coupled with selection. People selectively continue to interact more often with the people for whom they feel greater affection. Thus, the familiarity-accuracy hypothesis could probably be recast as predicting that we should be best at detecting the deception of people we like the most and to whom we feel closest.

In addition to the knowledge of whatever idiosyncratic cues a relational partner might exhibit when lying (discussed above), familiarity also brings an increased knowledge of personal facts. A person might be successful in convincing a stranger in a bar that his mother is a physician in private practice, but that will not work with his roommate who already knows that Mom is the Secretary of Health and Human Services. Close relationship partners may be advantaged at detecting each other's lies because they know more of the relevant facts than do strangers.

Finally, observers who are familiar with another person may be more accurate at detecting that person's truths and lies not only because they are more sensitive and knowledgeable, but also because the person telling the truths and lies may become rattled by their perceptions of the other person's knowledge. Apart from the question of whether people really are better at detecting the lies of people with whom they are familiar (addressed below), if the persons communicating the lies believe that familiar observers are more accurate, that very expectation can undermine their success at telling a convincing lie. A series of studies has shown that people do expect their lies to be more obvious to people who know them better (e.g., more detectable by friends than strangers) (Anderson, Ansfield, & DePaulo, 1997; Buller, Strzyzewski, & Comstock, 1991; Burgoon, Buller, Dillman, & Walther, 1995). In addition, liars may feel guiltier when their targets are close relationship partners than when they are strangers. With guilt may come more of the kinds of behaviors that are perceived as deceptive (Zuckerman et al., 1981).

As we noted above, the consequences of lies to relational partners may be more severe than the consequences of lies to strangers. This may result in a greater motivation for the liar to get away with the lie. Research on the motivational impairment effect (DePaulo & Kirkendol, 1989; DePaulo, Kirkendol, Tang, & O'Brien, 1988; DePaulo, Lanier, & Davis, 1983; DePaulo, Stone, & Lassiter, 1985b) has shown that when people are especially motivated to get away with their lies (as they may be when lying to people who know them better) but insecure about their ability to lie convincingly, their lies become even more obvious (DePaulo, LeMay, & Epstein, 1991). In most studies of the phenomenon, nonverbal cues were especially important. When judges had access to channels that included nonverbal cues, the lies of the highly motivated group were easier to detect than those of the less motivated group. The same was not true when the judges had access only to transcripts of the communications. A meta-analysis of motivational moderators of cues to deception (Zuckerman et al., 1981) indicated that highly motivated communicators, relative to less motivated ones, showed lower rates of nonverbal behaviors when lying than when telling the truth. In their attempts to control their nonverbal behaviors, they may have instead overcontrolled them. As a result, the highly motivated liars may have appeared unusually inhibited and stiff. This overcontrol can be just as much of a marker of deception as an increase in any of the reliable cues to deception mentioned earlier.

## Familiarity and Deception Detection: The Evidence

All of the lines of reasoning we reviewed justify the prediction that familiarity enhances accuracy at detecting deception, and that closer relationship partners will therefore be especially accurate at detecting each other's deception. There is, however, strikingly little support for this prediction. Three kinds of evidence are relevant. First, there are studies in which accuracy at detecting deception is compared across different relationship categories differing in closeness (e.g., strangers, friends, spouses, parents). Table 14.1 shows the results of all such studies in which the relevant data were reported. As shown in the table, in not one of these studies was there unqualified support for the prediction that partners in closer relationship categories are better at detecting each other's lies than partners in less close relationship categories. (The qualified support will be described later.) A second kind of evidence is correlational: Is relationship closeness correlated with success at detecting deception? Results from the four relevant studies, including multiple estimates from one of the studies (Anderson et al., 1997), are shown in the first column of Table 14.2. Once again, there is simply no support for the hypothesis that closeness is linked to accuracy.

Finally, the relationship between familiarity and accuracy can be studied longitudinally. In the one such study, one member of a same-sex friendship dyad told true or fabricated stories from their life in conversations with the other member, who tried to determine whether the first person's stories were lies or truths (Anderson et al., 1997). They engaged in four such conversations when they had known each other for only about 1.5 months, and then again when they had known each other for about 6.5 months. Once again, there was no unqualified support for the prediction that as relationships develop, people become more accurate at detecting each other's lies. Across all 52 pairs of friends in the study, accuracy was not significantly greater at six months than it had been at one month. (Again, the qualifications will be described later.)

Table 14.1 *Deception detection accuracy for different relationship categories*

|  | | Accuracy | |
| --- | --- | --- | --- |
| **Millar and Millar (1995)[w]** | | | |
| Study 1 | | | |
|  | Audio | Audiovisual | Overall |
| Stranger | .45$_a$ | .55$_{ab}$ | .50 |
| Friend or relative | .57$_b$ | .48$_a$ | .52 |
| Study 2 | | | |
|  | Visual | Audiovisual | Overall |
| Stranger | .48$_a$ | .61$_{ab}$ | .54 |
| Friend or relative | .56$_b$ | .51$_a$ | .54 |
| **Comadena (1982)[x]** | Male | Female | Average |
| Friend | 4.87$_{ab}$ | 4.75$_{ab}$ | 4.48 |
| Spouse | 4.08$_a$ | 5.80$_b$ | 5.28 |
| **Fleming, Darley, Hilton, and Kojetin (1990)[y]** | | | |
| Study 2 (Transcript) | | Average | |
| Strangers | | .30$_a$ | |
| Friends | | .30$_a$ | |
| Study 3 (Audiovisual) | | Average | |
| Strangers | | .34$_a$ | |
| Friends | | .34$_a$ | |

| **Fleming and Darley (1991)** | Secret meeting | Personal preference | Average | Average for familiar participants[z] |
| --- | --- | --- | --- | --- |
| Fellow Senders | .46$_a$ | .63$_a$ | .54$_a$ | |
| Friends | .44$_{ab}$ | .57$_a$ | .50$_a$ | .51 |
| Parents | .36$_b$ | .60$_a$ | .48$_a$ | |
| Adult Strangers | .36$_b$ | .56$_a$ | .46$_a$ | |

*Note:* Means marked with different subscripts differ from each other (within each study) at $p < .05$.

[w] Chance accuracy for these studies was .50. Strangers did not differ significantly from friends on accuracy in either reported study.

[x] There was a trend for spouses to do better than friends overall at detecting deception ($p = .07$).

[y] Chance accuracy for these studies was .25

[z] This average is based upon the Fellow Senders, Friends, and Parents categories.

Table 14.2. *Correlations of closeness with confidence, accuracy, and truth bias*

| | Relationship | Closeness and Confidence | | Closeness and Accuracy | | Closeness and Truth Bias | |
|---|---|---|---|---|---|---|---|
| McCornack and Parks (1986) | Dating Couples | .26 | | .02 | | .16 | |
| Levine and McCornack (1992) | Dating Couples | .38 | | .06 | | −.02 | |
| Stiff, Kim, and Ramesh (1992) | Close Friends | | | −.07 | | .01 | |
| Anderson, Ansfield, and DePaulo (1997) | Same-sex Friends | Time 1 | Time 2 | Time 1 | Time 2 | Time 1 | Time 2 |
| | (RCI[a]) | −.01 | .34 | .01 | .22 | −.22 | .22 |
| | (SCI[b]) | −.02 | .40 | −.11 | .10 | .03 | .20 |

[a] Relationship Closeness Inventory (Berscheid, Snyder, & Omoto, 1989).
[b] Subjective Closeness Inventory (Aron, Aron, & Smollan, 1992).

## Explaining the Weak Link

*Too Much Information?* What might explain this failure to find an unqualified link between relationship closeness and accuracy at detecting deception? One possibility is that it was misguided in the first place to assume that it is advantageous to have more information rather than less in one's quest to ferret out lies. Millar and Millar (1995) have proposed that the reverse is true. They believe that when close relationship partners try to detect each other's deception, they bring to mind a great deal of information about each other. When that information is called to mind in the context of all of the cues that are usually available (vocal, verbal, and visual), the total amount of available information is overwhelming. The deception detectors deal with this by processing cues selectively or heuristically, instead of carefully searching for genuine clues to deceit. When instead the new information available to relationship partners is limited, they will utilize their special knowledge about each other more effectively. In a pair of studies, Millar and Millar (1995) reported supportive results. Friends and relatives of senders did relatively better than strangers at detecting deception when they had only audio (speech) cues or only visual cues available to them than when they had both audio and visual cues; in contrast, they did relatively worse than strangers when they had both audio and visual cues available (see Table 14.1).

*Taken for Granted?* An explanation for the Millar and Millar (1995) results that the authors did not mention might be called the "taking each other for granted" effect. Perhaps under ordinary circumstances (e.g., when all of the usual information is available, as in the audiovisual condition), close relationship partners take for granted that they know each other well and do not have to pay very close attention to each other's cues in order to discern what the other is thinking or feeling. It is only when circumstances become more challenging (e.g., when only audio or only visual cues are available) that partners believe that they need to pay closer attention. When they are thereby prompted to observe more carefully, they can call on their greater knowledge and insights about each other to interpret each other's cues more accurately than can strangers who do not have the benefit of familiarity.

*Looking but Not Seeing?* Patterson (1995, 1997) posits a parallel process model of social interaction, in which participants must simultaneously engage in social behavior (i.e., self-presentation) and social cognition (i.e., decoding nonverbal cues). The division of cognitive resources necessary to serve multiple goals in social interaction can result in less involved processing of nonverbal behavior. This general model is particularly applicable to deception detection, since there are nonverbal cues that reliably differentiate lies from truths. These cues, if noticed and processed correctly, should lead to enhanced deception detection accuracy. But, if factors such as expectations about the relational partner (such as the expectation of honesty), heightened self-presentational concerns within a relationship (such as the need to appear supportive in a given interaction), or, as Millar and Millar (1995) suggest, a surfeit of social information to process about a relational partner interfere with this process, those cues to deception may never be noticed.

In order for attempts at deception detection to succeed, cognitive resources may need to be diverted from other goals and recommitted to the processing of cues to deception. For example, in the Millar and Millar studies, when one channel of social information is shut down (audio or video), the resources that ordinarily would be devoted to processing social information in those channels may be focused instead on those cues that still are available for processing. If those cues are valid indicators of deceit, accuracy may improve.

*The Other Side of Familiarity?* Another explanation for the findings of surprisingly low rates of accuracy for close relationship partners is that as relationships develop, the partners become more adept at crafting communications uniquely designed to fool each other. That is, perhaps as partners develop the potential to detect each other's lies more successfully, they are also faced with lies that are increasingly difficult to detect. This hypothesis is only helpful in explaining the low rates of deception detection accuracy in studies in which relationship partners interacted directly and uniquely with each other. It cannot account for the results of studies in which people from different relationship categories tried to detect the exact same truths and lies (as, for example, when the senders were in a room with people from several different relationship categories and told their truths and lies to all of them simultaneously).

There is some evidence for the possibility that people tell more convincing lies to people they know better. Buller and Aune (1987) found that strangers, when lying, exhibited less forward lean, were less vocally pleasant, and made more brief head and facial adaptors (touches) compared to when they were telling the truth. Intimates, however, showed a different pattern of behaviors. When they were lying, intimates showed more vocal activity, including more vocal clarity, loudness, pitch variety, pleasantness, rate, and fluency. Rate and fluency, at least, correlate with perceptions of truthfulness (Zuckerman et al., 1981), and it is possible that the other vocal behaviors might also enhance credibility. So, in short, strangers, when lying, exhibited some of the behaviors stereotypically associated with perceptions of deceptiveness, while intimates seemed to be projecting cues associated with truthfulness.

There were two noteworthy exceptions. When a person was lying to an intimate relationship partner, compared to when telling the truth, there were more periods of time when neither person was looking at the other. Also, in those intimate dyads, the targets of deception showed more one-sided gaze times when they were looking at their partner, but the partner was not looking at them. This may suggest that there is a general reluctance for the liar to look at the relationship partner when lying, and perhaps a tendency for the target also to avoid looking at the liar, except when the target knows the liar is not looking. This behavioral tendency may limit access to some visual cues in the situation, and if the liar is not focused on the target, then the liar's full focus may be on controlling his or her own behavior.

*Looking for Lies in All the Wrong Places?*   Since we know that some cues are accurate (though imperfect) indicators of deception, and that some channels are less controllable than others and therefore more informative about deception, it is possible to ask whether people are paying attention to the "correct" channels in their attempts to detect deceit. In the longitudinal study of friendship development and deception detection, Anderson and his colleagues (Anderson et al., 1997) asked participants what it was about each story that made them think it was either the truth or a lie. This was open-ended, and participants could report anything that they believed had probative value in determining the veracity of the story. In this study, participants were directed to try to discover whether their friends were telling the truth. It is precisely this sort of situation, involving direct instruction to uncover possible deceit, that should elicit careful consideration of all available information.

The responses were quite varied, ranging from specific nonverbal cues to mere restatement of the original guess of truth or lie ("I thought it was a lie . . ."). Overall, people most often mentioned cues relevant to the verbal component of the lie; that is, the content, the consistency of the story with the storyteller's personality, and the plausibility of the story. They did this more than they mentioned other cues, such as paralinguistic cues (e.g., tone of voice, speech errors, the "flow" of the story), or visual cues (e.g., specific perceived behaviors or visual impressions of the speaker's general demeanor). Men mentioned relatively more verbal cues than did women, while women mentioned relatively more visual cues than men. Mentioning these cues, however, was not related to accuracy. Men and women mentioned the paralinguistic cues equally, and those who did mention paralinguistic cues were more likely to be correct than those who did not. This finding mirrors earlier experimental work by DePaulo, Lassiter, and Stone (1982). In that study, participants specifically told to attend to tone of voice were better at detecting deception than those who were given no such hint. Perhaps some of the participants in the friendship study attended to these telltale paralinguistic cues without prompting from the experimenters and thereby achieved greater accuracy.

Participants in the friendship study were relatively more likely to mention visual cues (including the friend's general demeanor) when their friends were lying than when they were telling the truth. Further, they were relatively more likely to mention verbal cues (including consistency with the speaker's personality and plausibility) when their friends were telling the truth than when they were lying. Therefore, in the cues that they reported using, the participants successfully distinguished the truths from the lies. In an indirect or implicit way, they accurately detected deception. This is an especially noteworthy finding, because when the participants were asked directly whether their friend was lying, their accuracy was unimpressive. In fact, for the men, it was never better than chance. The friends seem to have a kind of knowledge of each other's truthfulness that they do not utilize effectively when asked directly to report whether or not a story is a lie.

*Overcoming the Barriers: Relationship Status and Sex Differences in Detecting Deception.* We began by suggesting that particular individuals may have their own idiosyncratic ways of lying, and if so, the people who know them best and have had the most exposure to such cues may be best at recognizing them. However, there may be another dynamic that works to obscure cues to deception, and that is the apparent tendency for liars to act in more stereotypically truthful ways when lying to people they know well. Further, in one study, participants who more often mentioned looking at one category of cues known to discriminate truths from lies, paralinguistic cues, were more accurate. Attention to this channel may yield greater deception detection accuracy. These suggestions are tentative, though, as the evidence is sparse or indirect. The questions merit further research attention.

Another set of explanations involves motivational mechanisms. These explanations posit that as relationships develop, partners become not only more knowledgeable about each other, but also more invested emotionally. They come to care deeply about what the other person is like and how the other person treats them. For example, in close personal relationships, partners may become invested in their belief that their relationship partner does not lie and especially that their partner does not lie to them. This emotional investment can blind them to a wide range of lies that their partner might tell.

There are also particular lies that hide information that could be especially hurtful – for example, information that is threatening to the relationship, such as the partner's feelings toward other attractive people (Simpson, Ickes, & Blackstone, 1995). In these instances, relationship partners may be especially insensitive to the lies, relative to strangers. They do not see through the lie to the information covered up by the lie, largely because they do not want to see it.

With both cognitive and motivational impediments to the accurate detection of the deceptions of close relationship partners, only certain kinds of people may be able to rise to the challenges and utilize the advantages that familiarity might then give them. For example, perhaps people who are securely attached to their relationship partner, or who have had a history of very positive and reassuring experiences within the particular relationship, are not so threatened by the possibility of deception by their partners. It may not be as important to have an entirely positive relationship history (which may be nearly impossible) as to have a history of successfully confronting and resolving challenges to the relationship (Holmes & Rempel, 1989).

Supportive evidence comes from the longitudinal study of same-sex friendships (Anderson et al., 1997). Pairs of friends were categorized as either "solid" friends or just "middling." In the solid friendship pairs, both friends in the dyad reported feeling close to each other at both time periods (1.5 months and 6.5 months into the friendship). Their feelings of closeness either remained stable over time or increased. The middling pairs, in contrast, reported lower overall levels of closeness and no marked increases in closeness from 1 month to 6. Consistent with predictions, it was only the solid friends who showed any significant improvement in their deception detection accuracy as their relationship developed over time.

Anderson and his colleagues reported one other important moderator of the link between relationship development and deception detection accuracy: the sex of the pair. In analyses that included all of the pairs of friends, they found that although there was no significant improvement with time across all of the pairs, there was significant improvement for the women. At 1.5 months into the friendships, neither the women nor the men could detect their friends' lies at better than chance accuracy. At 6.5 months into the friendships, the men were still at chance level, but the women had improved. The findings are paralleled by Comadena's comparisons of friends and spouses (see Table 14.1). When men were the observers, they were no better (and tended to be somewhat worse) at detecting the lies of their spouse than the lies of a friend. Women, in contrast, were significantly better at detecting the lies of their closer relationship partner – that is, they were better at reading their spouse than their friend.

The two sets of results are especially meaningful in light of a puzzle in the literature on sex differences in nonverbal sensitivity (Rosenthal & DePaulo, 1979a; 1979b). Women are better than men at reading nonverbal cues that do not involve deception, and they are better at other interpersonal sensitivity tasks such as face recognition and empathy (e.g., Hall, 1984; Hoffman, 1977). Yet, across all of the deception detection studies that involve strangers, women do not do any better than men (Zuckerman et al., 1981), and in at least one way (reading underlying emotions), they do even worse (DePaulo, Epstein, & Wyer, 1993). The studies of sex differences in deception detection in personal relationships suggest that women develop sensitivity to other people's truths and lies only when they have come to care about the other person and how that person really feels. When instead they are reading the truths and lies of strangers, they politely take what is communicated at face value.

*A Winding Road to Accuracy.* One final and very important explanation for the weak or nonexistent link between relationship closeness and deception detection accuracy is that the relationship between closeness and accuracy is not a direct one, but an indirect one. To see the links between closeness and accuracy, it is necessary to trace the steps in the hypothesized intervening process (McCornack & Parks, 1986; Levine & McCornack, 1992).

In a model formulated by McCornack and Parks (1986), relationship closeness is linked to confidence. As relationships develop, partners become more confident that their judgments about each other are accurate. This confidence, in turn, is linked to the truth bias (a bias toward guessing that someone is telling the truth). This hypothesized link represents the somewhat counterintuitive prediction that as relationship partners become more confident in their judgments of each other, they will be more likely to perceive each other as telling the truth (as opposed to the more intuitive prediction that as partners come to perceive each other as more truthful, they become more confident). The negative relationship between truth bias and accuracy is the final link in the model: As truth bias increases, accuracy should decrease. In sum, then, the McCornack and Parks (1986) model predicts that relationship closeness is linked to lower accuracy at detecting deception because closeness increases confidence which strengthens the truth bias which then undermines accuracy. We turn next to the literature on the truth bias.

## Truth Bias

> *Such are promises*
> *All lies and jest*
> *Still, a man hears what he wants to hear*
> *And disregards the rest.*
>
> Paul Simon and Art Garfunkel, "The Boxer"

> *Imagination is a powerful deceiver*
> *When you try to believe her just a little too much . . .*
>
> Elvis Costello, "Imagination Is a Powerful Deceiver"

In the literature on the communication of deception, the truth bias is defined as the tendency to see more communications as truths than as lies, even when truths and lies actually occur equally often in the set of messages being judged. Across the many studies in the literature – most of which involved senders and judges who were strangers to each other – the truth bias is a very robust phenomenon (Zuckerman et al., 1981).

The truth bias fits comfortably into several important perspectives on human communication. For example, Grice (1975) has postulated that ordinary conversation is predicated on the assumption that speakers try to convey messages that are truthful (as well as clear, unambiguous, and relevant). If we could not make these assumptions, social discourse would seem much more perilous.

Writing from a dramaturgical perspective, Goffman (1959) does not suggest that people really are truthful nor even that conversationalists believe each other to be truthful. Instead, he maintains that we all assume particular "faces" or identities that we present to our fellow interactants. They, in turn, go along with our self-presentational shows. They do not ordinarily challenge our faces, and they assume that their own self-presentations will be likewise accepted.

The truth bias also follows easily from Gilbert's (1991) model of how mental systems believe. Drawing from Spinozan philosophy, Gilbert argues that belief comes automatically; everything that is comprehended is initially taken to be true. To disbelieve requires an extra effort. Anything that increases our mental burdens (e.g., fatigue, distraction, a difficult task) will impair our ability to abandon the truth bias. The truth bias, then, is the default setting. It can be overcome only if the perceiver has ample motivation and sufficient cognitive resources to do the work of disbelieving. Patterson (1995; chapter 12 in this volume) echoes this in his parallel process model of nonverbal communication. The challenges of social interaction leave too few cognitive resources to process effectively all of the information available, perhaps including the extra step of disbelief.

The truth "bias" may simply be an accurate reflection of ordinary life. Because people really do tell the truth far more often than they lie, it is entirely appropriate for perceivers to develop an inclination to see other people's communications as truthful. Although this can seem like a mistake in laboratory paradigms in which lies are just as common as truths, outside of the lab it is not (Funder, 1987). For our purposes, the fact that the truth bias occurs reliably across many studies is less important than the question of whether people who are closer to each other are more inclined to see each other as truthful than are people who are less close.

### Closeness and Truth Bias: The Evidence

As we did when summarizing the results of the link between closeness and deception detection accuracy, we will review three kinds of evidence pertinent to the link between closeness and truth bias. First, there are studies in which truth bias is compared across different relationship categories that differ in closeness. There are only three such studies in the published literature. Millar and Millar (1995) found, in the results that were combined across their two studies, that friends and relatives showed a significantly greater truth bias than did strangers. Friends also showed a significantly greater truth bias than strangers in the one other relevant study (Buller et al., 1991).

Correlational support for the link between closeness and truth bias is unimpressive. As shown in the second column of Table 14.2, not a single study provides strong support for that link. Even taking all of the studies into account, meta-analytically, does not support a direct, linear relationship between closeness and truth bias (combined $r$ =

.05). If the McCornack and Parks (1986) model is correct, however, the zero-order correlation between closeness and truth bias is understandably unimpressive. According to their model, closeness should be positively correlated with confidence, and confidence, in turn, should be positively correlated with truth bias. Thus, the link between closeness and truth bias is indirect rather than direct.

There are several correlational reports in the literature of each of the first two links in the model, and those have been summarized quantitatively in a recent review (DePaulo, Charlton, Cooper, Lindsay, & Muhlenbruck, 1997). Across four studies (Anderson et al., 1997; Fleming, Darley, Hilton, & Kojetin, 1990; Levine & McCornack, 1992; McCornack & Parks, 1986), closeness was positively and significantly correlated with confidence, mean $r = .16$, as the model would predict. The support for this portion of the model is stronger for developed relationships. In the longitudinal study of same-sex friends, the correlations between closeness (feeling close and behaving close) and confidence were essentially zero when the friends had known each other for only a month, but were more impressive, mean $r = .37$, five months later. The other studies dealing exclusively with people who knew each other (dating partners: Levine & McCornack, 1992; McCornack & Parks, 1986), also showed relatively high correlations between closeness and confidence ($r = .34$ and .26, respectively).

The second hypothesized link, between confidence and truth bias, was also supported, but qualified. The mean correlation across nine estimates was also positive and significant, though not large, $r = .16$, $p < .05$. More importantly for this discussion, this correlation was significantly larger for studies in which the senders and judges were friends or were dating, $r = .35$, than it was for studies in which the senders and judges did not know each other, $r = .08$. Perhaps, then, those in closer relationships make the confident assumption that their partners are telling the truth, while confidence for those in more casual relationships can go toward either belief or disbelief. Whatever the interpretation, it appears that the link between confidence and truth bias is stronger for relationship partners than for strangers.

Preliminary indications, then, are that McCornack and Parks (1986) are correct in suggesting that relationship closeness is linked to truth bias, but the link is indirect, and may apply only to those in established relationships. Closeness is correlated with confidence, and confidence is correlated with truth bias, at least for relational partners. Studies reporting tests of all of the links within the same sample, including the third and final link between truth bias and lower deception detection accuracy, have also been supportive (Levine & McCornack, 1992; McCornack & Parks, 1986).

The link between closeness and truth bias can also be examined longitudinally. In the longitudinal study of same-sex friendships (Anderson et al., 1997), there was an unexpected drop in truth bias from the first or second month of the friendship (68%) to the sixth or seventh (58%). The men and women contributed in different ways to this effect. The men showed a weaker truth bias because at Time 2, compared to Time 1, they inaccurately perceived more of the truths as lies. Women, in contrast, showed a weaker truth bias because they were becoming more accurate over time at recognizing the lies as lies.

The unexpected drop in truth bias from Time 1 to Time 2 might also be attributable to the fact that in the sample as a whole, relationship closeness also declined. To see whether the truth bias might increase for the closest of the friends, we eliminated from the analysis a small number of pairs who were no longer friends at Time 2, and then compared the changes over time in truth bias for two remaining groups of friends – those in which both partners reported feeling especially close to each other at both time periods, and whose closeness remained stable or even increased over time; and another group of friends in which the partners also reported feeling close to each other, but not as close, or as stably close over time, as the first group. In this new analysis, the less close group still showed a decline in truth bias from Time 1 to Time 2. Like the men in the analysis of the complete sample, they were especially likely to misperceive truths as lies at Time 2. For the most solid subsample of friends, there was no decline over time in their truth bias, but there was no significant increase, either.

In sum, then, the evidence so far suggests that people in close relationship categories, such as friends and family members, are more inclined to see each other as truthful than are pairs of strangers. Within categories, such as dating couples, closeness is not directly linked to truth bias, but it may be indirectly linked to it.

## *Explaining the Link between Relationship Status and Truth Bias*

What might account for the greater truth bias shown by friends and relatives than by strangers? One possibility is that the truth bias is a cognitive shortcut through the barrage of information available to friends and relatives that is not available to strangers (Millar & Millar, 1995). Perhaps close relationship partners opt not to wade through all that they know about each other in order to weigh the likelihood that what they are hearing is deceptive; instead, they simply assume it is the truth. Strangers, in contrast, consider the message more closely, because the message itself is about all they have to go by.

The McCornack and Parks (1986) model suggests that close relationship partners assume truthfulness more often not because they are overwhelmed by what they have come to know about each other but because they are bolstered by it. Closeness, they propose, increases confidence. Partners who feel more confident may also feel that there is less need to scrutinize each other's behavior closely. Instead, they can simply assume that they are hearing the truth (Levine & McCornack, 1992).

The assumption of truthfulness may be a simple heuristic that develops directly from past experiences. Because relationship partners have had many past experiences of communicating with each other truthfully, they assume that the truth is being told in the present as well. This dynamic would fit well with what we know about the rates of everyday lying. People do tell fewer little lies (per social interaction) to their friends and relatives than to strangers.

Whether the truth bias is forged from confidence or follows more directly from past experience, it should be undermined by intimations that the partner may not be telling the truth at the present. McCornack and Levine (1990b) tested this hypothesis in a study in which they manipulated perceivers' current suspiciousness and measured their dispositional suspiciousness. Perceivers were told that their partner might be lying (medium state suspiciousness) or would definitely be lying at some point (high suspiciousness), or they were given no information about this (low suspiciousness). When manipulated suspiciousness was low, truth bias was high (about 80%) and accuracy at detecting deception was low (about 54%). However, when perceivers who were already dispositionally suspicious were made moderately suspicious of their partners' communications, their truth bias dropped (to 68%) and their accuracy improved markedly (to 70%).

The participants in the McCornack and Levine (1990b) study were couples who had been dating an average of about one year. They probably already had a history of truthful exchanges with each other, and they may have developed confidence in their judgments of truthfulness. But importantly, they probably also had the informational basis for discriminating lies from truths, once their confidence was undermined by the suggestion that their partner might be lying to them at that very moment. In another study in which suspiciousness was manipulated between pairs of strangers, there was no increment in accuracy (Toris & DePaulo, 1984). Instead, the suspiciousness served only to darken the participants' views of each other. Suspicious perceivers were more likely to see their partners as lying overall, but they were no more likely to see them as lying when they really were lying compared to when they were actually telling the truth.

The truth bias may also have an important motivational component that is especially significant in the context of close personal relationships. Perceivers may be motivated to believe that the people in their lives who are especially important to them are basically very honest people, and that they are especially honest to the perceivers in particular. Perceivers may assume that their close relationship partners are telling the truth because that is what they deeply hope and wish for.

In assuming truthfulness, perceivers risk missing a lie by ignoring potential verbal and nonverbal cues to deception. But perhaps in close personal relationships, that is seen as a potentially less damaging risk than the opposite error of disbelieving the truth. Unjustly accusing a relationship partner of lying may be very costly.

## Consequences

> *There ain't no need to act like I shot your dog,*
> *I was only tellin' a lie . . .*
> James Taylor, "I Was Only Telling a Lie"

Since communal relationships (Clark & Mills, 1979; Clark, Mills, & Powell, 1986) seem necessarily built upon trust, any breach of that trust is likely to have consequences for the relationship, and these consequences may place the relationship itself in jeopardy. Planalp and Honeycutt (1985) found deception to be a major category of uncertainty-increasing behavior within close relationships, reducing belief in the honesty of the partner, as well as changing beliefs about fairness in the relationship. Although communication is ordinarily thought of as reducing uncertainty in a relationship, cases such as deception clearly violate this assumption and can negatively impact the course of the relationship.

## Consequences and Motivations

Anecdotally, targets of serious lies sometimes claim that they were more distressed by the fact that their partner lied to them than they were by the information that their partner was trying to hide with the lie. But is this really so? McCornack and Levine (1990a) pursued this question by asking students to describe a recently discovered lie told by a relational partner. The students rated the importance to them of the information that was covered by the lie, the importance of the fact of the lie, the intensity of their emotional reaction upon discovering the lie, and the degree of their romantic love for their partner. The importance ascribed to the act of lying did indeed predict the intensity of targets' emotional reactions to the discovery of the lies, as did the importance of the information covered by the lie, and the targets' love for the liar. However, the strongest predictor of whether or not the relationship had been terminated was not the importance of lying, but instead the importance of the information that had been covered by the lie.

The consequences of this finding for nonverbal behavior in deceptive situations depend upon the liar's realization of the severe consequences that may come about should the deception be uncovered. In situations in which the truth being covered is likely to be deeply distressing to the target of the lie, the motivation for the liar to get away with the lie is sure to be greater than if the hidden truth is of no consequence to the target of the lie. A strong motivation may undermine the liar's chances for success (DePaulo & Kirkendol, 1989).

Women seem more sensitive than men to violations of the sanctity of close personal relationships. For example, there are more different kinds of behaviors that they view as relational transgressions (Metts, 1994). With regard to deception in particular, women regard it as more unacceptable than do men, both in friendships and in romantic relationships, and they regard the act of telling a lie as a more significant relational event than do men. They are also more distressed than are men upon discovering the deceit of a close relational partner (Levine, McCornack, & Avery, 1992). These sex differences may be especially problematic in opposite sex relationships, because the partners could feel very differently about the deception and its acceptability and significance, leading to conflict over discovered deception. Further, the sex differences may impact motivations, in that women may be more concerned with successfully lying than men, since lying is more significant for them. Again, this may undermine female liars' attempts at deception due to heightened motivation (DePaulo & Kirkendol, 1989).

Most analyses of the implications of lying for relationships focus on the reactions of the target upon discovering the deception. However, an intriguing phenomenon has been recently demonstrated, whereby liars denigrate the persons to whom they told their lies, and other people as well, even when their lies remain undiscovered (Sagarin, Rhoads, & Cialdini, 1997). The fact of telling a lie is threatening to the self-image of the liars; they can try to cope with the threat by telling themselves that other people are also dishonest and would have acted the same way. This "deceiver distrust" is still another potential impediment to the accurate detection of truths and lies in close personal relationships. People who have lied to their relationship partners may be motivated to see those partners as behaving deceptively themselves. Because the cues to deception in actual interactions are always somewhat ambiguous (there is no nose that always grows when lies are told, and never otherwise), confident misinterpretations that a partner is being deceitful may come easily. The targets may then be doubly victimized, first by the liars' lies and then by their misplaced suspicions.

### Accurate Deception Detection: Mixed Blessing?

Although accurate deception detection may seem like a worthwhile goal, would perfect deception detection really be a boon? Certainly, those "little white lies" that serve to bolster self-esteem may be welcome, at least to some, and seeing through such lies may leave one with both low self-esteem and a sense of distrust. More serious lies, however, may be a different story. Uncovering serious lies may mean the end of relationships, careers, and lifestyles. Moral issues aside, uncovering deception may not always be in the best interest of either the target of the deception or the liar. This is not an endorsement of deception, but merely a practical consideration in light of some of the motivational explanations we have described for low rates of deception detection accuracy. To maintain a relationship in the face of a threatening event covered by a lie, one might be motivated to believe the lie rather than have to deal with the reality of the threatening event.

## Summary

*She can ruin your faith with her casual lies*
*And she only reveals what she wants you to see . . .*
Billy Joel, "She's Always a Woman to Me"

*At lovers' perjuries*
*They say Jove laughs*
William Shakespeare, *Romeo and Juliet*

In theory, there are many reasons to expect close relationship partners to be better at detecting each other's lies than pairs of people who know each other only superficially, if at all. For example, close relationship partners, because of their many experiences with one another, should be far more familiar with each other's styles of lying and truth telling. As observers of each other's behavior, close relationship partners believe that they have special insights into each other's lies; anecdotally, they can often tell you what they think are the signs that their partner is lying. As perpetrators of deceit, close relationship partners hold analogous beliefs: They think their partners are more likely than strangers to recognize their lies. Apparently, all that is missing is the empirical evidence.

There are two ways in which the relevant data are missing. Very few studies of the communication of deception in different kinds of relationships exist; and, from those few studies that do exist, there is no unqualified support for a direct link between closeness and success at detecting deception. We will try to make sense of the missing link, but we also caution that at some point in the future, when a substantial literature exists, the link may in fact appear.

Theoretically, it is possible that close relationship partners never gain any special knowledge about each other's styles of lying because people in such relationships simply do not lie to each other. With regard to the little lies of everyday life, close relationships are in fact safe havens; the rate of such lies is markedly lower in closer relationships. But it is still nontrivial. For example, among adult pairs, the lowest rate of everyday lying reported in the literature is between spouses, and that rate is still about one lie in every 10 social interactions (DePaulo & Kashy, 1998). Moreover, in the domain of serious lies, close relationships are breeding grounds for deceit. More than 60% of the most serious lies in people's lives involve their closest and most important relationship partners (DePaulo et al., 1997).

Another possible explanation for why close relationship partners show no special insight into each other's lies is that there are no reliable cues to deception, or that there are no reliable cues to the lies that close relationship partners tell to each other. Meta-analytic reviews (e.g., Zuckerman et al., 1981) have shown that there are in fact moderately reliable cues to deception, though the vast majority of the studies in those reviews involved people who were unacquainted with each other. In the one study of the nonverbal behaviors characteristic of the truths and lies told to casual and close relationship partners (Buller & Aune, 1987), there were behaviors that distinguished truths from lies in both the casual and the close dyads, though in the close dyads, the cues were not the stereotypical ones. Accuracy at detecting the lies of close relationship partners is sometimes greater than chance; this is indirect evidence that useful cues are available. But it does not sate the need for further work on this topic.

If lies are told at a nontrivial rate in close relationships, and cues to those lies are potentially available, then perhaps deception is not detected very successfully because it is too difficult to notice and learn such cues. Cues to deception are in fact probabilistic. There is no one behavior that always occurs when a person is lying and never otherwise. It should, then, be difficult to learn these cues and to utilize them effectively. But apparently, it is not impossible. Participants in one study improved their ability to detect lies after receiving feedback on just eight trials (Zuckerman et al., 1984). However, the improvement was specific to the persons they saw during the training and did not generalize to others. This is more indirect evidence that ways of lying may be somewhat idiosyncratic. It is also evidence that people can learn to do better at recognizing the relevant information.

The Zuckerman et al. (1984) training study, and other studies reporting attempts to improve people's skill at catching liars (see Ansfield, DePaulo, & Cooper, 1997, for a review), all involved lie detectors who were strangers to the communicators. Such studies do not address the possibility that lies told to close relationship partners may be difficult to detect because intimates learn to craft lies that will be especially effective at fooling their particular partner. They also do not capture other special challenges to the detection of the lies of close relationship partners, such as the possibility that the tremendous amount of information that a person can bring to mind about a close partner when attempting to detect that person's deceit can undermine rather than augment success.

Because there are so many challenges to the accurate detection of the deception of a close relationship partner, it may be that only certain people learn to succeed at this task. And in fact, there are indications that women, but not men, learn to detect deception better as relationships progress, and that friends who are closer to each other show more improvement than friends who are not as close.

Another very different explanation for why close relationship partners show no overall advantage at detecting each other's deception is that, at some level, they really do not want to succeed at such a task. The "reward" of accurately spotting a lie may come at the cost of keeping the relationship whole. In some cases, the maintenance of the relationship will be more important than uncovering the lie or the truth behind it, and therefore the partner will opt to let the lie pass.

Relational partners may also be overconfident about their partner's honesty and simply assume truthfulness rather than scrutinizing each communication. In fact, there is evidence that the truth bias is stronger among intimates than strangers. The assumption of truthfulness in close relationships is not entirely irrational. In everyday life, truths are far more plentiful than lies, and the imbalance is even greater in closer relationships. Simply assuming truthfulness will yield reasonable accuracy in real life, though not in laboratory studies in which the persons to be judged are typically lying just as often as they are telling the truth. Moreover, it may be cognitively easier, and better for the relationship, to forgo the temptation constantly to scrutinize messages for signs of lies.

Our review of the dynamics of deception suggests that the forces at work within a relationship can both help and hinder deception detection. The net result will vary with the specific circumstances. For example, because the truth bias is undermined by suspicion, a stray credit card receipt for a hotel room may motivate one partner to scrutinize closely the behavior of the other partner while asking about the damning evidence. The liar, confronted with the evidence, is likely to display a great deal of anxiety. Further, since the liar may feel pressure to get away with the lie, or else be sued for divorce, the liar may try too hard to control all relevant nonverbal behaviors, and as a result, may end up looking overcontrolled and unnatural, and by implication, guilty. The net result in this case would be a caught lie.

Different situations could occur that would result in false accusations of lying, or correct judgments of truthfulness, or missed lies.

We have carefully considered the question of whether highly accurate detection of deception in close personal relationships is possible. We want to end with the question of whether it is desirable. In the realm of everyday lies, the kinds of lies that are relatively more frequent in close relationships than in casual ones are altruistic lies. If Juliet were to learn to detect such lies more successfully, she would more often realize that her new haircut reminded Romeo of his least favorite zoo animal; that in his heart, the dinner she slaved to prepare for him took second place to spam; and that her sweet declarations of love were, to him, sometimes cloying.

And what of the truly serious lies? Had Romeo been able to see through Juliet's most serious deception (her faked death), then the "star-cross'd lovers" might have lived, settled down in a house in Verona with a white picket fence, and had 2.4 children. The discovery of other serious lies may not be as beneficial to the relationship. If Juliet had lied about a clandestine affair, instead, then Romeo, and the relationship, might have been better off if the affair had remained hidden.

Although lying is ordinarily condemned as a bad act, some truths can hurt so much that the liar is loathe to inflict such pain on a loved one. Therefore, one relationship norm (honesty) is accorded lower status than another (avoiding hurting the partner). The Romeos of the world may be willing to collude in the deception (though this will not necessarily be a conscious decision), to avoid the pain that the discovery and acknowledgment of Juliet's cheating heart would cause. By remaining blithely oblivious to the deceit, Romeo can feel secure in Juliet's love for him, and in his idealized view of her as an honorable and trustworthy woman. As Shakespeare concluded, in a more pragmatic, yet less tragic work,

> *Therefore I lie with her, and she with me,*
> *And in our faults by lies we flattered be.*

William Shakespeare, Sonnet 138

### References

Altman, I., & Taylor, D. A. (1973). *Social penetration: The development of interpersonal relationships*. New York: Holt, Rinehart, & Winston.

Anderson, D. E., Ansfield, M. E., & DePaulo, B. M. (1997). Friendship development, nonverbal behavior, and deception detection. Manuscript in preparation.

Ansfield, M. E., DePaulo, B. M., & Cooper, H. (1997). Can accuracy at deception detection be improved? Manuscript in preparation.

Aron, A., Aron, E. A., & Smollan, D. (1992). Inclusion of the other in the self scale and the structure of interpersonal closeness. *Journal of Personality and Social Psychology, 63,* 596–612.

Bauchner, J. E., Brandt, D. R., & Miller, G. R. (1977). The truth/deception attribution: Effects of varying levels of information availability. In B. D. Ruben (Ed.), *Communication Yearbook 1* (pp. 229–243). New Brunswick, NJ: Transaction Books.

Berscheid, E., Snyder, M., & Omoto, A. M. (1989). The relationship closeness inventory: Assessing the closeness of interpersonal relationships. *Journal of Personality and Social Psychology, 57,* 792–807.

Bochner, A. P. (1982). On the efficacy of openness in close relationships. *Communications Yearbook, 5,* 109–124.

Brandt, D. R., Miller, G. R., & Hocking, J. E. (1980a). Effects of self-monitoring and familiarity on deception detection. *Communication Quarterly, 28,* 3–10.

Brandt, D. R., Miller, G. R., & Hocking, J. E. (1980b). The truth deception attribution: Effects of familiarity on the ability of observers to detect deception. *Human Communication Research, 6,* 99–110.

Brandt, D. R., Miller, G. R., & Hocking, J. E. (1982). Familiarity and lie detection: A replication and extension. *Western Journal of Speech Communication, 46,* 276–290.

Buller, D. B., & Aune, R. K. (1987). Nonverbal cues to deception among intimates, friends, and strangers. *Journal of Nonverbal Behavior, 11,* 269–290.

Buller, D. B., Strzyzewski, K. D., & Comstock, J. (1991). Interpersonal deception: I. Deceivers' reactions to receivers' suspicions and probing. *Communication Monographs, 58,* 1–24.

Burgoon, J. K., Buller, D. B., Dillman, L., & Walther, J. B. (1995). Interpersonal deception: IV. Effects of suspicion on perceived communication and nonverbal behavior dynamics. *Human Communication Research, 22,* 163–196.

Camden, C., Motley, M. T., & Wilson, A. (1984). White lies in interpersonal communication: A taxonomy and preliminary investigation of social motivations. *Western Journal of Speech Communication, 48,* 309–325.

Clark, M. S., & Mills, J. (1979). The difference between communal and exchange relationships: What it is and is not. *Personality & Social Psychology Bulletin, 19,* 684–691.

Clark, M. S., Mills, J., & Powell, M. C. (1986). Keeping track of needs in communal and exchange relationships. *Journal of Personality and Social Psychology, 51,* 333–338.

Comadena, M. E. (1982). Accuracy in detecting deception: Intimate and friendship relationships. *Communication Yearbook 6* (pp. 446–472). Beverly Hills, CA: Sage.

DePaulo, B. M., Ansfield, M. E., Kirkendol, S. E., & Boden, J. M. (1997). Serious lies: First person accounts. Manuscript in preparation.

DePaulo, B. M., Charlton, K., Cooper, H., Lindsay, J. J., & Muhlenbruck, L.

(1997). The accuracy-confidence correlation in the detection of deception. *Personality and Social Psychology Review, 1*, 346–357.

DePaulo, B. M., Epstein, J. A., & Wyer, M. M. (1993). Sex differences in lying: How women and men deal with the dilemma of deceit. In M. Lewis and C. Saarni (Eds.), *Lying and deception in everyday life* (pp. 126–147). New York: The Guilford Press.

DePaulo, B. M., & Friedman, H. S. (1998). Nonverbal communication. In D. Gilbert, S. T. Fiske, & G. Lindzey (Eds.). *Handbook of social psychology* (4th ed., pp. 3–40). New York: Random House.

DePaulo, B. M., & Kashy, D. A. (1998). Everyday lies in close and casual relationships. *Journal of Personality and Social Psychology, 74*, 63–79.

DePaulo, B. M., Kashy, D. A., Kirkendol, S. E., Wyer, M. M. & Epstein, J. A. (1996). Lying in everyday life. *Journal of Personality and Social Psychology, 70*, 979–995.

DePaulo, B. M., & Kirkendol, S. E. (1989). The motivational impairment effect in the communication of deception. In John C. Yuille (Ed.), *Credibility assessment. NATO Advanced Science Institutes series. Series D: Behavioural and social sciences, Vol. 47* (pp. 51–70). Dordrecht, Netherlands: Kluwer Academic Press.

DePaulo, B. M., Kirkendol, S. E., Tang, J., & O'Brien, T. P. (1988). The motivational impairment effect in the communication of deception: Replications and extensions. *Journal of Nonverbal Behavior, 12*, 177–202.

DePaulo, B. M., Lanier, K., & Davis, T. (1983). Detecting the deceit of the motivated liar. *Journal of Personality and Social Psychology, 45*, 1096–1103.

DePaulo, B. M., Lassiter, G. D., & Stone, J. I. (1982). Attentional determinants of success at detecting deception and truth. *Personality and Social Psychology Bulletin, 8*, 273–279.

DePaulo, B. M., LeMay, C. S., & Epstein, J. A. (1991). Effects of importance of success and expectations for success on effectiveness at deceiving. *Personality and Social Psychology Bulletin, 17*, 14–24.

DePaulo, B. M., Stone, J. I., & Lassiter, G. D. (1985a). Deceiving and detecting deceit. In B. R. Schlenker (Ed.), *The self and social life* (pp. 323–370). New York: McGraw-Hill.

DePaulo, B. M., Stone, J. I., & Lassiter, G. D. (1985b). Telling ingratiating lies: Effects of target sex and target attractiveness on verbal and nonverbal deceptive success. *Journal of Personality and Social Psychology, 48*, 1191–1203.

Feeley, T. H. (1997). Choosing deceptive communication. Submitted for publication.

Feeley, T. H., deTurck, M. A., & Young, M. J. (1995). Baseline familiarity in lie detection. *Communication Research Reports, 12*, 160–169.

Fleming, J. M., & Darley, J. H. (1991). Mixed messages: The multiple audience problem and strategic communication. *Social Cognition, 9*, 25–46.

Fleming, J. M., Darley, J. M., Hilton, B. A., & Kojetin, B. A. (1990). Multiple audience problem: A strategic communication perspective on social perception. *Journal of Personality and Social Psychology, 58*, 593–609.

Funder, D. C. (1987). Errors and mistakes: Evaluating the accuracy of social judgment. *Psychological Bulletin, 101*, 75–90.

Gilbert, D. T. (1991). How mental systems believe. *American Psychologist, 46,* 107–119.

Goffman, E. (1959). *The presentation of self in everyday life.* Garden City, New York: Doubleday.

Grice, H. P. (1975). Logic and conversation. In P. Cole & J. Morgan (Eds.), *Syntax and semantics: Vol. 3. Speech acts* (pp. 41–58). New York: Academic Press.

Hall, J. (1984). *Nonverbal sex differences: Communication accuracy and expressive style.* Baltimore, MD: Johns Hopkins University Press.

Hoffman, M. L. (1977). Sex differences in empathy and related behaviors. *Psychological Bulletin, 84,* 712–722.

Holmes, J. G., & Rempel. J. K. (1989). Trust in close relationships. In C. Hendrick (Ed.), *Review of personality and social psychology: Vol. 10, Close relationships* (pp. 187–220). Newbury Park, CA: Sage Publications.

Kashy, D. A., & DePaulo, B. M. (1997). Who lies? *Journal of Personality and Social Psychology, 70,* 1037–1051.

Kraut, R. E. (1980). Humans as lie detectors. Some second thoughts. *Journal of Communication, 30,* 209–216.

Levine, T. R., & McCornack, S. A. (1992). Linking love and lies: A formal test of the McCornack and Parks model of deception detection. *Journal of Social and Personal Relationships, 9,* 143–154.

Levine, T. R., McCornack, S. A., & Avery, P. B. (1992). Sex differences in emotional reactions to discovered deception. *Communication Quarterly, 40,* 289–296.

McCornack, S. A., & Levine, T. R. (1990a). When lies are uncovered: Emotional and relational outcomes of discovered deception. *Communication Monographs, 57,* 119–138.

McCornack, S. A., & Levine, T. R. (1990b). When lovers become leery: The relationship between suspicion and accuracy in detecting deception. *Communication Monographs, 57,* 219–230.

McCornack, S. A., & Parks, M. R. (1986). Deception detection and relational development: The other side of trust. In M. L. McLaughlin (Ed.), *Communication Yearbook 9* (pp. 377–389). Beverly Hills, CA: Sage.

Maier, R. A., & Lavrakas, P. J. (1976). Lying behavior and evaluation of lies. *Perceptual and Motor Skills, 42,* 575–581.

Metts, S. (1994). Relational transgressions. In W. R. Cupach & B. H. Spitzberg (Eds.), *The dark side of interpersonal communication* (pp. 217–239). Hillsdale, NJ: Lawrence Erlbaum.

Millar, K. U., and Tesser, A. (1988). Deceptive behavior in social relationships: A consequence of violated expectations. *Journal of Psychology, 122,* 263–273.

Millar, M., & Millar, K. (1995) Detection of deception in familiar and unfamiliar persons: The effects of information restriction. *Journal of Nonverbal Behavior, 19,* 69–84.

Miller, G. R., Mongeau, P. A., & Sleight, C. (1986). Fudging with friends and lying with lovers: Deceptive communication in personal relationships. *Journal of Social and Personal Relationships, 3,* 495–512.

Parks, M. (1982). Ideology in interpersonal communication: Off the couch and into the world. *Communications Yearbook, 5,* 79–107.

Patterson, M. L. (1995). Invited article: A parallel process model of nonverbal communication. *Journal of Nonverbal Behavior, 19,* 3–29.

Planalp, S., & Honeycutt, J. M. (1985). Events that increase uncertainty in personal relationships. *Human Communication Research, 11,* 593–604.

Rosenthal, R., & DePaulo, B. M. (1979a). Sex differences in accommodation in nonverbal communication. In R. Rosenthal (Ed.), *Skill in nonverbal communication* (pp. 68–103). Cambridge, MA: Oelgeschlager, Gunn, & Hain.

Rosenthal, R., & DePaulo, B. M. (1979b). Sex differences in eavesdropping on nonverbal cues. *Journal of Personality and Social Psychology, 37,* 273–285.

Sagarin, B. J., Rhoads, K. L., & Cialdini, R. B. (1997). Deceiver's distrust: Denigration as a consequence of undiscovered deception. Manuscript submitted for review.

Simpson, J. A., Ickes, W., & Blackstone, T. (1995). When the head protects the heart: Empathic accuracy in dating relationships. *Journal of Personality and Social Psychology, 69,* 629–641.

Stiff, J. B., Kim, H. J., & Ramesh, C. (1992). Truth bias and aroused suspicion in relational communication. *Communication Research, 19,* 326–345.

Thomas, G., & Fletcher, G. J. O. (1997). Empathic accuracy in romantic relationships. In W. Ickes (Ed.), *Empathic Accuracy* (pp. 194–217). New York: Guilford Press.

Thomas, G., Fletcher, G. J. O., & Lange, C. (1997). On-line empathic accuracy in marital interaction. *Journal of Personality and Social Psychology, 72,* 839–850.

Toris, C., & DePaulo, B. M. (1984). Effects of actual deception and suspiciousness of deception on interpersonal perceptions. *Journal of Personality and Social Psychology, 47,* 1063–1073.

Turner, R. E., Edgley, C., & Olmstead, G. (1975). Informational control in conversations: Honesty is not always the best policy. *Kansas Journal of Sociology, 11,* 69–89.

Zuckerman, M., DePaulo, B. M., & Rosenthal, R. (1981). Verbal and nonverbal communication of deception. In L. Berkowitz (Ed.), *Advances in experimental social psychology* (Vol. 14 pp. 1–59). New York: Academic Press.

Zuckerman, M., Koestner, R., & Alton, A. O. (1984). Learning to detect deception. *Journal of Personality and Social Psychology, 46,* 519–528.

# Author Index

# Subject Index

abused children, emotion recognition of, 159, 176
academic achievement, and family expressiveness, 140
action schemas, 330–331
action-tendency goals
  definition, 74
  and ethnotheories of emotion, 74
"action units," 290
affect, in social cognition, 336
affect infusion, 217
"affect program," 289–290, 301
affordances, and social inference, 328
African Americans
  anger expression, children, 89
  decoding judgments, 198
  facial expression perception, 27–28
age factors
  display rule use, and television, 174
  encoding/decoding ability, 172–173
aggression, and family expressiveness, 131–132
AIM model, 236
altruistic lies, 381–382
anger expression
  cultural influences, 89, 197
  decoding accuracy, cultural factors, 197
  family expressiveness effects, 125, 128
  high-status men, 194
  non-universality, 253
  sex differences, 52, 74, 84
  social context influences, 302
  and status differentials, 194
anger recognition, cultural differences, 23
Anglo Canadians, decoding, 198
appeasement, and smiling, 47–48, 61
approach-avoidance behavior
  in couple conflicts, 355–357, 367
  marital satisfaction indicator, 367
arousal

management of, children, 76–78
  in nonverbal exchange, 320–322
Asians; *see also* Japanese
  emotion decoding, 197
  facial expression perception, 27–28
at-risk children, emotion management, 88
attachment quality, and family expressiveness, 133–134
attributions
  cultural influences, 23–29
  dispositional versus situationist views, 249–252
  and facial expression intensity, 23–27
Australian children, decoding ability, 196–197
authoritarian parenting, 132–133
authoritative parenting, 132–133
automatic judgments, person perception, 327–329
avoidance behavior
  in couple conflicts, 356–357
  marital dissatisfaction indicator, 367–368

behavior problems, 88
behavioral ecology perspective
  contextual emphasis of, 295–296
  emotional expression view integration, 305–308
  facial displays, 288, 295–310
  and implicit audience effects, 299–300
  problems with, 300–308
behavioral inhibition, 136
blind children, 31
boys
  emotional displays, 77, 84–87
  family expressiveness effects, 120, 143–144
British children, display rules, 89–91
bullfighters' facial behavior, 254–255

*Studies in Emotion and Social Interaction*

First Series
Editors: Paul Ekman and Klaus R. Scherer